1997 Index
of Economic Freedom

Edited by Kim R. Holmes, Bryan T. Johnson, and Melanie Kirkpatrick

The Heritage Foundation

THE WALL STREET JOURNAL.

KIM R. HOLMES is Vice President and Director of Foreign Policy and Defense Studies at The Heritage Foundation

BRYAN T. JOHNSON is a Policy Analyst at The Heritage Foundation.

MELANIE KIRKPATRICK is Assistant Editor of *The Wall Street Journal* Editorial Page.

Robert L. Bartley is Editor of *The Wall Street Journal*.

William W. Beach is John M. Olin Senior Fellow in Economics at The Heritage Foundation.

Gareth Davis is a Research Assistant at The Heritage Foundation.

George Melloan is Deputy Editor (International) of *The Wall Street Journal*, in charge of the Editorial Pages of *The Wall Street Journal Europe* and *The Asian Wall Street Journal*.

ISBN 0–89195–240–3

Copyright © 1997 by The Heritage Foundation and Dow Jones & Company, Inc.

The Heritage Foundation
214 Massachusetts Avenue, N.E.
Washington, D.C. 20002
(202) 546-4400
http://www.heritage.org

The Wall Street Journal
Dow Jones & Company, Inc.
200 Liberty Street
New York, N.Y. 10281
(212) 416-2000
http://wsj.com

TABLE OF CONTENTS

Acknowledgments

We would like to express our appreciation to several individuals at The Heritage Foundation who helped with the third edition of the *Index of Economic Freedom*. We are grateful to the staffs of the Foreign Policy and Domestic Policy departments and the Asian Studies Center, who participated in The Heritage Foundation's internal peer review group. The expertise of these analysts greatly increased the accuracy of the *Index*. Members of the group are: Ariel Cohen, Senior Policy Analyst for Russian and Eurasian affairs; Richard D. Fisher, Senior Policy Analyst for Asian affairs; Robert P. O'Quinn, Policy Analyst for Asian trade and economics; James Phillips, Senior Policy Analyst for Middle East affairs; James J. Przystup, Director of The Heritage Foundation's Asian Studies Center; Thomas P. Sheehy, former Jay Kingham Fellow in International Regulatory Affairs at The Heritage Foundation; John P. Sweeney, Policy Analyst for trade and Latin American affairs; Ronald Utt, Senior Fellow; and Stephen J. Yates, Policy Analyst for China.

Brett Schaefer of the Foreign and Defense Policy Studies staff managed the data and assisted with research. Brett was instrumental in contributing a substantial amount of research. In addition, John Nixon, Research Services Coordinator, provided significant research skills in helping the authors track down vital information.

We also would like to thank Senior Editor Richard Odermatt, Director of Sales and Production Services Ann Klucsarits, and the team that managed the production of the book: Copy Editor William T. Poole; Design and Publishing Associate James V. Rutherford; and Deputy Director and Art Editor Thomas J. Timmons. Their editorial and design skills and knowledge were simply invaluable. The regional maps were taken from Cartesia Software's MapArt, while the detailed country maps were based on the CIA's *World Factbook, 1996*.

Countless individuals serving with various accounting firms, businesses, research organizations, U.S. government agencies, embassies in Washington, and other organizations cooperated in providing us with data. Their assistance is much appreciated. So, too, is the help of Heritage interns. In particular, Tami Puno and Daniele Schiffman were extremely helpful in producing the third edition of the *Index*. Like their predecessors the previous summer, they were the ones who did the legwork, cheerfully running down data throughout the humid Washington summer. We wish them the best in their new ventures. Also, fall semester intern Spencer Persson was instrumental in last-minute fact-checking and research.

We would like to thank Dr. Edward L. Hudgins, now of the Cato Institute, who deserves credit for laying down a foundation for the *Index* several years ago while serving as Director of the Center for International Economic Growth at The Heritage Foundation. We are grateful also to Heritage Trustee Ambassador J. William Middendorf, for encouraging us early to undertake such a study of global economic freedom. Many other people within The Heritage Foundation have generously lent their expertise to our effort. We would like to express our appreciation to the many people who enthusiastically praised the *Index of Economic Freedom*. We have been pleased indeed at how well the *Index* has been received. The support and encouragement of people worldwide has been important in inspiring us to produce this third edition in cooperation with the *Wall Street Journal* Editorial Page. We hope this effort matches their expectations.

K.R.H.

B.T.J.

M.K.

Foreword

As the 20th Century draws to its end, a cycle is closing. Mankind passed the year 1900 at an epitome of economic freedom, but these 19th Century ideas were quickly eclipsed by war and economic crisis. In our Century, advanced thinkers grew fascinated with assorted recipes for government economic manipulation and central planning. Now suddenly, as we approach the second millennium, everyone again understands that the path to economic progress starts with economic freedom.

The habits of our era run so deep we forget the remarkable era before it. The Century that ran from 1815 to 1914, from Waterloo to Sarajevo, was a time of previously unparalleled economic freedom and previously unparalleled economic advance. In Great Britain, repeal of the Corn Laws consolidated a second empire. In the United States, the Robber Barons punched five railroads across a continent. The produce of the Mississippi basin fed workers of Birmingham, and the City of London financed the development of the American continent.

The year 1820 marks the sharp acceleration in world economic growth, as measured in the careful studies of Angus Maddison.[1] He estimates per-capita world output in the "protocapitalist" era from 1500 to 1820, compared to the "present 'capitalist' epoch." In 1990 dollars, by 1820 per capita GDP crawled to $651 from $565 three centuries earlier. In half as much time, from 1820 to 1992, it soared to $5,145.

Technological progress was the most important element in this change, along with the accumulation of physical capital, the development of human capital and the integration of individual economies. But some economies fared far better than others; the growth was sparked in Western Europe and fueled by the "Western offshoots"—the

---

1   *Monitoring the World Economy, 1820–1992* (OECD Development Center, 1995).

United States, Canada, Australia, and New Zealand. It was in these areas that the Renaissance and the Enlightenment had done the most to open eyes to the possibility of change, and they profited from other freedoms as well: the end of feudal restrictions on land sales, legal systems protecting property rights and enforceable contracts, and, I would add, the intellectual heritage staked out by Adam Smith in 1776.

If new freedoms started capitalist development, our century has witnessed a turning away. Rapid growth is itself unsettling, especially because it inevitably creates losers as well as winners. Starting about the turn of the Century, there have been new concerns with making the process fair to the players, and in particular with protecting those left behind. The development of the welfare state may have protected the legitimacy of the capitalist process, as Maddison suggests. But it has been carried to levels—with, to take the extreme example, 65 percent of GDP passing through government hands in Sweden—that demonstrably impede economic growth.

Our Century, too, has been a century of war: World War I, the Great Depression amid the economic confusions of war debts and reparations, World War II, and the Cold War. Wars of course are huge centralizing influences, not least through creating high levels of taxation. And if a central government can mobilize the people and dispatch divisions, it is natural to believe it can also rationally direct resources and outguess markets. So our Century saw many experiments with central direction of the economy, from Keynesian fine-tuning through Fabian socialism to Communist five-year plans.

As our Century began late with an assassination in 1914, it ended early, with the fall of the Berlin Wall in 1989. The collapse of the centrally planned economies was utter and complete. Eyes turned to free economies, most particularly Asia's rapidly developing "tigers," which often seem an earlier and purer form of capitalism. With the decentralizing influence of the microchip, and with world financial markets bringing world-wide competition, the dawning century beckons a return to the free economy.

If the intellectual debate is reasonably settled, political practice is typically another matter. Politicians cling to the old perquisites of the nation-state, even at the expense of their citizens. Local private and public monopolists become substantial constituencies against change. Citizens are hesitant to give up old habits and old promises. Progress toward the intellectual ideal of economic freedom will always be uneven.

We at *The Wall Street Journal* have been fascinated observers in the drama sketched above. Our traditions reach back into the last century, and by now our name—and that of our publisher, Dow Jones & Co., Inc.—are redolent with the idea of capitalism. Our editorial policy, as we conceive it, is built on the bedrocks of free people and free markets. And as the financial markets are now world-wide, so is *The Wall Street Journal,* published every business day in three editions on three continents.

With this background, we have naturally looked with great admiration at the last two issues of *The Index of Economic Freedom,* conceived by The Heritage Foundation as a measure of where nations stand in progress toward economic freedom and development. It is an attempt to quantify something important to us, important to the new century, and indeed, important to mankind. We're delighted at the opportunity to co-sponsor this year's *Index,* in the hope that it will prove stimulating to investors, government officials, and thinkers throughout our increasingly indivisible world.

Robert L. Bartley,
Editor, *The Wall Street Journal*
November 1996

Preface

There may be many reasons why so much poverty exists in the world, but no reason is more important than the lack of economic freedom. Most of the world's economies are unfree and repressed. This is not a result of natural events beyond the control of governments. Nor is it the consequence mainly of war or natural disasters. Rather, it is mainly the result of man's actions. Indeed, poverty itself is not a natural condition, but the result of repressive economic policies that are the work of governments.

Development economists long have argued that the best way to alleviate poverty overseas is to transfer the wealth of the rich nations to the poor ones. This is not only unrealistic, it ignores the root cause of poverty. People around the world are poor mainly because they live in countries whose governments repress, and in some cases, even steal their livelihoods. For an economy to grow and prosper, people must be free to work, keep most of what they earn, and trade with whom they want. Businesses must be free to produce the kinds of products they want, in the quantities they decide, and to sell those products at the prices they and the market deem appropriate.

In America, we take it for granted that people are free to leave their jobs and open their own business if they desire. We also take it for granted that people are permitted to buy what they want and live in a place of their choosing.

In many less developed countries, this is not the case. In too many countries around the world, people are not free to work, establish their own businesses, buy the kinds of products they want, or seek legal protection of their wealth. For example, private property still is essentially against the law in Cuba. The fruits of people's labors is regularly confiscated by the government. There is no legal recourse for those who seek to protect their property from theft. This also is the case in countries like North Korea, where the government remains the center of all economic transactions. Because these countries and others like them are not economically free, their economies stagnate, miring their people in miserable poverty.

First published in 1994, The Heritage Foundation's *Index of Economic Freedom* provides a framework for understanding better how to eliminate global poverty. This third edition of *The Index of Economic Freedom*, published jointly with *The Wall Street Journal,* examines the economies of 150 countries. The *Index* shows that those countries that have liberated their economies are either the most prosperous or growing the most rapidly. Conversely, the *Index* shows that the countries whose governments most tightly control their economies are the poorest and are growing the most slowly. This edition of the *Index* also demonstrates through economic modeling that countries that become economically free are more likely to grow faster in the future.

The Index of Economic Freedom is the first, most accurate, comprehensive, and up-to-date measurement of the status of economic freedom around the world. It examines ten broad economic factors and over 50 independent criteria in 150 countries around the world, the most of its kind. New this year is an intensive analysis on the statistical linkage between economic freedom and economic wealth. Moreover, *The Wall Street Journal* Editorial Page, now a co-publisher of the *Index* with The Heritage Foundation, has provided a substantial chapter analyzing the impact of economic freedom and foreign investment.

The Index of Economic Freedom has many conclusions. But one of its most important is a resounding condemnation of foreign aid. It demonstrates that countries with free economies generally don't need U.S. development assistance, because their economies are growing and prospering, while countries that receive U.S. aid don't deserve it, because their economies are not free and the money will just be wasted.

Policymakers and scholars the world over are awaking to the importance of economic freedom to global economic development. We hope the *Index of Economic Freedom* continues to point to this vital connection: To be free is to grow and prosper.

Edwin J. Feulner, Ph.D.
President
The Heritage Foundation
November 1996

Executive Summary

by Kim R. Holmes, Bryan T. Johnson, and Melanie Kirkpatrick

The idea of producing a "user-friendly" *Index of Economic Freedom* for policymakers was born at The Heritage Foundation in 1989. The purpose then, as it remains today, was to develop an index that empirically measures the level of economic freedom in countries around the world. To this end, a set of objective economic criteria has been established to grade 150 countries. Although there are many theories about the origins and causes of economic development, the findings of this study are conclusive: Those countries with the most economic freedom have higher rates of economic development than those with less economic freedom.

The Index of Economic Freedom measures how well these countries score on a list of ten economic factors. The higher the score, the more government interference in the economy (hence, the less economic freedom there is). The factors are:

- Trade Policy
- Taxation Policy
- Government Intervention in the Economy
- Monetary Policy
- Capital Flows and Foreign Investment
- Banking Policy
- Wage and Price Controls
- Property Rights
- Regulation
- Black Market

In each of these ten broad categories, the authors used some 50 independent economic criteria to develop an empirical snapshot of the level of economic freedom in each country (these independent criteria are listed at the end of Chapter 4, "The Factors of the Index of Economic Freedom"). The study demonstrates unequivocally that countries with the highest levels of economic freedom also have the highest living standards. Similarly, countries with the lowest levels of economic freedom also have the lowest living standards.

A comparison of scores from the first and second editions of the *Index* demonstrates an interesting phenomenon: Wealthy and economically free countries tend to reintroduce restrictions on economic freedom over time. As they become wealthy, countries begin adding welfare and other social programs that were not affordable when they were poorer. Thus, after they have become economically "liberated," countries like Germany and France tend to fall back down the scale of economic freedom, getting worse scores than newly emerging free economies like Hong Kong or Singapore. These Asian "tigers" are still growing and developing, and may be just beginning to restrict their economies with post-industrial welfare and environmental policies. This phenomenon, when displayed graphically, is called the Curve of Economic Freedom. It shows that economic freedom can rise and fall, and that the seeds of destruction can exist in the fruits of success.

The third edition of the *Index* seems to substantiate this trend. Of the ten highest ranking countries in last year's edition, four received worse scores this year, five remained the same, and only one was better. Switzerland, the Netherlands, Denmark, and Luxembourg received worse scores because of increased restrictions on economic freedom. Switzerland, the Netherlands, and Luxembourg all are characterized by increased government intervention in the economy; and both the Netherlands and Denmark have higher tax burdens than they did last year.

With eight more countries this year, and 49 new countries since the first edition, the *Index* provides a clearer vision of the world's economically freest and most repressed regions. As was true last year, most of the world's economies remain economically unfree. Of the 150 countries graded, 72 are mostly free or free, up from 65 last year, while 78 are mostly unfree or repressed, up from 77 last year. Of the top ten freest countries, five are from North America or Europe, four are from Asia, and one is from the Middle East. Most of the world's freest economies are in North America and Europe, while most of the world's most economically repressed countries are in Africa and the Middle East. Asia has a mixture of free and unfree economies.

By region, many interesting developments have occurred since last year's edition. For example:

Europe. Switzerland is the economically freest country in Europe. The economies of the United Kingdom, the Netherlands, the Czech Republic, and Denmark are the next freest. Former Marxist countries continue to make progress toward maximizing economic freedom. The best examples are the Czech Republic and Estonia, which score well on the *Index*. These countries are following the models of Hong Kong and Singapore to promote large economic growth rates by maximizing economic freedom. Germany is the only country in Europe that has received a worse score each year than in the previous year's edition. The most recent cause is an increase in government intervention in the economy, primarily a result of the failure to complete the privatization of state-owned industries.

Latin America. Chile is the economically freest country in Latin America. Chile has further reduced barriers to trade and has eliminated additional price controls. Panama is the second freest economy in Latin America. El Salvador now is tied with Trinidad and Tobago. There has been little progress in Mexico, which remains mostly unfree. Despite a rush of media reports on purported economic reform in Cuba, the facts show that Havana continues to pursue economically repressive policies. Cuba remains the most economically unfree country in Latin America and one of the three most economically repressed countries in the world. Guatemala, Peru, and Ecuador have recorded better scores in each edition of the *Index*. Colombia and Venezuela are the only two countries in which economic freedom has worsened each year.

Asia. Despite the enthusiasm of the investment community, Vietnam remains economically unfree, ranking fifth in a listing of the world's most economically repressed countries. It also continues to suffer from corrupt border officials, an inadequate foreign investment law, and a legal system that provides little protection for private property. Vietnam remains a centrally planned economy with a marginal, albeit growing, free market. Japan's score did not change from last year, indicating that its spiraling economic recession may be over. China is still among the most economically unfree countries in the world.

Sub-Saharan Africa. As a whole, sub-Saharan Africa remains the most economically unfree, and by far the poorest, area in the world. Of the 38 sub-Saharan African countries graded, none received a score of free. Only ten received a score of mostly free, 22 scored mostly unfree, and six were rated repressed. Of the 19 countries categorized as repressed, the majority are in sub-Saharan Africa. The *Index* demonstrates quite clearly that sub-Saharan Africa's poverty is not the result of insufficient levels of foreign aid, weather patterns, or internal strife; on a per-capita basis, many sub-Saharan African countries are among those receiving the highest levels of economic assistance in the world. Rather, the main cause of poverty in sub-Saharan Africa is a lack of economic freedom, embodied in the policies these nations have imposed on themselves.

The findings of the *Index* with respect to sub-Saharan Africa cast doubt on the assertion that economic growth can be achieved by huge transfers of wealth from the industrialized economies to the less developed world. The people of Angola, Mozambique, Haiti, and Ukraine are not poor because wealthy people in the West do not share their riches. They are poor because their governments pursue destructive economic policies that depress free enterprise. Only when they increase the economic freedom of their citizens and unleash the phenomenal power of the free market will the poor nations of the world begin to achieve true prosperity and economic growth. Anything short of this is not only economically unwise, but inhumane.

This year's *Index* features a chapter by George Melloan, of *The Wall Street Journal's* Editorial Page, on the importance of economic freedom to foreign investment. With the explosion of investment in emerging markets, there is an increasing need for sound country risk analysis. Although many economic risk factors exist, perhaps one of the most important is economic freedom. In 1995, U.S. investors bought foreign stocks worth $51.2 billion and foreign bonds worth $46.8 billion. With American overseas investment at such levels, it is all the more important that countries be evaluated based on their chances of achieving sustainable levels of economic growth. The *Index* provides such an analysis, and investors may find it useful in determining which countries are dedicated to economic reform and which ones are not.

Also new this year is a chapter by Heritage Foundation economists on the statistical connection between economic freedom and economic growth. The authors examine the economic benefits that flow from economic freedom and conclude that there is strong evidence, both from the emerging field of New Growth Theory and from statistical tests which they themselves conduct, linking the concepts measured in the *Index* to higher growth rates and greater prosperity. They conclude that introducing the sorts of reforms that would boost a nation's score on the *Index of Economic Freedom* could well produce massive improvements in the living standards experienced by people in many of the world's poorest and most unfree economies.

Understanding the Data: A Guide to the Charts and Graphs

by Bryan T. Johnson

The following charts and graphs are designed to assist the reader in understanding the data contained in the *Index of Economic Freedom*. What follows is a description of the content and implications of the charts and graphs.

The Curve of Economic Freedom. The Curve of Economic Freedom is a graphical representation of the correlation between economic freedom and wealth. As the findings in the *Index* indicate, those countries with the highest level of economic freedom are the richest, while those countries with the least economic freedom are the poorest. As countries introduce new economic reforms, represented by higher levels of economic freedom, they also increase their chances of creating more wealth.

Global Distribution of Economic Freedom: This is a world map with all of the 150 countries graded in the *Index* colored to represent one of four broad economic freedom categories: "free," "mostly free," "mostly unfree," and "repressed." The map indicates that Africa is the region with the greatest number of "mostly unfree" and "repressed" economies, while Europe is the area with the greatest number of "mostly free" and "free" countries.

The Curve of Economic Freedom by Region: The subsequent four charts represent the Curve of Economic Freedom divided into four geographical regions: (1) Africa and the Middle East, (2) Asia and Pacific Region, (3) Latin America and the Caribbean, and (4) Europe and North America. After each chart, is a colored map that divides all the countries graded in the *Index* into one of four categories: (1) "free," (2) "mostly free," (3) "mostly unfree," and (4) "repressed."

Country Rankings. This table lists all 150 countries in order of their 1997 *Index* scores. It summarizes each country's grade for the ten *Index* factors and includes the scores from 1995 and 1996 for comparison.

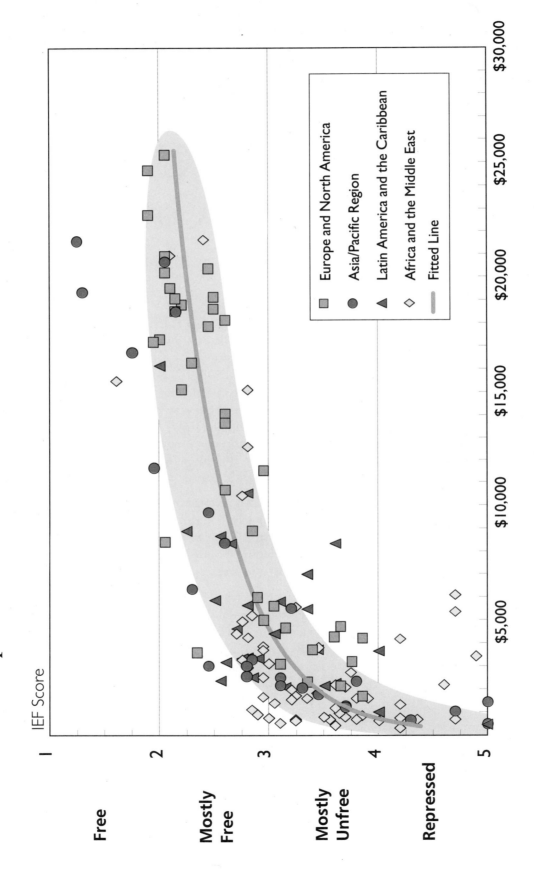

1997 CURVE OF ECONOMIC FREEDOM
A Comparison of Economic Freedom and Wealth

IEF Score

Free

Mostly
Free

Mostly
Unfree

Repressed

Europe and North America
Asia/Pacific Region
Latin America and the Caribbean
Africa and the Middle East
Fitted Line

Per Capita GDP 1993 (in Purchasing Power Parity)

GLOBAL DISTRIBUTION OF ECONOMIC FREEDOM

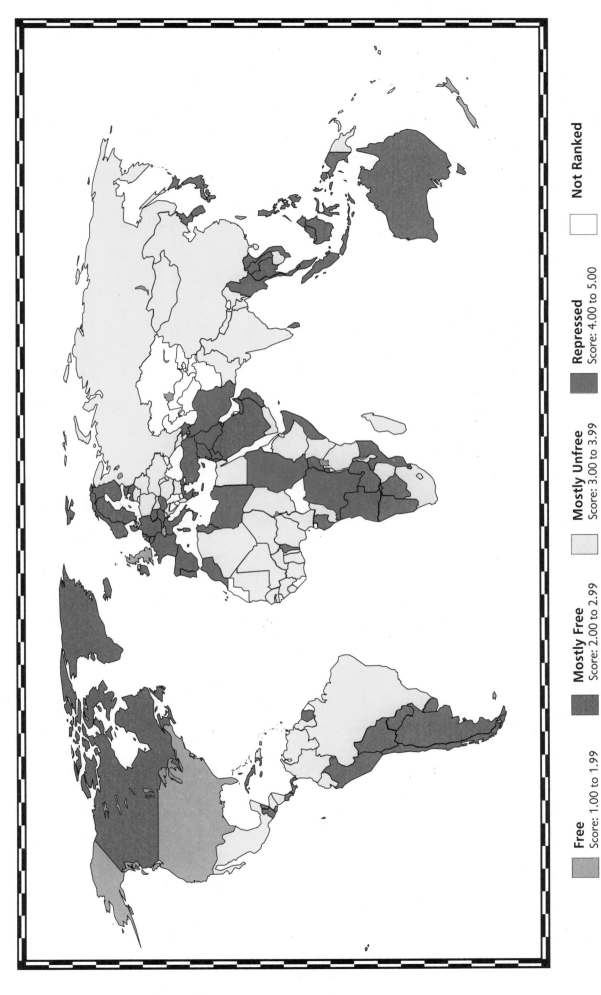

Free
Score: 1.00 to 1.99

Mostly Free
Score: 2.00 to 2.99

Mostly Unfree
Score: 3.00 to 3.99

Repressed
Score: 4.00 to 5.00

Not Ranked

ECONOMIC FREEDOM:
AFRICA AND THE MIDDLE EAST
A Comparison of Economic Freedom and Wealth

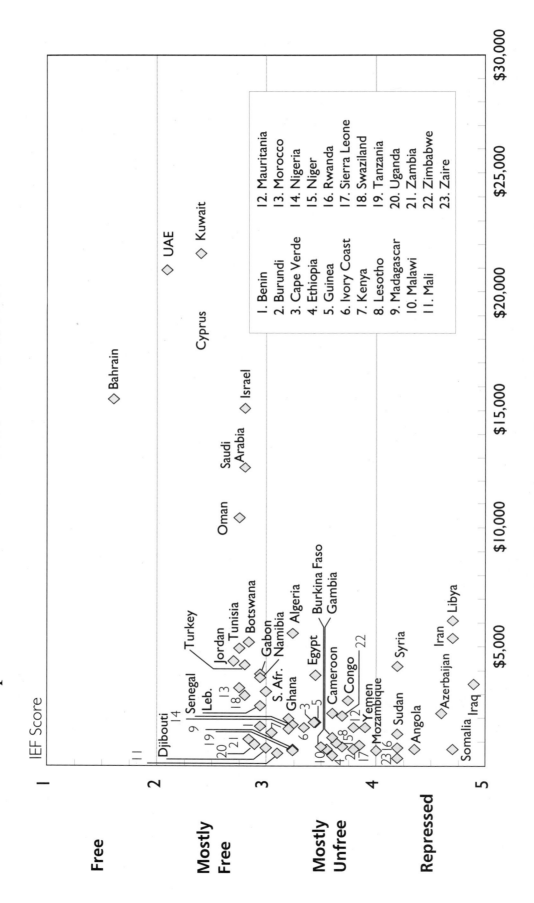

Legend:
1. Benin
2. Burundi
3. Cape Verde
4. Ethiopia
5. Guinea
6. Ivory Coast
7. Kenya
8. Lesotho
9. Madagascar
10. Malawi
11. Mali
12. Mauritania
13. Morocco
14. Nigeria
15. Niger
16. Rwanda
17. Sierra Leone
18. Swaziland
19. Tanzania
20. Uganda
21. Zambia
22. Zimbabwe
23. Zaire

IEF Score

Free

Mostly Free

Mostly Unfree

Repressed

Per Capita GDP 1993 (in Purchasing Power Parity)

$5,000 $10,000 $15,000 $20,000 $25,000 $30,000

ECONOMIC FREEDOM IN AFRICA AND THE MIDDLE EAST

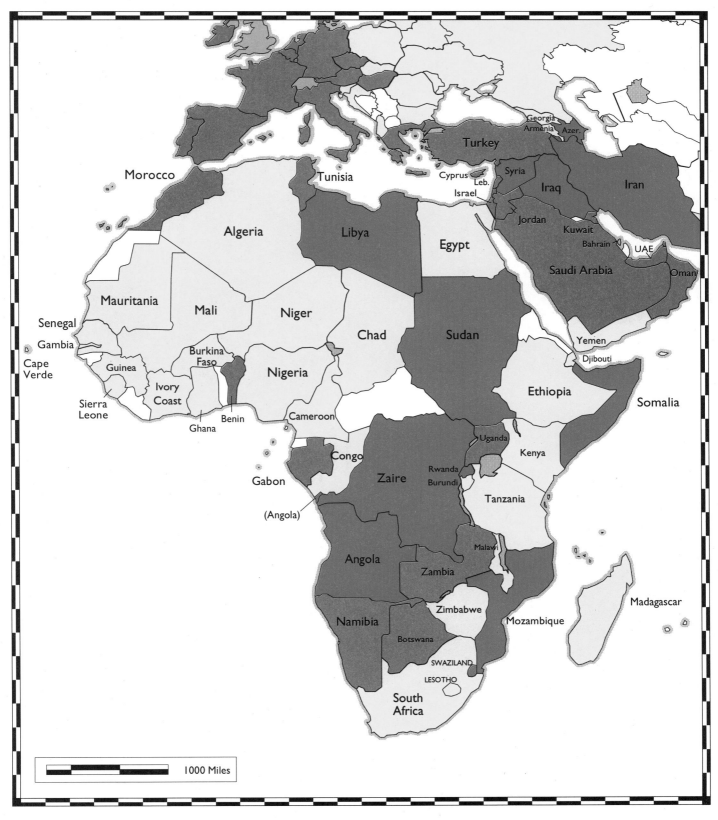

	Free		Mostly Free		Mostly Unfree		Repressed		Not Ranked
	Score: 1.00 to 1.99		Score: 2.00 to 2.99		Score: 3.00 to 3.99		Score: 4.00 to 5.00		

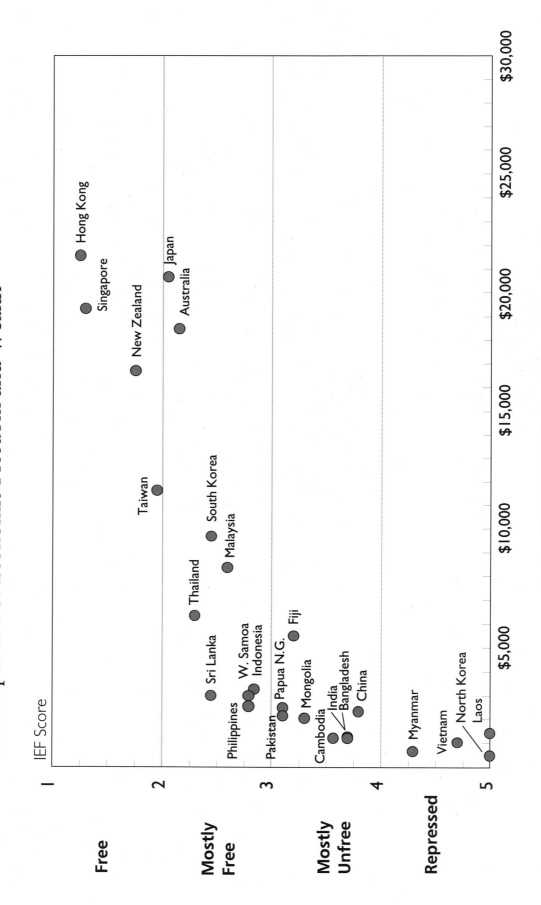

ECONOMIC FREEDOM:
THE ASIA/PACIFIC REGION
A Comparison of Economic Freedom and Wealth

IEF Score

Free

Mostly
Free

Mostly
Unfree

Repressed

Per Capita GDP 1993 (in Purchasing Power Parity)

ECONOMIC FREEDOM IN THE ASIA-PACIFIC REGION

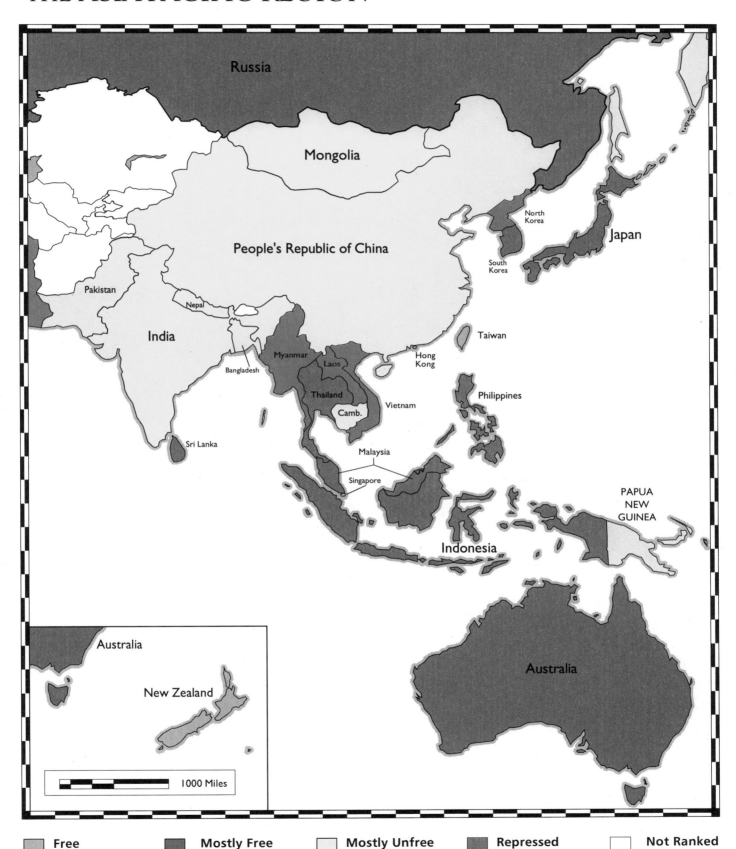

Free
Score: 1.00 to 1.99

Mostly Free
Score: 2.00 to 2.99

Mostly Unfree
Score: 3.00 to 3.99

Repressed
Score: 4.00 to 5.00

Not Ranked

Note: Fiji (Mostly Unfree) and Western Samoa (Mostly Free) are not shown on this map.

ECONOMIC FREEDOM:
EUROPE AND NORTH AMERICA
A Comparison of Economic Freedom and Wealth

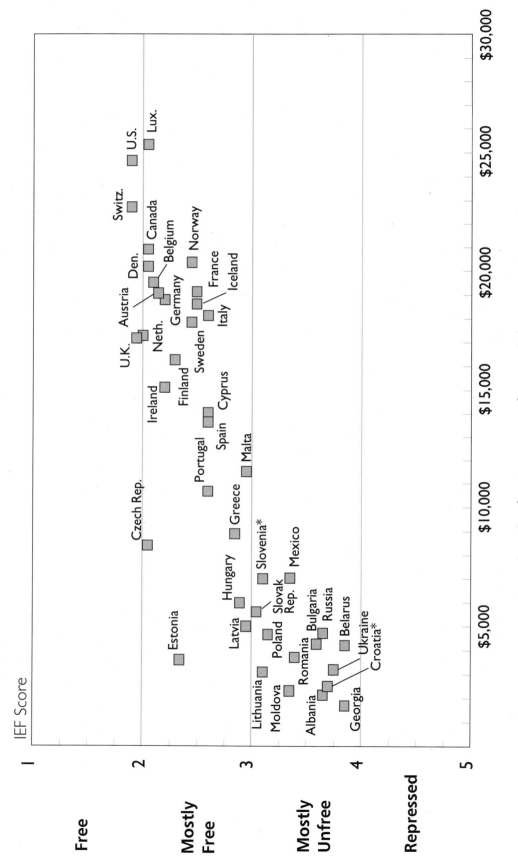

*Croatia and Slovenia's per capita GDP figures are estimates.

ECONOMIC FREEDOM IN
NORTH AMERICA AND EUROPE

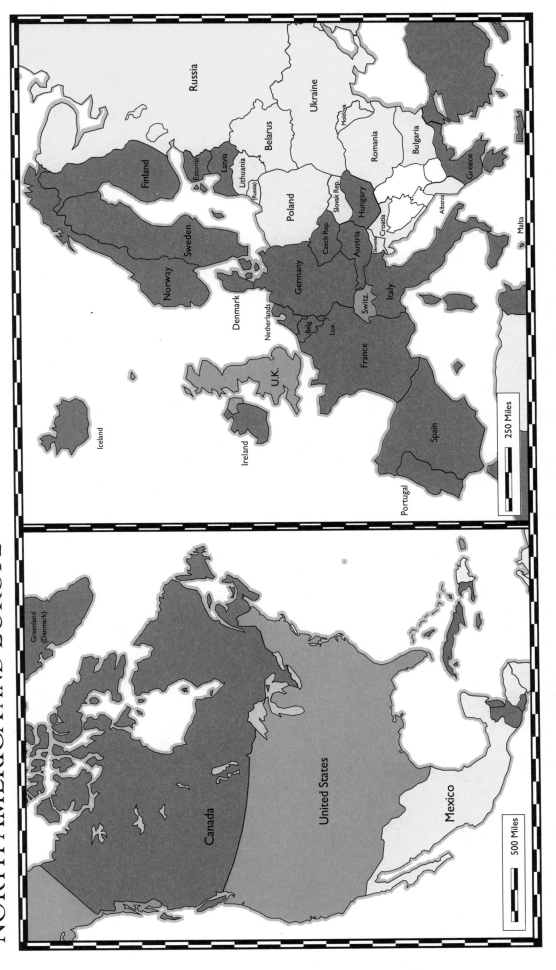

Free
Score: 1.00 to 1.99

Mostly Free
Score: 2.00 to 2.99

Mostly Unfree
Score: 3.00 to 3.99

Repressed
Score: 4.00 to 5.00

Not Ranked

ECONOMIC FREEDOM:
LATIN AMERICA AND THE CARIBBEAN
A Comparison of Economic Freedom and Wealth

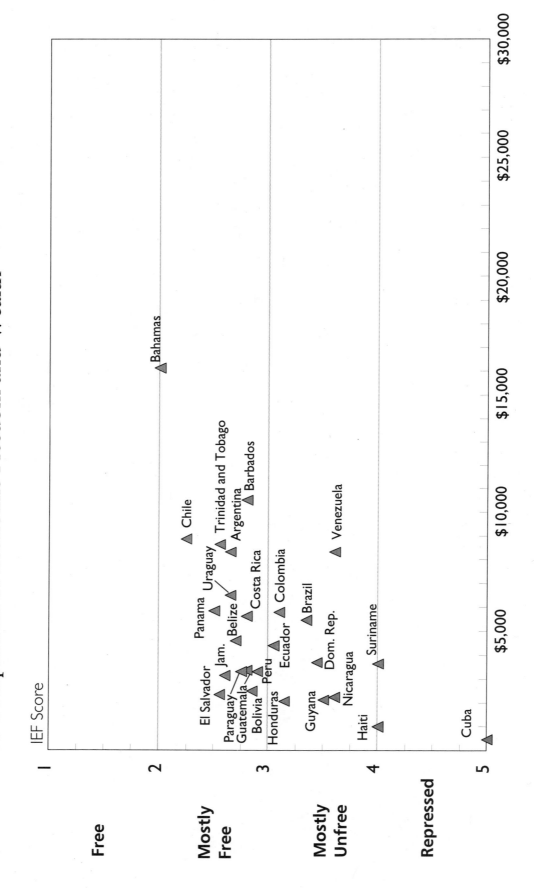

ECONOMIC FREEDOM IN SOUTH AMERICA

Venezuela

Guyana
Surimane

Colombia

Ecuador

Peru

Brazil

Bolivia

Paraguay

Chile

Argentina

Uruguay

1000 Miles

| | **Free**
Score: 1.00 to 1.99 | | **Mostly Free**
Score: 2.00 to 2.99 | | **Mostly Unfree**
Score: 3.00 to 3.99 | | **Repressed**
Score: 4.00 to 5.00 | | **Not Ranked** |

ECONOMIC FREEDOM IN CENTRAL AMERICA AND THE CARIBBEAN

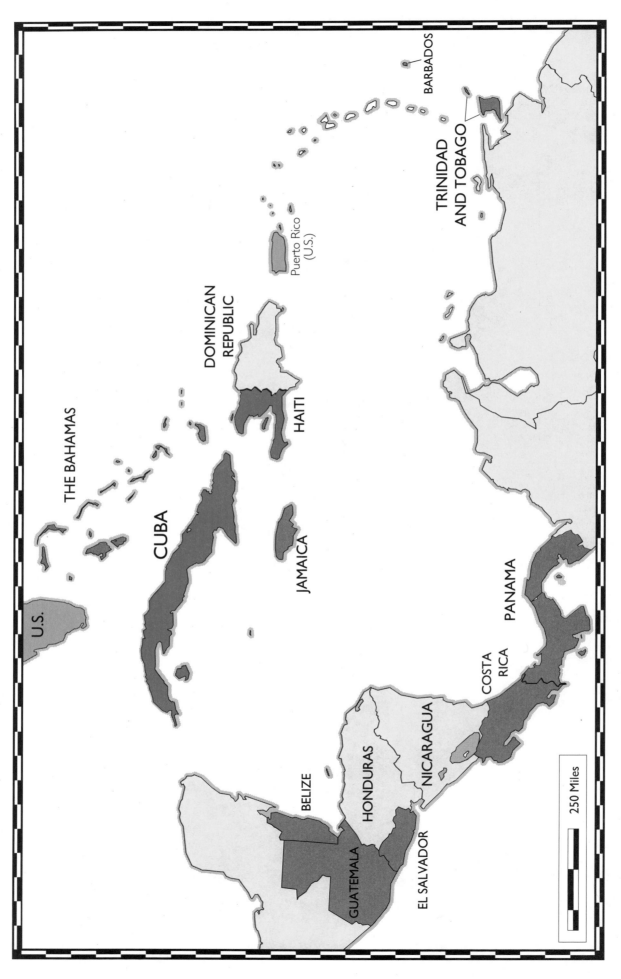

Free
Score: 1.00 to 1.99

Mostly Free
Score: 2.00 to 2.99

Mostly Unfree
Score: 3.00 to 3.99

Repressed
Score: 4.00 to 5.00

Not Ranked

250 Miles

U.S.

THE BAHAMAS

CUBA

JAMAICA

DOMINICAN REPUBLIC

HAITI

Puerto Rico (U.S.)

BARBADOS

TRINIDAD AND TOBAGO

BELIZE

GUATEMALA

EL SALVADOR

HONDURAS

NICARAGUA

COSTA RICA

PANAMA

1997 INDEX OF ECONOMIC FREEDOM RANKINGS

Rank	Trade	Taxation	Government Intervention	Monetary Policy	Foreign Investment	Banking	Wage/ Prices	Property Rights	Regulation	Black Market	1995 Score	1996 Score	1997 Score
1 Hong Kong	1	1.5	1	2	–	1	2	1	1	–	1.25	1.25	1.25
2 Singapore	–	3	1	1	–	2	2	1	1	–	1.25	1.30	1.30
3 Bahrain	2	1	3	1	2	2	2	1	–	–	1.60	1.70	1.60
4 New Zealand	2	3.5	2	2	2	1	2	1	2	–		1.75	1.75
5 Switzerland	2	3	3	1	2	2	2	1	3	–		1.80	1.90
5 United States	2	4	2	1	2	2	2	1	2	–	1.90	1.90	1.90
7 United Kingdom	2	4.5	2	1	2	2	2	1	2	–	1.95	1.95	1.95
7 Taiwan	2	2.5	2	1	3	3	2	1	2	–	1.95	1.95	1.95
9 Bahamas	5	1	2	–	3	2	2	1	1	2	2.10	2.00	2.00
9 Netherlands	2	5	3	1	2	2	2	1	2	–		1.85	2.00
11 Czech Republic	–	3.5	2	2	2	–	2	2	–	4	2.10	2.00	2.05
11 Denmark	2	4.5	4	–	2	2	–	1	2	–		1.95	2.05
11 Japan	2	4.5	1	–	3	3	2	1	2	–	1.95	2.05	2.05
11 Luxembourg	2	4.5	3	–	2	2	2	1	2	–		1.95	2.05
15 Canada	2	5	2	–	3	2	2	1	2	–	2.00	2.00	2.10
15 Belgium	2	5	2	–	2	2	2	1	3	–		2.10	2.10
15 United Arab Emirates	2	1	3	–	4	3	3	1	2	–		2.10	2.10
18 Australia	2	4.5	3	–	2	2	2	1	3	2	2.20	2.10	2.15
18 Austria	3	4.5	3	–	2	2	2	1	3	–	2.05	2.05	2.15
20 Ireland	2	5	2	–	2	2	2	1	2	3	2.20	2.20	2.20
20 Germany	2	5	3	–	2	2	2	1	3	1	2.00	2.10	2.20
22 Chile	2	3.5	1	3	2	3	2	2	2	3	2.50	2.45	2.25
23 Finland	2	4	3	–	2	3	3	1	3	–		2.30	2.30
23 Thailand	3	3	1	–	3	3	3	2	3	2	2.30	2.30	2.30
25 Estonia	2	3.5	2	4	1	2	2	2	2	3	2.25	2.35	2.35
26 Kuwait	2	1	4	2	4	3	3	2	2	2		2.40	2.40
27 Norway	3	4.5	3	–	2	3	3	1	3	–		2.45	2.45
27 So. Korea	3	4.5	2	2	3	2	2	2	3	2	2.15	2.30	2.45
27 Sri Lanka	3	3.5	2	2	3	2	–	3	2	3	2.80	2.65	2.45
27 Sweden	2	4.5	5	–	2	2	2	2	3	–	2.65	2.55	2.45
31 France	2	5	3	–	3	3	3	2	2	–	2.30	2.30	2.50
31 Iceland	2	4	3	3	2	3	3	1	3	–			2.50
31 Panama	4	3	3	–	2	–	2	3	3	3	2.70	2.40	2.50
34 El Salvador	3	2.5	2	3	2	2	2	3	3	3	2.65	2.45	2.55
34 Trinidad and Tobago	5	4.5	2	2	1	2	2	1	3	3		2.50	2.55
36 Cyprus	3	4	3	1	2	2	3	3	2	3	2.50	2.60	2.60
36 Italy	3	5	3	2	2	2	2	2	3	2		2.70	2.60

1997 INDEX OF ECONOMIC FREEDOM RANKINGS

Rank		Trade	Taxation	Government Intervention	Monetary Policy	Foreign Investment	Banking	Wage/ Prices	Property Rights	Regulation	Black Market	1995 Score	1996 Score	1997 Score
36	Jamaica	2	3	2	4	2	2	3	2	3	3	2.80	2.70	**2.60**
36	Malaysia	5	3	2	1	3	3	3	2	2	2	2.15	2.40	**2.60**
36	Portugal	2	5	3	2	2	3	2	2	3	2	2.80	2.60	**2.60**
36	Spain	2	5	2	2	2	3	3	2	3	2	2.60	2.70	**2.60**
42	Argentina	4	3.5	2	5	2	2	2	3	2	2	2.85	2.65	**2.65**
43	Belize	5	4	2	1	2	3	2	2	3	3	2.70	2.70	**2.70**
43	Jordan	4	3	2	2	2	2	3	2	3	4	2.90	2.80	**2.70**
43	Uruguay	2	3	3	5	2	2	3	2	3	3	2.90	2.80	**2.70**
46	Paraguay	2	2.5	2	4	1	2	3	3	3	5	2.75	2.65	**2.75**
46	Morocco	4	3.5	3	1	2	3	3	2	3	3	2.90	2.70	**2.75**
46	Oman	3	3.5	4	1	3	4	3	2	2	2	2.65	2.85	**2.75**
46	Tunisia	5	3.5	3	2	2	2	2	3	2	3	2.85	2.65	**2.75**
50	Costa Rica	4	3	2	3	2	3	2	3	3	3	2.90	2.80	**2.80**
50	Barbados	4	5	3	1	2	2	2	3	3	3		3.00	**2.80**
50	Guatemala	3	3	1	3	3	2	3	3	4	3	3.05	2.85	**2.80**
50	Israel	2	5	4	3	1	3	2	2	2	4	3.10	2.90	**2.80**
50	Philippines	5	3	1	2	3	3	2	3	3	4	3.30	2.90	**2.80**
50	Saudi Arabia	4	4	4	1	4	3	3	1	3	2		2.90	**2.80**
50	Swaziland	4	3	2	2	2	3	3	2	3	4	2.90	2.90	**2.80**
50	Turkey	1	5	2	5	2	2	3	3	3	3	3.00	3.00	**2.80**
50	Western Samoa	3	4	2	2	3	3	3	3	3	2		2.80	**2.80**
59	Bolivia	2	2.5	5	3	2	2	1	3	4	4	3.20	2.75	**2.85**
59	Botswana	5	2.5	4	2	3	2	2	2	3	3	3.05	2.80	**2.85**
59	Greece	2	3.5	3	3	2	4	3	3	3	3	2.80	2.80	**2.85**
59	Indonesia	2	3.5	1	2	2	3	3	3	4	5	3.35	2.85	**2.85**
59	Zambia	2	3.5	2	5	2	2	2	3	4	3	3.05	2.95	**2.85**
64	Hungary	4	4	3	4	2	2	2	2	3	3	2.80	2.90	**2.90**
64	Peru	3	3	1	5	2	2	2	3	4	4	3.40	3.00	**2.90**
64	Uganda	4	4	3	5	2	3	1	2	3	2	2.94	2.83	**2.90**
67	Benin	4	3.5	3	1	3	3	3	3	3	3		2.95	**2.95**
67	Gabon	5	4.5	3	1	2	2	3	3	3	3	3.06	3.05	**2.95**
67	Latvia	4	2.5	3	5	2	2	2	2	3	4		3.05	**2.95**
67	Lebanon	2	2.5	2	5	3	2	2	3	3	5		2.95	**2.95**
67	Malta	4	3.5	2	1	2	3	4	3	3	4	3.25	3.05	**2.95**
67	Namibia	4	3.5	4	2	2	2	3	2	4	3			**2.95**
73	Djibouti	4	2	3	1	3	3	3	3	4	4			**3.00**
73	So. Africa	5	4	3	3	2	3	2	3	2	3	3.00	3.00	**3.00**
75	Ecuador	3	2.5	1	5	2	3	3	3	4	4	3.25	3.15	**3.05**

1997 INDEX OF ECONOMIC FREEDOM RANKINGS

Rank		Trade	Taxation	Government Intervention	Monetary Policy	Foreign Investment	Banking	Wage/ Prices	Property Rights	Regulation	Black Market	1995 Score	1996 Score	1997 Score
75	Kenya	4	3.5	3	2	3	2	3	3	4	3	3.05	3.05	3.05
75	The Slovak Republic	2	4.5	3	3	3	3	3	3	3	3	2.75	2.95	3.05
78	Colombia	4	4	2	4	2	2	2	3	3	5	2.90	3.00	3.10
78	Ghana	4	3	3	4	3	3	2	3	4	2	3.30	3.20	3.10
78	Lithuania	2	3	3	5	2	3	3	3	3	4		3.50	3.10
78	Mali	3	5	3	1	2	3	3	3	3	5	3.50	3.10	3.10
78	Pakistan	5	4	3	2	3	3	3	2	4	3	3.15	3.05	3.10
78	Papua New Guinea	5	3	3	1	3	4	3	3	3	3		3.10	3.10
78	Slovenia	4	4	3	3	3	2	3	3	3	3		3.35	3.10
85	Honduras	4	3.5	3	2	3	3	3	3	4	4	3.15	3.15	3.15
85	Poland	4	3.5	3	5	2	3	3	2	3	3	3.25	3.05	3.15
87	Fiji	5	3	3	1	3	3	3	3	4	4	3.30	3.10	3.20
87	Nigeria	5	3	2	4	2	4	2	3	4	3	3.15	3.25	3.20
89	Algeria	5	3.5	3	3	3	3	3	3	3	3	3.15	3.25	3.25
89	Madagascar	4	3.5	2	3	4	4	2	3	3	4	3.50	3.35	3.25
89	Senegal	5	4.5	3	1	3	3	4	2	4	3		3.40	3.25
89	Tanzania	3	3.5	3	4	3	3	2	3	4	4	3.50	3.45	3.25
93	Mongolia	3	4	3	5	3	3	3	3	3	3	3.33	3.50	3.30
94	Brazil	4	2.5	3	5	3	3	3	3	3	4	3.30	3.45	3.35
94	Ivory Coast	5	3.5	3	1	3	3	3	4	4	4	3.25	3.25	3.35
94	Mexico	3	3.5	3	5	2	4	3	3	4	3	3.05	3.35	3.35
94	Moldova	3	3.5	3	5	3	3	3	3	3	4	4.10	3.45	3.35
98	Romania	2	5	3	5	2	3	2	4	4	4	3.55	3.70	3.40
99	Cape Verde	5	N/A	3	2	2	5	4	2	4	4		3.44	3.44
100	Armenia	2	3.5	3	5	4	3	3	3	4	4		3.75	3.45
100	Dominican Republic	5	2.5	2	5	3	3	2	4	3	4	3.40	3.45	3.45
100	Guinea	5	4.5	2	3	3	2	2	4	4	5	3.35	3.35	3.45
100	Egypt	5	4.5	3	3	3	3	3	3	4	3	3.50	3.45	3.45
104	Burkina Faso	5	4	3	1	2	4	4	3	4	5		3.70	3.50
104	Guyana	4	4	3	5	3	3	2	3	4	4		3.35	3.50
106	Cambodia	5	2.5	4	4	3	3	3	4	4	3			3.55
106	Malawi	5	4.5	3	3	3	3	3	3	4	4	3.40	3.40	3.55
108	Bulgaria	3	5	3	5	3	3	3	3	4	4	3.50	3.50	3.60
108	Cameroon	5	4	3	1	3	4	3	4	4	5	3.60	3.60	3.60
108	Ethiopia	4	4	3	2	4	4	3	4	4	4	3.80	3.70	3.60
108	Gambia	4	4	3	2	4	4	4	2	4	5			3.60
108	Nepal	4	3	3	2	4	4	4	3	4	5		3.50	3.60

1997 INDEX OF ECONOMIC FREEDOM RANKINGS

Rank		Trade	Taxation	Government Intervention	Monetary Policy	Foreign Investment	Banking	Wage/ Prices	Property Rights	Regulation	Black Market	1995 Score	1996 Score	1997 Score
108	Nicaragua	5	3	2	5	2	3	3	4	4	5	3.90	3.60	3.60
108	Venezuela	4	4	3	5	3	3	3	3	3	5	3.00	3.50	3.60
115	Albania	3	3.5	5	5	2	4	3	3	3	5	3.55	3.45	3.65
115	Lesotho	4	4.5	3	3	3	4	4	3	4	4		3.65	3.65
115	Russia	5	3.5	4	5	3	2	3	3	4	4	3.50	3.50	3.65
118	Bangladesh	5	4	2	2	3	3	4	4	5	5	3.90	3.65	3.70
118	Croatia	3	3	5	5	3	3	4	4	4	3		3.70	3.70
118	India	5	4	3	2	3	4	4	3	4	5	3.70	3.75	3.70
118	Niger	5	4	3	1	4	4	4	3	4	5		3.70	3.70
118	Zimbabwe	5	4	3	4	4	3	3	3	4	4	3.50	3.70	3.70
123	Congo	5	4.5	3	1	4	4	3	4	4	5	3.90	3.80	3.75
123	Ukraine	4	4.5	3	5	3	4	3	3	4	4	3.90	4.00	3.75
125	Burundi	5	4	3	1	4	4	4	4	4	5			3.80
125	Chad	5	4	3	1	4	4	3	4	4	5			3.80
125	China	5	4	5	3	3	3	3	4	4	4	3.80	3.80	3.80
125	Mauritania	5	4	3	2	3	5	3	4	4	4		3.80	3.80
129	Belarus	5	4.5	3	5	4	3	3	3	3	5	3.65	3.55	3.85
129	Georgia	3	2.5	4	5	3	4	4	4	4	5		3.85	3.85
129	Sierra Leone	4	4.5	3	5	3	4	3	4	3	5	3.75	3.75	3.85
132	Yemen	5	3	4	5	2	4	3	4	4	5	3.75	3.75	3.90
133	Haiti	4	3	3	3	4	4	4	5	5	5	4.20	4.20	4.00
133	Mozambique	3	4	3	5	4	4	3	4	5	5	4.40	4.05	4.00
133	Suriname	5	5	3	5	3	4	3	3	4	5		3.90	4.00
136	Rwanda	5	5	4	1	4	5	3	5	5	5			4.20
136	Sudan	5	5	3	5	4	4	4	4	4	4	4.22	4.10	4.20
136	Syria	5	5	3	5	4	5	4	4	2	5		4.20	4.20
136	Zaire	4	5	3	5	4	4	4	4	4	5		4.20	4.20
140	Myanmar	5	3	5	4	4	4	4	4	5	5		4.30	4.30
141	Angola	5	3.5	4	5	4	4	4	4	5	5	4.35	4.35	4.35
142	Azerbaijan	5	4	5	5	5	4	5	4	4	5		4.70	4.60
143	Iran	5	5	5	4	5	5	4	5	4	5		4.70	4.70
143	Libya	5	5	5	2	5	5	5	5	5	5		4.70	4.70
143	Somalia	5	5	5	5	4	5	3	5	5	5		4.70	4.70
143	Vietnam	5	5	5	5	4	4	4	5	5	5	4.70	4.70	4.70
147	Iraq	5	5	5	5	5	5	5	5	4	5		4.90	4.90
148	Cuba	5	5	5	5	5	5	5	5	5	5	5.00	5.00	5.00
148	Laos	5	5	5	5	5	5	5	5	5	5		5.00	5.00
148	North Korea	5	5	5	5	5	5	5	5	5	5	5.00	5.00	5.00

1997 Index
of Economic Freedom

Edited by Kim R. Holmes, Bryan T. Johnson,
and Melanie Kirkpatrick

1

The *Index of Economic Freedom* and Economic Growth

by William W. Beach and Gareth Davis

The central question that should occupy all people concerned about their economic future is simple: How can my country achieve higher, sustainable economic growth? People asking that question can gain significant insight about how to answer it by carefully studying the *Index of Economic Freedom*.

Not only does the *Index* clearly identify successful countries that can serve as models for achieving higher levels of economic performance, but it also identifies those policies that can lead to higher growth. As this chapter will demonstrate, the *Index* draws on a rich body of scholarship about economic growth that encompasses insights as old as Adam Smith's and as recent as the New Growth Theory of the 1990s. Countries with good *Index* scores tended to grow faster over the past two decades. In short, the *Index of Economic Freedom* is more than an interesting annual snapshot of international progress toward freer markets and freer people; it can also be a roadmap to helping reduce poverty and expand economic horizons.

IMPORTANCE OF THE INSTITUTIONAL CONTEXT FOR ECONOMIC GROWTH

Adam Smith, the 18th century Scottish philosopher and founder of modern economics, devoted the whole of his *Inquiry into the Nature and Causes of the Wealth of Nations*[1] to a seemingly simple question: Why do some countries prosper while others do not? For Smith and his many followers, the answer was obvious: All economic growth flourishes from the single root of creatively dividing labor in the production of desirable goods, and blossoms in a political environment that protects private property and the justly deserved fruits of labor. Nations will experience opulence and peace, Smith argued, once they create the institutions that encourage entrepreneurship and savings (the stock of capital upon which all production takes place). On the other hand, nations reap only poverty and despair when they discourage business and thrift.

Subsequent generations of economists—in fact, nearly all major schools of economic thought since Smith—have begun their work with the same question: What is economic growth? And all of these perspectives on economic life—from Alfred Marshall and Karl Marx to John Maynard Keynes and Friedrich Hayek—have emphasized the critical relationship between economic activity and its institutional setting when explaining the phenomenon of economic growth. Perhaps more important, much of the policymaking community and intellectually active public already recognizes that sustainable, long-term growth stems in some fashion from the synergy between freewheeling capitalism and the institutions that sustain the civil society.

Even so, experts and laymen alike differ on what is meant by economic growth and the nature of its mediating institutions. Is economic growth merely the expansion of an economy's size, or is it the extension of improved well-being to all of a nation's citizens? Do a country's imperial designs executed in the name of economic growth count at all in answering the basic question of what constitutes growth, or does growth in any meaningful sense occur only when peaceful domestic and international exchange leaves, as in David Ricardo's felicitous example, the English and the Portuguese both better off through trade in cloth and wine?[2] If government policy puts labor behind and capital ahead in the struggle for income shares, or strips capital owners of their property in the name of improved welfare for labor, is that really growth? Does public policy play any role at all in the long-term growth of an economy, or does economic expansion really stem only from changes in population and technology that are not related to public policy?

Given these difficult questions, many of which are raised by experts on economic growth, is it any wonder that non-experts, from oil tycoons to short-order cooks, wonder what to believe? Nearly everyone lives in the massive currents of economic change, the swirl and rush of markets, the rise and tumble of great companies, and the ebb and flow of everyday working life. These are the economic rhythms that shape people's lives and punctuate their everyday work, and they leave precious little time for abstracting the big questions from the minutiae of living.

Although most people can sense that more income, more goods and services, and more economic opportunities promote economic growth, they, like many of the experts, puzzle over what ingredients are essential to facilitate that growth. They wonder about what public policies they should support, about which politicians they

---

1   Adam Smith, *An Inquiry into the Nature and Causes of the Wealth of Nations*, ed. R. H. Campbell and A. S. Skinner, Glasgow Edition (Oxford: Oxford University Press, 1976); originally published in 1776.

2   David Ricardo, *On the Principles of Political Economy and Taxation*, Third Edition, ed. Piero Sraffa (Cambridge: Cambridge University Press, 1951); originally published in 1821. See especially Chapter 7, "On Foreign Trade," for Ricardo's discussion of how two economies can grow by trading commodities in which each has a comparative advantage.

should believe, and about what they can do to ensure a bigger economy for their children and grandchildren.

It is on these questions that The Heritage Foundation/ *Wall Street Journal's Index of Economic Freedom* sheds much-needed light. The *Index* measures a country's degree of economic freedom using a composite score consisting of ten elements, each of which forms a major part of that country's institutional setting. These ten elements are trade policy, taxes, government consumption of economic output, monetary policy, capital flows and foreign investment policy, banking regulation, wage and price controls, protection of property rights, business regulation, and the strength of the black market. Each element is scored separately, with the average of all elements for a country constituting a rating of that country's level of economic freedom.

What does this year's *Index of Economic Freedom* suggest about a country's prospects for superior economic growth? This chapter takes takes two approaches to answering this question. First, many economists of the "New Growth Theory" school believe that the institutional setting strongly influences the rate of economic growth. A review of recent developments in this new field of research supports the position that low *Index* (greater economic freedom) scores imply the superior rates of economic growth. Second, statistical work conducted independently by The Heritage Foundation also links *Index* scores to economic growth.

A SHORT PRIMER ON THE ECONOMICS OF GROWTH

From the 1960s to the mid-1980s, the dominant academic theory of what causes economic growth was the "Solow Growth Model," named after Nobel Laureate Robert Solow. From a factual or a policy viewpoint, this theory has performed poorly.

First, the theory offered meager advice to policymakers on to how to generate economic growth. Solow argued that the only way a nation could boost its level of growth was to save more and therefore accumulate physical capital. Even an increase in the rate of capital accumulation, however, would bring only a one-time boost in income and have only a short-term or medium-term increase in economic growth rates. The long-run rate of economic growth (the "steady state" level) was determined by "technological innovation." This technological innovation was a mysterious force within Solow's model that neither could be analyzed by economists nor influenced by government policy. In the Solow model, to paraphrase the famous Cambridge economist Joan Robinson, technology and growth fall like manna from heaven.

Second, the major factual prediction of traditional growth theory (that poorer countries generally would grow faster and "converge" to the economic status of richer countries) clearly is not coming true in the real world.[3]

---

3   Some economists have found evidence of convergence when they control for countries' differing savings rates, but this convergence has been very weak. In any case, the traditional model of growth has no explanation for what causes these international differences in savings rates, and therefore no policy prescriptions in this regard.

What is the New Growth Theory?[4]

In 1983, Professor Paul Romer, then at the University of Rochester, published a paper entitled "Increasing Returns and Long Run Growth."[5] Some 35 pages long and accessible only to those with a firm grasp of mathematics, this paper revolutionized the field of growth theory and led to the emergence of the New Growth Theory. The New Growth Theory can be distinguished from its predecessor by the following:

✔ **The long-run costs and benefits of economic policies are much greater than previously thought due to "increasing returns."**

Romer argued that an initial increase in a society's productive capacity can feed on itself (because of what are known technically as *increasing returns*) to produce permanently higher rates of growth. This feedback effect stands in sharp contrast to the *decreasing returns* contained in the old theory, under which the growth effects of an increase in a society's capacity are only temporary. In other words, under the old theory of decreasing returns, policy changes would produce only a one-time boost to economic activity, after which the economy would return to its long-term growth path. Under the new theory of increasing returns, however, it is possible to affect the long-term growth path itself.

The old growth theory predicted that establishing sound policies would lead only to a one-time boost in income (and therefore only a transitory increase in economic growth rates). The theory of increasing returns implies that instituting sensible policies can result in a GDP growth rate that is permanently higher. This means that the benefits of instituting wise economic policies and the costs of pursuing misguided policies are much greater than was the case under the old theories that assumed decreasing returns. In this model, introducing a "good" policy can create an economic expansion that will feed on itself to bring about a permanent acceleration in the growth of prosperity. "Bad" policies, however, mean permanently lower growth rates and cost society more than earlier theorists thought.

Policy Lessons from the New Growth Theory

(1) **Accumulate capital.** Increasing the stock of physical capital per worker is one of the best ways to increase per capita income.

(2) **Keep government small.** Government spending consumes scarce resources that could be used for investment and distorts the incentives faced by individuals and firms. State ownership of capital stock means that the output from a society's productive assets will be lower than if they were in private hands.

(3) **Open the economy to foreign trade and investment.** New Growth Theory has uncovered many previously unknown gains from foreign trade and investment, including the faster and deeper diffusion of technology, an increase in competition, and more rapid capital accumulation.

---

4   For a brief review of the New Growth literature, see Appendix, "Evidence from New Growth Economics on Components of the *Index of Economic Freedom*," *infra*.

5   Published in *Journal of Political Economy*, Vol. 94 (1986), pp. 1002–1037.

(4) **Respect property rights and the rule of law.** Without adequate property rights and a secure political environment, individuals and firms will face severe disincentives to invest and to engage in productive activities.

(5) **Do not burden the productive sector with government regulations and controls.** Regulations, mandates, and wage and price controls are a drag on economic growth. They raise the cost of producing goods and services and make innovation and invention more expensive. Government controls also increase the opportunities for rent seeking and the corruption of the bureaucracy and political system.

(6) **Invest in "human capital."** Education, which increases worker productivity, is very important to growth, according to many leading New Growth economists. In this context, it is important that education systems operate primarily to educate students rather than to serve the ends of "social justice" or of powerful political groups.

✔ **Greater emphasis on the importance of technology, institutions, and human capital to economic growth.**

The New Growth Theory is also sometimes referred to as *Endogenous Growth Theory* because key factors in economic growth (human capital, technology, innovation, and institutions) are now examined within and form an integral part of (are "endogenous" to) this theory. No longer seen as mysterious and unfathomable, these factors are treated as concrete entities over which policymakers can exercise influence, whether for good or ill. The focus of Romer's original paper was technology. Other theorists, such as 1995 Nobel Laureate Robert Lucas, have examined the growth implications of human capital, institutions, and other factors.

In the old growth theory, the only things for which its advocates could account were the accumulation of physical capital and population growth. None of the other factors that cause economic growth could be explained, predicted, or influenced by public policies.

✔ **A new emphasis on investigating the causes of economic growth using statistical tests.**

New Growth Economics extends beyond mere theory. Economists have been inspired by these new theories to use statistical models. In the past seven years, a massive volume of econometric research has been carried out on the differences in growth rates across countries. This has been made possible by the recent emergence of internationally compatible and reliable long-run economic data for developing and developed countries. Even though this work is ongoing and in a state of relative infancy, several generalized findings have begun to emerge.

There is a striking correspondence between the elements of the *Index of Economic Freedom* and the key findings of the New Growth Theory. New Growth economists show that high levels of growth are positively associated with (1) the level of private investment (especially in machinery); (2) "openness" to international trade and finance; (3) the educational attainment level of the population; and (4) the rule of law, political stability, and the protection of property rights. Economists in this field also associate slow or negative economic growth with hyperinflation, high levels of government consumption and taxation, and excessive regulation. The *Index* considers nearly all of these factors to be crucial in evaluating international economic freedoms.

New Growth Theory strongly suggests that public policies do matter. In a recent essay on why some countries enjoy better economic performance than others, Mancur Olson, one of the world's leading economic theorists, observed that "[t]hose countries with the best policies and institutions achieve most of their potential, while other countries achieve only a tiny faction of their potential income."[6] Olson further notes that

> the large differences in per capita income across countries cannot be explained by differences in access to the world's stock of productive knowledge or to its capital markets, by differences in the ratio of population to land or natural resources, or by differences in the quality of marketable human capital or personal culture.... The only remaining plausible explanation is that the great differences in the wealth of nations are mainly due to differences in the quality of their institutions and economic policies.[7]

STATISTICAL RELATIONSHIP OF THE *INDEX* TO ECONOMIC GROWTH

In addition to the strong support this scholarship affords the *Index* as an indicator of future economic performance, statistical tests performed by The Heritage Foundation further underscore the applicability of the *Index* to discussions of economic growth. Using one of the largest datasets designed for inter-country growth comparisons,[8] Heritage analysts found statistically significant relationships (at the 99 percent confidence level) both between the *Index* and country-by-country levels of economic development and between the *Index* and economic growth rates.

Chart 1.1 shows the type of relationship observed between economic growth and *Index* values. In Chart 1.1, the vertical axis contains the percentage change in real GDP per person between 1976 and 1991. The horizontal axis shows the *Index* values for 1997. This graph clearly shows a distinct association between countries with lower *Index* numbers (freer economies) and higher levels of economic growth. In other words, the Heritage analysis of these data strongly suggests that countries with free-market public policies grow faster than countries that have repressed economies.[9]

---

6   Mancur Olson, Jr., "Big Bills Left on the Sidewalk: Why Some Nations Are Rich, and Others Are Poor," *Journal of Economic Perspectives*, Vol. 10 (Spring 1996), p. 6.

7   *Ibid.*, p. 19.

8   This is the 138 country dataset modified and expanded by Harvard economists Robert Barro and Jong-Wha Lee. The data are presented in five-year intervals from 1960 and fall generally into seven categories: national income, education, population/fertility, government expenditures, price deflators, political variables, and trade variables. See Robert Barro and Xavier Sala-I-Martin, *Economic Growth* (New York: McGraw-Hill, 1995).

9   A number of qualifications must be made about the association contained in Chart 1.1. First, a number of factors outside the sphere of economic policy affect a country's growth rate: natural disasters, mineral discoveries, commodity price shifts, war, pestilence, and the policies of other countries, to name just a few. A prudent use of the relationship illustrated above is valid, however; at the very least, it emphasizes a connection between economic performance and public policies. Second, the Heritage analysis compares growth rates ending in 1991 to *Index* numbers based on 1995–1996 data. The *Index* measures institutional dimensions, however, that typically change very little over the short run; a correlation of 96 percent was found between the *Index* for 1995 and the *Index* for 1996. Thus, the four-year gap between the two variables most probably would not obliterate the relationship that appears to exist. Indeed, it can be argued that had contemporary data been available the true underlying relationship would have been proved to have been much stronger. Third, data on growth were not available for a number of countries with closed political systems between 1976 and 1991. Had such data been available, we believe that the relationship shown here would be stronger.

Chart 1.1

RELATIONSHIP OF LONG-TERM
ECONOMIC GROWTH TO INDEX VALUES FOR 1997

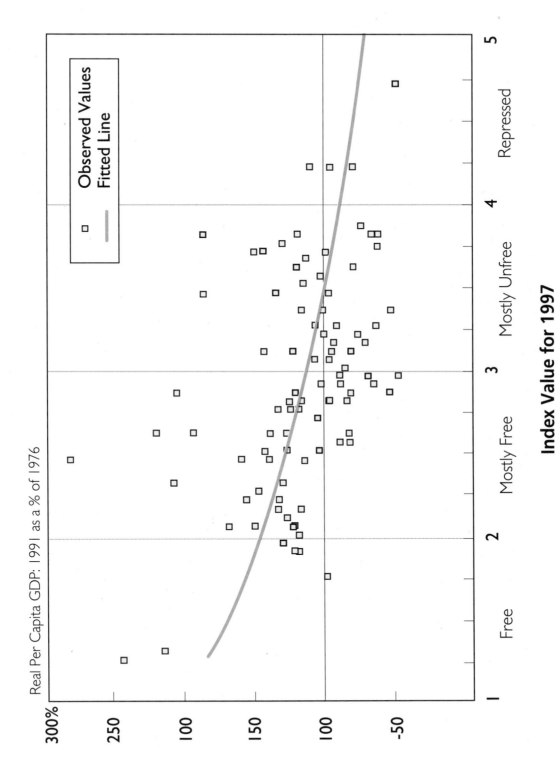

Note: Per Capita GDP is expressed in Purchasing Power Parities. This data used in these calculations are taken from the 138 country economic dataset modified and expanded by Harvard economists Robert Barro and Jong-Wha Lee.
Source: Heritage calculations based on Robert Barro and Xavier Sala-I-Martin, *Economic Growth*, 1995.

Chart 1.2 demonstrates this correlation between economic freedom and wealth as well, by describing the average annual real per-capita growth rate of nations in each *Index* category. Nations with repressed economies or mostly unfree economies experienced negative per-capita income growth on average. Free economies, and to a lesser extent mostly free economies, on average experienced positive real income growth.

Despite the limitations of these and other data used to explore the implications of policy changes on cross-country growth rates, numerous other eminent scholars have found similar and significant relationships between economic growth and government policies. For example, Robert Barro, a Harvard professor and contributing editor of *The Wall Street Journal,* has found a strong positive relationship between growth rates and data that measure the degree to which a country rules itself by law as opposed to the whims and edicts of political strongmen. He also has found that growth rates are better in those countries in which government consumes a lower share of GDP than they are in those countries in which government consumes higher percentages of GDP. Barro has determined that other policy and institutional or non-economic variables significantly related to growth include the inflation rate, political rights, the fertility rate, years of secondary and higher education, and the initial level of GDP.[10]

HOW HIGHER GROWTH RATES COULD AFFECT POOR COUNTRIES

Enormous benefits will accrue for human welfare if countries solve the riddle of what causes economic growth. An indication of this can be obtained by taking the case of Bangladesh, one of the world's poorest and most destitute nations, and seeing how much faster it would grow if its economy expanded at the long-term rates sustained by a diverse group of market-oriented economies.

In 1992, Bangladesh had a real, average income per capita of $1,510 in inflation-adjusted 1985 U.S. dollars—just one-twelfth of per-capita income in the United States. Over the period 1980–1993, the World Bank estimated that real income per person in Bangladesh (as measured by GDP) grew at an average annual rate of 2.1 percent.[11] Over this same period, countries such as Hong Kong, South Korea, Singapore, Botswana, and Thailand all sustained high long-term growth rates. The Heritage Foundation therefore analyzed what would happen if Bangladesh implemented policies that enabled it to grow at the same long-term rates experienced by these countries over the 1980–1993 period. The implications for Bangladeshi living standards are staggering.

As can be seen from Table 1.1, if the Bangladeshi economy continues to grow at the same 2.1 percent rate it experienced during the 1980s and early 1990s, a decade's worth of growth would raise income levels by only 23 percent, from $1,510 to $1,859 per

---

we believe that the relationship shown here would be stronger.

10   Robert J. Barro, presentation to Heritage Foundation Roundtable on Economic Growth, June 26, 1996; copies available upon request from The Heritage Foundation. See also Robert J. Barro, "Economic Growth in a Cross-Section of Countries," *Quarterly Journal of Economics,* Vol. 106 (1991), pp. 407-443.

11   Bangladesh's growth performance of 2.1 percent per annum over 1980–1993 is by no means relatively poor. Indeed, Bangladeshi incomes grew faster than was the norm for Third World countries over the same period; many nations actually had average incomes that fell on aggregate over this period. If we assume that the alternative to growth-enhancing policies is zero or negative growth, then the gains from reform are even larger.

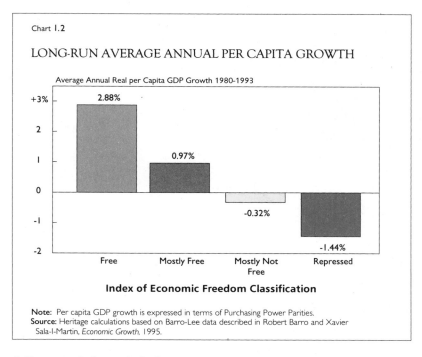

Chart 1.2

LONG-RUN AVERAGE ANNUAL PER CAPITA GROWTH

Average Annual Real per Capita GDP Growth 1980-1993

2.88%

0.97%

-0.32%

-1.44%

Free   Mostly Free   Mostly Not Free   Repressed

Index of Economic Freedom Classification

Note: Per capita GDP growth is expressed in terms of Purchasing Power Parities.
Source: Heritage calculations based on Barro-Lee data described in Robert Barro and Xavier Sala-I-Martin, *Economic Growth,* 1995.

capita in real 1985 dollars. And if Bangladeshi per-capita income grew at 2.1 percent per annum for 50 years, real per-capita income would reach only $4,268—roughly the same as the standard of living enjoyed by Turkey or Brazil today.

By contrast, if Bangladesh adopted the policies necessary to attain the long-term growth rates of those countries listed in Table 1.1, it would rapidly escape poverty.

- If Bangladesh's growth rate rose to the same level as the long-term rate achieved by Singapore, Botswana, or Thailand, its living standards within 25 years would roughly approximate those currently enjoyed by such European nations as Greece, Spain, and Portugal.

- Within 40 years, Bangladeshi income levels would be roughly equivalent to those currently enjoyed by such nations as the United States and Switzerland, and would exceed those currently enjoyed by Japan, Sweden, and Germany.

- Also within 40 years, even at the lower Hong Kong growth rate, Bangladesh would have attained living standards equivalent to levels currently enjoyed by Great Britain or Austria.

At the growth rate experienced over 1980–1993—which is by no means the worst experienced by any Third World nation—it would take Bangladesh 102 years to achieve the living standards currently enjoyed in the industrial world. The typical Bangladeshi born in 1995 with a life expectancy of 55[12] would not be alive to experience these income levels. If, however, Bangladeshi policymakers helped their country achieve growth rates equivalent to those in Hong Kong, Singapore, Botswana, Thailand, or South Korea, the typical Bangladeshi child born in 1995 would live to experience living standards equivalent to those enjoyed today by the world's richest societies.

---

12   Based on an estimate contained in the 1995 *CIA World Factbook.*

Table 1.1

WHAT WOULD IT MEAN FOR BANGLADESHI LIVING STANDARDS IF THE GROWTH RATE INCREASED?

If it grew as fast as . . .	Real GDP Growth Rate 1980-1993	Income Per Person After 10 Years	Income Per Person After 25 Years	Income Per Person After 40 Years	Income Per Person After 50 Years
Bangladesh (1980-1993)	2.1 %	$1,859	$2,539	$3,467	$4,268
Hong Kong	5.4 %	$2,555	$5,623	$12,377	$20,941
Singapore	6.1 %	$2,730	$6,635	$16,128	$29,157
Botswana	6.2 %	$2,756	$6,793	$16,748	$30,563
Thailand	6.4 %	$2,808	$7,121	$18,057	$33,578
South Korea	8.2 %	$3,321	$10,831	$35,324	$77,686

Note: All figures are in 1985 inflation-adjusted U.S. dollars.
Source: Heritage calculations based on data from 1994 World Bank World Development Report and Penn World Tables Version 5.5.

Indeed, assuming that the G–7 nations continued to grow at the 1980–1993 long-term rate of 2.1 percent, and that Bangladesh grew at the same rate as Botswana or Singapore grew over the 1980–1993 period, Bangladeshi living standards could overtake those of the G–7 nations within 59 to 60 years. If Bangladesh grew at South Korean rates, its living standards would overtake those of the world's wealthiest nations within 40 years, again well within the lifetime of a Bangladeshi child born in 1995.

The growth rates necessary for Bangladesh, one of the world's poorest nations, to achieve these feats are well within reach. With the sorts of income levels that are produced by faster economic growth, more resources would be available for individuals to meet their own basic human wants and needs, such as food, housing, medical care, education, and other goods. The result would be large numbers of people who are healthier, better fed, and better educated, and who have more resources with which to experience life. The economic growth rates used in this analysis were achieved for a sustained period of time by a diverse group of nations ranging from Hong Kong to Thailand (with its formerly rice-based subsistence economy) to the sub-Saharan African nation of Botswana. What they all have in common are relatively high levels of economic freedom.[13]

---

13   All of the high-growth nations mentioned here have relatively high levels of economic freedom. Among sub-Saharan African nations, Botswana had by far the best 1996 *Index of Economic Freedom* ranking and has enjoyed its economic success in a region ravaged by widespread declines in average income levels. Hong Kong and Singapore are the first and second most economically free nations in the 1997 *Index of Economic Freedom*. Thailand and South Korea (ranked 23rd and 27th, respectively, out of 150) also receive relatively good scores. Bangladesh was ranked 118th. Many commentators have argued that rapid population growth and "culture" bar such countries as Bangladesh from enjoying rapid income growth even if the proper policies are implemented. This is a fallacy. The societies mentioned in this analysis are very different from each other. Indonesia, a country that has been "diagnosed" in the past as suffering the same "structural problems" as Bangladesh (rapid population growth and a high population density, being predominantly Muslim, and having a history of political unrest), instituted a partial set of reforms that gave it an above-average level of economic freedom (59th out of 150 in the 1997 *Index of Economic Freedom*); this enabled it to sustain an average per-capita annual GDP growth rate of 4.2 percent over 1980–1993 (more than twice that achieved in Bangladesh). Most likely, full reform would have brought even higher growth.

Chart 1.3

HOW LONG WOULD IT TAKE BANGLADESH TO ATTAIN THE SAME INCOME LEVELS AS THOSE CURRENTLY ENJOYED BY THE G-7 DEVELOPED NATIONS?

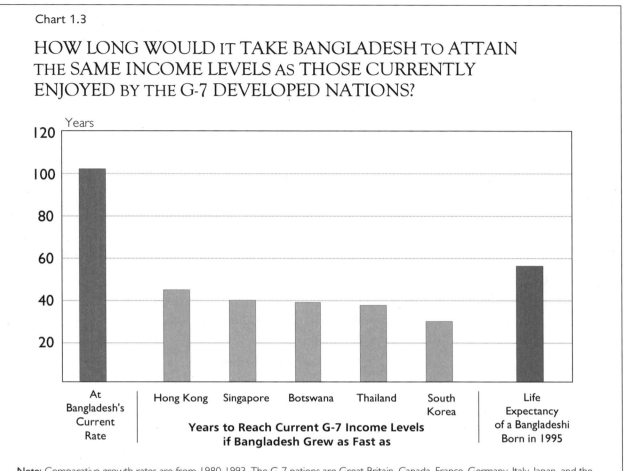

Note: Comparative growth rates are from 1980-1993. The G-7 nations are Great Britain, Canada, France, Germany, Italy, Japan, and the United States. The income levels enjoyed by the G-7 nations are calculated by means of an unweighted average of their real GDP per capita. **Source:** Heritage Foundation calculations based on data from 1994 World Bank World Development Report and Penn World Tables Version 5.5.

CONCLUSION

What could happen in Bangladesh could also occur in scores of other countries caught in the grip of poverty and economic decline. In fact, the powerful effects of pro-growth economic policies could be produced by any country willing to embrace the policies of economic freedom. Although cultural and political factors (including the frequency of wars) will make every country's response somewhat different, it appears to be a universal truth that free trade, free markets, and free men and women create stronger economies and better lives than any other "mix" of public policies.

The *Index of Economic Freedom* clearly points to those policies that reduce want and increase life spans. This makes the *Index* more than an intellectual exercise. This chapter began with a discussion of Adam Smith and ended with Bangladesh. Although this progression may strike some as odd, Adam Smith, whose economics lived squarely in the real world, certainly would understand.

of economic freedom (59th out of 150 in the 1997 *Index of Economic Freedom*); this enabled it to sustain an average per-capita annual GDP growth rate of 4.2 percent over 1980–1993 (more than twice that achieved in Bangladesh). Most likely, full reform would have brought even higher growth.

Appendix

Evidence from New Growth Economics on Components of the *Index of Economic of Freedom*

Evidence from the New Growth Literature, combined with the work of earlier economists, supports the argument that the concepts measured by the *Index of Economic Freedom* are related to economic growth. That is, conclusions from the New Growth Economics link differences in the rate of economic growth across countries to a number of policy variables, many of which the *Index* attempts to measure.

Econometric studies by economists at Harvard, the World Bank, and the Federal Reserve Bank have found that long-term growth rates rise as restraints on foreign trade and investment are lowered.[14] Calculations by Columbia economist Richard Baldwin have demonstrated that old models of growth tend to underestimate drastically the magnitude of gains from free trade.[15]

Likewise, numerous cross-country studies have established that high levels of government spending will slow the long-term rate of economic growth.[16] An econometric model calibrated by Professors Robert King and Sergio Rebelo of the University of Rochester found that traditional growth models underestimated the growth effect of taxes by a magnitude of 40.[17] Studies also have found links between inflation (particularly hyperinflation) and lower long-term GDP growth rates.[18] Recent statistical evidence also indicates the special importance of a strong, sophisticated, and unencumbered banking and financial system as a conduit for economic growth.[19]

---

14 Ross Levine and David Renelt, "A Sensitivity Analysis of Cross-Country Growth Regressions," *American Economic Review,* Vol. 82 (1990), pp. 943–963; David Gould and Roy Ruffin, "What Determines Economic Growth?" *Economic Review,* Federal Reserve Bank of Dallas, 1993, pp. 25–40.

15 Richard Baldwin, "The Growth Effects of 1992," *Economic Policy,* November 1989, pp. 248–283.

16 Barro, "Economic Growth in a Cross-Section of Countries"; Barro and Sala-I-Martin, *Economic Growth,* p. 434; Daniel Landau, "Government and Economic Growth in the Lesser Developed Countries: An Empirical Study for 1960–80," in *Economic Development and Cultural Change,* Vol. 35 (October 1986), p. 68; Michael Marlow, "Links Between Taxes and Economic Growth: Some Empirical Evidence," *Journal of Economic Growth,* Vol. 1, No. 4 (1986); Eric Engen and Jonathan Skinner, "Fiscal Policy and Economic Growth," *NBER Working Paper* No. 4223, 1992; and Kevin Grier and Gordon Tullock, "An Empirical Analysis of Cross-National Economic Growth, 1951–80," *Journal of Monetary Economics,* Vol. 24 (1989), pp. 259–276.

17 Robert King and Sergio Rebelo, "Public Policy and Economic Growth: Developing Neoclassical Implications," *Journal of Political Economy,* Vol. 98 (1990).

18 For a full discussion of the evidence, see Kevin Dowd, "The Costs of Inflation and Disinflation," *Cato Journal,* Fall 1994. A 1993 panel and cross-sectional study by top MIT economist Stanley Fischer concludes that "high growth is not sustainable in the presence of high inflation." See Stanley Fischer, "The Role of Macroeconomic Factors in Growth," *Journal of Monetary Economics,* Vol. 32, No. 3 (1993), pp. 485–512.

19 Robert King and Ross Levine, "Finance, Entrepreneurship and Growth: Theory and Evidence," *Journal of Monetary Economics,* Vol. 32, No. 3 (December 1993), pp. 513–542; see also Robert

Robert Barro of Harvard and Xavier Sala-I-Martin of Yale University have found a correlation between lower growth rates and measures of the distortions caused by wage, price, and exchange controls and other forms of government regulation.[20] Economists also have succeeded recently in uncovering a robust empirical link between cross-country long-term economic growth and the degree to which governments abide by the rule of law and respect and enforce property rights and contracts.[21]

After a decade of New Growth Economics, there is stronger scientific evidence than ever before that the concepts measured in the *Index of Economic Freedom* strongly indicate the degree to which a country's current economic policies and institutions are friendly or unfriendly to economic growth.

King and Ross Levine, "Finance and Growth: Schumpeter Might Be Right," *Quarterly Journal of Economics,* Vol. 108, No. 3 (August 1993), pp. 717–737.

20   Barro and SalaI-Martin, *Economic Growth,* pp. 434–435.

21   Steven Knack and Philip Keefer "Institutional and Economic Performance: Cross-Country Tests Using Alternative Institutional Measures," *Economics and Politics,* Vol. 7 (1995), pp. 207–227, and Barro and Sala-I-Martin, *Economic Growth,* pp. 439–440.

2

Economic Freedom, Foreign Aid, and Economic Development

by Bryan T. Johnson

U.S. foreign aid bureaucrats have argued for years that foreign assistance is vital to the economic well-being of less developed countries. J. Brian Atwood, administrator of the U.S. Agency for International Development (AID), the agency responsible for handing out most of America's $12 billion foreign aid budget, has further stretched such claims by suggesting that the overall economic prosperity of the post–World War II era can be attributed largely to the Marshall Plan and successive foreign aid efforts.[1] This grossly exaggerates the benefits of development aid while ignoring its many harmful effects. Not only has the U.S. foreign aid program failed to promote economic growth in less developed countries, but many recipient countries are worse off because of it.

The *Index of Economic Freedom* demonstrates that economic freedom is the single most important factor in creating the conditions for economic growth and prosperity. The data in this chapter further demonstrate that instead of helping poor countries lift themselves out of poverty, development aid often impedes their economic growth while

---

1   Remarks by AID Administrator J. Brian Atwood to Center for National Policy, Washington, D.C., December 14, 1994.

damaging their fragile economies. Economic freedom, not aid, is what matters most in achieving economic development.

The *Index* also shows that many long-term U.S. foreign aid recipients have unfree or repressed economies. No matter how much money the United States and other donors spend on foreign aid recipients like Tanzania, Sudan, and Ethiopia, economic development and wealth will not be forthcoming. Indeed, no country scored by the *Index* as having a mostly unfree or repressed economy has generated substantial levels of wealth. On the other hand, those that rank at the very top are among the richest in the world.

Countries graduating to the developed world in the past two decades—Hong Kong, Singapore, Taiwan, South Korea, and Chile—largely have done so without the crutch of foreign aid. All, to varying degrees, have used the free market as the major engine of economic development. At the same time, countries in sub-Saharan Africa, a region receiving large amounts of foreign aid, have remained poor and impoverished. The reason is that they have refused to make the market reforms necessary to produce economic growth. If history is any guide, foreign aid clearly is no prerequisite to, or major factor in, economic prosperity.

FOREIGN AID AND WORLD POVERTY

The facts show that poverty is largely a condition imposed on people by ill-conceived and repressive economic policies. Other factors such as history, culture, war, and climate influence a country's development, but none is as important as economic freedom. The facts also show that no amount of foreign aid can make up for the conditions that result from economically unfree economies. Some countries have received U.S. foreign aid for over 50 years and still are no better off than they were before such aid. A close look at recipients of U.S. foreign aid and their economic performance over the last several decades proves the point:

- Of the 78 countries ranked as mostly unfree or repressed on the *Index,* 35 have received U.S. foreign aid for over 35 years—many for as long as 52 years;

- Of these 35 countries, 25 are no better off today than they were in 1965; and

- Of these 25 countries, 13 actually are poorer today than they were in 1965.

These facts raise several questions: If development aid is so important to economic growth, why are so many long-term recipients of foreign aid still so poor? If development aid is essential for economic growth and development, why are so many long-term recipients—over one-third—becoming poorer?[2] If development aid is essential to economic prosperity, why has there been so little progress by the countries that are most dependent on foreign aid? The answer is simple: Economic freedom, not aid, is the key to economic development. Consider the following examples:

---

2   Some aid recipients in sub-Saharan Africa and elsewhere have at least doubled their wealth in the past 30 years. In 1965, for example, Lesotho's per-capita GDP in constant 1987 dollars was $126; by 1994, its per-capita wealth had reached $319. Nevertheless, Lesotho obviously remains an extremely poor country. The growth rates for Lesotho and other aid-dependent countries pale in comparison to those of the Asian tigers, most of which increased their wealth over 500 percent during the same period. Thus, foreign aid recipients that have doubled or even tripled their economic wealth since 1965 are still worse off than the Asian tigers, which had much higher growth rates without receiving much foreign aid. The reason for the difference: the free market economic policies of the Asian tigers.

Haiti. Haiti has depended on U.S. foreign aid for 52 years, yet it is one of the world's poorest countries.[3] During this time, Haiti has received almost $1 billion in foreign aid from the United States alone, not including the money the United States spent in its military operation to "restore" democracy in Haiti in 1994. In 1965, Haiti's per-capita GDP was $360; in 1994, it was even lower: $225.[4]

Peru. Peru also has been a U.S. foreign aid recipient for 52 years, receiving almost $2 billion in foreign aid during that time. Its per-capita GDP in 1965 was $1,126; by 1994, it had fallen to $1,103.

Somalia. The Clinton Administration argues that cutting foreign aid to less developed countries will result in "more Somalias." Yet almost $1 billion in U.S. foreign aid over the past 41 years has failed to contribute to the development of Somalia's economy. Somalia's per-capita GDP was $123 in 1965; by 1987, it had shrunk to $111.

Niger. Niger has received over $500 million in U.S. foreign assistance over the last 37 years, but its per-capita wealth shrank by more than 60 percent from 1965 to 1994, falling from $617 to only $272.

Defenders of foreign aid often argue that poor people around the world rely on assistance for their daily existence, but some 70 percent of U.S. foreign aid spending never even reaches the poor overseas.[5] It stays in the United States, used to fund American contractors and consultants, many of whom provide useless and duplicative services to AID. Some examples:[6]

- A U.S. company called Planning & Development Collaborative International contracted with AID to sponsor a 1993 study tour in the United States for the Romanian Union of Architects. AID never explained how acquainting Romanians with American architecture would help to build a prosperous free-market economy in Romania.

- The Academy for Educational Development of Washington, D.C., in 1993 undertook a study for AID to determine how Indonesian health workers can improve their interpersonal communication skills. One recommendation of this study: Conduct further study.

- Four organizations collaborated to perform an AID contract worth over $2 million that culminated in a study of "ecotourism" in Central America. The study includes a section on the "cultural and socioeconomic impacts of tourism" and a list that ranks the "desirability of native fauna for the tourist industry by marketing value and observation satisfaction."

---

3   Figures include both military and economic assistance, although most assistance to less developed countries generally has been in the form of economic aid. For example, of the $932.5 million in U.S. foreign aid Haiti received from 1946 to 1990, $917.2 million was economic assistance. For more information, see *Foreign Operations, Export Financing, and Related Programs Appropriations Bill, 1994,* Report No. 103–142, U.S. Senate, September 14, 1993.

4   All figures are GDP per capita, expressed in constant 1987 dollars; from *World Data 1995 on CD–ROM* (Washington, D.C.: The World Bank, 1996).

5   Atwood remarks, *op. cit.*

6   See Thomas P. Sheehy, "Clinton Blows Smoke Over Foreign Aid Cuts," Heritage Foundation *Executive Memorandum* No. 416, June 7, 1995.

Even though the real winners from such aid programs are U.S. contractors, the real losers are countries that continue to depend on foreign aid. There is little chance that steps taken this year by the Clinton Administration will improve the prospects of aid-dependent countries like Niger. Until these countries adopt the principles of economic freedom, prosperity will not be forthcoming—no matter how much foreign aid they receive. Low taxes, open trade and investment policies, free banking institutions, and other economic freedoms cannot be bought with foreign aid dollars. Only the governments of these countries can make these changes. If history sheds any light on the current status of the world's poor, these countries will remain impoverished until they become economically free.

ECONOMIC FREEDOM AND PROSPERITY

Although many aid-dependent countries have remained poor, the few that have eschewed foreign aid have achieved impressive levels of economic growth and wealth. They have done so because they have maximized economic freedom. The key to economic growth is a set of policies that minimize government control of the economy. Consider the success stories of economic freedom:

Hong Kong. Ranked the world's economically freest country by the *Index*, Hong Kong is an example of what economic freedom can achieve. In 1965, Hong Kong had a per-capita GDP of $2,279. Then AID, the World Bank, and International Monetary Fund began to withdraw foreign aid from the region, forcing Hong Kong and other Asian countries to reform their economies. As a result of years of economic reform, Hong Kong's economy soared; because it cut taxes, privatized banks, slashed regulation, and made other market reforms, its per-capita wealth rose nearly ten times to $21,650.[7]

Singapore. The world's second economically freest country according to the *Index*, Singapore also was cut off from most foreign aid in the mid to late 1960s. As a result, its economy shot up like Hong Kong's. Singapore's per-capita wealth was only $1,863 in 1965; by 1994, it had risen to $23,360—a more than tenfold increase.[8]

The surest way to create the most economic wealth for the most people is for a government to cut or eliminate taxation and tariffs, privatize state enterprises, deregulate the economy, and generally reduce its role in the economy. These lessons have been lost on the U.S. foreign aid bureaucracy.

THE STATE OF THE U.S. FOREIGN AID PROGRAM

In 1995, expectations were high that the 104th Congress would make major reforms in the U.S. foreign aid program. The need for such reform had been recognized for many years. At least since 1989, when a congressional task force report on foreign aid conducted by Representatives Lee Hamilton (D–IN) and Benjamin Gilman (R–NY) was published, there has been a strong bipartisan consensus in favor of revamping foreign aid. Almost everyone who follows foreign aid recognizes that it lacks a focus and is burdened with too many, sometimes overlapping objectives. In 1994, the Clinton Administration recognized the need for reform, but its Peace, Prosperity and Democracy Act failed to generate much support in Congress.

---

7   Based on 1994 per capita GDP, using purchasing power parity; from *The World Bank World Atlas 1996* (Washington, D.C.: The World Bank, 1996).

8   *Ibid.*

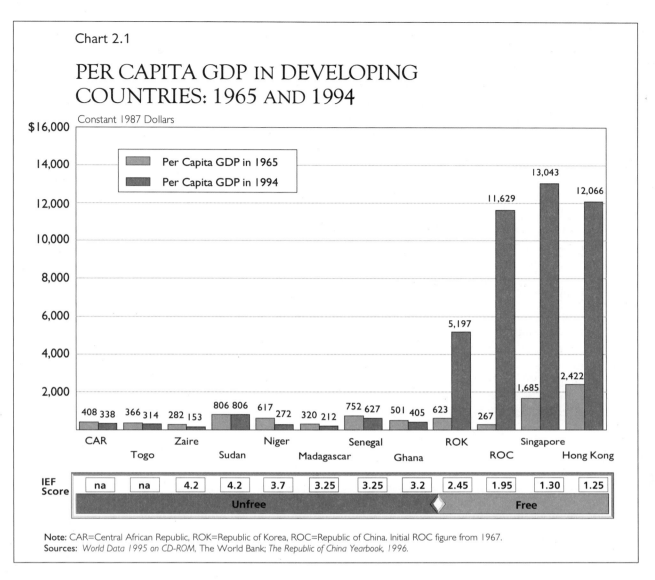

Chart 2.1

PER CAPITA GDP IN DEVELOPING COUNTRIES: 1965 AND 1994

Constant 1987 Dollars

Legend:
- Per Capita GDP in 1965
- Per Capita GDP in 1994

	CAR	Togo	Zaire	Sudan	Niger	Madagascar	Senegal	Ghana	ROK	ROC	Singapore	Hong Kong
1965	408	366	282	806	617	320	752	501	623	267	1,685	2,422
1994	338	314	153	806	272	212	627	405	5,197	11,629	13,043	12,066

| IEF Score | na | na | 4.2 | 4.2 | 3.7 | 3.25 | 3.25 | 3.2 | 2.45 | 1.95 | 1.30 | 1.25 |

Unfree ◄——————————————————————————► Free

Note: CAR=Central African Republic, ROK=Republic of Korea, ROC=Republic of China. Initial ROC figure from 1967.
Sources: *World Data 1995 on CD-ROM,* The World Bank; *The Republic of China Yearbook, 1996.*

Then came the new Republican-led Congress in 1995. The new majority tried to reorganize the U.S. foreign aid bureaucracy. In June 1995, the House of Representatives passed the American Overseas Interests Act (H.R. 1561), which would have dismantled several executive branch agencies, including AID, and consolidated their activities within the State Department.

The Senate version, introduced by Mitch McConnell (R–KY), set out to abolish AID and condition economic aid on how well a recipient country scores on a set of criteria similar to the *Index of Economic Freedom.* But because Senator McConnell sits on the Appropriations Committee, not the Foreign Relations Committee where such legislation usually originates, his bill was never brought up for a vote. Instead, the Foreign Relations Committee approved the Foreign Relations Revitalization Act (S. 908). The brainchild of Foreign Relations Committee Chairman Jesse Helms (R–NC), S. 908 was supposed to abolish AID, as well as the Arms Control and Disarmament Agency (ACDA) and U.S. Information Agency (USIA), moving some of their functions into the State Department. Faced with opposition from the Clinton Administration and filibuster threats by Senate Democrats, however, Senator Helms was unable to bring his bill to the Senate floor for a vote.

Senator Helms also drafted the Foreign Aid Reduction Act of 1995, which would alter substantially the way the United States spends foreign aid dollars. Originally, this legislation would have required the President to certify (1) that money spent on military and security aid, as well as development aid, was in the U.S. national interest; (2) that countries receiving development aid have sufficient levels of economic freedom, based on the findings of a study like the *Index;* and (3) that a sunset provision for the funding is included in all foreign aid projects. Like the State Department reorganization bill, however, the Foreign Aid Reduction Act fell victim to threats of a Senate filibuster and a presidential veto. Thus, though approved by the Senate Foreign Relations Committee, it was never voted on by the full Senate. Instead, as in every other year since 1985, Congress appropriated funds for a foreign aid program without authorizing legislation.

When Congress reconvened in January 1996, there was no attempt to pass authorizing legislation for foreign aid. Instead, it immediately took up the various spending bills. The House version called for appropriations of $11.9 billion for foreign aid, a $200 million reduction over FY 1995 and $1 billion less than the President requested. The Senate version, passed in July 1996, called for $12.2 billion in foreign aid, $300 million more than the House version and $100 million more than last year (but still $700 million less than President Clinton's request). In September, a House–Senate conference committee met to resolve the differences between the two bills. Under the final version, passed in October, U.S. foreign aid programs will receive $12.1 billion in FY 1997, $800 million less than President Clinton requested.

One of the reasons foreign aid legislation has been stymied is that AID Administrator Atwood persuaded the real beneficiaries of development aid—the legions of U.S.-based AID contractors—to lobby against foreign aid reorganization and cuts. Atwood also has resorted to charges of isolationism against those who question the worth of development aid. For now, at least, AID has prevailed. It will continue to spend billions of dollars to subsidize statist economic policies worldwide, with no reforms having taken place.

An important victory for Congress came in 1995 when Senators Connie Mack (R–FL) and Rod Grams (R–MN) introduced an amendment to the foreign aid appropriations bill. This amendment, based on the *Index of Economic Freedom,* requires AID to address the issue of economic freedom in its annual report to Congress. The amendment was approved by Congress and signed into law by the President in February 1996. It is clear that Congress regards AID's lack of attention to economic freedom as no longer tolerable. The report was due in summer 1996. As of November 1996, AID had not submitted a final version of its report to Congress.

If the *Index* provides any insight into the development process, it is not to show which countries deserve economic development aid—no country does. Rather, it is to show the general futility of providing economic development assistance in the first place. Although some well-intentioned foreign aid program may help a newly independent country pay for the development of a commercial code, it is far more likely that the crutch of foreign aid will hinder the economic development process by prolonging the implementation of needed reforms such as privatization, the lowering of taxes and tariffs, and the other factors of the *Index of Economic Freedom*. The next time the foreign aid issue arises, policymakers would do well to reject the fantasies of those who argue that such aid helps the poor. It is time to abolish programs that perpetuate the very poverty foreign aid's advocates claim to abhor.

Table 2.1

ECONOMIC FREEDOM AND ECONOMIC PROSPERITY

	Index of Economic Freedom Score 1997	GDP per Capita 1965, Constant 1987 US$	GDP per Capita 1994, Constant 1987 US$	Increase in GDP per Capita 1965 - 1994	Years Receiving Aid
Free Countries					
Hong Kong	1.25	2422	12066	398%	—
Singapore	1.3	1685	13043	674	—
Taiwan ‡	1.95	267	11629	4,255	—
Unfree Countries					
Ecuador	3.05	626	1237	97	52
Kenya	3.05	221	372	68	44
Colombia	3.1	690	1326	92	52
Mali	3.1	227	247	9	37
Honduras	3.15	746	939	26	52
Ghana	3.2	501	405	-19	40
Nigeria	3.2	335	352	5	37
Tanzania	3.25	134	**135**	0	40
Madagascar	3.25	320	212	-34	39
Senegal	3.25	752	627	-17	37
Mexico	3.35	1136	1857	63	51
Dominican Republic	3.45	372	832	123	45
Egypt	3.45	300	712	138	45
Guinea *	3.45	386	413	7	39
Guyana	3.5	479	519	8	44
Burkina Faso	3.5	180	**242**	35	37
Malawi	3.55	113	116	3	42
Ethiopia **	3.6	187	154	-18	49
Nicaragua	3.6	1752	801	-54	49
Nepal	3.6	151	198	31	46
Gambia	3.6	225	276	23	40
Cameroon	3.6	618	668	8	38
Lesotho	3.65	126	319	152	37
India	3.7	217	399	84	51
Niger	3.7	617	272	-56	37
Mauritania	3.8	516	490	-5	38
Burundi	3.8	124	181	46	37
Chad	3.8	202	176	-13	36
Sierra Leone	3.85	137	139	1	43
Haiti	4	360	225	-37	52
Zaire †	4.2	282	153	-46	43
Sudan	4.2	806	**806**	0	40
Rwanda	4.2	229	**280**	22	36
Myanmar/Burma	4.3	210	267	27	38
Somalia ††	4.7	111	**111**	0	41

Note: Shaded countries experienced growth of less than 1% per year. Figures in **Bold** are from 1993.
   * First GDP/capita from 1986.   ** First GDP/capita from 1983.
   † Second GDP/capita from 1992   †† Second GDP/capita from 1990   ‡ First GDP/capita from 1967

Sources: *World Data 1995 CD-ROM*, The World Bank, 1996; *Foreign Aid Reduction Act of 1995*, Committee on Foreign Relations; Taiwan Figures from *The Republic of China Yearbook, 1996*, Government Information Office, Republic of China., pg. 155.

Table 2.2

LONG-TERM RECIPIENTS OF U.S. FOREIGN AID AND THEIR ECONOMIC PERFORMANCE: 1965-1994

	GDP per Capita 1965, Constant 1987 US$	GDP per Capita 1994, Constant 1987 US$	Increase in GDP per Capita 1965-1994	Years Receiving Aid
Bolivia	$682	$780	14%	52
Chile	1236	2359	91	52
Colombia	690	1326	92	52
Costa Rica	1128	1905	69	52
Ecuador	626	1237	97	52
El Salvador	913	1022	12	52
Guatemala	690	907	31	52
Haiti	360	225	-37	52
Honduras	746	939	26	52
Panama	1371	2379	74	52
Peru	1126	1103	-2	52
Philippines	464	623	34	52
India	217	399	84	51
Indonesia	189	628	233	51
Mexico	1136	1857	63	51
Turkey	834	1758	111	51
Uruguay	434	626	44	51
Liberia ††	627	486	-22	50
Ethiopia **	187	154	-18	49
Nicaragua	1752	801	-54	49
Lebanon	—	—	—	48
Thailand	366	1680	358	48
Israel	4654	**9887**	112	47
Jordan **	2253	1559	-31	47
Morocco	500	934	87	46
Nepal	151	198	31	46
Dominican Republic	372	832	123	45
Egypt	300	712	138	45
Tunisia	638	1428	124	45
Guyana	479	519	8	44
Kenya	221	372	68	44
Afghanistan	—	—	—	43
Sierra Leone	137	139	1	43
Sri Lanka	213	510	139	43

Note: Shaded figures indicate countries whose per capita GDPs rose less than 1% per year. Figures in **Bold** are from 1993.
　* First GDP/capita from 1986.　　** First GDP/capita from 1983.　　‡ Second GDP/capita from 1990.
　† Second GDP/capita from 1992.　　†† Second GDP/capita from 1987.

Sources: *World Data 1995 CD-ROM,* The World Bank, 1996; *Foreign Aid Reduction Act of 1995,* Committee on Foreign Relations.

Table 2.2 (con't)

LONG-TERM RECIPIENTS OF U.S. FOREIGN AID AND THEIR ECONOMIC PERFORMANCE: 1965-1994

	GDP per Capita 1965, Constant 1987 US$	GDP per Capita 1994, Constant 1987 US$	Increase in GDP per Capita 1965-1994	Years Receiving Aid
Zaire †	282	153	-46	43
Belize	830	2133	157	42
Jamaica	1272	1588	25	42
Malawi	113	116	3	42
Somalia ‡	111	111	0	41
Uganda **	452	514	14	41
Gambia	225	276	23	40
Ghana	501	405	-19	40
Portugal	1849	5048	173	40
Sudan	806	806	0	40
Tanzania	134	135	0	40
Benin	346	367	6	39
Guinea *	386	413	7	39
Madagascar	320	212	-34	39
Togo	366	314	-14	39
Zambia	478	253	-47	39
Cameroon	618	668	8	38
Gabon	2798	3689	32	38
Mauritania	516	490	-5	38
Mauritius	968	2372	145	38
Myanmar/Burma	210	267	27	38
Burkina Faso	180	242	35	37
Burundi	124	181	46	37
Central African Rep.	408	338	-17	37
Lesotho	126	319	152	37
Mali	227	247	9	37
Niger	617	272	-56	37
Nigeria	335	352	5	37
Senegal	752	627	-17	37
Seychelles	1918	4847	153	37
Swaziland	478	752	57	37
Chad	202	176	-13	36
Rwanda	229	280	22	36

Note: Shaded figures indicate countries whose per capita GDPs rose less than 1% per year. Figures in **Bold** are from 1993.
 * First GDP/capita from 1986.   ** First GDP/capita from 1983.   ‡ Second GDP/capita from 1990.
 † Second GDP/capita from 1992.   †† Second GDP/capita from 1987.

Sources: *World Data 1995 CD-ROM,* The World Bank, 1996; *Foreign Aid Reduction Act of 1995,* Committee on Foreign Relations.

3

Freedom and Risk

by George Melloan

An explosion of investment in emerging markets in the 1990s has generated a corresponding boomlet in a rather esoteric intellectual pursuit called country risk analysis. Every significant money manager in the developed world with some responsibility for global investments is a customer for the risk estimates that try to analyze the political and economic stability of the world's nation states.

Country risk analysis involves a lot of guesswork, simply because of the range of possibilities for unpleasant surprises in any national political system. But it goes without saying that open systems, in which there is a high degree of economic and political freedom—and hence a larger supply of objective information available—are easier to assess than closed or partly closed systems. And the very existence of a free flow of information makes the economic players in open systems—whether they be government policymakers or managers of private firms—better able to adapt to changing economic circumstances. Hence, these economies are more stable and more attractive to risk-averse investors than highly autarkic systems.

Appearances, of course, often suggest the contrary. Italy's revolving-door governments and large national debt often suggest instability at times. But Italy is fundamentally democratic and has a thriving private sector. It does not make the top ranking in our assessments of economic freedom—it ranks only Number 36 on our *Index* —but there is sufficient freedom of information that Italy's problems are well-publicized, with the result that the country's political class is under heavy pressure for reform. Despite its heavy debt burden, its bonds are near the top of Standard & Poor's ratings.

NO ECONOMIC FREEDOM HERE

By contrast, we heard little about the deep-seated economic and social problems of the Soviet Union in the mid-1980s, simply because the outside world had little access to facts about the state of government finances or the instabilities of the political system. There was an illusion, even at high levels of the U.S. foreign policy establishment, that the Soviet Empire was essentially stable and that careful management of the U.S.–Soviet relationship could and would continue to contribute to world order. Mikhail Gorbachev's *glasnost* and *perestroika* were hailed as sound steps toward reform that gradually would fold the Soviet Union and its satellite states into the world economic order. What a shock it was to people who held that view, largely implanted by skillful Soviet propaganda, when the entire empire collapsed at the beginning of this decade.

The assessments of country risk in the Soviet Empire made by Western banks were going wrong well before the collapse. Poland, for example, had run up huge debts that had to be renegotiated and restructured by the lenders. The experience of Western bankers with the Soviet bloc proved beyond a doubt the high degree of fallibility in risk assessments applying to closed national systems. That was most particularly true of closed systems functioning as command economies, which of course embody the very antithesis of economic freedom.

Fortunately, Soviet Empire borrowing never got much beyond the bank loan stage. The Soviets and their satellites never gained significant access to the more rigorous competition for funds in the international bond market, and so the exposures of the outside world to the financial consequences of the empire's collapse was limited largely to banks. Even there, they were not so extensive as to do any serious damage to the world financial system.

THE EMERGING MARKET PHENOMENON

It is an understatement to say that the world of finance has changed dramatically in the five years since the demise of the Soviet Union. Indeed, former Soviet republics and satellites have been a central part of the emerging market phenomenon. Mutations are taking place as well in the communist countries of Asia. The opening up of China in the 1980s by Deng Xiaoping provided the world with the keystone of the emerging market phenomenon and has been a fascinating study for country risk analysts ever since. The ability of China to attract foreign investment despite its low ranking on the economic freedom scale will get further attention later on in this chapter, but first comes a description of why country risk analysis has become such an important endeavor in the international investment community.

The answer is that capital investment has become globalized to an extent unprecedented in history. In 1995, U.S. investors bought foreign stocks with a dollar value of $51.2 billion and foreign bonds with a value of $46.8 billion. That was not as high as the record level of purchases in 1993 but it was impressive in light of the fact that U.S. stock prices were rising throughout the year and thus U.S. stocks were very attractive relative to foreign securities. The U.S. bond market also was recovering from its 1994 slump.

Michael R. Sesit, writing in the May 8, 1996, *Wall Street Journal*, noted as well that Americans allocated 17 percent of their 1995 stock purchases to investments in emerging markets, despite the setback those markets suffered from the Mexican peso crisis at the end of 1994. One important factor is that U.S. institutional investors are turning increasingly to overseas securities as a way of improving returns on their investments.

Mr. Sesit quoted InterSec Resarch Corp., an investment advisory firm in Stamford, Conn., as estimating that U.S. pension funds will have 14 percent of their funds invested abroad by 2000, compared with about 9 percent today and only 4 percent in 1990. Arthur McCain, an InterSec vice president, noted that while pension fund assets have expanded at the rate of about 10 percent a year over the past five years, their cross-border investments have been rising at a 32 percent annual rate. The scope of that investment power can be judged by the fact that U.S. pension fund assets now total more than $3.5 trillion. U.S. mutual funds also have been expanding rapidly in the 1990s, mainly because the low interest rates available on bank savings in the early 1990s prompted Americans to make a major transfer of their savings to securities, mainly by way of mutual funds. In their eagerness to offer new products and better yields to investors, mutual fund managers have created an array of overseas investment funds. The amount of money flowing into overseas funds shifts rapidly according to the yield on these funds relative to yields on domestic investment.

TYPES OF INVESTMENT

Country risk assessments vary with the type of investment. Bond rating agencies, such as Standard & Poor's and Moody's, assess "sovereign risk" in rating the bonds issued by national governments, taking into account the usual factors in credit rating, such as a government's past record in servicing its debt and the level of national debt relative to the country's gross national product. A finer tuning method for rating bonds issued by a government that are denominated in a foreign currency is to measure the government's annual cost of servicing its foreign debt relative to the country's ability to generate foreign currency through exports. If this "export coverage" drops, the bond is likely to be downgraded.

Bond rating agencies obviously can't ignore issues of economic freedom. The ability of a country to acquire foreign reserves will depend heavily on such factors as the liberality of its trade policies, the stability of its currency and the degree to which it stifles economic growth through overregulation and arbitrary interference by political officials with the workings of markets. The political stability of the country is necessarily associated with the degree to which it maintains a functioning system for selecting its leaders through democratic processes.

Yet another important phenomenon is the amount of foreign direct investment flowing into emerging nations. Direct investment refers to actual physical facilities, like factories or fast food outlets. According to the World Bank, foreign direct investment in developing countries reached a record $90 billion in 1995, an increase of 13 percent from the year before and triple the amount of five years earlier. Most of that was private capital as opposed to government or multilateral development bank aid.

So obviously, a lot of private companies are engaged in country risk assessments along with banks and securities firms. But a different kind of risk assessment is made by General Motors or Toyota when they are deciding whether to build a plant in a country that seems to offer a tempting market for their products or provide a good base for regional exports. Here, the level of commitment is higher than that made by a bond buyer, who can simply sell his bond if he becomes nervous about the country that issued it, and thus the stakes are higher. The direct investor is going to have physical facilities in the country and hopes that they will function and turn a profit for a long time.

Selection of a plant location is a complex form of analysis that involves country risk certainly, but many other factors as well, such as the quantity and quality of labor available and the availability of transportation and basic services. Assessments that would be made when a company is building a plant in the country in which it is headquartered take on the added dimension of country risk when the company is going abroad.

IS CHINA WORTH THE RISK?

The importance of economic freedom in this equation becomes more complex also. The other side of the risk coin is opportunity, the time-honored equation of risk versus reward. A direct investor has his eyes fixed on opportunities and his eyes get very wide indeed when he stares at a place like China, a market of 1.2 billion people. As its rating on our *Index* shows, China ranks low—Number 125—on the economic freedom scale. But nonetheless it has attracted a veritable flood of direct investment from abroad in the past five years.

At an Asia Society conference co-sponsored by Dow Jones in Seoul, South Korea, on May 10, 1996, Li Guohua, vice minister of Foreign Trade and Economic Cooperation of the People's Republic of China, revealed the remarkable extent of this inflow of money. She said that "by the end of 1995, 120,000 projects with foreign investment had started their operation and the actually paid-in investment amounted to US$135.4 billion." International Monetary Fund figures show that foreign direct investment in China surged in 1993, when it jumped to $27.5 billion from $11.2 billion the year before and only $4.3 billion in 1991.

It seems clear from this that the folks who make country risk assessments for business corporations throughout the developed world suddenly decided that the huge China market was worth the risks. That doesn't, however, invalidate this volume's stress on the importance of economic freedom to a nation's social, political and economic development. What it reflects instead is first of all the attractiveness of the huge Chinese market to foreign direct investors and secondarily, the skillful way China has gone about the process of attracting direct investment.

But there is another side to this success. It seems certain that unless the People's Republic moves further toward the reduction of government economic intervention it will be in for trouble down the road. The tiger it is now riding will not offer an easy dismount. China has attracted foreign money essentially by offering investors franchises in its special economic zones (SEZs). Franchises, with their suggestion of an absence of competition, are hard for business corporations to resist. China has gone about this in a special sort of way. The foreign investor achieves his relative freedom to set up in a special economic zone by going into business with the local government, for example the Shenzhen municipal authority in the very prosperous Shenzhen SEZ or the Shanghai local government in the ambitious Pudong development zone rising as a new port city within Shanghai's environs.

At first the foreign investors were invited in to make use of an abundant supply of Chinese labor but were restricted to exporting from the zone to other countries as opposed to marketing their products inside China itself. That was mainly to protect inefficient Chinese state industries from competition. The first investors were the rich "overseas Chinese" who have made fortunes in places like Hong Kong, Singapore or Taiwan and could see opportunities in returning to the land of their ancestors. They cautiously limited their projects to light industry for the most part and planned for a quick return on investment in case the mainland authorities changed their minds.

But from that initial start, and under heavy pressure from the local authorities, China is gradually opening up its domestic market to the products of foreign firms, thus providing the incentive that the foreign manufacturers were yearning for. This still falls a great deal short of the free and competitive market system that would exist under conditions of true economic freedom. The attraction of the SEZs to Chinese workers from the rural provinces also has caused enormous internal migration, with attendant social and political difficulties.

But despite the successes, development has been uneven. China may get a General Motors plant in Pudong, and Shanghai and Shenzhen hope to have thriving stock markets, but the country is making only slow progress in developing a modern banking system. The result is that capital formation inside the country is subject to great misallocation because of the central role the government plays in that process. If at some point China is no longer able to keep foreign investment flowing in, the flaws in this uneven development process will become glaringly evident. China will be faced with serious social and political unrest. If the central government is wise, therefore, it will continue to follow the lead of the local authorities toward economic liberalization.

David Malpass, a senior managing director at Bear Stearns who devotes a great deal of his time to country risk analysis, believes that China has done one thing that any developing country would do well to emulate. It has stabilized its currency, the yuan. Indeed, Mr. Malpass would give currency convertibility and stability a very heavy weighting in any criteria for assessing economic freedom. "The most important thing to me about a country is whether I can buy a given amount of its currency for a dollar when I go into the country and get my dollar back for the same amount when I go out again," he says.

Monetary stability and convertibility do indeed figure into our ratings of economic freedom in this book, but Mr. Malpass would give those elements a higher weighting than we do. On his scale, Peru, the Philippines and China, for example, would get good marks for their currency achievements whereas such countries as Russia and Venezuela would score badly.

COMPETITION FOR INVESTMENT

As Mr. Malpass's comments indicate, country risk analysts give varying weights to the many factors they consider in assessing the safety of a given investment environment. Their job has become more complex as the number of countries vying for direct and portfolio investment has ballooned. David Beers, manager of sovereign risk analysis at Standard & Poor's, says that "the number of rated sovereign governments has grown enormously over the last 15 years. In the early 1980s, they were a small homogeneous group of about a dozen countries in Europe, North America and the Pacific and their bonds were mostly rated triple-A." In 1997, by contrast, he expects to be rating the sovereign-risk bonds of more than 60 countries and the ratings will range from triple-A down to B. "The number has doubled just in the last three years," he says.

The rating agencies are of course cautious when assessing the credit-worthiness of countries that are newcomers to the international bond markets. China's bonds were assigned a triple-B rating when a rating was first assigned in February 1992, and the rating has remained there since, even though S&P's latest report lists the outlook for China as positive. China doesn't have much of a track record in the international bond market but it does have a relatively low level of government debt and a relatively high level of export earnings.

Argentina ranks significantly higher than China on our scale of economic freedom—it is at Number 42 and gets a 2.65 compared with China's 3.8—but it is still eyed with suspicion by the bond raters. It earned its position on our *Index* as a result of its dramatic moves to stabilize its currency and open the country up to outside competition. That has not gone unnoticed by bond raters. But Argentina's bonds still earn only a BB- rating from S&P, mainly because bond raters have long memories and remember Argentina's bouts with hyper-inflation and sovereign debt delinquencies that persisted in the 1970s and 1980s. Its outlook is termed "stable" as opposed to the "positive" estimate granted China. Both countries, in essence, are on trial, the one because it has a past and the other because it doesn't, at least in terms of international credit-worthiness.

Although there can be little doubt that over-regulation retards economic growth and correctly figures into our *Index of Economic Freedom*, Mr. Malpass reminds us that under-regulation in some sectors can be a problem, too. He cites Venezuela's failure to adequately supervise its banks with resulting troubles for the deposit insurance system. The bond raters don't think highly of Venezuela either. Its bond rating has slumped to B+ from BB in 1991.

HOW RUSSIA IS FARING

One factor in country risk assessment is how badly off the country was at the time it came to the attention of the international investment community. Russia is a case in point. Since the fall of the Soviet Union it has emerged from having the closest thing to autarky any nation in history, with the possible exception of North Korea, has ever suffered. But Russia now rates 3.65 on our *Index*, at Number 115. This puts it higher than China, on the strength of its widespread efforts at privatization of industry and a genuine opening up of the political and economic system to inspection by a free press and the public.

But unlike China it hasn't even made it to the international bond market yet and its flow of direct investment is a scant $1 billion or so annually, far below that of China. One of its weaknesses has been an inability to manage the ruble, which supports the views of Mr. Malpass on the importance of currency stability. His suggestion that sometimes a country can be under-regulated in a certain sense also applies to Russia. Clearly its difficulties in attracting foreign investment are related to its problems with enforcement of contracts and the business risks associated with a free-wheeling criminal underground.

But some other things are happening in Russia that are not happening in China and it may well be that Russia is on a path of economic development that is more normal and sound than that being followed by China. Its relative lack of direct foreign investment has a positive as well as a negative side. To a greater extent than China it is beginning to develop a homegrown private business sector as young Russian *biznezmen* try out their wings at new ventures. And there are signs that its private banks, which were largely nothing more than bucket shops when they first emerged, are beginning to develop into real banks, with a greater sense of responsibility about handling other people's money and a growing inclination toward financing legitimate ventures with promising prospects. It still is too early to predict whether the rather anarchic Russian model for development will eventually outstrip the controlled Chinese model, but it is by no means certain that it won't, even though at this moment Western country risk assessments rate Russia a larger risk than China.

The experience of former communist countries that never suffered the extremes of central control that Russia experienced supports the thesis that economic freedom and development go hand in hand. A case in point is Poland, which has climbed to a 3.15 rating and a rank of 85 in our index on the strength of its immediate post-communist "big bang" approach to economic policy. One of the most important things it did was to make the zloty convertible—with some limitations. That opened the door to foreign investment and foreign competition for moribund state industries. Poland was high on the sick list of the international banking community in the early 1980s, but now has earned some respect from the bond raters. Its S&P rating has moved up to BBB- from the BB first assigned to its bonds in June of last year.

ADVANCED MARKET DEMOCRACIES

But of course the most important testament to the importance of economic freedom is right before our eyes. As Mr. Beers of S&P noted, the highest bond ratings have for years gone to the handful of countries that are the most advanced market democracies. The sovereign risk bonds of countries like the United States, the United Kingdom, the Netherlands, and Germany get straight A's as they have for years. These are also countries that are in the top tier of our *Index of Economic Freedom*. The United States, of course, stands alone as an economic phenomenon and surely everyone knows by now that it is not just because of the size of its population or its abundance of arable land and natural resources. In our *Index*, it ranks fifth, tied with Switzerland, behind only four small countries as having the freest economic system. The United Kingdom is only one step behind. Both countries, despite advanced levels of economic development, are magnets for foreign investment of all kinds.

In 1995, the United States earned the top score among 42 nations for competitiveness in the World Competitiveness Scoreboard published by the World Economic Forum of Davos, Switzerland. It drew special mention for domestic economic strength. And even though emerging markets are important players for investors there can be little doubt that they are instinctively judged by how likely they are to duplicate the free market policies that have made the U.S. economy a powerhouse that accounts for more than 20 percent of the world's GNP.

Country risk assessment is a complex art form and the many people who do it go about it in many different ways. Some banks, J. P. Morgan, for example, no longer try to give numerical risk ratings to countries, preferring instead to judge each investment prospect on its individual merits as they can be defined currently. But country risk assessment is a little bit like critiquing art. Most of the specialists think they know a good risk when they see it and the more freedom of decision making they see in any given system, the more likely they are to judge it favorably. That is why this *Index of Economic Freedom* is a valuable tool for the investor.

4

Factors of the *Index of Economic Freedom*

by Bryan T. Johnson

Economic freedom may sound like a vague term that is open to interpretation. It is not. The dictionary defines "freedom" as "the absence of necessity, coercion, or constraint on choice or action."[1] The dictionary defines "economic" as "of, relating to, or based, on the production, distribution, and consumption of goods and services."[2] Therefore, economic freedom can be defined as the "absence of government coercion or constraint on the production, distribution, or consumption of goods and services." There are all kinds of "constraints" placed on economic activity.

> **Factors of the Index of Economic Freedom**
>
> 1. Trade Policy
> 2. Taxation Policy
> 3. Government Intervention in the Economy
> 4. Monetary Policy
> 5. Capital Flows and Foreign Investment
> 6. Banking Policy
> 7. Wage and Price Controls
> 8. Property Rights
> 9. Regulation Policy
> 10. Black Market

Accordingly, economic freedom is measured best by determining the degree to which individuals are free to produce, distribute, and consume goods and services. In looking at specific countries, determining the level of economic freedom is done best by examining government policies and conditions that either maximize personal economic choices or restrict them. Since its inception, the *Index* has used some 50 independent economic factors to determine the level of economic freedom for each country.[3] These 50 independent variables can be classified into ten broad factors. These

---

1   *Webster's Ninth New Collegiate Dictionary*, Merriam Webster, Inc., Springfield, MA. 1987.

2   *Ibid.*

3   A list of these variables can be found at the end of this chapter.

are: trade, taxation, government intervention in the economy, monetary policy, foreign investment, banking, wage and price policies, property rights, regulation, and black markets.

Inputs vs. Outputs. Most of these factors should be considered as "inputs" in the economic freedom equation. In other words, they are factors that measure the governmental policies that either maximize or restrict economic freedom. These factors do not represent "outputs" in the economic freedom equation. That is, they do not measure the results or consequences of policies that are economically free or unfree.[4] Students of economic freedom may want to evaluate how free individuals are to open bank accounts in foreign countries or to measure the difference between a country's official currency exchange rate and the unofficial black market exchange rate. Yet these are not "inputs." They are not governmental polices, but how people and companies react to governmental policies — i.e., "outputs."

The Grading Scale. Under each factor is a grading scale. The scale runs from 1 to 5 with 1 being the most free and 5 the least free. Each of the ten scores then are averaged to produce an overall economic freedom score. After each score is either a "-," "+," or "stable" mark. These indicate whether a country is getting worse, better, or staying the same, respectively, when compared with last year's score.

Weighting. Some students of economic freedom argue that certain factors are more important than others in their impact on economic freedom. They argue that these factors should be "weighted," that is, given more or less importance in measuring the overall score. Proponents argue that this is objective. Yet, by its very nature, weighting factors is an exercise in subjectivity, requiring a value judgment by someone. Moreover, even it if were possible to identify which factors are more important and by how much, it would not be possible to argue that the various weightings assigned to any given factor would be true for all countries in the world. Who is to say that taxation is equally and exactly more important than trade in Russia, the United States, North Korea, and Mozambique—countries with vastly different economies? The only objective way to measure economic freedom fairly and comprehensively is to measure all factors equally. This is what the authors of *The Index of Economic Freedom* have done.

Countries were ranked according to four categories of economic freedom. Countries receiving a score of 1.99 or less are considered to have economies that are "free." Countries scoring between 2.00 and 2.99 have economies that are "mostly free." For scores of between 3.00 and 3.99, economies were ranked as "mostly not free." And economies that obtained a score of 4.00 and above are "repressed." Last year's *Index* graded 142 countries. This year's edition grades 150.

New This Year. Like last year's edition, this year's includes a comprehensive listing of all countries graded with their corresponding scores in each of the ten factors. Added to this list at the end of each country row are its 1995 index score, its 1996 index score, and its score this year. This provides the reader with an indication of whether a country is increasing, reducing, or maintaining the same level of economic freedom.

---

4   The black market factor is the only factor that measures outputs.

THE FACTORS
Factor #1: Trade Policy.[5]

Trade policy is a key factor in measuring economic freedom. The degree to which a government hinders the free flow of foreign commerce has a direct bearing on economic growth. Trade policy, in fact, is a key factor in the industrialization of developing economies. International trade enables a country's industries to maximize production by allowing them to import raw materials and foreign goods and services that are cheaper than those produced at home. It also can offer a country greater access to a large world market, which can be the source of much wealth.

Methodology: The average tariff rate is used to score a country's trade policy. A score of 1 through 5 is given based on a country's tariff rate—the higher the tariff rate, the worse the score. Sources to determine the average tariff rate were derived from reports issued by the General Agreement on Tariffs and Trade (GATT) and the International Monetary Fund (IMF). When the average tariff rate was not available in these sources, the authors determined the average rate by calculating the revenue raised from tariffs and duties as a percentage of total imports. In some cases, adequate average tariff rate figures do not exist. In these cases, the authors used publications from the Office of the United States Trade Representative, the Commerce Department, and the State Department. These instances are footnoted. Such non-tariff barriers as trade quotas, overly strict licensing, or import inspections also were examined. If they existed in sufficient quantity, a country's score based solely on tariff rates was moved one point higher on the scale, representing decreased economic freedom.

Grading Scale

Score	Levels of Protectionism	Criteria
1	Very low	Average tariff rates less than 4 percent and/or very low non-tariff barriers.
2	Low	Average tariff rate 5 percent to 9 percent and/or low non-tariff barriers.
3	Moderate	Average tariff rate 10 percent to 14 percent and/or moderate non-tariff barriers.
4	High	Average tariff rate 15 percent to 19 percent and/or high non-tariff barriers.
5	Very high	Average tariff rate 20 percent and higher and/or very high non-tariff barriers that virtually close the market to imports

---

5   Unless otherwise noted, the following sources were used in determining scores for this factor: Office of the United States Trade Representative, *1996 National Trade Estimate Report on Foreign Trade Barriers;* U.S. Bureau of the Census, *Statistical Abstract of the United States;* Department of State, *Country Reports on Economic Policy and Trade Practices;* U.S. Department of Commerce, *Country Commercial Guide,* official government publications of respective countries.

Factor #2: Taxation.[6]

Taxes are a key factor in measuring economic freedom. All taxes are harmful to economic activity. A tax is essentially a government-imposed disincentive to perform the activity being taxed. For this reason, exorbitant taxes slow economic growth. When analyzing this factor, taxes on corporate profits, income, and other significant activities are measured.

Methodology: Two types of taxation are scored: income taxes and corporate taxes. First, each country was scored based on these two major types of taxation, which many economists agree have the most negative economic impact on individuals. These scores then were averaged to get a single taxation score. Then, other taxes such as value-added taxes, sales taxes, and state and local taxes also were examined. If they existed in sufficient quantity, a country's taxation score was moved one-half point higher on the scale, representing decreased economic freedom. This one-half-point increase represents the relative impact of these other taxes on individual freedom.

The authors considered examining the level of tax revenues as a percentage of the economy, based on the assumption that the higher the percentage, the lower the economic freedom. According to this assumption, taxes are higher when they equal a higher percentage of the overall economy. This approach was rejected. When countries cut taxes, in most cases revenues increase. Thus, the percentage of tax revenues to the overall economy may initially increase. To be sure, it is also true that these tax cuts also will result in a growing economy. Thus, the economy may grow faster than revenues over time. But the lag time can cause distortions in the measurements and the percentage eventually will decrease. Measuring tax revenues as a percentage of the economy may initially "penalize" those countries which cut their taxes.

Likewise, when taxes are increased, revenues usually drop. Consequently, revenues as a percentage of the economy may initially drop as well. While it is true that as taxes go up the economy may slow or shrink faster than the shrinking revenues, it also is true that the effect is not immediate. Measuring taxation this way could "reward" countries that increase taxes. Thus, the best way to measure a country's tax structure is to examine tax rates and which rates apply to the average taxpayer. Such is the method employed by the *Index*. Using this method, the *Index* can immediately account for an increase, or a decrease, in economic freedom as countries either reduce or raise their taxation rates.

1) Income taxes

Some countries have relatively high top income tax rates, but they apply to very few people. For example, Japan has a top income tax rate of 50 percent, but it is levied on such large amounts of income that very few people fall into this high tax bracket. The tax rate that applies to the average Japanese taxpayer is much lower. Thus, to measure taxation policy more accurately, it is necessary to examine not only the top income tax rate, but the rate that applies to the average taxpayer.

---

6   For each country, the following sources were used unless otherwise footnoted: *Worldwide Executive Tax Guide and Directory, 1996 Edition,* Ernst & Young, New York, 1996; *Worldwide Corporate Tax Guide and Directory,* Ernst & Young, New York, 1996; The Economist Intelligence Unit, *ITL Reports,* official government publications of respective countries.

To discover the average income tax rate, a country's per capita gross domestic product (GDP) was used.[7] Once this was ascertained, each country was scored on (1) the top tax rate and (2) the tax rate that applies to average income.

Income Tax Grading Scale

This scale lists a score from 1 through 5. The higher the score, the higher the tax rate. The highest level for which a country qualifies is the score that the country receives.

Score	Tax Rates	Criteria
1	Very low taxes	No taxes on income; or a flat tax rate on income of 10 percent or less.
2	Low taxes	A top tax rate of 25 percent or below; or a flat income tax between 10 percent and 20 percent; or a top rate of 40 percent or below, and a tax on average income below 10 percent.
3	Moderate taxes	A top tax rate of 35 percent or below; or a tax on average income below 15 percent.
4	High taxes	A top income tax rate of 36 percent to 50 percent; or an average tax level between 15 percent and 20 percent.
5	Very high taxes	A top rate above 50 percent and a tax on average income between 20 percent and 25 percent; or a tax rate on average income of 25 percent or above regardless of the top rate.

2) Corporate taxes

The second type of tax analyzed is the corporate tax. Each country is scored according to a sliding scale based on corporate tax rates.

Corporate tax grading scale

Score	Tax Rates	Criteria
1	Very low taxes	Considered a tax haven. Limited or no taxes are imposed on corporate profits.
2	Low taxes	Flat corporate tax less than 25 percent or a progressive top tax of less than 25 percent.
3	Moderate taxes	A progressive corporate tax system with top rate between 26 percent and 35 percent, or a flat tax system with tax levels above 25 percent.
4	High taxes	A progressive corporate tax system with a top rate between 36 percent and 45 percent.
5	Very high taxes	A cumbersome progressive tax system with top corporate tax rates above 46 percent.

---

7   This method allowed the authors to generate an average income level for nearly all countries, because these figures are readily available.

Factor #3: Government Intervention in the Economy.[8]

The greater the degree to which the government intrudes in the economy, the less individuals are free to engage in their own economic activities. By taking government consumption as a percentage of gross domestic product, one can begin to determine the level of government intervention in the economy. The higher the rate of government consumption as a percentage of gross domestic product, the higher the *Index* score, and hence the lower the economic freedom.

Methodology: Measuring a country's government consumption as a percentage of GDP reveals only an approximation of the government's role in the economy.[9] In the United States, for example, the federal budget is about 24 percent of GDP. This figure includes servicing the federal budget deficit and transfer payments through entitlements like Medicaid. Other government consumption figures for most less developed countries do not include funds spent on servicing the budget deficit and some transfer payments. Although government consumption figures probably understate total government intervention in the economy, they are a useful tool and starting point for gauging the degree of government intervention in the economy.

The next step in scoring a country on government consumption is to determine the size of the state-owned sector of the economy. If a country has many state-owned enterprises, or if a large portion of its GDP is produced by the state-owned sector, it was moved one point higher on the scale, representing decreased economic freedom.

Grading Scale

Score	Level of Government Intervention in the Economy	Criteria
1	Very low	Less than 10 percent of GDP. Virtually no government-owned enterprises.
2	Low	11 percent to 25 percent of GDP. A few government-owned enterprises, like the postal service.
3	Moderate	26 percent to 35 percent of GDP. Several government-owned enterprises, like telecommunications, some banks, energy production.
4	High	36 percent to 45 percent of GDP. Many government-owned enterprises, like transportation, goods distributors, manufacturing companies, etc.
5	Very high	46 percent or above of GDP. Mostly government-owned industries, few private companies.

---

8   For each country, the following sources were used unless otherwise noted: The Economist Intelligence Unit, *Country Reports*, United Nations Development Project, *United Nations Human Development Report: 1995;* International Monetary Fund, *Government Finance Statistics Yearbook: 1994;* World Bank, *World Tables, 1995.*

9   GDP is used in most cases. When only GNP figures were available, it is so stated.

Factor #4: Monetary Policy.[10]

The value of a country's currency is based largely on its monetary policy. If a government maintains a "tight" monetary policy—the supply of currency does not exceed demand—individuals have the economic freedom to engage in productive and profitable economic activities. If the government maintains a "loose" monetary policy—it supplies more money than demand requires—money loses its value and individuals are less free to engage in productive and profitable economic activities. The best way to measure monetary policy is to analyze the inflation rate over a period of time. It is linked directly to the government's ability to manage the money supply in the economy.

Methodology: The average inflation rate was the main criterion for this factor. The inflation rate is the best measure of how a country manages its money supply. Countries with high inflation rates have a loose monetary policy and are graded higher because they have less economic freedom than countries with lower inflation rates. Countries with a low inflation rate have a tight monetary policy and are graded lower because they have more economic freedom. Countries of the former Soviet Union pose a unique problem in determining average inflation rates. Because these countries had command economies, annual inflation rate averages from 1985 to 1993 are misleading. Without a market-based system, prices can be held constant because they are controlled by the state. Therefore, countries of the former Soviet Union are graded solely on an estimated average inflation rate since 1992. Although these figures are high, especially due to their transformation to a market-based system, they are more accurate reflections of current conditions than are figures from the Soviet era.

Moreover, measuring inflation on a historical basis may understate the current economic conditions within certain countries. If, for example, a country had high inflation rates in the early 1980s, but low rates today, the average inflation rate might still be quite high. In these instances, it is important to include information giving the most current inflation rate figures possible. These figures appear at the end of the Monetary Factor section for each country. For purposes of grading monetary policy, however, they are used only to determine whether inflation is going down, increasing, or staying even with historical levels.

Grading Scale

Score	Inflation Rate	Criteria
1	Very low	Below 6 percent.
2	Low	Between 7 percent and 13 percent.
3	Moderate	Between 14 percent and 20 percent.
4	High	Between 21 percent and 30 percent.
5	Very high	Over 30 percent.

10   Unless otherwise noted, the main source for this factor was *World Bank World Atlas 1996*, The World Bank, Washington, D.C, 1996. Inflation figures for countries without an average inflation rate, or for countries of the former Soviet Union, were gathered from The Economist Intelligence Unit, *Country Reports* and *ILT Reports*, and from the U.S. Department of State, *Country Reports on Economic Trade Policy and Trade Practices 1996*. For some countries, the average inflation rate was not available. In other cases, the consumer price index or only retail inflation rates were used.

Factor #5: Capital Flows and Foreign Investment Policy.[11]

Foreign investment funds economic expansion. Investors from abroad supply capital to domestic investors who then start or expand their businesses. Restrictions on foreign investment hamper economic freedom and thus limit the inflow of foreign capital. By contrast, little or no restriction of foreign investment maximizes economic freedom and thus increases the flow of investments. For this category, the more restrictions a country imposes on foreign investment, the higher the score and the lower the economic freedom.

Methodology: A country's foreign investment policies were scrutinized in order to determine the overall investment climate. Among the specific questions asked: Are there foreign ownership limits placed on domestic industries? Is there an existing foreign investment code that defines the country's investment laws and procedures? Does the government encourage foreign investment through fair and equitable treatment of investors? Are foreign corporations treated under the law the same as domestic corporations? Are specific industries closed to foreign investment? These questions were answered to develop an overall description of the investment climate of the country being examined. Each country was graded based on its investment climate.

Grading Scale

Score	Barriers to Foreign Investment	Criteria
1	None	An open and impartial treatment of foreign investment. Open and accessible foreign investment code.
2	Low	Restrictions on investments like utilities, companies vital to national security, and natural resources.
3	Moderate	Restrictions on many investments, but government policy conforms to established foreign investment code.
4	High	Investments permitted on a case-by-case basis.
5	Very high	Government actively seeks to prevent foreign investment.

---

11 For each country, the following sources were used unless otherwise footnoted: Office of the United States Trade Representative, *1996 National Trade Estimate Report on Foreign Trade Barriers;* U.S. Bureau of the Census, *Statistical Abstract of the United States;* U.S. Department of State, *Country Reports on Economic Policy and Trade;* The Economist Intelligence Unit, *ITL Reports;* U.S. Department of Commerce, *Country Commercial Guide;* and official government publications of the respective countries.

Factor #6: Banking.[12]

In most countries, banks provide the economy with the financial means to operate. They lend money to start businesses; provide services such as real estate, insurance, and securities investments; and furnish a safe place for individuals to store their earnings. The more government controls banks, the less they are free to engage in these activities. The consequence of heavy regulation of banks is restricted economic freedom. Therefore, the more a government restricts its banking sector, the higher its *Index* score and the lower its economic freedom.

Methodology: This factor is measured by determining the openness of a country's banking system. Among the questions asked: Are foreign banks able to operate freely? How difficult is it to open domestic banks? How heavily regulated is the banking system? Are banks free to provide customers with insurance, sell real estate, and invest in securities? The answers to these questions were used to develop a description of the country's banking climate. The *Index* represents a sliding scale that measures the relative openness of a country's banking system.

Grading Scale

Score	Restrictions on Banks	Criteria
1	Very low	Very few restrictions on foreign banks. Banks can engage in all types of financial services. Government controls few, if any, commercial banks. No government deposit insurance.
2	Low	Few limits on foreign banks. The country may maintain some limits on financial services and have interstate banking restrictions and deposit insurance. Domestic bank formation may face some barriers.
3	Moderate	Barriers to new bank formation. Heavy influence on banks by government. Government owns or operates some banks. Strict government control of credit. Domestic bank formation may face significant barriers.
4	High	Banks tightly controlled by government. Corruption may be present. Domestic bank formation is virtually nonexistent.
5	Very High	Financial institutions in chaos. Corruption is rampant.

---

12   For each country, the following sources were used unless otherwise noted: U.S. Department of State, *1996 Country Reports on Economic Policy and Trade Practices;* The Economist Intelligence Unit, *ITL Reports;* U.S. Department of Commerce, *Country Commercial Guide;* the National Trade Data Bank of the United States, official government publications of the respective countries; and The World Bank.

Factor #7: Wage and Price Controls.[13]

A free economy is one that allows individuals to set not only the prices on the goods and services they sell, but also the wages they pay to the workers they employ. Some governments mandate wage and price controls. By doing so, they restrict economic activity, and thus curtail economic freedom. Therefore, the more a government intervenes and controls prices and wages, the higher the Index score and the lower the economic freedom.

Methodology: This factor is measured by how much a country lets the market or the government set wages and prices. Among specific questions asked: Are there any products whose prices are set by the government? If so, which products? Does the government affect prices by controlling such things as utilities? Does the government have a minimum wage policy? Are other wages set by the government? A sliding scale is developed to measure the relative degree of government control over wages and prices. A 1 or "very low" score represents wages and prices being set completely by the market, whereas at the other end of the scale, a "very high" score of 5 means that wages and prices are set completely by the government.

Grading Scale

Score	Wage and Price Controls	Criteria
1	Very low	Wages and prices determined by the market. No minimum wage.
2	Low	Most prices determined by supply and demand. Some prices are determined by the government or monopolies such as utilities. May or may not have minimum wage laws.
3	Moderate	Mixture of market forces and government-determined wages and prices, or heavy government control of either prices or wages.
4	High	Rationing, wage and price controls on most jobs and items.
5	Very high	Wages and prices completely controlled by the government.

Factor #8: Property Rights.[14]

The accumulation of private property is the main motivating force in a market economy. The rule of law is vital to a fully functioning, efficient market economy. This factor examines the extent to which private property is protected by the government and how safe it is from expropriation. The less protection private property receives, the higher the score and the lower the economic freedom.

---

13   For each country, the following sources were used unless otherwise noted: U.S. Department of State, *1996 Country Reports on Economic Policy and Trade Practices;* The Economist Intelligence Unit, *ITL Reports;* and The World Bank.

14   For each country, the following sources were used unless otherwise noted: The National Trade Data Bank of the United States; U.S. Department of Commerce, *Country Commercial Guide;* The Economist Intelligence Unit, *ITL Reports;* Price Waterhouse; and The World Bank.

Methodology: The degree to which private property is a guaranteed right is measured. So, too, is the extent to which the government protects and enforces laws to protect private property. The probability that the state will expropriate private property also is examined. This factor also takes into account the country's court and legal system. The less legal protection of private property, the higher the score. The higher the chance of government expropriation of private property, the higher the score.

Grading Scale:

Score	Protection of Private Property	Criteria
1	Very high	Private property guaranteed by the government, and efficient court system enforces contracts. Adequate justice system to punish those who unlawfully confiscate private property. Expropriation not likely.
2	High	Private property guaranteed by the government, but enforcement is lax. Expropriation unlikely.
3	Moderate	Government recognizes some private property rights, such as land, but property can be nationalized. Expropriation possible.
4	Low	Property ownership is limited to personal items with little legal protection. Communal property is the rule. Expropriation likely, and the government does not protect private property adequately. The legal system has collapsed.
5	Nonexistent	Private property is outlawed. Everything belongs to the people or the state. Expropriation is certain, or the country is so corrupt and chaotic that property protection is nonexistent.

Factor #9: Regulation. [15]

In many less developed economies, obtaining a business license to sell a good or service is nearly impossible. With so many hoops for the entrepreneur to jump through, it is very difficult to create new businesses. In some cases, government officials frown upon private sector initiative, and it may even be illegal. Although there are many regulations that hinder business, the most important ones are those associated with licensing new companies and businesses. In some countries, like the United States, obtaining a business license is as simple as mailing in a registration form with a minimal fee. In others, especially in sub-Saharan Africa and parts of South America, obtaining a business license requires endless trips to a government building and countless bribes, and may take up to a year.

---

15   For each country, the following sources were used unless otherwise noted: The National Trade Data Bank of the United States; U.S. Department of Commerce, *Country Commercial Guide;* official government publications of the respective countries.

Once a business is open, that is not necessarily the end of government regulation. In some cases, it is just the beginning. Some countries apply their regulations haphazardly. For example, an environmental regulation may be used to shut down one business while another is not penalized. Business owners become confused over which regulations must be obeyed. Moreover, the existence of many regulations can cause corruption as confused and harassed business owners try to work around the red tape.

Methodology: The purpose is to measure how easy or difficult it is to open a business and keep it open. The more regulations on business, the harder it is to open. In addition, the degree of corruption was examined, as was whether regulations are applied uniformly to all businesses. Another factor was whether the country has any state planning agencies that set production limits and quotas. The scale was established by listing a set of conditions for each of the five possible scores. These conditions include such items as the extent of government corruption, how uniformly the regulations are applied, and the extent to which the regulations pose a burden on business. At one end of the scale is the "very low" score of 1, where corruption is nonexistent and regulations are minimal and uniformly applied. At the other end of the scale is the "very high" score of 5, where corruption is rampant, regulations are applied randomly, and the general level of regulation is very high. A country need only meet a majority of the conditions in each score to receive that score.

Grading Scale

Score	Levels of Regulation	Criteria
1	Very low	Corruption-free. Existing regulations are straightforward and applied uniformly to all businesses. Regulations are not much of a burden to business.
2	Low	Simple licensing procedure. No bribes. Existing regulations are relatively straightforward and applied uniformly most of the time. Regulations, however, prove to be a burden to business in some instances.
3	Moderate	Existing regulations may be applied haphazardly and in some instances are not even published by the government. Complicated licensing procedure. Regulations are a substantial burden to business. A significant state-owned sector exists. However, no bribes.
4	High	Government-set production quotas and state planning. Major barriers to opening a business. Complicated licensing process, very high fees, bribes sometimes necessary. Regulations a great burden to business.
5	Very high	Government discourages new business creation. Bribes mandatory. Regulations applied randomly.

Factor #10: Black Market.[16]

Black markets are a direct result of government intervention in the market. In fact, a black market activity is one that government has outlawed. The larger the black market is in a country, the lower the economic freedom. The smaller the black market, the higher the economic freedom. This factor considers the size of a country's black market as a percentage of GDP. The higher the percentage, the higher the score and the lower the economic freedom.

Methodology: Information available on the size of black markets in less developed countries is extremely scarce. Nevertheless, estimates can be made of the size of black market activities by answering several questions. For example, does the country have a large smuggling market? If so, this could be an indication that the government imposes too many restrictions on foreign imports. Do consumers need to turn to the black market to buy such items as televisions and video-cassette recorders? If so, this could be an indication that these products cannot be bought in stores legally or that their prices are too high because of very high tariffs. Are there large numbers of workers who work illegally? If so, this could be an indication that the economy is overly regulated and that labor must be supplied by the black market. Does there exist a black market in pirated trademarked or copyrighted material? If so, this usually means that there are insufficient laws protecting intellectual property. Although this may be considered a property rights issue, it is treated here as a black market issue because most of these pirating activities occur in the black market.[17]

Although this factor does measure black market activities in the production, distribution, or consumption of goods and services, it does not measure such things as black market exchange rates, gambling, illegal narcotics, illegal arms, or related activities. Such activities are very difficult to quantify objectively.

The existence or absence of these and other activities was used to estimate the level of economic activity that occurs in the black market, The higher the activity, the higher the score, which represents lower economic freedom. In cases where black market information exists for specific countries, it is noted. At one end of the scale is the score of 1, where the black market constitutes less than 10 percent of GDP. At the other end is the score of 5, where the black market makes up 30 percent or more of GDP.

---

16   For this factor, unless other noted, the following sources were used: U.S. State Department, *Country Reports on Economic Policy and Trade Practices;* official U.S. government cables supplied by the U.S. Departments of Commerce and State, available on The National Trade Data Bank of the United States; U.S. Department of Commerce, *Country Commercial Guide;* official government publications of the respective countries.

17   There is a difference between government-tolerated or -sanctioned violation of intellectual property rights, such as in China, where in the past the government has overlooked intellectual property rights violators, and informal violations that occur without government approval, such as when government restrictions on entrepreneurship drive individuals into the informal market in order to conduct business.

Grading Scale

Score	Black Market Activity	Criteria
1	Very low	Very low level of black market activity. Economies with this rating are free markets with black markets in such things as drugs, weapons, etc.
2	Low	Low level of black market activity. Economies with this rating may have some labor or pirating of intellectual property.
3	Moderate	Moderate level of black market activity. Countries with this rating may have some black market activities in the labor, agriculture, and transportation sectors, and moderate levels of piracy in intellectual property.
4	High	High level of black market activity. Countries with this rating may have substantial levels of black market activity in areas like labor, pirated intellectual property, smuggled consumer goods, services such as transportation, electricity, and telecommunications.
5	Very high	Very high level of black market activity. Countries with this rating have black markets that are larger than the formal economy.

SUMMARY OF VARIABLES COVERED BY THE TEN FACTORS

In grading each country, there are some 50 independent factors used to determine the overall level of economic freedom. Below is a list of those 50 factors.

Factor #1: Trade

1) What is the average tariff rate?

2) Are there any significant non-tariff barriers?

3) Is there corruption in the customs service?

Factor #2: Taxation

4) What is the top income tax rate?

5) What tax rate applies to the average income level?

6) What is the top corporate tax rate?

7) What other taxes exist?

Factor #3: Government Intervention in the Economy

8) What is the government consumption level as a percentage of the economy?

9) To what extent does the government own businesses and industries?

10) How much of the economy's output is produced by the government?

Factor #4: Monetary Policy

11) What is the average inflation rate from 1985 to 1994?

12) What is the average inflation rate for 1995?

Factor #5: Capital Flows and Foreign Investment

13) Does the country have an investment code?

14) Does it provide 100 percent foreign ownership?

15) Are there restrictions on which industries and companies foreign investors can invest in?

16) Are there restrictions and performance requirements on foreign companies?

17) Can foreigners own land?

18) Are foreign and domestic companies treated the same under the law?

19) Does the country allow foreign companies to repatriate their earnings?

20) Can foreign companies receive local financing?

Factor #6: Banking

21) Does the government own any banks?

22) Can foreign banks open branches and subsidiaries?

23) Does the government influence the allocation of credit?

24) Are banks free to operate without government regulations such as deposit insurance?

25) Are banks free to offer all types of financial services like buying and selling real estate, securities, and insurance policies?

Factor #7: Wage and Price Controls

26) Does the government have a minimum wage?

27) Are businesses free to set their own prices without government influence?

28) Does the government set prices for any products?

29) If so, to what extent?

30) Does the government provide subsidies to businesses to affect prices?

Factor #8: Property Rights

31) Is the legal system free from government influence?

32) Is there a commercial code defining contracts?

33) Does the country allow foreign arbitration of contract disputes?

34) Can property be expropriated by the government?

35) Is there corruption within the judiciary?

36) Are there major delays in receiving judicial decisions?

37) Is private property legally granted and protected?

Factor #9: Regulation

38) Is a license required to operate a business?

39) Is it easy to obtain a business license?

40) Is there corruption within the bureaucracy?

41) Does the government force businesses to subscribe to established work weeks, paid vacations, maternity leave, etc.?

42) Does the government force businesses to subscribe to strict environmental, consumer safety, and worker health regulations?

43) Does the existence of regulations pose a burden on business? To what extent?

Factor #10: Black Market

44) Is there a significant level of a country's labor supplied on the black market?

45) Is there a significant level of a country's transportation supplied on the black market?

46) Is there a significant level of a country's agricultural production supplied on the black market?

47) Is there a significant level of a country's manufacturing supplied on the black market?

48) Is there a significant level of a country's services supplied on the black market?

49) Is there a significant level of piracy of intellectual property in the black market?

50) Is there a significant level of smuggling in the country?

The 1997 *Index of Economic Freedom:* The Countries

by Bryan T. Johnson

This section is a compilation of countries, each graded in all ten factors of *The Index of Economic Freedom*. Each country receives a 1 through 5 score for all ten factors. Those scores then are averaged to get the final *Index of Economic Freedom* score. Countries with a score between 1 and 2 have the freest economies. Countries with a score around 3 are less free. Countries with a score near 4 are over-regulated and need significant economic reforms to achieve even the most basic increases in economic growth. Countries with a 5 score are the most economically oppressive nations in the world.

ALBANIA

Located in Southeastern Europe, the Balkan country of Albania gained its independence from the Ottoman Empire in 1912. Its struggle for independence, however, resulted in the loss of about half its territory and 40 percent of its citizenry to neighboring Greece and Serbia. During World War I, Albania became a battlefield, and much of the country was destroyed. Following the war, Albania was an independent state ruled by a monarchy. Although King Zog sought economic self-sufficiency, Albania became increasingly dependent on Italy. In 1939, Benito Mussolini occupied parts of Albania. The Albanian Communist Party was formed in 1941, and after World War II Albania became one of the world's most oppressive communist states. The communist regime was deposed in 1991, and current President Sali Berisha was first elected in 1992 and re-elected in 1996. Albania has made significant progress in reducing inflation and increasing agricultural production.

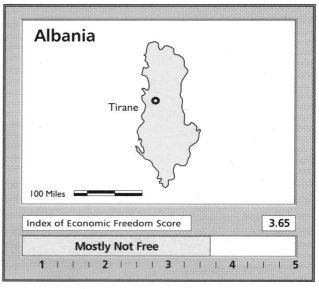

Albania	
Index of Economic Freedom Score	3.65
Mostly Not Free	

1 | | | 2 | | | 3 | | | 4 | | | 5

Factor #1: Trade Policy

Score: 3+ (Moderate level of protectionism)

Most of Albania's tariffs range from 5 percent to 30 percent, although most products enter at a rate of about 10 percent to 15 percent. Tariffs range from 0 percent on heavy machinery used in agriculture to 5 percent on mineral fuels, 30 percent on electronic equipment, and 20 percent on precision equipment like oscilloscopes. No import licenses are required.

Factor #2: Taxation

Score - Income taxation: 2-Stable (Low tax rates)
Score - Corporate taxation: 3-Stable (Moderate tax rates)
Final Taxation Score: 3.5-Stable (High tax rates)

Albania has a top income tax rate of 24 percent.[1] Albania's top corporate tax rate is 30 percent. It also has a small business tax, a social contributions tax, and a turnover tax.

Factor #3: Government Intervention in the Economy

Score: 5-Stable (Very high level of government intervention)

The public sector generates about 50 percent of GDP.[2] Albania has made significant progress in privatizing some industries like agriculture, however, which is likely to result in reduced government intervention in the economy.

---

1   Information with which to determine the tax on the average income level is not available.

Factor #4: Monetary Policy
Score: 5- (Very high level of inflation)

Although inflation in Albania has been very high, it dropped from 226 percent in 1992 to 31 percent in 1993. The inflation rate was below 20 percent in 1994 but increased to 22 percent in 1995. Although there are not enough data to develop an average inflation rate from 1985 to 1994, it is possible to estimate an average inflation rate from 1992 to 1995. Thus, Albania's average inflation rate since 1992 is well over 30 percent. This moves Albania into the "5" category.

Factor #5: Capital Flows and Foreign Investment
Score: 2-Stable (Low barriers to foreign investment)

Albania has moved quickly to open its borders to desperately needed foreign capital and has passed laws forbidding state expropriation of foreign property. Foreign firms and domestic firms are treated equally under Albanian law. No sectors are closed to foreign investment.

Factor #6: Banking
Score: 4- (High restrictions on banking)

Although Albania has made significant strides in replacing the communist central bank and providing the avenues for a competitive market-driven system, the financial system is still not fully private. Albania's financial system consists of seven major banks. Of these, four are state-owned, two are joint ventures between state-owned banks and private banks, and only one is fully private. There are few government restrictions on foreign banks. According to the Economist Intelligence Unit, "The government is anxious to liberalize Albania's unsophisticated financial services which are a serious impediment to the expansion of the economy."[3]

Factor #7: Wage and Price Controls
Score: 3-Stable (Moderate level of wage and price controls)

Albania has a minimum wage. Although the government has ended officially established prices, most prices are controlled by the huge state-owned sector of the economy, which still receives government subsidies. These enterprises often are able to control prices because they can undercut prices determined by the market.

Factor #8: Property Rights
Score: 3-Stable (Moderate level of protection of private property)

Although the government has made some strides in privatization, the private sector remains small when compared with the size of public holdings. In addition, the court system is not sufficiently developed to handle a growing caseload of property disputes. Thus, the biggest threats to private property remain a large state-owned sector and an inadequate legal system.

---

2   Budgetary figures are not available for Albania. Thus, it is not possible to generate a government consumption figure. Albania's grade is based strictly on the fact that 50 percent of gross domestic product is generated by the public sector.

3   Economist Intelligence Unit, *EIU Country Reports*, 1996.

Factor #9: Regulation
Score: 3-Stable (Moderate level of regulation)

Albania has made some progress in streamlining its bureaucracy. Nevertheless, the bureaucracy has been unable to adapt to the emerging private sector. It is still too large and inefficient.

Factor #10: Black Market
Score: 5-Stable (Very high level of black market activity)

Although Albania's legal market may be growing, many consumers and entrepreneurs find it easier and more profitable to deal in the black market. Taxi and bus transportation still are provided by black marketeers. Smugglers find that the scarcities caused by high tariffs on auto parts provide them with ample opportunities for profit on the black market. Moreover, many agricultural items are still being provided by black marketeers. For example, according to the U.S. Department of Commerce, "Customs tax evasion also results in Albanian import statistics that undercount the true quantity/value of imported poultry by almost half. Black market sales of perishable food items have also presented problems for the Albanian Food Inspection Service."[4]

Summary

Albania				Overall Score	3.65
Trade	3	Monetary Policy	5	Property Rights	3
Taxation	3.5	Foreign Investment	2	Regulation	3
Government Intervention	5	Banking	4	Black Market	5
		Wage and Prices	3		

---

4   U.S. Department of Commerce, *Country Commercial Guide, 1996.*

ALGERIA

The North African country of Algeria has had a state-controlled socialist economy since gaining independence from France in 1962. Years of government mismanagement and low oil prices in the mid-1980s led to anti-government riots in 1988. In 1989, Algeria adopted a new constitution that ended one-party rule and called for multi-party elections. But the elections were canceled in January 1992 after the results of the first round of voting made it clear that the radical Islamic Salvation Front would have taken power. This precipitated a rebellion by Islamic radicals against the military-backed government. Since 1992, more than 50,000 Algerians have been killed in a brutal civil war. Islamic terrorists have targeted foreigners to cut Algeria's economic links to the outside world and fuel discontent. In this uncertain climate, economic growth has been negligible over the last several years. Under pressure from the international financial community, Algeria has committed to economic liberalization. The pursuit of economic reform, however, has been erratic.

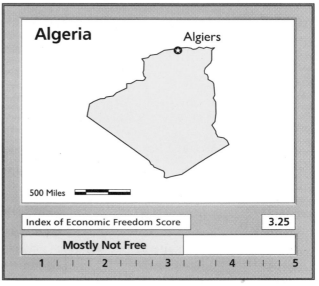

Algeria — Algiers

| Index of Economic Freedom Score | 3.25 |

Mostly Not Free

1 2 3 4 5

Factor #1: Trade Policy

Score: 5-Stable (Very high level of protectionism)

The government reformed the tariff schedule in 1992, cutting the top tariff rate from 120 percent to 60 percent and reducing the number of tariff categories. In addition to tariffs, importers must pay two other taxes, adding a combined 17 percent to 90 percent to the cost of imports.[5] Tariffs may increase in the future as the government moves to eliminate its substantial non-tariff barriers. The government bans the importation of some 70 goods, including textiles and shoes.

Factor #2: Taxation

Score - Income taxation: 3-Stable (Moderate tax rates)
Score - Corporate taxation: 3-Stable (Moderate tax rates)
Final Taxation Score: 3.5-Stable (High tax rates)

The top income tax rate in Algeria is 50 percent. There is no tax on average income. Income earned by foreigners is taxed at a flat 20 percent; in the past, the rate has been as high as 70 percent. The corporate tax rate is 50 percent for business profits and 20 percent for earnings that are reinvested. Tax breaks are available for companies locating in poorer areas. Algeria also maintains a value-added tax of 21 percent.

---

5   Algeria's average tariff rate was unavailable.

Factor #3: Government Intervention in the Economy
Score: 3-Stable (Moderate level of government intervention)

State-controlled enterprises dominate most commerce and industry. Private-sector involvement is increasing slowly. The government consumes 17 percent of Algeria's GDP.[6] Algeria's state sector is large, accounting for some 60 percent of national production. An announced privatization effort has made little progress while opposition to it mounts.

Factor #4: Monetary Policy
Score: 3-Stable (Moderate level of inflation)

Algeria's average annual rate of inflation between 1985 and 1994 was 22.3 percent. Inflation was estimated at 15 percent for 1995.[7]

Factor #5: Capital Flows and Foreign Investment
Score: 3-Stable (Moderate barriers to foreign investment)

A 1993 investment code does not distinguish between foreign and domestic investment and includes incentives for foreign investors, although the wording is vague. Laws governing hydrocarbons and natural gas exploration have been liberalized, resulting in increased foreign investment. The large role played by state enterprises limits investment opportunities. Moreover, it is not uncommon for foreign investors to spend two years negotiating with government officials charged with overseeing investments. Radical Islamic groups attacked and killed several foreign oil workers in 1995.

Factor #6: Banking
Score: 3-Stable (Moderate restrictions on banking)

Algeria's heavily state-controlled banking sector has been liberalized. Foreign banks may establish operations in Algeria but must maintain the same level of capital as Algerian banks. A private Algerian bank was established and another licensed in the past year. The central bank assumes non-performing commercial loans made by five state banks, many of which are carried by state-controlled enterprises. The government enjoys a monopoly on insurance activities.

Factor #7: Wage and Price Controls
Score: 3-Stable (Moderate wage and price controls)

The Algerian government controls the profit margins and sales of medicine, school supplies, tobacco, sugar, coffee, and vegetable oil. There has been substantial progress, however, toward eliminating price controls. Eighty-nine percent of the goods in the consumer price index were freely determined in 1994; this figure was 10 percent in 1989. The government's widespread participation in the economy, however, limits pricing competition. Subsidies on food items exist, although many were reduced in 1995. A minimum wage exists.

---

6   The World Bank, *World Bank World Development Report 1996* (Washington, D.C.: 1996).

7   First two quarters only.

Factor #8: Property Rights
Score: 3-Stable (Moderate level of protection of private property)

Government expropriation is unlikely. Collective farms recently have been parceled into lease properties, a modest advance for property rights. Overall, private property is reasonably well protected in Algeria, but this would change drastically if the Islamic fundamentalists were to come to power.

Factor #9: Regulation
Score: 3-Stable (Moderate level of regulation)

Algerian private sector enterprises, of which there are relatively few, must contend with burdensome regulations. Algerian workers cannot be dismissed easily; the norm is employment for life. This represents a considerable burden to foreign companies and the private sector. Setting up a business is fairly straightforward, and there has been some lessening of the difficulties encountered in hiring expatriate workers.

Factor #10: Black Market
Score: 3-Stable (Moderate level of black market activity)

Subsidies on foodstuffs have led to smuggling to neighboring countries. There is considerable smuggling of high-tariff electronics and textiles. Algeria has advanced, efficient laws protecting such intellectual property rights. Enforcement is strict.

Summary

Algeria				Overall Score	3.25
Trade	5	Monetary Policy	3	Property Rights	3
Taxation	3.5	Foreign Investment	3	Regulation	3
Government Intervention	3	Banking	3	Black Market	3
		Wage and Prices	3		

ANGOLA

The Southern African country of Angola began a war of independence from Portugal in 1961 and won its independence in 1975. After that, Angola became embroiled in a civil war. The government adopted a socialist economic system and maintained close ties with Cuba and the Soviet Union. Years of civil war between the government and Jonas Savimbi's UNITA movement have left Angola economically devastated. A peace agreement signed in late 1994 opened the door to a renewed United Nations peacekeeping mission involving over 7,000 personnel. Economic liberalization efforts launched since 1991 have had modest impact. Considerable opposition to economic liberalization exists inside the government.

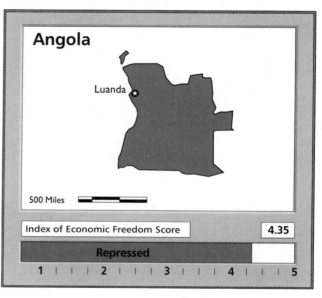

Factor #1: Trade Policy
Score: 5-Stable (Very high level of protectionism)

Angola is virtually a closed market. Although figures on Angola's tariff rates are virtually non-existent, its market is highly protected behind a wall of trade quotas and import licenses, which are required for all imports. Corruption in the customs services hampers foreign imports, and politically well-connected firms continue to dominate trade. According to the U.S. Department of Commerce, "State owned firms in some service industries have in the recent past attempted to keep out foreign competition, sometimes with success."[8]

Factor #2: Taxation

Score - Income taxation: 2-Stable (Low tax rates)
Score - Corporate taxation: 4-Stable (High tax rates)
Final Taxation Score: 3.5-Stable (High tax rates)

Angola maintains a top marginal income tax rate of 40 percent. For the average income level, the rate is 4 percent. Angola has a top corporate tax rate of 40 percent, a 40 percent capital gains tax, and a 7 percent social contributions tax.

Factor #3: Government Intervention in the Economy
Score: 4-Stable (High level of government intervention)

Government consumption as a percentage of GDP is 35.2 percent.[9] Progress with privatization has been minimal, and the government continues to control most of the modern sectors.

---

8   U.S. Department of Commerce, *Country Commercial Guide*, 1996.

9   The most recent information is for 1989.

Factor #4: Monetary Policy
Score: 5-Stable (Very high level of inflation)

Inflation in Angola has reached astronomical levels. The annual inflation rate is hovering around 1,000 percent, and the government exercises no fiscal discipline. Angola simply plans to delete three zeros from newly designed currency notes. Angola's average annual rate of inflation from 1990 through 1994 was over 500 percent.

Factor #5: Capital Flows and Foreign Investment
Score: 4-Stable (High barriers to foreign investment)

Angola is effectively closed to most foreign investment, which is prohibited in several sectors. There is considerable red tape and corruption in the investment approval bureaucracy. The economic and political crisis in Angola also serves to deter foreign investment. Although there has been some easing of investment restrictions, a number of proposed projects are languishing because of government roadblocks. The U.S. Department of Commerce reports that "Regulations and the lack of execution of reforms continue to prohibit or limit foreign investment in defense, banking, public telecommunications, media, energy, and transport."[10]

Factor #6: Banking
Score: 4-Stable (High restrictions on banking)

Banks are controlled mainly by the government. Despite recent attempts to allow foreign investment in banks, little progress has been made.

Factor #7: Wage and Price Controls
Score: 4-Stable (High wage and price controls)

Although price controls have been lifted on many items, they still exist for many goods and services. The Ministry of Labor and Social Security sets wages and benefits. Petroleum price subsidies recently were eliminated, and gas no longer is 12 cents per gallon. Large subsidies remain, however, on a wide array of services, including transportation and telecommunications.

Factor #8: Property Rights
Score: 4-Stable (Low level of protection of private property)

The Angolan government has few means to protect private property, and expropriation is likely. Despite pervasive corruption and bureaucratic inefficiency, however, the protection of property rights should improve if the cease-fire in Angola lasts.

Factor #9: Regulation
Score: 5-Stable (Very high level of regulation)

Government regulations are overbearing and a severe hindrance to business. Labor regulations are particularly onerous. Corruption and bureaucratic red tape have created an environment in which legal businesses find it nearly impossible to operate. According to the U.S. Department of Commerce, "Administrative chaos, corruption, hyperinflation, and war have vitiated normal economic activity and attempts at reform."[11]

---

10   U.S. Department of Commerce, *Country Commercial Guide,* 1996.

Factor #10: Black Market
Score: 5-Stable (Very high level of black market activity)

A significant share of Angola's economic output is in the black market. Although the government has been cracking down on these "parallel economic activities," both medicine and food are sold on the black market, and there is considerable smuggling of goods. An illegal diamond trade also exists. The civil war has boosted black market activity. According to the Commerce Department, "To date, Angola has not adhered to any of the principal international intellectual property rights conventions."[12]

Summary

Angola				Overall Score	4.35
Trade	5	Monetary Policy	5	Property Rights	4
Taxation	3.5	Foreign Investment	4	Regulation	5
Government Intervention	4	Banking	4	Black Market	5
		Wage and Prices	4		

---

11   *Ibid.*

12   *Ibid.*

ARGENTINA

By the 1930s, Argentina had achieved the status of fourth richest country in the world. Just before World War II, Argentina had a living standard equal to that of the United States and much of Europe. Following the war, however, it introduced a host of social and economic policies that sent the economy into a spiraling decline. Argentina then retreated into a foreign policy of isolationism that lasted until 1989. Under the leadership of President Carlos Menem, Argentina in 1990 began a free-market revival that has increased economic freedom. As a result, inflation has stabilized and the economy is growing. Corruption is still rampant, but Argentina today is one of the richest countries in South America. President Menem won re-election in May 1995.

Factor #1: Trade Policy
Score: 4-Stable (High level of protectionism)

Argentina has an average tariff rate of just under 10 percent. Some non-tariff barriers remain in Argentina's quickly opening market. For example, in response to the global proliferation of antidumping laws and duties, especially U.S. duties on Argentine exports to the United States, Argentina responded by enforcing its antidumping laws more aggressively. The result was higher duties on some items like textile products. There also are trade quotas for some imported automobiles.

Factor #2: Tax Policy

Score - Income taxation: 3-Stable (Moderate tax rates)
Score - Corporate taxation: 3-Stable (Moderate tax rates)
Final Taxation Score: 3.5-Stable (High tax rates)

Argentina has reduced its tax rates to stimulate the economy. The top income tax rate is 30 percent, the tax rate on the GDP per capita level is 11 percent, and the top marginal corporate tax rate is 30 percent. Argentina also maintains a 30 percent capital gains tax and a 21 percent to 27 percent value-added tax.

Factor #3: Government Intervention in the Economy
Score: 2-Stable (Low level of government intervention)

Government consumes about 15 percent of Argentina's GDP. Moreover, Argentina has undertaken a massive privatization program that is open to both foreign and domestic investors. Even some nuclear power plants are being partially privatized. If completed, this program will reduce government involvement in the economy significantly and expand opportunities for investors.

Factor #4: Monetary Policy
Score: 5-Stable (Very high level of inflation)

From 1985 to 1994, the average annual rate of inflation in Argentina was 317 percent. In 1995, however, it was around 1.6 percent; in 1996, it is likely to be only 2.5 percent. These lower inflation rate figures demonstrate Argentina's commitment to reducing inflation and pursuing sound monetary policies.

Factor #5: Capital Flows and Foreign Investment
Score: 2-Stable (Low barriers to foreign investment)

There are few investment barriers in Argentina. Firms do not need to gain permission from the government to invest, foreign investors may own most local companies wholly, and no permission is needed to own investment shares in the local stock exchange. Foreign investment is prohibited in the following industries, however: ship building, fishing, insurance, and nuclear power generation. In addition, many foreign investors complain about bureaucrats seeking bribes.

Factor #6: Banking
Score: 2-Stable (Low level of restrictions on banking)

Argentina's banking system is becoming more competitive as a result of privatization. As banks have become profit-driven, they have streamlined and modernized their business practices. The government recently reduced most barriers to foreign banking. There no longer are any distinctions between foreign and domestic banks, and both types are treated equally.

Factor #7: Wage and Price Controls
Score: 2-Stable (Low level of wage and price controls)

Under the leadership of President Menem, the government has liberalized prices. Today, no major items are subject to price controls, and most wages are determined by the market. The government fixes wages for public sector employees, however, and there is a minimum wage.

Factor #8: Property Rights
Score: 2-Stable (High level of protection of private property)

Private property is secure in Argentina. The likelihood of property expropriation is low; however, court protection of private property can be weak.

Factor #9: Regulation
Score: 2-Stable (Low level of regulation)

Argentina has reduced cumbersome registration requirements. Thus, opening a business is generally easy. Existing regulations are relatively straightforward and, in general, are applied uniformly.

Factor #10: Black Market
Score: 2-Stable (Low level of black market activity)

In the past, most of Argentina's GDP was produced in the black market. As Argentina's market becomes more integrated into the world economy, however, the black market is shrinking.

Summary

Argentina					Overall Score	2.65
Trade	4	Monetary Policy	5	Property Rights	2
Taxation	3.5	Foreign Investment	2	Regulation	2
Government Intervention	2	Banking	2	Black Market	2
		Wage and Prices	2		

ARMENIA

Armenia was an independent country from 1918 until 1922, at which time it was incorporated into the Soviet Union. Before 1918, it was divided between the Russian and Ottoman Empires. On September 23, 1991, Armenia became independent once again. In the years since, it has attempted to shed its centrally planned, communist past by adopting a system based on democratic free markets. But the entrenched bureaucracy, war with Azerbaijan over the enclave of Nagorno-Karabakh, trade embargoes imposed by Azerbaijan and Turkey, and civil unrest in neighboring Georgia have hindered Armenia's move toward a free market. Interruptions in supplies of fuel, natural gas, and electricity also have damaged the Armenian economy. Armenia recently has reduced tariffs, government spending, and wage and price controls.

Armenia

Yerevan

100 Miles

| Index of Economic Freedom Score | 3.45 |
| Mostly Not Free | |

1   2   3   4   5

Factor #1: Trade Policy
Score: 2+ (Low level of protectionism)

Armenia has an average tariff rate of about 1 percent. It maintains non-tariff barriers in the form of licensing requirements for several products, including some pharmaceuticals.

Factor #2: Taxation
Score - Income taxation: 3+ (Moderate tax rates)
Score - Corporate taxation: 3- (Moderate tax rates)
Final Taxation Score: 3.5-Stable (High tax rates)

Armenia has a top income tax rate of 30 percent. The tax on the average income level, however, is 12 to 15 percent. The top marginal corporate tax rate is 30 percent. Armenia also maintains a 20 percent value-added tax.

Factor #3: Government Intervention in the Economy
Score: 3+ (Moderate level of government Intervention)

Government consumes about 18 percent of Armenian GDP.[13] Moreover, a substantial state sector exists, and the war with Azerbaijan consumes considerable resources. "Despite strong pressure from the IMF and the World Bank," reports the Economist Intelligence Unit, "the government again failed to meet new targets to sell off

---

13   World Bank, *World Development Report 1996.*

some 700 large and medium sized enterprises by the end of 1995. Only about half that number were sold."[14]

Factor #4: Monetary Policy
Score: 5-Stable (Very high level of inflation)

Armenia has been plagued by high inflation rates. Although the inflation rate was 26 percent in 1995, it was 2,331 percent in 1994, 3,732 percent in 1993, and 729 percent in 1992. In 1996, inflation is expected to drop to around 20 percent. Thus, since gaining its independence, Armenia has had an average annual inflation rate well above 500 percent.

Factor #5: Capital Flows and Foreign Investment
Score: 4-Stable (High barriers to foreign investment)

Few official restrictions exist on investment in Armenia, and investors are welcome in most industries. There are many informal but nonetheless substantial barriers to investment, however, including a slow privatization process, inadequate infrastructure, inefficient banking system, and insufficient court system. "At the same time," according to the U.S. Department of State, "the following factors acted as significant barriers to U.S. exports to Armenia: low purchasing power of the population and local companies; absence of local long-term financing; generally underdeveloped banking services and high interest rates charged by Armenian banks...reluctance of U.S. financial institutions to finance trade with Armenia; inadequate, unreliable and expensive cargo transportation services; the continuing blockade of the country's principal transportation land and rail routes; insufficient telecommunications services; absence of information on Armenian market demands; poor intellectual property rights protection; insufficient guarantees for foreign investments; and lack of a dispute resolution mechanism."[15]

Factor #6: Banking
Score: 3-Stable (Moderate restrictions on banking)

The banking system in Armenia is becoming more efficient. For example, there are now over 40 private banks. These banks offer few services and inadequate lending potential to the private sector (see Factor #5), however, and the government still owns and operates several banks.

Factor #7: Wage and Price Controls
Score: 3+ (Moderate level of wage and price controls)

Most prices now are set by the market. Price controls on rent, electricity, and public transportation, however, remain in effect.

Factor #8: Property Rights
Score: 3-Stable (Moderate level of protection of private property)

Private property is guaranteed in Armenia. The legal and judicial system provides inadequate protection, however. "According to the Foreign Investment Law," reports the U.S. Department of Commerce, "all disputes that may arise between a foreign inves-

---

14   Economist Intelligence Unit, *EIU Country Profiles*, 1996, p. 19.

15   State Department Report, 1996, p. 121.

tor and the Republic of Armenia must be settled in the Armenian courts."[16] This restricts the ability of property owners, especially foreign investors, to receive an impartial hearing.

Factor #9: Regulation
Score: 4-Stable (High level of regulation)

Establishing a business in Armenia is becoming easier. A corrupt bureaucracy, however, often applies regulations haphazardly. According to the U.S. Department of Commerce, "Corruption is a widespread and growing phenomenon in the majority of state organizations in Armenia, including such controlling bodies as the police and the customs department. Though foreigners are largely exempt, there may be cases where officials will delay approval of your application to rent an office from a state agency, for transportation, licensing, and let you know directly or indirectly that a good 'tip' may fix things immediately."[17]

Factor #10: Black Market
Score: 4- (High level of black market activity)

Some black market activities are found in the transportation and labor sectors of the economy. Moreover, Armenia does not provide sufficient protection of intellectual property, and piracy in these products is rampant. "Piracy of U.S. video and audio records, books, and software is widespread through illicit local copying and importation from neighboring states," reports the U.S. Department of State. "Armenian state television and numerous private cable channels regularly show video materials of U.S. origin, many of which are unlicensed."[18]

Summary

Armenia				Overall Score	3.45
Trade	2	Monetary Policy	5	Property Rights	3
Taxation	3.5	Foreign Investment	4	Regulation	4
Government Intervention	3	Banking	3	Black Market	4
		Wage and Prices	3		

---

16   U.S. Department of Commerce, *Country Commercial Guide,* 1996.

17   *Ibid.*

18   State Department Report, 1996, p. 121.

AUSTRALIA

In 1901, six self-governing British colonies federated to form the Commonwealth of Australia, which became fully independent in 1932. Throughout most of its history, Australia has maintained high trade barriers to promote industrialization, has shunned trade with its Asian neighbors, and has based its wages and working conditions on principles of social justice rather than market conditions. With the election of a Labor Party government in 1983, Australia began to deregulate financial markets, remove hefty trade barriers, improve ties to Asia, and privatize many federally owned firms. Today, Australia is a leading force seeking trade liberalization in the World Trade Organization and the emerging Asia Pacific Economic Cooperation forum. The new Liberal-National Party coalition government elected on March 2, 1996, has pledged both to reform the Awards System to achieve substantial deregulation of the labor market and to privatize Telstra, a telecommunications firm.

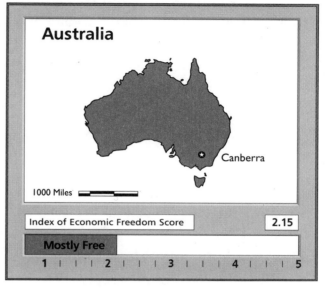

Australia

Canberra

1000 Miles

| Index of Economic Freedom Score | 2.15 |

Mostly Free

1　　2　　3　　4　　5

Factor #1: Trade Policy
Score: 2-Stable (Low level of protectionism)

Australia has an average tariff rate of less than 4 percent. Nevertheless, it does maintain high tariffs on some items, such as duties of 25 percent on automobiles and up to 37 percent on textiles, clothing, and footwear. Textiles, apparel, and footwear also are subject to import quotas.

Factor #2: Taxation
Score - Income taxation: 4-Stable (High tax rates)
Score - Corporate taxation: 4- (High tax rates)
Final Taxation Score: 4.5- (Very high tax rates)

Australia's top income tax rate is 47 percent; the average income level is taxed at a rate of 20 percent. The top corporate tax rate is 36 percent, up from 33 percent in 1995. Australia has a 12 percent to 45 percent sales tax. Capital gains, after adjusting for inflation, are taxed at the same rate as other personal or corporate income.

Factor #3: Government Intervention in the Economy
Score: 3-Stable (Moderate level of government intervention)

The Australian government consumes 17 percent of GDP and plays a significant role in such industries as telecommunications, electricity, and railways.

Factor #4: Monetary Policy
Score: 1-Stable (Very low level of inflation)

From 1985 to 1994, inflation in Australia averaged 4.1 percent annually. In 1995, the inflation rate was 4 percent; and for the first half of 1996, it still was about 4 percent.

Factor #5: Capital Flows and Foreign Investment
Score: 2-Stable (Low barriers to foreign investment)

Australia has opened its economy to foreign investment. It provides equal treatment for domestic and foreign firms and has opened particular service industries such as insurance and accounting to some foreign participation.

Factor #6: Banking
Score: 1-Stable (Very low restrictions on banking)

Banks in Australia are relatively free from intrusive government control. Foreigners are allowed to establish wholly owned institutions or branches. The banking system, once dominated by a few banks, has been substantially deregulated. In 1985, Australia allowed foreign banks to enter the market; so far, over 30 foreign banks have obtained banking licenses.

Factor #7: Wage and Price Controls
Score: 2-Stable (Low level of wage and price controls)

Minimum wages and working conditions are determined through a mandatory and centralized arbitration process involving labor, government, and business. Most wages and almost all prices are determined by the market, however.

Factor #8: Property Rights
Score: 1-Stable (Very high level of protection of private property)

Property is very secure in Australia, which has an efficient legal and judicial system that enforces contracts and settles disputes. Government expropriation is very unlikely.

Factor #9: Regulation
Score: 3-Stable (Moderate level of regulation)

Some regulations are cumbersome, especially those affecting labor, occupational safety and health standards, and the environment.

Factor #10: Black Market
Score: 2-Stable (Low level of black market activity)

Australia has a small black market in labor services and a growing market in pirated computer software and prerecorded music. Recent regulations requiring that all television broadcasts include a specified amount of local content have created a black market in pirated video cassettes of TV programs produced in the United States and Europe. Nevertheless, the level of these activities is relatively low when compared with the size of the Australian economy.

Summary

Australia		Overall Score	2.15

Trade	2	Monetary Policy	1	Property Rights	1
Taxation	4.5	Foreign Investment	2	Regulation	3
Government Intervention	3	Banking	1	Black Market	2
		Wage and Prices	2		

AUSTRIA

Austria has long played an important role in European history and culture. Following World War I, the government intervened deeply in the economy, causing massive economic recession in the 1930s. At the end of World War II, Austria was occupied by U.S. and Soviet troops; in 1955, it was freed from occupying armies and became an independent neutral country. Although Austria has been ruled mainly by socialist parties since then, it also has pursued some free-market policies. This has helped Austria maintain a relatively high standard of living. Austria became a member of the European Union (EU) in 1995. Since then, most economic changes have been designed to bring the country's economy into alignment with EU standards. In certain areas (such as tariffs), however, Austria's laws are more restrictive than the EU's.

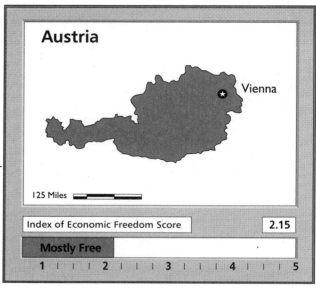

Factor #1: Trade Policy

Score: 3- (Moderate level of protectionism)

When Austria entered the EU in 1995, 63 percent of its tariffs were lowered. Some 31 percent, however, were increased. According to the Economist Intelligence Unit, "Although Austria has reduced its customs duties in recent years, import tariffs at an average of 10.7 percent are higher than the EU average of 7.3 percent...."[19] For the first half of 1996, the average rate was about 9 percent. The government plans to bring its tariffs into line with those of the rest of the EU eventually. Austria also limits imports by imposing quotas, particularly on textiles.

Factor #2: Taxation

Score - Income taxation: 5-Stable (Very high tax rates)
Score - Corporate taxation: 3-Stable (Moderate tax rates)
Final Taxation Score: 4.5-Stable (Very high tax rates)

Austria has a top income tax rate of 50 percent, and the average income level is taxed at a rate of 32 percent. The top corporate tax rate is 34 percent. Austria also imposes several other taxes, including (among others) a 34 percent capital gains tax, a 20 percent value-added tax, and a 3.5 percent real estate tax.

---

19   Economist Intelligence Unit, *ILT Reports: Austria,* September 1995, updated March 1996.

Factor #3: Government Intervention in the Economy
Score: 3-Stable (Moderate level of government intervention)

Austria's government consumes 19 percent of GDP. Austria has a large state-owned industrial sector, however, and its recent privatization program is slowing. For example, one-third of the country's work force remains in the public sector. The government either owns outright or has controlling stakes in Austrian Radio and Television, Austrian Airlines, postal services, and long-distance busing. Still, by global standards, Austria's involvement in the economy is relatively moderate.

Factor #4: Monetary Policy
Score: 1-Stable (Very low level of inflation)

Austria had an average annual inflation rate of 3.2 percent from 1985 to 1994. Inflation was about 2 percent in 1995 and around 1.8 percent for the first half of 1996.

Factor #5: Capital Flows and Foreign Investment
Score: 2-Stable (Low barriers to foreign investment)

Austria depends heavily on foreign investment and welcomes it openly. There are few restrictions. Foreign investors, however, at times must deal with slow bureaucratic procedures to gain approval for new operations.

Factor #6: Banking
Score: 1-Stable (Very low restrictions on banking)

Foreign banks can operate in Austria as long as they have prior government approval. Austrian banks are permitted to engage in all kinds of services, including the underwriting of loans and the brokering of securities and mutual funds. They also may own subsidiaries that underwrite and sell insurance policies, and are allowed to invest in, develop, and manage real estate ventures.

Factor #7: Wage and Price Controls
Score: 2-Stable (Low level of wage and price controls)

Most wages and prices are set by the market. Austrian businesses voluntarily cooperate with the government, however, to set prices. Thus, prices in Austria are not completely free. Some price controls are still in effect on rail travel, telecommunications, and some energy. Austria maintains a minimum wage.

Factor #8: Property Rights
Score: 1-Stable (Very high level of protection of private property)

Property is very secure in Austria, which has an efficient and well-established legal system that respects and protects private property and contractual agreements.

Factor #9: Regulation
Score: 3-Stable (Moderate level of regulation)

Although Austria experienced long periods of economic growth after World War II, it also allowed the state to become involved in regulating the economy. A growing environmental movement threatens to shackle many Austrian businesses with burdensome regulations. Business competitiveness is hindered further by Austria's extensive worker health and safety standards. According to the U.S. Department of Commerce,

"Terms of employment are closely regulated by law, including working hours, minimum vacation time, maternity leave, juvenile work allowances, statutory separation notice, protection against dismissal...and the right to severance payments."[20] Nevertheless, by global standards, Austria's economy is only moderately regulated.

Factor #10: Black Market
Score: 1-Stable (Very low level of black market activity)

The black market is relatively small to nonexistent in Austria. Goods and services move fairly freely across the border, limiting the incentives for smuggling. The government passed legislation in 1995 to protect many intellectual property products, including satellite broadcasting and cable TV. Nevertheless, there still exists some piracy of video cassettes and computer software, although these activities are minuscule when compared with the size of the Austrian economy.

Summary

Austria					Overall Score	2.15
Trade	3	Monetary Policy	1		Property Rights	1
Taxation	4.5	Foreign Investment	2		Regulation	3
Government Intervention	3	Banking	1		Black Market	1
		Wage and Prices	2			

---

20   U.S. Department of Commerce, *Country Commercial Guide, 1996.*

AZERBAIJAN

What today is the territory of Azerbaijan was ceded by Iran to Russia in 1813 and 1828. Azerbaijan gained its independence in 1918 but was conquered by Soviet Russia in 1920. In 1989, Azerbaijan claimed its sovereignty from the Soviet Union. By 1991, it had become fully independent. Since then, the government has embarked on a haphazard course of reform, the success of which is threatened by a well-entrenched bureaucracy. The discovery of significant oil deposits on the shelf of the Caspian Sea (deposits equal to those of the North Sea) has attracted the attention of foreign investors; a consortium led by Amoco is about to begin work on an oil field. Recently, Azerbaijan has reduced some government regulations.

Azerbaijan

Baku

150 Miles

| Index of Economic Freedom Score | 4.60 |

Repressed

1 2 3 4 5

Factor #1: Trade Policy
Score: 5-Stable (Very high level of protectionism)

The average tariff rate for Azerbaijan is unavailable. Nevertheless, tariffs range from 10 percent to 50 percent on most items, with most of them around 25 percent. Among the non-tariff barriers are corrupt customs officials who often confiscate imports and exports. Most trade must take the form of barter because Azerbaijan has little in foreign currency reserves.

Factor #2: Taxation

Score - Income taxation: 5-Stable (Very high tax rates)
Score - Corporate taxation: 3-Stable (Moderate tax rates)
Final Taxation Score: 4-Stable (High tax rates)

Azerbaijan has a top income tax rate of 55 percent[21] and a top marginal corporate tax rate of 35 percent. Azerbaijan also maintains a 28 percent value-added tax.

Factor #3: Government Intervention in the Economy
Score: 5-Stable (Very high level of government intervention)

Azerbaijan is privatizing its large state-owned sector. This initiative has slowed, however, and the economy remains dominated by large state enterprises, particularly in the agricultural sector.

---

21   The tax on the average income level is not available. Therefore, Azerbaijan is graded strictly on its top income tax rates.

Factor #4: Monetary Policy
Score: 5-Stable (Very high level of inflation)

Azerbaijan has been plagued by hyperinflation. Although inflation was projected to be less than 40 percent in 1995, it was 1,742 percent in 1994, 833 percent in 1993, and 1,066 percent in 1992.

Factor #5: Capital Flows and Foreign Investment
Score: 5-Stable (Very high barriers to foreign investment)

Although the government wants to promote increased foreign investment, little non-petroleum investment has been forthcoming, chiefly because of an ineffective legal environment, a stubborn and corrupt bureaucracy, and a weak infrastructure. Moreover, nearly all foreign investment must be approved by the government, and ownership of land is forbidden. In addition, as the U.S. Department of Commerce reports, "Azerbaijan is not a member of the International Center for the Settlement of Investment Disputes."[22] This is an international agreement among some 104 countries that stipulates the rights of investors to a non-partial hearing.

Factor #6: Banking
Score: 4-Stable (High restrictions on banking)

The banking system in Azerbaijan is collapsing. Most banks are owned either wholly or partially by the government, and many of these are insolvent. Although there are some foreign banks in Azerbaijan, few have the ability or the capital to operate independently, without government involvement.

Factor #7: Wage and Price Controls
Score: 5-Stable (Very high level of wage and price controls)

Both wages and prices in Azerbaijan are controlled by government ministries and the large state-owned sector, and the government continues to set prices on bread and other products. According to the U.S. Department of Commerce, "Several key commodities, including bread, natural gas and gasoline, remain under price controls. While the government raises these controlled prices periodically, they remain artificially low, and shortages of these goods occur along with corruption and black market activity." [23]

Factor #8: Property Rights
Score: 4-Stable (Low level of protection of private property)

Private property is not sufficiently protected by the legal system. Foreigners may not own land, and government expropriation is possible. The U.S. Department of Commerce reports that "the Azeri legal system is in a state of flux and is not transparent."[24]

---

22   U.S. Department of Commerce, *Country Commercial Guide*, 1996.

23   *Ibid.*

24   *Ibid.*

Factor #9: Regulation
Score: 4+ (Moderate level of regulation)

Establishing a business in Azerbaijan is a tedious and time-consuming procedure that requires individuals to overcome numerous bureaucratic barriers. Some private businesses are opening in the retail sector, but racketeering and corruption are widespread. Azerbaijan is developing a formalized process, however, by which businesses will be able to register and obtain licenses.

Factor #10: Black Market
Score: 5-Stable (Very high level of black market activity)

Smuggling in Azerbaijan is rampant. Because bartered trade is the norm, substantial underground economies exist in the trading of all kinds of goods.

Summary

Azerbaijan				Overall Score	4.60
Trade	5	Monetary Policy	5	Property Rights	4
Taxation	4	Foreign Investment	5	Regulation	4
Government Intervention	5	Banking	4	Black Market	5
		Wage and Prices	5		

THE BAHAMAS

The Bahamas, an archipelago about 50 miles east of Florida, consists of some 700 islands, only 30 of which are inhabited. The country is both a parliamentary democracy and a member of the British Commonwealth. Its biggest industry is tourism, and with a few notable exceptions, the economy is essentially free from government control. Recently, the government passed a new foreign investment code, opening its borders to more investment.

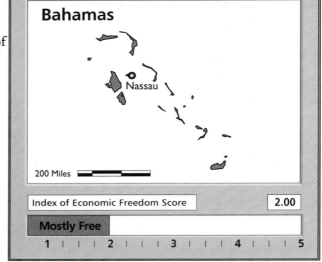

Bahamas

Nassau

200 Miles

| Index of Economic Freedom Score | 2.00 |

Mostly Free

1   2   3   4   5

Factor #1: Trade Policy

Score: 5-Stable (Very high level of protectionism)

Import duties are a main source of revenue for the Bahamian government, and tariff rates are very high. The general rate of duty charges on imports is 33 percent. The Bahamas maintains no other significant barriers to trade.[25]

Factor #2: Taxation

Score - Income taxation: 1-Stable (Very low tax rates)
Score - Corporate taxation: 1-Stable (Very low tax rates)
Final Taxation Score: 1-Stable (Very low tax rates)

The Bahamas has no income tax, no corporate income tax, no capital gains tax, and no value-added tax.

Factor #3: Government Intervention in the Economy

Score: 2-Stable (Low level of government intervention)

The Bahamian government consumes 12.8 percent of GDP and plays only a limited role in the economy.

---

25   It is impossible to generate an average tariff rate for the Bahamas because information on tax revenues generated from imports is not available. For purposes of this study, therefore, the country's general tariff rate of 33 percent, which applies to most imports, was used. Other tariff rates range from 0 percent (foodstuffs) to 47 percent (luxury items) to a top rate of 200 percent. Because most imports fall into the general category, however, the 33 percent figure most closely represents the Bahamas' average tariff rate. For more information, see *The Bahamas,* International Tax and Business Guide, 1994 edition (New York, N.Y.: Deloitte Touche Tohmatsu International, 1994).

Factor #4: Monetary Policy
Score: 1-Stable (Very low level of inflation)

From 1985 to 1994, the average annual rate of inflation in the Bahamas was 3.3 percent. Today, the inflation rate is about 2.5 percent.

Factor #5: Capital Flows and Foreign Investment
Score: 3-Stable (Moderate barriers to foreign investment)

The Bahamas has passed a new foreign investment law and seeks increased investment. The government restricts foreign investment in areas that compete directly with Bahamian-owned businesses, however, such as construction and restaurants (except gourmet and ethnic restaurants). It does this by preventing foreign companies from obtaining business licenses and by imposing other requirements in areas in which Bahamian businesses already exist.

Factor #6: Banking
Score: 2-Stable (Low level of restrictions on banking)

The Bahamas is one of the financial centers of the Caribbean. The government seeks to attract foreign banks, and the financial sector is extremely open to foreigners.

Factor #7: Wage and Price Controls
Score: 2-Stable (Low level of wage and price controls)

The Bahamas maintains some price controls on such items as automobiles, auto parts, flour, gasoline, public transportation, and utilities, but wages are determined mainly by the market. There is no minimum wage, although the government plans to introduce one soon.

Factor #8: Property Rights
Score: 1-Stable (Very high level of protection of private property)

Private property is easy to acquire and protect in the Bahamas. An advanced and efficient legal system based on English common law adequately protects property. The Bahamian government has never expropriated private property and is very unlikely to do so in the future.

Factor #9: Regulation
Score: 1-Stable (Very low level of government regulation)

Regulation is virtually nonexistent in the Bahamas; the government follows a hands-off approach to business. There are no specific requirements for establishing a business, and English common law is used to enforce contracts. In addition, profits are not taxed, and businesses are free from burdensome regulations.

Factor #10: Black Market
Score: 2-Stable (Low level of black market activity)

The black market in the Bahamas is like those in most developed countries: restricted to guns and drugs. Gambling is legalized. Because the government outlaws few things and businesses are free to operate as they see fit, the black market is very small, although high trade barriers encourage smuggling in such items as auto parts and electronics. According to the U.S. Department of State, "Although local intellectual property laws exist, enforcement is generally weak."[26] Thus, there is a growing black market in pirated materials such as compact discs and video cassettes.

Summary

Bahamas					Overall Score	2.0
Trade	5	Monetary Policy	1		Property Rights	1
Taxation	1	Foreign Investment	3		Regulation	1
Government Intervention	2	Banking	2		Black Market	2
		Wage and Prices	2			

---

26   State Department Report, 1996.

BAHRAIN

Bahrain declared its independence from the United Kingdom in 1971 and became a member of the United Nations and the Arab League in the same year. Bahrain also has maintained a free-market economic system. The country's principal export product is oil. With oil reserves expected to last only 20 more years, the government is pursuing ways to diversify and modernize Bahrain's economy. In addition, government spending has been reduced.

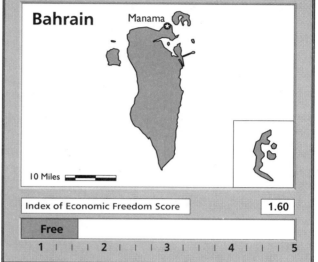

Index of Economic Freedom Score — 1.60

Factor #1: Trade Policy

Score: 2-Stable (Low level of protectionism)

With an average tariff rate of 4 percent, Bahrain has few barriers to trade. It does maintain, however, non-tariff barriers through strict labeling requirements on imported products. This limits imports because exporters do not wish to spend the extra money to meet the requirements.

Factor #2: Taxation

Score - Income taxation: 1-Stable (Very low tax rates)
Score - Corporate taxation: 1-Stable (Very low tax rates)
Final Taxation Score: 1-Stable (Very low tax rates)

Bahrain has no taxes on income or corporate profits. There is no capital gains tax or value-added tax.

Factor #3: Government Intervention in the Economy

Score: 3+ (Moderate level of government intervention)

Bahrain's government consumes 24.4 percent of GDP, down from 26 percent. The government owns significant portions of some industries, including oil, which contributes most of the country's GDP. Bahrain has privatized industrial and service companies within the last year, however. According to the U.S. Department of Commerce, "The Government of Bahrain has set out to make the country into the Singapore or Hong Kong of the Gulf, and hopefully, of the whole Middle East plus South Asia."[27]

Factor #4: Monetary Policy

Score: 1-Stable (Very low level of inflation)

The average annual inflation rate from 1985 to 1994 was a 0.3 percent. Inflation leaped to 3 percent in 1995, however, and remains around 3 percent today.

---

27   U.S. Department of Commerce, *Country Commercial Guide*, 1996.

Factor #5: Capital Flows and Foreign Investment
Score: 2-Stable (Low level of barriers to foreign investment)

Bahrain maintains few barriers to foreign investment and has no foreign investment law. Instead, it relies on various commercial codes to govern foreign investment. For example, there are no ownership requirements on new industrial investments. Moreover, because of a recent change in the law, foreigners now can own non-industrial companies wholly, although they are not permitted to purchase and own land.

Factor #6: Banking
Score: 2-Stable (Low level of restrictions on banking)

Over the past 20 years, Bahrain has established itself as a financial center for the Gulf region and the Arab world. "As of the beginning of 1995," reports the U.S. Department of Commerce, "there were 19 full commercial banks, two specialized banks, 50 off-shore banks, 39 representative offices, 23 investment banks, five foreign exchange and money brokers, and 27 money-changing companies registered in Bahrain."[28] Bahrain has a vibrant and competitive banking market with few government restrictions. The government has made it easy to establish a bank, both by streamlining the paperwork process and by placing few, if any, restrictions and requirements on new banks. Foreign banks are welcome.

Factor #7: Wage and Price Controls
Score: 2-Stable (Low level of wage and price controls)

Most wages and prices in Bahrain are set by the market. Price controls remain only on some basic foodstuffs such as bread. Bahrain requires importers of certain goods to pay a 5 percent fee to a local agent, thus increasing the cost of these goods. However, several other price controls have been removed. Bahrain has a minimum wage.

Factor #8: Property Rights
Score: 1-Stable (Very high protection of private property)

Property is secure in Bahrain, and expropriation remains unlikely. The court system protecting private property is efficient. According to the U.S. Department of Commerce, "The Bahraini legal system adequately protects and facilitates acquisition and disposition of other property rights."[29]

Factor #9: Regulation
Score: 1-Stable (Very low level of regulation)

Bahrain has an efficient and unobtrusive bureaucracy that poses no significant threat to business. Businesses are free to operate as they see fit. Opening a business is straightforward; Bahrain has a "fast track" business application process under which companies can be registered and licensed within seven days, with most registered and licensed within only five days.

---

28   *Ibid.*

29   *Ibid.*

Factor #10: Black Market

Score: 1-Stable (Very low level of black market activity)

Bahrain has virtually no black market. With practically no barriers to imports, smuggling is not a problem, and there is almost no black market in pirated intellectual property.

Summary

Bahrain				Overall Score	1.60
Trade	2	Monetary Policy	1	Property Rights	1
Taxation	1	Foreign Investment	2	Regulation	1
Government Intervention	3	Banking	2	Black Market	1
		Wage and Prices	2		

BANGLADESH

Bangladesh, a small country on the northeast border of India, seceded from Pakistan in 1971. Since gaining its independence, it has experienced several coups and political turmoil. One of the world's most densely populated nations, Bangladesh has struggled to produce and import enough food to feed its population. Some 60 percent of the labor force is engaged in agriculture. Since becoming independent, Bangladesh has received massive infusions of foreign aid, much of which has been squandered on under-utilized buildings, roads, and bridges rather than used to develop a free market. In 1991, Bangladesh embarked on a path of economic reform.

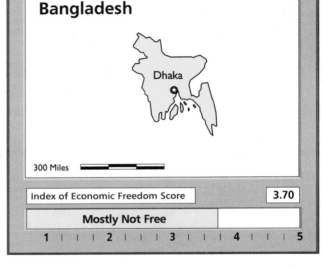

Bangladesh

Dhaka

300 Miles

Index of Economic Freedom Score	3.70

Mostly Not Free

1 2 3 4 5

Factor #1: Trade Policy

Score: 5-Stable (Very high level of protectionism)

Bangladesh has an average tariff rate of 21 percent, down from 40 percent in 1992.[30] Moreover, according to the U.S. Department of State, "Customs procedures are lengthy and burdensome, and further complicated by rent-seeking activity [bribes]."[31]

Factor #2: Taxation

Score - Income taxation: 2-Stable (Low tax rates)
Score - Corporate taxation: 5- (Very high tax rates)
Final Taxation Score: 4- (High tax rates)

The top marginal income tax rate is 25 percent, down from 50 percent in 1991. The tax on the average income level is zero percent. Bangladesh has a top corporate tax rate of 47.5 percent as well as a value-added tax.

Factor #3: Government Intervention in the Economy

Score: 2-Stable (Low level of government intervention)

Government consumption as a percentage of GDP is 7 percent, up from 6.3 percent in 1980. The state presence in the economy continues to be large, with government owning many industries and companies.[32]

---

30 State Department Report, 1996, p. 515.

31 *Ibid.*

32 *Ibid.*

Factor #4: Monetary Policy
Score: 2-Stable (Low level of inflation)

Bangladesh's average annual rate of inflation from 1985 to 1994 was 6.6 percent. The inflation rate was 4.9 percent in 1995.

Factor #5: Capital Flows and Foreign Investment
Score: 3-Stable (Moderate barriers to foreign investment)

Some industries, like power generation, forestry, telecommunications, air transportation, railways, and mining, are closed to foreign investment. Nevertheless, Bangladesh has made some modest efforts recently to attract foreign investment. Foreign and domestic investors, for example, now enjoy equal treatment.

Factor #6: Banking
Score: 3-Stable (Moderate level of restrictions on banking)

The government has initiated reforms that limit its control of the banking system, but the central bank still restricts some types of lending. Although some reforms have aimed at increasing poor people's access to banking services, some parts of the banking system are chaotic and corrupt. Moreover, the state still owns some banks; of the 23 commercial banks operating in Bangladesh, for example, 14 are privately owned and nine are state-owned.

Factor #7: Wage and Price Controls
Score: 4-Stable (High level of wage and price controls)

Some price reform has been accomplished. Nevertheless, prices in Bangladesh continue to be influenced by large state-owned industrial sectors, such as textile production and jute and sugar processing, which also are subsidized by the state. Heavy government subsidies negatively affect prices.

Factor #8: Property Rights
Score: 4-Stable (Low level of protection of private property)

Even though private property is guaranteed by law, according to the U.S. Department of Commerce, "[Bangladesh's] legal system is outdated and inefficient. A large and recalcitrant bureaucracy often views its role more as controlling commercial activity than as stimulating it. Corruption is endemic...."[33] Thus, private property remains at risk.

Factor #9: Regulation
Score: 5-Stable (Very high level of regulation)

The largest regulatory problems in Bangladesh are corruption and outdated business laws. Private businesses often are faced with laws that do not protect private contracts.

---

33   U.S. Department of Commerce, *Country Commercial Guide*, 1996.

Factor #10: Black Market
Score: 5-Stable (Very high level of black market activity)

According to the U.S. Department of State, "The local media have highlighted an apparent increase in smuggling of Indian salt, sugar, textiles, fruit, leather, livestock, automotive spares, and cement."[34]

Summary

Bangladesh				Overall Score	3.70
Trade	5	Monetary Policy	2	Property Rights	4
Taxation	4	Foreign Investment	3	Regulation	5
Government Intervention	2	Banking	3	Black Market	5
		Wage and Prices	4		

---

34   State Department Report, 1996, p. 506.

BARBADOS

Barbados, a former British colony with a parliamentary democracy, has few natural resources and must import most of what it consumes, including energy, food, and most consumer goods. With a history of high tariffs, restrictions on foreign investment, and heavy government controls, the economy actually shrank in the early 1990s, by 4.2 percent in 1992 and 6.2 percent in 1993. Recent reforms, however, have established a generally free-market economy. Since 1990, Barbados has achieved significant economic reform in specific areas of the economy. For example, it recently lowered some barriers to trade, reformed its banking system, allowed more foreign investment, and slashed price controls.

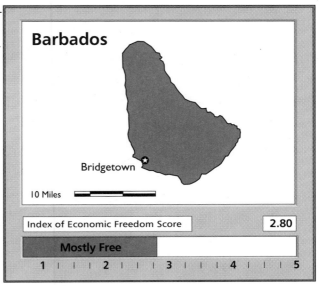

Barbados

Bridgetown

10 Miles

| Index of Economic Freedom Score | 2.80 |

Mostly Free

1 2 3 4 5

Factor #1: Trade Policy

Score: 4+ (High level of protectionism)

Import duties range from 0 to 70 percent (with a 100 percent duty on certain luxury items). As a member of the Caribbean Community (CARICOM) region, Barbados has brought its import tariffs in line with the rest of the region, although the most recent figures available show that Barbados still has an average tariff rate of about 18 percent.[35] "The commercial environment is generally favorable," reports the U.S. Department of Commerce, "although the local business community would like to see lower tax rates and import tariffs, and fiscal policies that would favor more investment...."[36] Moreover, there is some question as to whether the Barbados customs service prevents imports from entering the country. For example, according to the U.S. Department of State, "Customs procedures are often alleged to be administered in a manner that is neither transparent nor predictable."[37]

Factor #2: Taxation

Score - Income taxation: 5-Stable (Very high tax rates)
Score - Corporate taxation: 4-Stable (High tax rates)
Final Taxation Score: 5-Stable (Very high tax rates)

Barbados has a top income tax rate of 40 percent. The tax on the average income level, however, is 25 percent. Barbados also has a top marginal corporate tax rate of 40 percent and maintains a 5 percent sales tax and another consumption tax.

---

35   From International Monetary Fund, *Government Financial Statistics, 1994* (Washington, D.C.: 1995).

36   U.S. Department of Commerce, *Country Commercial Guide,* 1996.

37   State Department Report, 1996, p. 330.

Factor #3: Government Intervention in the Economy
Score: 3-Stable (Moderate level of government intervention)

Government in Barbados consumes about 20.3 percent of GDP, and the public sector is rather large. According to the U.S. Department of Commerce, "Successive Barbadian governments have used indicative planning, in keeping with the existence of (and desire for) a mixed economy. Indicative planning is designed to enable governments to plan and implement developmental activity in partnership and collaboration with the private sector.... In short, the Government has, and likely will continue to have a large role in Barbados' economy."[38] Major state-owned enterprises include the only commercial dairy, the Barbados Hilton, sugar refineries and lands, and an oil exploration company. Still, by global standards, the Barbados government intervenes only moderately in the economy.

Factor #4: Monetary Policy
Score: 1-Stable (Very low level of inflation)

Barbados had an average inflation rate of 2.8 percent from 1985 to 1994. In 1995, the inflation rate was 2 percent.

Factor #5: Capital Flows and Foreign Investment
Score: 2-Stable (Low barriers to foreign investment)

Barbados permits 100 percent foreign ownership of enterprises and provides equal treatment for both domestic and foreign firms. There are few restrictions on investments. Prior government approval is needed for investments in utilities, broadcasting, banking, and insurance.

Factor #6: Banking
Score: 2-Stable (Low level of restrictions on banking)

The banking system is fairly open to competition. Some foreign banks already operate there, but government approval is needed for foreign investment in banks.

Factor #7: Wage and Price Controls
Score: 2-Stable (Low level of wage and price controls)

Wages and prices are set mainly by the market. But Barbados still sets prices on some goods and services (for example, some household appliances and food staples).[39]

Factor #8: Property Rights
Score: 3-Stable (Moderate level of protection of private property)

Private property in Barbados is a legal right, based on British common law. Courts operate independently from the government. Some delays in court decisions can occur, however, and trademark law often allows the outright theft of trademarked property. According the U.S. Department of State, "The Barbados law provides that whoever first registers a [trade]mark has the right to use the [trade]mark. There are cases where some-

---

38   U.S. Department of Commerce, *Country Commercial Guide,* 1996.

39   State Department Report, 1996, p. 328.

one other than the original owner of the mark has registered it in Barbados, and therefore could demand royalty payments from the original owner."[40]

Factor #9: Regulation

Score: 3-Stable (Moderate level of regulation)

Establishing a business in Barbados is simple if the business does not compete directly with the large state-owned sector. Some newer regulations, like the country's environmental "green tax," hinder business formation and raise costs to consumers.

Factor #10: Black Market

Score: 3+ (Moderate level of black market activity)

Because of high levels of trade protectionism, illegal reproduction of video cassettes, recorded music, and computer software is rampant; so is trademark infringement on items like T-shirts. "There have been no recent court challenges or settlements for patent, trademark, or copyright infringements," reports the U.S. Department of Commerce, "although infringement is commonplace in certain sub-sectors of the economy (e.g., rentals and sales of films on videocassettes, tee-shirt production of unlicensed copyrighted images, unlicensed use of trademarks as store names, software piracy, satellite signal piracy)."[41] According to the State Department, "The major problem is illegal copying from promotional tapes provided by movie distributors or from U.S. hotel 'pay-per-view' movies and shows or from satellite transmissions."[42] By global standards, however, all of this represents only a moderate level of black market activity.

Summary

Barbados				Overall Score	2.80
Trade	4	Monetary Policy	1	Property Rights	3
Taxation	5	Foreign Investment	2	Regulation	3
Government Intervention	3	Banking	2	Black Market	3
		Wage and Prices	2		

---

40   *Ibid.*, p. 330.

41   U.S. Department of Commerce, *Country Commercial Guide*, 1996.

42   State Department Report, 1996, p. 331.

BELARUS

Lying between Poland and Russia, Belarus had one of the highest income levels in the former Soviet Union. The collapse of the Soviet Union, however, has left the country's heavily industrialized economy in a shambles. Market reforms have been half-hearted, and recent trends suggest a resurgence of old socialist economic policies. As a result, the size of the economy has shrunk.

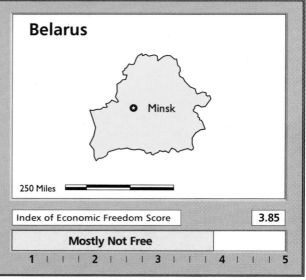

Belarus

● Minsk

250 Miles

Index of Economic Freedom Score	3.85
Mostly Not Free	

1   2   3   4   5

Factor #1: Trade Policy
Score: 5- (Very high level of protectionism)

Belarus maintains relatively high barriers to trade. Its average tariff rate was 3.9 percent in 1994,[43] down from 11 percent in 1992. Belarus entered a customs union with Russia in 1995, the effective result of which has been to eliminate tariffs on goods shipped between Russia and Belarus. As a condition of the customs union with Russia, however, Belarus also raised its tariffs on all imported goods not originating in Russia; these tariffs, which had ranged from 5 percent to 10 percent, now are from 20 percent to 40 percent. Thus, the average tariff rate is closer to Russia's 17 percent. Belarus maintains non-tariff barriers through heavy user fees on imports and through some currency requirements on businesses trying to import raw materials.

Factor #2: Taxation

Score - Income taxation: 5-Stable (Very high tax rates)
Score - Corporate taxation: 3-Stable (Moderate tax rates)
Final Taxation Score: 4.5-Stable (Very high tax rates)

Income taxes in Belarus are among the highest in Europe. The top income tax rate is 60 percent. Belarus has a top corporate income tax of 30 percent, but the rate can be as high as 80 percent for income earned in auctions and through leases. Belarus also maintains a value-added tax of 20 percent.

Factor #3: Government Intervention in the Economy
Score: 3-Stable (Moderate level of government intervention)

The government of Belarus is very active in the economy. Most enterprises are still government-owned, and government consumes about 22 percent of GDP.

---

43   Based on taxes raised from international trade taken as a percentage of imports in 1994. From World Bank, "Statistical Handbook 1995, States of the Former USSR" (Washington, D.C.: 1995).

Factor #4: Monetary Policy
Score: 5-Stable (Very high level of inflation)

Belarus has chronically high inflation rates. Inflation was 308 percent in 1995, down from 2,059 percent in 1994 and 2,096 percent in 1993.[44]

Factor #5: Capital Flows and Foreign Investment
Score: 4- (High barriers to foreign investment)

Foreign investment in Belarus is hindered by political instability, anti-Western sentiment, inefficient bureaucracy, corruption, and lack of privatization. In addition, foreigners are not permitted to own land. According to the U.S. Department of Commerce, "It should be specifically noted that although the provisions necessary to start up foreign investment in Belarus are in place, foreign businesses often encounter unexpected problems. Although there are profitable trade opportunities, the political climate in Belarus is still not hospitable to foreign investment, which sometimes results in extreme and sudden new regulations, mainly in the tax and leasing spheres."[45]

Factor #6: Banking
Score: 3- (Moderate restrictions on banking)

Banking is one area in which Belarus outpaces most of its former communist neighbors. In 1994, the government adopted a hands-off approach to commercial banking, abolishing most regulations. The result was a boom in small banks. Belarus has over 44 commercial banks, one of which has as many as 20 branches. The government, however, still influences the country's largest banks. According to the U.S. Department of State, for example, "The National Bank of Belarus (NBB) is a weak financial institution hampered by a lack of technical and financial expertise, as well as by political interference."[46]

Factor #7: Wage and Price Controls
Score: 3-Stable (Moderate level of wage and price controls)

Belarus has a very high minimum wage. Moreover, although many prices and wages are free from government control, price controls remain on some items (for example, some forms of energy and various foodstuffs).

Factor #8: Property Rights
Score: 3-Stable (Moderate level of protection for private property)

Property is at risk in Belarus. The legal system does not protect private property fully, the primary problem being that contracts are not always enforced by the inefficient court system. A framework for the protection of private property is being established, however.

---

44   Based on the Consumer Price Index.

45   From U.S. Department of Commerce, "Belarus—Foreign Investment Regs—IM1950711 Market Research Reports," June 11, 1995.

46   State Department Report, 1996, p. 132.

Factor #9: Regulation

Score: 3-Stable (Moderate level of regulation)

The government of Belarus imposes significant regulations on businesses. Corruption exists, and regulations are not always applied evenly.

Factor #10: Black Market

Score: 5-Stable (Very high level of black market activity)

Belarus has a large black market that, generally left over from the days when the country was a part of the former Soviet Union, has increased in size because of the slow pace of economic reform. Black market activity occurs in the smuggling of consumer goods, in transportation, and in some services.

Summary

Belarus				Overall Score	3.85
Trade	5	Monetary Policy	5	Property Rights	3
Taxation	4.5	Foreign Investment	4	Regulation	3
Government Intervention	3	Banking	3	Black Market	5
		Wage and Prices	3		

BELGIUM

Belgium gained its independence from the Netherlands in 1830, but the Dutch did not recognize the country's independence officially until 1839. Belgium was occupied by Germany in both World War I and World War II, and the monarchy fell victim to internal political strife immediately following World War II. Civil unrest between the French-speaking Walloons and the Flemings during the late 1960s resulted in the collapse of the government in 1968. In the 1970s, a socialist regime gained power and severely restricted economic freedom by expanding government authority over the economy. In the 1990s, however, the government has undertaken some limited economic reforms.

Belgium

Brussels

100 Miles

| Index of Economic Freedom Score | 2.10 |

Mostly Free

1   2   3   4   5

Factor #1: Trade Policy

Score: 2- Stable (Low level of protectionism)

The average Belgian tariff rate is 3.6 percent. Nevertheless, as a member of the European Union (EU), Belgium also maintains non-tariff barriers common to the EU (for example, government restrictions on trade in the telecommunications industry, stemming mainly from government ownership and operation of the telephone company).

Factor #2: Taxation

Score - Income taxation: 5-Stable (Very high tax rates)
Score - Corporate taxation: 4-Stable (High tax rates)
Final Taxation Score: 5-Stable (Very high tax rates)

Belgium has a top income tax rate of 55 percent, and the average taxpayer is in the 40 percent bracket. The top marginal corporate tax rate is 40 percent. Belgium also maintains a 40 percent capital gains tax and a 20.5 percent value-added tax.

Factor #3: Government Intervention in the Economy

Score: 2-Stable (Low level of government intervention)

Belgium's government consumes 15.3 percent of GDP. Unlike some of its neighbors, Belgium has achieved significant progress in privatization; the government currently is engaged in selling off its telecommunications, mail, energy, and transportation services.

Factor #4: Monetary Policy

Score: 1-Stable (Very low level of inflation)

From 1985 to 1994, the average rate of inflation in Belgium was 3.2 percent. In 1995, the inflation rate was 1.5 percent; for the first half of 1996, it was about 2 percent.

Factor #5: Capital Flows and Foreign Investment
Score: 2-Stable (Low barriers to foreign investment)

Belgium's investment policy is one of the most open in Europe. Foreign and domestic firms are treated equally, and there are no restrictions on foreign investment that do not apply also to domestic investment, except in industries vital to national defense.

Factor #6: Banking
Score: 2-Stable (Low level of restrictions on banking)

Foreign banks are allowed to operate in Belgium, and are subject to relatively few government restrictions. The domestic banking system often is tightly regulated by the government, however, although progress is being made to free up this sector.

Factor #7: Wage and Price Controls
Score: 2-Stable (Low level of wage and price controls)

Wages and prices in Belgium are determined mainly by the market. State ownership of some industries and a massive program of government subsidies, however, both affect pricing in many areas, such as electricity and some agricultural products. Some price controls remain on household rent and certain pharmaceuticals. Belgium also maintains a minimum wage policy.

Factor #8: Property Rights
Score: 1-Stable (Very high level of protection of private property)

Private property generally is safe from government expropriation in Belgium. The legal and judicial system is like that of any other advanced industrial nation.

Factor #9: Regulation
Score: 3-Stable (Moderate level of regulation)

Establishing a business in Belgium can be easy if the business does not compete directly with government-owned industries (such as some utilities), and regulations are applied evenly in most cases. Belgium requires generous worker benefits, and regulations on business are making it harder for some companies to survive.

Factor #10: Black Market
Score: 1-Stable (Very low level of black market activity)

The black market in Belgium is negligible. According to U.S. State Department estimates, some 20 percent of the video cassette and compact disc market is in pirated material, and some 46 percent of all software in Belgium also is pirated.[47] This is small, however, when compared to the size of Belgium's economy.

---

47   State Department Report, 1996, p. 138.

Summary

Belgium				Overall Score	2.10
Trade	2	Monetary Policy	1	Property Rights	1
Taxation	5	Foreign Investment	2	Regulation	3
Government Intervention	2	Banking	2	Black Market	1
		Wage and Prices	2		

BELIZE

Located just south of Mexico's Yucatan Peninsula, the Central American country of Belize is among the region's fastest-growing. Belize's economy stagnated in the early 1980s because the main export (sugar cane) was hit by disease. Since then, however, Belize has had extremely high rates of economic growth because of sound policies and favorable conditions in Latin and North America, to which many of its goods are exported.

Belize

Belmopan

50 Miles

| Index of Economic Freedom Score | 2.70 |

Mostly Free

1   2   3   4   5

Factor #1: Trade Policy

Score: 5-Stable (Very high level of protectionism)

Trade is a main source of government revenue in Belize. Tariffs are very high and average 26 percent. Belize requires import licenses for 26 different products, including citrus, flour, meats, jams and jellies, pepper sauce, pasta, matches, and peanut butter, among others. A special stamp duty of 12 percent is added to various products.

Factor #2: Taxation

Score - Income taxation: 4-Stable (High tax rate)
Score - Corporate taxation: 3-Stable (Moderate tax rate)
Final Taxation Score: 4-Stable (High tax rate)

Taxes in Belize are high. The top marginal income tax rate is 45 percent, and the average income level is taxed at 15 percent. The corporate income tax rate is a flat 35 percent. Belize also has a social contributions tax.

Factor #3: Government Intervention in the Economy

Score: 2-Stable (Low level of government intervention)

Government consumes 17 percent of GDP in Belize.

Factor #4: Monetary Policy

Score: 1-Stable (Very low level of inflation)

From 1985 to 1994, the average annual inflation rate in Belize was 3.5 percent. In 1995, it was 2.9 percent.

Factor #5: Capital Flows and Foreign Investment

Score: 2-Stable (Low barriers to foreign investment)

Foreign investment is not permitted in a variety of industries and economic activities, including accounting, beekeeping, commercial fishing, merchandising and distribution, sugar cane production, and transportation. Belize offers tax holidays, however, which eliminate taxes on investments over a specified period, for investments in many other areas. This encourages investments that result in increased exports and more jobs.

Factor #6: Banking

Score: 3-Stable (Moderate level of restrictions on banking)

Bank loans in Belize are closely regulated, and banks are under tight government control. Moreover, recently promulgated regulations have increased government oversight of some banks. Foreigners need to acquire permission from the government to operate in Belize, and competition among banks is limited because new bank formation is hindered by government restrictions.

Factor #7: Wage And Price Controls

Score: 2-Stable (Low level of wage and price controls)

Most wages and prices are set by the market, although there are price controls on some foodstuffs. Belize maintains a minimum wage.

Factor #8: Property Rights

Score: 2-Stable (High level of protection of private property)

The chances for expropriation are remote. An adequate court system is in place.

Factor #9: Regulation

Score: 3-Stable (Moderate level of regulation)

Some regulations, like health and safety standards, can be onerous in Belize, especially for smaller companies. Regulations often are applied haphazardly, and existing regulations pose a burden on business. Obtaining a business license can be complicated.

Factor #10: Black Market

Score: 3-Stable (Moderate level of black market activity)

Black market activity in Belize takes many forms. Some construction, transportation, and other cash transactions are done primarily in the black market. Moreover, although the government is engaged in updating its copyright laws and other laws pertaining to intellectual property, there is a growing black market in pirated trademarks and prerecorded music and video tapes.

Summary

Belize				Overall Score	2.70
Trade	5	Monetary Policy	1	Property Rights	2
Taxation	4	Foreign Investment	2	Regulation	3
Government Intervention	2	Banking	3	Black Market	3
		Wage and Prices	2		

BENIN

Located in West Africa on the Gulf of Guinea, Benin gained its independence from France in 1960 under the name of Dahomey. The country was renamed Benin in 1975 by a Marxist government that had seized power in a 1972 coup. Free and fair elections were held in 1991 and 1996, and Benin currently is one of Africa's more vibrant democracies, although its old dictator returned to power via the ballot box in 1996. Benin's economy has been improving gradually since the beginning of its liberalization in 1989. Two decades of Marxism had devastated Benin's economy, which is based primarily on agriculture, mining, and regional trade; but economic growth today is in the 5 percent range. Benin maintains close political and economic ties with France.

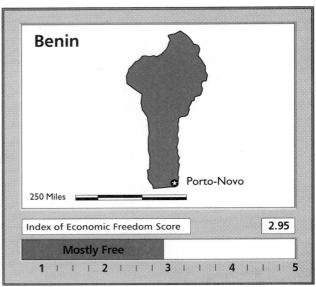

Factor #1: Trade Policy

Score: 4-Stable (High level of protectionism)

Benin is liberalizing its trade policies. The tariff structure was simplified in 1993, although Benin still has an average tariff rate of 20.2 percent.[48] Import licensing controls were removed in 1993, and overall tariff rates were reduced in 1994. Thus, the average tariff rate probably is much less than 20 percent. Few if any non-tariff barriers exist.

Factor #2: Taxation

Score - Income taxation: 3-Stable (Moderate tax rates)
Score - Corporate taxation: 3-Stable (Moderate tax rates)
Final Taxation Score: 3.5-Stable (High tax rates)

Benin has a top income tax rate of 35 percent.[49] The corporate tax recently was reduced from 48 percent to 38 percent. An 18 percent value-added tax covering most goods was introduced in 1991.

Factor #3: Government Intervention in the Economy

Score: 3-Stable (Moderate level of government intervention)

Government consumes about 11.4 percent of Benin's GDP. Although there has been significant progress with the privatization and liquidation of state enterprises over

---

48   1996 World Bank figure based on 1994 data; from World Bank, "African Development Figures, 1996."

49   The tax on the average income level is not available. Thus, Benin's income tax score is based solely on the top rate.

the past several years, some 30 enterprises remain in state hands. Further privatization is planned.

Factor #4: Monetary Policy
Score: 1-Stable (Very low level of inflation)

Benin had an average inflation rate of 2.9 percent from 1985 to 1994. More recently, however, it has been on the upsurge, running at 35 percent in 1995.

Factor #5: Capital Flows and Foreign Investment
Score: 3-Stable (Moderate barriers to foreign investment)

Benin has improved its foreign investment climate considerably over the past few years. Investment incentives have been established, foreign investment has increased, and a one-stop foreign investment approval center is being planned. In the meantime, however, foreign investors must contend with numerous hurdles imposed by inefficient bureaucracies subject to corruption. The mining, energy, water, forestry, transport, and communications sectors all remain under state control.

Factor #6: Banking
Score: 3-Stable (Moderate level of restrictions on banking)

The banking sector collapsed in the late 1980s. Several state-controlled banks became bankrupt and subsequently were liquidated. Today, five private banks operate in Benin. The government remains involved in providing agricultural credit, and interest rates are dictated by the Central Bank of West Africa. New banks must meet minimum capital and other requirements.

Factor #7: Wage and Price Controls
Score: 3-Stable (Moderate level of wage and price controls)

An elaborate price control scheme has been dismantled. Price controls on several foodstuffs have been reimposed, however, in an attempt to combat inflation. There also are price controls on cement, medicine, school equipment, electricity, and water, as well as a producer price for cotton, Benin's largest export commodity. There is a minimum wage, and the government plays a significant role in guiding private-sector wage negotiations.

Factor #8: Property Rights
Score: 3-Stable (Moderate level of protection of private property)

Although private property is legal, two decades of Marxist rule have left Benin's court and legal system in disarray.

Factor #9: Regulation
Score: 3-Stable (Moderate level of regulation)

Benin's government has recognized the need to simplify business licensing procedures, as well as to revise the labor code to allow employers increased flexibility in hiring and firing decisions. The licensing tax was reduced recently.

Factor #10: Black Market

Score: 3-Stable (Moderate level of black market activity)

The reimposition of price controls on several products has led to the establishment of surveillance teams charged with combating smuggling.

Summary

Benin				Overall Score	2.95
Trade	4	Monetary Policy	1	Property Rights	3
Taxation	3.5	Foreign Investment	3	Regulation	3
Government Intervention	3	Banking	3	Black Market	3
		Wage and Prices	3		

BOLIVIA

B olivia, a landlocked country in central South America, is a constitutional democracy. Although much of Latin America has undergone several years of economic liberalization, Bolivia has done so only recently. Thus, although the government has controlled inflation and the economy has grown somewhat, Bolivia is behind its neighbors in both economic growth and freedom. Bolivia recently has reformed its banking sector by selling off government-owned banks, and the government has been able to reduce inflation. The success of the Sanchez de Lozada government's economic reform plan will depend to a significant degree on the success of a program to privatize six of Bolivia's largest companies.

Bolivia

La Paz

500 Miles

Index of Economic Freedom Score	2.85

Mostly Free

1　　2　　3　　4　　5

Factor #1: Trade Policy

Score: 2-Stable (Low level of protectionism)

In 1990, the government reduced the average tariff rate from 16 percent to 10 percent on all but capital goods, whose rate is 5 percent. Thus, Bolivia's average tariff rate is between 5 percent and 9 percent. Bolivia maintains few if any non-tariff barriers.

Factor #2: Taxation

Score - Income taxation: 2-Stable (Low tax rates)
Score - Corporate taxation: 2-Stable (Low tax rates)
Final Taxation Score: 2.5-Stable (Moderate tax rates)

Bolivia has a flat income tax of 13 percent and a top corporate tax rate of 25 percent. Bolivia also has a 13 percent value-added tax and a variety of other transaction and property taxes.

Factor #3: Government Intervention in the Economy

Score: 5-Stable (Very High level of government intervention)

Total government spending accounts for some 40 percent of GDP,[50] largely because state-owned industries account for almost 50 percent of GDP. The government is undergoing a massive privatization program. When this program is complete, Bolivia's government spending is very likely to decrease.

50　Based on current 1995 dollars; from U.S. Department of Commerce, *Country Commercial Guide,* 1996.

Factor #4: Monetary Policy
Score: 3+ (Moderate level of inflation)

Bolivia's average inflation rate was 20 percent from 1985 to 1994 and 10 percent in 1995. It has been 8 percent so far in 1996.

Factor #5: Capital Flows and Foreign Investment
Score: 2-Stable (Low barriers to foreign investment)

Bolivia encourages foreign investment. Few restrictions remain on foreign investment; and although some restrictions remain on the petroleum and mining industries, they are minimal.

Factor #6: Banking
Score: 2-Stable (Low level of restrictions on banking)

Bolivia's banking system has been reformed, and government-owned banks no longer exist. The banking industry is composed primarily of 18 banks, 13 of which are private domestic banks and five of which are foreign-owned.

Factor #7: Wage and Price Controls
Score: 1-Stable (Very low level of wage and price controls)

There are few price controls in Bolivia, although the government does maintain the right to limit the prices of foodstuffs. Wages and prices are being set more freely as more state-owned companies are privatized. There are no minimum wage laws in Bolivia.

Factor #8: Property Rights
Score: 3-Stable (Moderate level of protection of private property)

Legal protection of private property is lax. Large property owners are particularly vulnerable to official corruption as property can be seized without just compensation and "taxed" by corrupt government officials.

Factor #9: Regulation
Score: 4-Stable (High level of government regulation)

Bolivia's economy is heavily regulated through haphazardly applied government requirements on business, and there are many complaints of corruption. Although the government maintains no occupational or environmental regulations, corruption poses a significant burden on business.

Factor #10: Black Market
Score: 4-Stable (High level of black market activity)

Bolivia's black market is being reduced. Some estimates place this activity at about 30 percent of GDP. In addition, piracy of intellectual property is widespread. Piracy in motion pictures, sound recordings, computer software, and books, for example, cost U.S. companies over $14 million in Bolivia in 1995.

Summary

Bolivia				Overall Score	2.85
Trade	2	Monetary Policy	3	Property Rights	3
Taxation	2.5	Foreign Investment	2	Regulation	4
Government Intervention	5	Banking	2	Black Market	4
		Wage and Prices	1		

BOTSWANA

The Southern African country of Botswana was named a British protectorate in 1885 and remained under the protection of Britain until 1966, when it was granted independence. Botswana is sparsely populated. It also is one of the few African countries to experience continuous civilian rule since gaining its independence. Botswana achieved annual economic growth rates near 10 percent through the 1980s. Although this growth has slowed over the past few years, the economy remains one of the most vibrant in Africa. Botswana is highly dependent on neighboring South Africa, which supplies about 85 percent of its imports and even administers its customs procedures. Despite significant progress in cutting taxes, reforming the banking sector, and curbing the black market, Botswana recently increased its barriers to trade and ex-

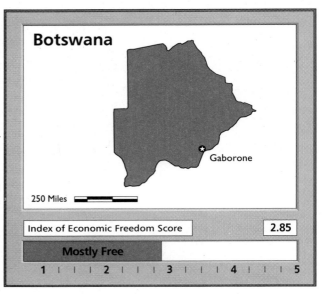

perienced higher levels of black market activity. It also has reduced taxes, however, and eliminated some wage and price controls.

Factor #1: Trade Policy
Score: 5- (Very high level of protectionism)

Botswana has moderately high tariffs but few, if any, non-tariff barriers. The average tariff rate is 30 percent.[51] Botswana is part of a customs union with South Africa, Lesotho, Swaziland, and Namibia.

Factor #2: Taxation

Score - Income taxation: 2-Stable (Low tax rates)
Score - Corporate taxation: 2+ (Low tax rates)
Final Taxation Score: 2.5+ (Moderate tax rates)

Botswana recently cut taxes and now has one of the lower tax burdens in Southern Africa. The top marginal income tax rate is 30 percent, and the average income level is taxed at 0 percent. Botswana also has a 25 percent corporate income tax;[52] a 25 percent capital gains tax; a 10 percent sales tax, which recently was extended to a greater range of goods and services; and a 35 percent capital transfer tax on such transfers as inheritance.

---

51   This rate is based on IMF figures, and taxes on international trade are computed as a percentage of total imports for 1992; from International Monetary Fund, *Government Financial Statistics, 1995.*

52   The basic corporate tax rate is 15 percent, but some companies pay an additional 10 percent tax.

Factor #3: Government Intervention in the Economy
Score: 4-Stable (High level of government intervention)

Government consumes 28.6 percent of Botswana's GDP, down from 34.9 percent. Moreover, the state sector owns a sizable portion of the country's enterprises.

Factor #4: Monetary Policy
Score: 2-Stable (Low level of inflation)

Botswana's average annual inflation rate was 11.8 percent from 1985 to 1994 and 10.5 percent in 1995.

Factor #5: Capital Flows and Foreign Investment
Score: 3-Stable (Moderate barriers to foreign investment)

Some sectors, including most utilities, some smaller retail stores, and some restaurants and bars, are closed to private investment. The requirement that licenses be obtained for expatriate employees deters some foreign investors because it can be cumbersome. Botswana permits 100 percent foreign equity and has some tax holidays for specific investments.

Factor #6: Banking
Score: 2-Stable (Low level of restrictions on banking)

Botswana's banking system is both competitive and advanced compared with those of most other African nations. Three new foreign-controlled commercial banks were established recently. The state plays a significant regulatory role in banking (for example, by limiting credit to foreign-owned companies), however.

Factor #7: Wage and Price Controls
Score: 2+ (Low level of wage and price controls)

Price controls have been eliminated. Some agriculture prices, however, are established through negotiated agreements with the government.

Factor #8: Property Rights
Score: 2-Stable (High level of protection of private property)

Property is relatively safe in Botswana, and there is little history of property expropriation. Because of financial constraints, however, the court system does not always operate efficiently.

Factor #9: Regulation
Score: 3-Stable (Moderate level of regulation)

Government bureaucracy often imposes a burden on businesses. A business license is relatively easy to obtain, but the bureaucracy plays a significant role in running the economy. For example, the government regulates the length of the work week, maternity leave, and standards for hiring and firing. Moreover, admitting that corruption often is prevalent in Botswana, the government recently established an oversight agency to root out corrupt bureaucrats. In 1995, this agency recovered over $2 million in unnecessary fines, fees, and bribes. The government of Botswana also recently stepped up its prosecution of corrupt bureaucrats. Thus, by global standards, regulation in Botswana is moderate.

Factor #10: Black Market
Score: 3- (Moderate level of black market activity)

By African standards, Botswana's black market is moderate. The elimination of price controls has diminished the level of black market activity. Still, according to the U.S. Department of Commerce, "Copyright protection is virtually nonexistent in Botswana. The pirating of videos, software, and television programming for local consumption is common."[53] The government recognizes this problem and is working to establish copyright laws and enforcement.

Summary

Botswana			Overall Score	2.85
Trade	5	Monetary Policy	2	Property Rights	2
Taxation	2.5	Foreign Investment	3	Regulation	3
Government Intervention	4	Banking	2	Black Market	3
		Wage and Prices	2		

---

53   U.S. Department of Commerce, *Country Commercial Guide*, 1996.

BRAZIL

Brazil, the largest country in Latin America, once was a colony of Portugal. Under President Fernando Collor de Mello, who was impeached in 1992, Brazil reduced trade barriers, privatized state-owned enterprises, controlled inflation, and maintained a tight monetary policy. Collor's successor, Itamar Franco, stalled economic reforms, raised taxes, and increased government control of credit. Brazil's new president, Fernando Henrique Cardoso, is reducing tax and tariff rates and privatizing many state-owned businesses.

Brazil

Brasilia

1000 Miles

Index of Economic Freedom Score	3.35
Mostly Not Free	

1   2   3   4   5

Factor #1: Trade Policy

Score: 4-Stable (High level of protectionism)

Brazil maintains an average tariff rate of 14 percent.[54] It has other barriers to trade as well, such as import licenses and other duties. "Import licenses are now used primarily for statistical purposes and generally are issued automatically within five days," according to the U.S. Department of State. "However, obtaining an import license can occasionally still be difficult."[55]

Factor #2: Taxation

Score - Income taxation: 2-Stable (Low tax rates)
Score - Corporate taxation: 2+ (Low tax rates)
Final Taxation Score: 2.5+ (Moderate tax rates)

Brazil has a top income tax rate of 25 percent, down from 35 percent in 1995. The government determines tax brackets based on what it calls a "fiscal unit of reference." By using this method to determine the amount of an individual's annual income after a year's worth of inflation (which was very high in Brazil until mid-1994 when the government cracked down on inflation), the government theoretically obtains the maximum amount of revenue from income that is continuously inflating. The average Brazilian, however, does not pay income taxes. Using the per capita GDP of $2,800 expressed in U.S. dollars, the average Brazilian taxpayer falls into the lowest tax bracket, in which no taxes are owed. Brazil has a maximum corporate tax rate of 15 percent, down from 25 percent in 1995, and recently abolished a surtax that was as high as 18 percent. In addition, Brazil has a capital gains tax of 15 percent, a top federal value-added tax of 365.6 percent, a state value-added tax of 7 percent to 25 percent, and a maximum municipal service tax of 10 percent.

---

54   Economist Intelligence Unit, *ILT Reports*, 1996.

55   State Department Report, 1996, p. 341.

Factor #3: Government Intervention in the Economy
Score: 3- (Moderate level of government intervention)

Government consumes 17 percent of GDP.[56] The Brazilian privatization program has not reduced the extent of government intervention in the economy significantly. The government still owns companies in petroleum, electricity, mining, railways, and banking, for example, although it gradually is selling off some of these assets to private investors. According to the Economist Intelligence Unit, "Apart from its extensive direct control of enterprises, Brazil continues to regulate business activities to a greater extent than most industrialized countries but less than many developing countries."[57] Thus, by global standards, government intervention in Brazil's economy is moderate.

Factor #4: Monetary Policy
Score: 5-Stable (Very high level of inflation)

From 1985 to 1994, the annual inflation rate was 913 percent. In 1995, however, it was reduced to about 23 percent.[58]

Factor #5: Capital Flows and Foreign Investment
Score: 3-Stable (Moderate barriers to foreign investment)

Brazil still maintains barriers to foreign investment, and restrictions on investments in the service industries can be high. For example, foreign capital investments in petroleum, banking, insurance, and mining are limited; and other investments (for example, in transportation, utilities, media, real estate, and shipping) are prohibited. The Brazilian Congress recently passed a new foreign investment law, however, that allows equal treatment for domestic and foreign firms and opens the overall economy to increased foreign investment.

Factor #6: Banking
Score: 3-Stable (Moderate level of restrictions on banking)

Few foreign banks that exist in Brazil. All are restricted from expanding their number of branches or doing business with state-owned companies. Private banks, both foreign and domestic, must compete with a substantial number of state-owned banks.

Factor #7: Wage and Price Controls
Score: 3-Stable (Moderate level of wage and price controls)

Brazil has a long history of wage and price controls. It last froze prices in 1990, but has been easing controls gradually since that time. Nevertheless, Brazil still maintains price controls on a variety of goods and services, such as some foodstuffs, and many prices of products manufactured by state-owned companies also are controlled.

---

56 World Bank, *World Development Report 1996.*

57 Economist Intelligence Unit, *ILT Reports, 1996.*

58 Based on the Consumer Price Index.

Factor #8: Property Rights
Score: 3-Stable (Moderate level of protection of private property)

There is little chance that the private property of foreign investors will be expropriated in Brazil. With a number of major multinational corporations operating in the country, and with the government trying to attract foreign investment, the protection of foreign-owned property is adequate. The court system often is inefficient, however; according to the U.S. Department of Commerce, "An overburdened court system is available for enforcing property rights; [but] decisions take years."[59]

Factor #9: Regulation
Score: 3+ (Moderate level of regulation)

Government regulation in Brazil has begun to fall from its previously high level, and the economy now is moderately regulated compared to global standards. Nevertheless, environmental, health, consumer, labor, financial, and a host of other regulations still restrain business activity, and regulations are not always applied evenly or consistently. "Although some administrative improvements have been made in recent years," reports the U.S. Department of Commerce, "the Brazilian legal and regulatory system is far from transparent. The government has historically exercised considerable control over private business through extensive and frequently changing regulations."[60]

Factor #10: Black Market
Score: 4-Stable (High level of black market activity)

Black market activity is increasing. Even though Brazil has adopted a new intellectual property rights law, enforcement is not yet vigorous enough to discourage black market activity in these areas. For example, there is a growing black market in pirated technologies (especially in pharmaceuticals, chemicals, and biotechnological inventions) and in pirated video cassettes, computer software, and other intellectual property. According to the U.S. Department of State, "Brazil's regime for the protection of intellectual property rights is inadequate. Serious gaps exist in current statutes with regard to patent protection for pharmaceuticals, chemicals, and biotechnology inventions; trademarks and trade secrets; and copyrights."[61]

Summary

Brazil				Overall Score	3.35
Trade	4	Monetary Policy	5	Property Rights	3
Taxation	2.5	Foreign Investment	3	Regulation	3
Government Intervention	3	Banking	3	Black Market	4
		Wage and Prices	3		

---

59   U.S. Department of Commerce, *Country Commercial Guide,* 1996.

60   *Ibid.*

61   State Department Report, 1996, p. 343.

BULGARIA

The Southeast European country of Bulgaria began to move away from its communist past after the fall of the Berlin Wall in 1989. It was not until 1991, however, that Bulgaria was free from communist control. Pressures to slow economic reforms are growing because of economic hardship. Elections in 1994 returned a neo-communist majority to the parliament, and this has resulted in a new cabinet controlled by former Communist Party members and a substantial slowdown of the reform process. In November 1996, Bulgarians elected reformist anti-communist Petar Stoyanov as president. Bulgaria remains behind the Czech Republic, Hungary, and Poland in economic reform, although progress has been made both in restoring land to its original owners and in small business privatization, primarily in the trade and services sectors. Recently, however, barriers to foreign investment have increased.

Factor #1: Trade Policy
Score: 3-Stable (Moderate level of protectionism)

Bulgaria's average tariff rate is about 7 percent. There also are non-tariff barriers in the form of import quotas that remain on such items as oranges, pulp and paper products, and fabrics.

Factor #2: Taxation
Score - Income taxation: 5-Stable (Very high tax rates)
Score - Corporate taxation: 4-Stable (High tax rates)
Final Taxation Score: 5-Stable (Very high tax rates)

Bulgaria has very high taxes. The top income tax rate is 50 percent, the average income level is taxed at 33 percent, and the top corporate tax rate is 40 percent. Bulgaria also has a 40 percent capital gains tax, an 18 percent value-added tax, and a 10 percent municipality tax.

Factor #3: Government Intervention in the Economy
Score: 3-Stable (Moderate level of government intervention)

Government consumption of GDP in Bulgaria is 15 percent and falling. Some state-owned industries still make up a significant portion of the economy, however. Although some smaller businesses have been privatized, most large state-owned industries have yet to be sold off to the private sector.

Factor #4: Monetary Policy
Score: 5-Stable (Very high level of inflation)

The inflation rate was 110 percent to 120 percent in 1994. The annual rate was brought down to 35 percent in 1995, but this is still very high.

Factor #5: Capital Flows and Foreign Investment
Score: 3- (Moderate barriers to foreign investment)

Bulgaria proclaims that foreign investment is welcome and has a non-restrictive foreign investment code. Tax incentives are offered in some cases. There are no restrictions on foreign ownership, and requirements for local content of goods and services produced in Bulgaria have been eliminated. A well-entrenched bureaucracy is the biggest obstacle to foreign investment, which also is discouraged by the large state-owned sector and weak infrastructure. Some Western companies have complained of a growing demand for bribes and kickbacks.

Factor #6: Banking
Score: 3-Stable (Moderate restrictions on banking)

Foreign participation in Bulgarian banks requires permission from the government. Moreover, a law postponing debt payments to private Western commercial banks has hindered the willingness of foreign banks to move into Bulgaria. A few banks from the Netherlands, Austria, and Greece have set up branches.

Factor #7: Wage and Price Controls
Score: 3-Stable (Moderate level of wage and price controls)

Despite attempts to adopt a free market, Bulgaria still has a mixed economy. Some prices are still affected by government-owned corporations, which supply subsidized raw materials to companies producing goods. Thus, the end prices of these goods and services are affected by the government's heavy-handed control of the economy. Bulgaria has a minimum wage.

Factor #8: Property Rights
Score: 3-Stable (Moderate level of protection of private property)

Private property has gained greater protection from a legal code and increasingly efficient legal system. There is a lack of progress, however, in land privatization and in the protection of real estate ownership.

Factor #9: Regulation
Score: 4-Stable (High level of regulation)

Bureaucrats held over from the communist era impose a significant burden on businesses. Licenses occasionally require a bribe, and existing regulations may be applied unevenly. Moreover, many businesses complain of an arbitrary bureaucracy that applies regulations haphazardly. This confusion often results in conflicting information from different government agencies.

Factor #10: Black Market
Score: 4-Stable (High level of black market activity)

Bulgaria has a large black market. Because economic reforms have yet to become fully established, many activities like construction, transportation, and food production remain in the black market. Although Bulgaria maintains laws to protect intellectual property, enforcement is lax. As a result, there is substantial black market activity in pirated materials such as computer software and prerecorded music and video.

Summary

Bulgaria				Overall Score	3.60
Trade	3	Monetary Policy	5	Property Rights	3
Taxation	5	Foreign Investment	3	Regulation	4
Government Intervention	3	Banking	3	Black Market	4
		Wage and Prices	3		

BURKINA FASO

The West African country of Burkina Faso, formerly Upper Volta, gained its independence from France in 1960. Ninety percent of this landlocked country's population depends on subsistence agriculture; and because it must import nearly all of its consumer goods, there is a chronic trade deficit. Although Burkina Faso instituted a significant economic reform program in 1991, it still maintains many restrictions on economic freedom. Little progress has been made.

Burkina Faso

Ouagadougou

250 Miles

| Index of Economic Freedom Score | 3.50 |

Mostly Not Free

1 2 3 4 5

Factor #1: Trade Policy

Score: 5-Stable (Very high level of protectionism)

Burkina Faso maintains a 5 percent customs fee, a variable import duty, a variable value-added tax, a 4 percent statistical tax (an administrative fee), a 1 percent solidarity tax, and a 1 percent tax to support government enforcement of trade laws, among other taxes. All of these taxes bring the average tariff rate to over 15 percent of the imported item's value. Burkina Faso also maintains some trade restrictions in the form of import bans and quotas.

Factor #2: Taxation

Score - Income taxation: 3-Stable (Moderate tax rates)
Score - Corporate taxation: 4-Stable (High tax rates)
Final Taxation Score: 4-Stable (High tax rates)

Burkina Faso has a top income tax rate of 35 percent and a top marginal corporate tax rate of 45 percent. It also maintains a 25 percent capital gains tax as well as real estate and other taxes.

Factor #3: Government Intervention in the Economy

Score: 3-Stable (Moderate level of government intervention)

The government of Burkina Faso consumes about 17.1 percent of GDP. Burkina Faso has a significant public sector.

Factor #4: Monetary Policy

Score: 1-Stable (Very low level of inflation)

Burkina Faso had an average inflation rate of 1.7 percent from 1985 to 1994. Inflation was 5 percent in 1995, however.

Factor #5: Capital Flows and Foreign Investment
Score: 2-Stable (Low barriers to foreign investment)

There are few restrictions on investments in Burkina Faso. In 1992, the government adopted a new investment code that treats foreign and domestic firms equally. Some tax incentives are granted. Corruption, however, remains a problem.

Factor #6: Banking
Score: 4-Stable (High level of restrictions on banking)

The banking system in Burkina Faso is heavily regulated and controlled by the government, although the government does plan to privatize some of its banks.

Factor #7: Wage and Price Controls
Score: 4-Stable (High level of wage and price controls)

Wages and prices in Burkina Faso are affected mainly by significant government involvement in the economy. The government continues to subsidize many domestically produced products.

Factor #8: Property Rights
Score: 3+ (Moderate level of protection of private property)

Private property in Burkina Faso still is subject to government expropriation. The legal and judicial system is becoming more efficient, however. According to the U.S. Department of Commerce, "Burkina Faso has a legal system which protects and facilitates acquisition and disposition of all property rights, including intellectual property."[62] Some cases, however, can take years to resolve.

Factor #9: Regulation
Score: 4+ (High level of regulation)

Establishing a business in Burkina Faso can be difficult if the business competes with a state-owned company. Regulations at times are applied unevenly and inconsistently.

Factor #10: Black Market
Score: 5-Stable (Very high level of black market activity)

The black market in Burkina Faso, by some estimates, is almost half the formal economy. According to the U.S. Department of Commerce, "The tertiary sector, contributing about 41 percent in value added to the economy, is poised for growth. This sector is dominated by the so-called 'informal sector' (70 percent)...."[63]

---

62   U.S. Department of Commerce, *Country Commercial Guide, 1996.*

63   *Ibid.*

Summary

Burkina Faso		Overall Score	3.50

Trade	5	Monetary Policy	1	Property Rights	3
Taxation	4	Foreign Investment	2	Regulation	4
Government Intervention	3	Banking	4	Black Market	5
		Wage and Prices	4		

BURUNDI

The East Central African country of Burundi gained its independence from a Belgian-administered United Nations (UN) trusteeship in 1962. The economy is primarily agricultural, with some 90 percent of the population engaged in farming. After gaining its independence, it was one of the poorest countries in sub-Saharan Africa and quickly became embroiled in civil unrest and political instability. Today, Burundi is trying to attract foreign investment. Yet, located just south of Rwanda, it still is struggling to develop both a market system and a stable political system, and the situation remains chaotic. There was a *coup d'état* in 1996, and ethnic tension and violence continue. The UN may consider a peacekeeping operation.

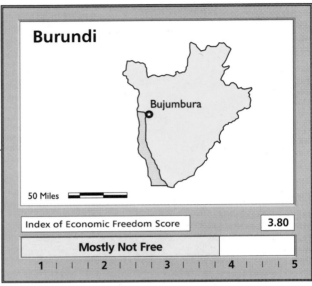

Burundi

Bujumbura

50 Miles

Index of Economic Freedom Score	3.80

Mostly Not Free

1   2   3   4   5

Factor #1: Trade Policy
Score: 5-Stable (Very high level of protectionism)

The average tariff rate was 7.4 percent in 1993. Yet the biggest deterrent to trade remains an unsafe and insecure border with Rwanda. According to the U.S. Department of State, "Sporadic violence remains a problem, in Bujumbura as well as in the interior where large numbers of displaced persons are encamped or in hiding.... Burundi periodically has closed its border without notice and suspended air travel and telephone service in response to political disturbances."[64] Thus, trade is severely restricted.[65]

Factor #2: Taxation
Score - Income taxation: 4-Stable (High tax rates)
Score - Corporate taxation: 4-Stable (High tax rates)
Final Taxation Score: 4-Stable (High tax rates)

Burundi's tax revenue as a percentage of GDP has averaged over 20 percent since 1990. Tax evasion is pervasive, indicating that the actual tax burden is quite high.

Factor #3: Government Intervention in the Economy
Score: 3-Stable (Moderate level of government intervention)

Burundi's government consumes about 15.6 percent of GDP. The public sector, however, generates most GDP. Burundi also has a large number of government-owned companies.

---

64   U.S. Department of State Department Travel Advisory, 1996.

65   Burundi's grade in trade is based solely on the government's unpredictable policy toward its borders. With commerce across its borders routinely stifled, Burundi's barriers to trade were considered very high.

Factor #4: Monetary Policy
Score: 1-Stable (Very low level of inflation)

Burundi had an average annual inflation rate of 5.2 percent from 1985 to 1994. Inflation rates are not available for 1995.

Factor #5: Capital Flows and Foreign Investment
Score: 4-Stable (High barriers to foreign investment)

Burundi provides equal treatment for both domestic and foreign firms and is actively seeking investment. It remains a country in turmoil, however. The biggest barriers to investment are underdeveloped financial institutions, unsafe conditions, and insecure borders.

Factor #6: Banking
Score: 4-Stable (High level of restrictions on banking)

The banking system in Burundi is heavily controlled by the government and severely underdeveloped.

Factor #7: Wage and Price Controls
Score: 4-Stable (High level of wage and price controls)

Wages and prices in Burundi are affected by the large public sector, import substitution policies, and government subsidies.

Factor #8: Property Rights
Score: 4-Stable (Low level of protection of private property)

Private property in Burundi is subject to government expropriation and armed bandits. The government is attempting to privatize many government-owned enterprises, but crime and theft remain problems. According to the U.S. Department of State, "Street crime in Burundi poses a high risk for visitors. Crime involves muggings, purse-snatching, pickpocketing, burglary, and auto break-ins. Criminals operate individually or in small groups. There have been reports of muggings of persons jogging or walking alone in all sections of Bujumbura, and especially on public roads bordering Lake Tanganyika."[66]

Factor #9: Regulation
Score: 4-Stable (High level of regulation)

Establishing a business in Burundi is difficult because of a massive and corrupt government bureaucracy. Bribery is sometimes present, as is embezzlement by government officials collecting fees.

Factor #10: Black Market
Score: 5-Stable (Very high level of black market activity)

Burundi's black market is larger than the formal market and growing. Most of this activity occurs in smuggled consumer goods, labor, and pirated intellectual property.

---

66   U.S. Department of State Travel Advisory, 1996.

Summary

Burundi			Overall Score	3.80
Trade	5	Monetary Policy	1	Property Rights	4
Taxation	4	Foreign Investment	4	Regulation	4
Government	3	Banking	4	Black Market	5
Intervention		Wage and Prices	4		

CAMBODIA

In recent history, Cambodia has been ruled by the French, a Cambodian monarch, and a military regime. After Washington ended military and economic aid, Cambodia fell to the Khmer Rouge, which killed over a million Cambodians. In 1979, Vietnam invaded Cambodia and placed its puppet Cambodia People's Party (CPP) in charge in Phnom Penh. This government was opposed by remnants of the Khmer Rouge and Western-backed non-communist factions in a war that continued until the 1991 Paris Peace Agreement, which called for a transitional government run by the United Nations until elections could be held in 1993.

These elections saw the defeat of the CPP by the royalist party of Prince Ranariddh. But the CPP managed to force a coalition government on Ranariddh and today is again in charge of Cambodia. Early confidence caused by democracy and free-market economic reforms has been eroded by CPP oppression of democratic opponents and widespread government corruption.

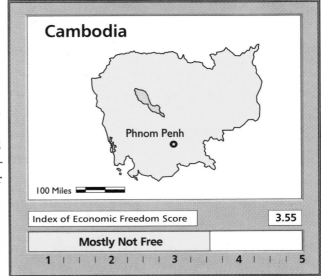

Index of Economic Freedom Score: 3.55

Mostly Not Free

Factor #1: Trade Policy

Score: 5-Stable (Very high level of protectionism)

Cambodia's tariffs range from 7 percent to 50 percent, with most goods coming into the country at the 35 percent level. Although import licenses have been abolished for most items, they remain on pharmaceuticals.

Factor #2: Taxation

Score - Income taxation: 2-Stable (Low tax rates)
Score - Corporate taxation: 2-Stable (Low tax rates)
Final Taxation Score: 2.5-Stable (Moderate tax rates)

Cambodia has a top marginal income tax rate of 20 percent[67] and a top corporate income tax rate of 20 percent. It also has a 4 percent sales tax as well as other taxes.

Factor #3: Government Intervention in the Economy

Score: 4-Stable (High level of government intervention)

The percentage of Cambodia's GDP that is consumed by government is unknown. It is known, however, that the government sector produces most of the country's GDP.

---

67   The tax on the average income level was unavailable. Therefore, Cambodia's score is based solely on the top rate.

Factor #4: Monetary Policy
Score: 4-Stable (High level of inflation)

Cambodia's average annual inflation rate between 1985 and 1994 is unavailable; however, inflation was 176 percent in 1992, 31 percent in 1993, 26 percent in 1994, 18 percent in 1995, and so far in 1996, inflation is around 10 percent.[68] Thus, the average inflation rate over the past several years is over 20 percent.

Factor #5: Capital Flows and Foreign Investment
Score: 3-Stable (Moderate barriers to foreign investment)

For the most part, Cambodia welcomes foreign investment. It treats foreign and domestic firms equally and has an established foreign investment code. Most foreign investments, however, still must be approved by the government.

Factor #6: Banking
Score: 3-Stable (Moderate restrictions on banking)

Cambodia's banking system remains under the influence of the government. There are two major state-owned banks and 17 private banks. Nevertheless, by global standards, Cambodia has only moderate restrictions on banking.

Factor #7: Wage and Price Controls
Score: 3-Stable (Moderate level of wage and price controls)

Most wages and prices are determined by the market. There are some controls, however, on such items as foodstuffs and some energy products. Moreover, companies in Cambodia's large state-owned sector receive subsidies that allow them to offer goods and services at artificially low prices.

Factor #8: Property Rights
Score: 4-Stable (Low level of protection of private property)

Cambodia's legal system does not protect private property effectively. "Cambodia's court system is weak," says the U.S. Department of Commerce. "Judges have been trained either for a short period at home or under other systems of law, have little access to published Cambodian law and, because paid a minimal salary (USD20/month), are susceptible to corruption."[69]

Factor #9: Regulation
Score: 4-Stable (High level of regulation)

Government corruption in Cambodia remains pervasive and often manifests itself in bribes, kickbacks, and payoffs. Moreover, the bureaucracy is cumbersome and inefficient, making it difficult to open businesses and to keep them open.

---

68   U.S. Department of Commerce, *Country Commercial Guide,* 1996; and "Investment in Cambodia," KPMG Peat Marwick, Phnom Penh, Cambodia, 1996.

69   U.S. Department of Commerce, *Country Commercial Guide,* 1996.

Factor #10: Black Market

Score: 3-Stable (Moderate level of black market activity)

Cambodia has a moderate level of black market activity, most of which occurs in labor and pirated intellectual property.

Summary

Cambodia				Overall Score	3.55
Trade	5	Monetary Policy	4	Property Rights	4
Taxation	2.5	Foreign Investment	3	Regulation	4
Government Intervention	4	Banking	3	Black Market	3
		Wage and Prices	3		

CAMEROON

Germany, the United Kingdom, and France at various times laid colonial claim to Cameroon. By 1961, however, this sub-Saharan African country had gained its independence from all European powers. A one-party state was established soon afterward, and political repression followed. By 1992, increasing pressure for democratization led to elections and the creation of a multi-party state. These elections, however, were neither free nor fair, and long-time president Paul Biya has stifled democratic progress. The United States has closed its aid mission in response to this lack of progress. Although a country of considerable resources, Cameroon has been in economic decline for the past 10 years.

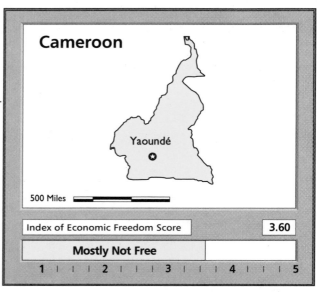

Index of Economic Freedom Score	3.60
Mostly Not Free	

Factor #1: Trade Policy

Score: 5-Stable (Very high level of protectionism)

Cameroon's average tariff rate is around 30 percent.[70] Almost 40 percent of government revenue is raised through these tariffs. Cameroon also uses countervailing and antidumping duties to protect its inefficient domestic industries. Import licenses are required, and at least 100 items are subject to import quotas. Used clothes and heavy vehicle imports are banned.

Factor #2: Taxation

Score - Income taxation: 3-Stable (Moderate tax rates)
Score - Corporate taxation: 4-Stable (High tax rates)
Final Taxation Score: 4-Stable (High tax rates)

Cameroon has a top income tax rate of 60 percent,[71] and the tax rate on the average income level is 0 percent. The top corporate tax rate is 38.5 percent. Cameroon also has a 38.5 percent capital gains tax and a 10.9 percent turnover tax.

Factor #3: Government Intervention in the Economy

Score: 3-Stable (Moderate level of government intervention)

Cameroon's government consumes 11.7 percent of GDP. The public sector is large, inefficient, and corrupt, and the privatization effort has been sluggish and scandal-plagued. President Biya recently announced plans to privatize the telephone, electricity, and water services.

---

70 Based on total taxes on international trade as a percentage of total imports. From International Monetary Fund, *Government Financial Statistics 1995*.

71 Some estimates place the top income tax rate at 66 percent.

Factor #4: Monetary Policy

Score: 1-Stable (Very low level of inflation)

Cameroon had an average annual inflation rate of 1.1 percent from 1985 to 1994. In 1995, inflation ran around 7.5 percent.

Factor #5: Capital Flows and Foreign Investment

Score: 3-Stable (Moderate barriers to foreign investment)

Cameroon has opened its borders to foreign investment in most industries, but it remains partial to investments from France and in some cases blocks them from other countries. Cameroon's corrupt bureaucracy and unstable legal institutions provide little comfort to foreign investors. Investment is approved on a case-by-case basis. Foreign direct investment is declining due to deteriorating economic conditions. "Cameroon's policies, as defined in law, meet all necessary elements of an open investment regime," says the U.S. Department of Commerce. "However, current practice does not permit a fair, transparent and impartial implementation of the country's laws."[72]

Factor #6: Banking

Score: 4-Stable (High level of restrictions on banking)

The banking sector is in crisis. Several government-owned banks are near collapse, and several French banks are reducing their presence in Cameroon. Banks in Cameroon are heavily influenced by the state and by France. Interest rates, for example, are controlled by the government and often do not reflect market conditions. There is a domestic banking industry, however. According to the U.S. Department of Commerce, "Cameroon's banking system is controlled by the *Banque des Etats de l'Afrique Centrale* (BEAC), a common central bank serving five other member countries of the Central African (UDEAC) subregion. BEAC is monitored closely and regulated by the French Treasury."[73]

Factor #7: Wage and Price Controls

Score: 3-Stable (Moderate level of wage and price controls)

Although most prices are set by the market, the government directly controls prices on some items, both by owning and operating enterprises and by officially dictating the prices of some goods that are produced by private firms and farms. There is corruption in the price control bureaucracy. Coffee prices recently have been liberalized. The government plays an active role in determining wages and benefits.

Factor #8: Property Rights

Score: 4-Stable (Low level of protection of private property)

Private property, although legal, is not entirely safe in Cameroon. A corrupt government and an uncertain legal environment can result in the confiscation of private property. According to the U.S. Department of Commerce, "Cameroon's judiciary remains effectively controlled by the Executive Branch. Firms have difficulties obtaining a fair and expeditious hearing before the courts. It is very difficult and costly to enforce

---

72   U.S. Department of Commerce, *Country Commercial Guide,* 1996.

73   *Ibid.*

contract rights in Cameroon. Property rights are ill-defined and inadequately protected in important respects, especially with respect to land tenure. Corruption within the judiciary system is widespread and unchecked. The execution of judgments is slow and fraught with administrative and legal bottlenecks."[74]

Factor #9: Regulation
Score: 4-Stable (High level of regulation)

Cameroon's economy is heavily regulated, and corruption is rampant. According to the U.S. Department of Commerce, "Corruption and a dysfunctional and arbitrary judicial system severely disrupt Cameroon's economy and society."[75] Existing regulations are applied unevenly and impose a huge burden on businesses. Establishing a business is a complicated procedure. It is difficult to hire expatriate employees.

Factor #10: Black Market
Score: 5-Stable (Very high level of black market activity)

Cameroon's black market is nearly as large as its legal market. Smugglers regularly bring in beef and other food products to circumvent the government's 40 percent countervailing duty on agricultural products.

Summary

Cameroon				Overall Score	3.60
Trade	5	Monetary Policy	1	Property Rights	4
Taxation	4	Foreign Investment	3	Regulation	4
Government Intervention	3	Banking	4	Black Market	5
		Wage and Prices	3		

---

74   *Ibid.*

75   *Ibid.*

CANADA

In 1759, Great Britain conquered France's North American colonies; in 1867, these colonies federated into the self-governing Dominion of Canada within the British Empire. Canada became fully independent in 1932. Today, with the world's seventh-largest market economy, Canada is moving away from many of the interventionist economic policies it had pursued since federation. In 1992, Alberta elected Conservative Premier Ralph Klein on a platform of spending cuts and deregulation. In 1995, Ontario elected Conservative Premier Mike Harris, who had pledged to cut provincial income taxes 30 percent, balance the budget, and reduce regulations. By 1996, even Quebec had joined this trend; new Parti Quebecois Premier Lucien Bouchard proposed sharp spending reductions and a deregulation program. At the federal level, Liberal Prime Minister Jean Chretien is curbing spending to reduce Ottawa's budget deficit. Last year, Ottawa privatized the state-owned Canadian National Railway.

Canada

1000 Miles

Ottawa

| Index of Economic Freedom Score | 2.05 |

Mostly Free

1 | | | 2 | | | 3 | | | 4 | | | 5

Factor #1: Trade Policy
Score: 2-Stable (Low level of protectionism)

Canada, a party to the North American Free Trade Agreement along with the United States and Mexico, generally supports free trade policies. Its average tariff rate is just over 4 percent. Canada does maintain trade barriers against dairy products, liquor, poultry, and wheat, however; import tariffs on some of these products are over 350 percent. According to the Office of the U.S. Trade Representative, Canada's Special Import Measures Act has been used to reduce imports. Since the early 1980s, the country also has increased its use of antidumping laws.

Factor #2: Taxation
Score - Income taxation: 4-Stable (High tax rates)
Score - Corporate taxation: 5- (Very high tax rates)
Final Taxation Score: 5- (Very high tax rates)

Canada's top marginal income tax rate is 53.19 percent,[76] with the average income level taxed at a rate of 17 percent. The top marginal corporate tax rate is 46.12 per-

---

76   This is a combined rate for 1995 in Ontario, which consists of a 31.32 percent federal tax and a 21.87 percent provincial tax. It is included here because both federal and provincial taxes are collected at the federal level. Thus, for all intents and purposes, the two tax rates are combined into one overall tax rate. Ontario is used because this is the rate reported in *The Worldwide Executive Tax Guide and Directory*, 1996 edition (New York, N.Y.: Ernst & Young, 1996). Other provinces may have higher or lower taxes, but the average for all of Canada is about 53 percent.

cent.[77] Canada also has a 21.84 percent capital gains tax and a 7 percent value-added tax, called a Goods and Services Tax.

Factor #3: Government Intervention in the Economy
Score: 2-Stable (Low level of government intervention)

Canada's government consumes 19.2 percent of GDP. Since 1984, the government has undertaken substantial privatization. Canada's provinces also are privatizing provincially owned firms, especially utilities.

Factor #4: Monetary Policy
Score: 1-Stable (Very low level of inflation)

Monetary policy is set by the Bank of Canada. The average annual rate of inflation from 1985 to 1994 was 3.1 percent. Today, the inflation rate is around 2 percent per year.

Factor #5: Capital Flows and Foreign Investment
Score: 3-Stable (Moderate barriers to foreign investment)

Canada maintains several restrictions on investment. The Investment Canada Act, for example, requires the government to review each foreign investment to determine whether there is a "net benefit to Canada." Although most such investments are approved, the Investment Canada Act often is used to restrict foreign investment in energy, publishing, telecommunications, broadcasting, and cable television.

Factor #6: Banking
Score: 2-Stable (Low level of restrictions on banking)

Canada has a private financial system with some restrictions. In mid-1992, the government implemented a financial sector reform package that increased competition among banks, trust companies, and insurance companies. The Canadian banking system, however, prohibits entry by foreign-owned branches.

Factor #7: Wage and Price Controls
Score: 2-Stable (Low level of wage and price controls)

Most prices in Canada are set by the market without government involvement. Some notable exceptions include government-owned utilities, the health care system, and such agricultural goods as eggs, poultry, and dairy products.

Factor #8: Property Rights
Score: 1-Stable (Very high level of protection of private property)

Private property is a fundamental principle of the Canadian economy. Canada's legal and judicial system affords adequate protection of private property.

---

77   This rate includes both federal and provincial rates and was provided by *Worldwide Corporate Tax Guide and Directory,* 1996 edition, Ernst & Young Online (*http://www1.ey.com*).

Factor #9: Regulation
Score: 2-Stable (Low level of regulation)

It is relatively easy to establish a business in Canada. Every business must be registered in its province, except in New Brunswick, which does not require any kind of registration. Canada does not have a single, uniform internal market, and regulations differ from province to province. The various provincial governments currently are seeking agreements that would establish common regulatory policies.

Factor #10: Black Market
Score: 1-Stable (Very low level of black market activity)

The Canadian black market is confined to the sale of goods and services that are considered harmful to public safety: weapons, drugs, and stolen merchandise. High taxes on alcohol and cigarettes encourage some smuggling of these products.

Summary

Canada					Overall Score	2.05
Trade	2	Monetary Policy	1	Property Rights	1
Taxation	4.5	Foreign Investment	3	Regulation	2
Government Intervention	2	Banking	2	Black Market	1
		Wage and Prices	2		

CAPE VERDE

The island nation of Cape Verde, located off the Western Coast of Africa in the Atlantic Ocean, remains a dependent territory of the United Kingdom. Cape Verde has few natural resources and is very dependent on imports. Even so, it maintains many restrictions on economic activity.

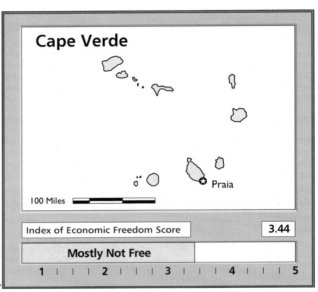

Cape Verde

Index of Economic Freedom Score — 3.44
Mostly Not Free
1   2   3   4   5

100 Miles

Praia

Factor #1: Trade Policy

Score: 5-Stable (Very high level of protectionism)

Cape Verde's tariff rates range from 5 percent to 50 percent; the average rate is about 20 percent. Imports also are subject to another 7 percent tax on top of the tariff rate, in addition to a 5 percent to 20 percent consumption tax. Cape Verde also maintains non-tariff barriers in the form of strict import licenses and documentation requirements.

Factor #2: Taxation

Score - Income taxation: Not Scored
Score - Corporate taxation: Not Scored
Final Taxation Score: Not Scored

Tax information for Cape Verde is not available.

Factor #3: Government Intervention in the Economy

Score: 3-Stable (Moderate level of government intervention)

Cape Verde's government consumes about 18 percent of GDP. The country has a significant state-owned sector.

Factor #4: Monetary Policy

Score: 2-Stable (Low level of inflation)

Cape Verde had an average inflation rate of 7.2 percent from 1985 to 1994. In 1995, inflation was 4.5 percent.

Factor #5: Capital Flows and Foreign Investment

Score: 2-Stable (Low barriers to foreign investment)

Although nearly all sectors of the economy now are open to investment, some restrictions remain. For example, delays often occur when revenue is converted to another currency and sent to the investor's home country.

Factor #6: Banking

Score: 5-Stable (Very high restrictions on banking)

The banking system in Cape Verde is underdeveloped. According to the U.S. Department of Commerce, "Financial services to the private sector are limited, with the result that the existing system is considered inadequate to efficiently and effectively satisfy the private sector's needs for credit."[78] There is no stock market and no capital market, and banking accounting systems, although clear, are not always consistent with international norms. The government owns most of the banks in Cape Verde.

Factor #7: Wage and Price Controls

Score: 4+ (High level of wage and price controls)

Wages and prices in Cape Verde are affected by a large public sector and the transfer of government subsidies to those institutions.

Factor #8: Property Rights

Score: 2-Stable (High level of protection of private property)

Private property is guaranteed in Cape Verde, and the legal and judicial system is based on English law. Private property can be expropriated, however, if such action is deemed to be in the national interest.

Factor #9: Regulation

Score: 4-Stable (High level of regulation)

Establishing a business can be cumbersome if the business competes with Cape Verde's state-owned sector. Regulations are applied evenly in most cases, but some corruption and a growing domestic monopoly in certain industries make it difficult to open new businesses.

Factor #10: Black Market

Score: 4-Stable (High level of black market activity)

Cape Verde has a growing and pervasive black market, mainly in consumer goods, luxury items, and Western books, video and audio cassettes, and movies.

Summary

Cape Verde				Overall Score	3.44
Trade	5	Monetary Policy	2	Property Rights	2
Taxation	N/A	Foreign Investment	2	Regulation	4
Government Intervention	3	Banking	5	Black Market	4
		Wage and Prices	4		

---

78 U.S. Department of Commerce, *Country Commercial Guide*, 1996.

CHAD

The Central African country of Chad gained its independence from France in 1960. It is primarily an agricultural economy. After independence, it was one of the poorest and least politically cohesive of the former colonies, and experienced constant and pervasive civil unrest and political instability. Little has changed. About 85 percent of Chadians make their living from subsistence agriculture, fishing, and ranching.

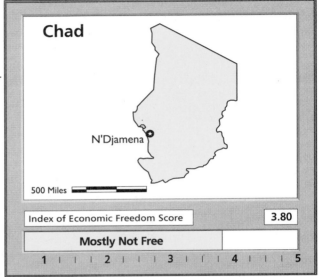

Chad
N'Djamena
500 Miles

Index of Economic Freedom Score	3.80
Mostly Not Free	

1 | | | 2 | | | 3 | | | 4 | | | 5

Factor #1: Trade Policy

Score: 5-Stable (Very high level of protectionism)

Chad's average tariff rate is 15.8 percent, but the biggest deterrent to trade remains an unsafe and un-navigable road system. "Roads are in poor condition and dangerous," reports the U.S. Department of State. "No emergency services exist. Travelers on roads in all areas of the country are subject to attacks by armed bandits. Overland travel after dark is especially dangerous."[79]

Factor #2: Taxation

Score - Income taxation: 4-Stable (High tax rates)
Score - Corporate taxation: 4-Stable (High tax rates)
Final Taxation Score: 4-Stable (High tax rates)

Chad's tax system is constantly changing, and evasion is endemic. The main form of taxation is government expropriation of agricultural crops and goods produced by merchants. Such action—by armed bandits as well as government officials—is common at the local level.

Factor #3: Government Intervention in the Economy

Score: 3-Stable (Moderate level of government intervention)

Chad's government consumes about 17 percent of GDP, and most of the country's GDP is generated by the public sector. Many companies are government-owned.

Factor #4: Monetary Policy

Score: 1-Stable (Very low level of inflation)

Chad had an average annual inflation rate of 1.8 percent from 1985 to 1994. Inflation rates are not available for 1995.

---

79   U.S. Department of State Travel Advisory, 1996.

Factor #5: Capital Flows and Foreign Investment
Score: 4-Stable (High barriers to foreign investment)

Although Chad provides equal treatment for both domestic and foreign firms, its international reputation for hostility to foreign investment and its conflict with Libya remain the biggest impediments to foreign investment. According to the U.S. Department of Commerce, "The effects of the war on foreign investment are still felt today, as investors who left Chad between 1979–82 have only recently begun to regain confidence in the country's future."[80] Some restrictions exist in the form of a strict investment review process, a hostile government-owned sector, and corruption. In addition, a cumbersome bureaucracy often delays investments.

Factor #6: Banking
Score: 4-Stable (High level of restrictions on banking)

The banking system in Chad is heavily controlled by the government, although some recent progress has been made on increasing foreign investment in this area.

Factor #7: Wage and Price Controls
Score: 4-Stable (High level of wage and price controls)

Wages and prices in Chad are affected by the large public sector, import substitution policies, and government subsidies.

Factor #8: Property Rights
Score: 4-Stable (Low level of protection of private property)

Private property is subject to government expropriation in Chad, although there are few recent examples of nationalization. Chad's government is attempting to privatize many government-owned enterprises, but crime and theft remain problems. According to the U.S. Department of State, "Pickpockets and purse snatchers are endemic in market and commercial areas. Burglary and vehicle thefts increase during times of political instability."[81]

Factor #9: Regulation
Score: 4-Stable (High level of regulation)

Establishing a business in Chad is difficult because of the massive and corrupt government bureaucracy. Bribery is sometimes present, as is embezzlement by government officials collecting fees. Regulations often are applied haphazardly.

Factor #10: Black Market
Score: 5-Stable (Very high level of black market activity)

Chad's black market is larger than the formal market and growing. Most of this activity occurs in smuggled consumer goods, labor, and pirated intellectual property.

---

80   National Trade Data Bank and Economic Bulletin Board—products of STAT–USA, U.S. Department of Commerce.

81   *Ibid.*

Summary

Chad				Overall Score	3.80
Trade	5	Monetary Policy	1	Property Rights	4
Taxation	4	Foreign Investment	4	Regulation	4
Government	3	Banking	4	Black Market	5
Intervention		Wage and Prices	4		

CHILE

Although most of the economic success stories since 1960 come from Asia, Chile is the greatest example of a Latin American country enjoying economic success. Chile underwent a massive economic transformation in the 1980s that has made it the envy of Latin America. Following this continuing transformation, which has resulted in some of the fastest economic growth rates in the Western Hemisphere,[82] Chile underwent a series of political reforms that culminated in democratic elections in 1989. The Chilean Constitution defines and protects individual liberties, and President Eduardo Frei is continuing the country's free-market course. Chile recently increased taxes on income, but it also has slashed tariffs and narrowed price controls.

Chile	
Santiago ☆	
1000 Miles	
Index of Economic Freedom Score	2.25
Mostly Free	
1 2 3 4 5	

Factor #1: Trade Policy
Score: 2+ (Low level of protectionism)

International trade is the cornerstone of the Chilean economy. Chile has a flat tariff rate for most products of 11 percent. Because it has opened its borders to many of its neighbors (many items enter duty free), however, the average tariff rate is less than 6 percent. Moreover, Chile recently has removed most of its non-tariff barriers. Thus, since Chile's average tariff has been reduced, its score improves.

Factor #2: Taxation
Score - Income taxation: 4- (High tax rates)
Score - Corporate taxation: 2-Stable (Low tax rates)
Final Taxation Score: 3.5- (High tax rates)

Chile's top income tax rate is 45 percent, up from 20 percent in 1995. The average taxpayer is in the 10 percent bracket. The top corporate income tax rate is 15 percent. Chile also maintains a 15 percent capital gains tax and an 18 percent value-added tax.

Factor #3: Government Intervention in the Economy
Score: 1-Stable (Very low government intervention)

Chile is an example of how reduced government intervention produces solid rates of economic growth. Chile's government consumes 9 percent of GDP. Chile has achieved this low rate by permitting private enterprises to supply such "public" services as education, pension funds, social security, and some utilities.[83] Chile's social security system, for example, is privately owned and operated.

---

82   Inter-American Development Bank, *Economic and Social Progress in Latin America: 1993 Report* (Washington, D.C., 1993).

Factor #4: Monetary Policy
Score: 3-Stable (Moderate level of inflation)

Chile's average annual rate of inflation from 1985 to 1994 was 18.5 percent. In 1995, the inflation rate was 8.2 percent.

Factor #5: Capital Flows and Foreign Investment
Score: 2-Stable (Low barriers to foreign investment)

Chile aims to attract foreign investors by granting them quick government approval in some industries. Nevertheless, although Chile has reformed its foreign investment code to attract investment, some barriers still exist. For example, all foreign investors must gain permission from the government's Foreign Investment Committee (although this rarely proves to be a barrier), and the government maintains restrictions on investment in the fishing, maritime transport, and oil and gas industries.

Factor #6: Banking
Score: 3-Stable (Moderate restrictions on banking)

Chile's banking system is relatively free from government corruption, but it is not totally competitive and market-oriented. Chile requires a license for foreign banks, and all licenses have been frozen. Thus, as a practical matter, no new foreign banks are allowed. Only 20 foreign banks operate in Chile. Domestic banks, especially those in the lending business, often find themselves in competition with the government-owned banks, and this distorts market operations. A state-operated agency provides subsidized loans to the public and private sectors, but the 40 percent default rate has swallowed up lending capital and skewed the banking system with bad loans. Banks are not permitted to engage in insurance, real estate, or investment services.

Factor #7: Wage and Price Controls
Score: 2+ (Low level of wage and price controls)

Chile's price policy is determined mainly by the market, although there are some exceptions such as prices for urban and public transport and some utilities. Minimum wages, hours worked, and safety regulations are controlled by the government, but most price controls have been removed.

Factor #8: Property Rights
Score: 1-Stable (Very high level of protection of private property)

Private property is gaining increased protection from the Chilean government through greater efficiency in the court system and legal institutions. Since the early 1980s, Chile has had a comprehensive program of privatization, and it continues today. The likelihood of private property expropriation is very low.

---

83   Cristian V. Larroulet, ed., *The Chilean Experience: Private Solutions to Public Problems,* Instituto Libertad y Desarrollo and Center for International Private Enterprise, Chile, 1991.

Factor #9: Regulation
Score: 2-Stable (Low level of regulation)

Government regulation in Chile runs from nonexistent in some areas to overbearing in others. Opening a business in Chile is far easier than in many other Latin American countries. Regulations are moderate, although some can be burdensome for private businesses. The Public Health Ministry, for example, directly regulates the production, storage, distribution, sale, and import of all food and drug products.

Factor #10: Black Market
Score: 3-Stable (Moderate level of black market activity)

Like most other Latin American countries, Chile has a black market. Although piracy of intellectual property is decreasing, there continues to be a large black market business in this area. As much as 65 percent of computer software in Chile is pirated, for example, and there still is a large black market in pirated U.S. pharmaceuticals.

Summary

Chile					Overall Score	2.25
Trade	2	Monetary Policy	3	Property Rights	1
Taxation	3.5	Foreign Investment	2	Regulation	2
Government Intervention	1	Banking	3	Black Market	3
		Wage and Prices	2		

CHINA, PEOPLE'S REPUBLIC OF

Although often criticized for its human rights abuses and its communist political system, China is more open and advanced economically than it was several decades ago. Despite some twists and turns, economic reforms have remained on track, gathering steam and expanding since they began in the late 1970s. As a result, economic growth reached 12 percent in 1993. At the same time, however, an overwhelmingly large part of China's economy remains under state control. In addition, disputes over intellectual property rights, trade surpluses, and protectionism have kept China from becoming a member of the World Trade Organization and have soured relations with the country's most important trade partner, the United States.

China, People's Republic of

Beijing

1000 Miles

Index of Economic Freedom Score	3.80

Mostly Not Free

1　　2　　3　　4　　5

Factor #1: Trade Policy

Score: 5-Stable (Very high level of protectionism)

China's average tariff rate is about 25 percent, although some high-tech companies may be exempt from tariffs altogether. Non-tariff barriers include licensing requirements, trade quotas, and local content restrictions. In 1992, China signed a trade agreement with the United States to reduce trade restrictions by 1997. It also is applying for membership in the General Agreement on Tariffs and Trade, forcing the government to take some steps toward freer trade. Although trade is increasing in China, most is restricted to "free trade zones" along the coast.

Factor #2: Taxation

Score - Income taxation: 4-Stable (High tax rates)
Score - Corporate taxation: 3-Stable (Moderate tax rates)
Final Taxation Score: 4-Stable (High tax rates)

China's top marginal income tax rate is 45 percent, with the average income level taxed at a rate of 15 percent. The top corporate tax rate is 30 percent. China also has a 33 percent capital gains tax, a 17 percent value-added tax, and a 3 percent to 20 percent business tax.

Factor #3: Government Intervention in the Economy

Score: 5-Stable (Very high level of government intervention)

Because China is a communist system, most property is owned by the state. The World Bank reports that China's government consumes only 13 percent of GDP, up from 8.3 percent in 1980. Nevertheless, the state-owned sector accounts for almost all

GDP. By definition, therefore, China's government consumes a very high percentage of economic output because the state owns most of the property and means of production.

Factor #4: Monetary Policy
Score: 3-Stable (Moderate level of inflation)

As a command economy, China's annual rate of inflation averaged only 5.8 percent from 1980 to 1991. Subsequent inflation rates were 8.1 percent (1992), 14.5 percent (1993), 19 percent (1994), and 17 percent (1995). This underestimates the real rate of inflation, however, because the communist government controls prices.

Factor #5: Capital Flows and Foreign Investment
Score: 3-Stable (Moderate barriers to foreign investment)

China always has maintained barriers to foreign investment. The government, which has no foreign investment code, uses foreign investment policy to prevent investments in some government-owned industries while channeling them into other state-owned enterprises, such as power, telecommunications, aviation, and information technologies. China's special foreign investment zones in the South, however, give it a somewhat better score.

Factor #6: Banking
Score: 3-Stable (Moderate level of restrictions on banking)

In 1998, China liberalized its banking industry and allowed the creation of domestic and foreign-owned banks. The government also owns many banks, however, and tries to prevent foreign banks from operating in China.

Factor #7: Wage and Price Controls
Score: 3-Stable (Moderate level of wage and price controls)

China has a history of price controls. After the 1993 recession, the government imposed controls on the prices of such items as foodstuffs and utilities. Controls on the prices of foodstuffs recently have been removed, but the production of some items in some areas still is centrally planned by the government. China has a minimum wage.

Factor #8: Property Rights
Score: 4-Stable (Low level of protection of private property)

Because China remains a communist system, most property remains in government hands, although the government currently is privatizing some major industries, thus moving some state-owned assets into private hands. Nevertheless, private property is still far from common, and the court system is both inefficient and far from impartial. According to the U.S. Department of Commerce, "Litigation is considered only reluctantly as a final option. Many foreign investors have found the Chinese approach time-consuming and unreliable."[84]

---

84 U.S. Department of Commerce, *Country Commercial Guide*, 1996.

Factor #9: Regulation
Score: 4-Stable (High level of regulation)

In an attempt to boost the private sector, the Chinese bureaucracy sometimes does not enforce cumbersome regulations. China still has a state planning agency that makes significant business and economic decisions, and this central planning results in high levels of regulation. Corruption is also a problem. According to the U.S. Department of Commerce, "Rapid price inflation, corruption, lay-offs from state-run enterprises, the growing gap between coastal regions and the interior, and economic disparities between rural and urban areas have contributed to dissatisfaction among the populace."[85]

Factor #10: Black Market
Score: 4-Stable (High level of black market activity)

Because of existing trade restrictions and central economic planning, the black market in China is rather large. There is extensive smuggling, both of automobiles from Hong Kong and of such consumer electronic products as TVs and video cassette recorders.

Summary

China, People's Republic of				Overall Score	3.80
Trade	5	Monetary Policy	3	Property Rights	4
Taxation	4	Foreign Investment	3	Regulation	4
Government Intervention	5	Banking	3	Black Market	4
		Wage and Prices	3		

---

85   *Ibid.*

CHINA, REPUBLIC OF (TAIWAN)

The Republic of China on Taiwan (ROC) has become one of the world's fastest-growing economies. In the late 1950s, mired in conflict with mainland China, Taiwan was held back by an inefficient and over-regulated economy. Taipei began to reform its economy in the late 1960s, however. It guaranteed private property, set up a legal system to protect it, reformed its banks and financial sectors, stabilized taxes, gave away public lands to private individuals, and allowed the free market to expand. These policies have launched Taiwan, as one of Asia's famous "tigers," into the industrialized world.[86] Today, the ROC has annual economic growth rates of around 6 percent. It also is developing a functional democracy and has conducted successful multi-party elections in both the legislative and executive branches of government.

Factor #1: Trade Policy
Score: 2-Stable (Low level of protectionism)

Taiwan's average tariff rate is only 4.9 percent. The government, however, maintains rather high barriers to the importation of agricultural goods like chicken, meat, peanuts, and pork; tariffs on these goods can reach 50 percent. Moreover, Taiwan's rather inefficient distribution system adds to the price of many products, making imports uncompetitive.

Factor #2: Taxation
Score - Income taxation: 2-Stable (Low tax rates)
Score - Corporate taxation: 2-Stable (Low tax rates)
Final Taxation Score: 2.5-Stable (Moderate tax rates)

Taiwan's top income tax rate is 40 percent, and the average income level is taxed at a rate of 6 percent. The maximum corporate tax rate is 25 percent. Taiwan also has a 25 percent capital gains tax and a 5 percent value-added tax.

Factor #3: Government Intervention in the Economy
Score: 2-Stable (Low level of government intervention)

Taiwan's government consumes 14.3 percent of GDP. The government continues to privatize its remaining public companies.

---

86   Lawrence J. Lau and Lawrence R. Klein, *Models of Development: A Comparative Study of Economic Growth in South Korea and Taiwan* (San Francisco, Cal.: ICS Press, 1990).

Factor #4: Monetary Policy
Score: 1-Stable (Very low level of inflation)

Taiwan's average annual rate of inflation rate during the 1980s was less than 2 percent.[87] From 1990 to 1994, the inflation rate was only 3.8 percent; in 1995, it was 4.3 percent; and for most of 1996, it remained around 3.5 percent.

Factor #5: Capital Flows and Foreign Investment
Score: 3-Stable (Moderate barriers to foreign investment)

Foreign investment has been a major concern of Taiwanese government officials. For the first half of 1995, reforms caused investment to rise 57 percent compared to 1994. Foreign investment in agriculture, cable television, cigarette manufacturing, housing construction, liquor manufacturing, and the refining of petroleum, however, is still banned, and foreign ownership is limited in the mining, shipping, and securities industries. Companies must use local parts in the manufacture of automobiles and motorcycles.

Factor #6: Banking
Score: 3-Stable (Moderate level of restrictions on banking)

Taiwan limits foreign ownership of securities investment companies, as well as some activities in the banking industry, and privatization of the country's commercial banks has yet to be implemented fully. In addition, there still are some restrictions on the opening of new banks. Nevertheless, banks are competitive and serve as an important source of capital for Taiwan's expanding economy.

Factor #7: Wage and Price Controls
Score: 2-Stable (Low level of wage and price controls)

Taiwan maintains a minimum wage policy and requires equal pay for men and women. Prices are monitored regularly by the Commodity Price Supervisory Board, which is comprised of members from the Ministry of Finance, the Ministry of Economic Affairs, the Agricultural Commission, and the Ministry of Communications (although the board does not have the power to set prices directly).

Factor #8: Property Rights
Score: 1-Stable (Very high level of protection of private property)

Property rights are fully protected in Taiwan.

Factor #9: Regulation
Score: 2-Stable (Low level of regulation)

Even though the government has established some moderately burdensome regulations, entrepreneurs can open a business in Taiwan with little difficulty. By global standards, Taiwan's level of regulation is low.

---

87   *Ibid.*, p. 187.

Factor #10: Black Market
Score: 1-Stable (Very low level of black market activity)

Because Taiwan has a free economy, its black market is very small. Taiwan has developed an advanced and efficient intellectual property rights protection law, consistent with the World Trade Organization. Although there is some trade in pirated material, it is minuscule in comparison with the size of its economy.

Summary

China, Republic of (Taiwan)					Overall Score	1.95
Trade	2	Monetary Policy	1	Property Rights	1
Taxation	2.5	Foreign Investment	3	Regulation	2
Government Intervention	2	Banking	3	Black Market	1
		Wage and Prices	2		

COLOMBIA

olombia's political system has come under growing pressure in recent years as drug traffickers have increased their influence within the government, corrupting executive, legislative, and judicial institutions. Although Colombia has enjoyed many years of economic stability and growth because of free-market reforms first applied in 1990 by President Cesar Gaviria, its economy has been slowing since the end of 1994. This is due mainly to a drug-related scandal involving current President Ernesto Samper. Samper has called for increased government spending on social welfare programs that could jeopardize Colombia's recent economic gains. The level of government intervention in the economy has increased, and the Samper government has imposed more burdensome regulations on the economy. Bureaucratic corruption and a thriving drug trade both are on the rise.

Colombia

⊕ Bogata

500 Miles

Index of Economic Freedom Score	3.10

Mostly Not Free

1   2   3   4   5

Factor #1: Trade Policy

Score: 4-Stable (High level of protectionism)

Colombia has an average tariff rate of 12 percent, down from 35.5 percent in 1990,[88] and maintains many non-tariff barriers. For example, it requires importers to gain licenses for automobile, dairy, poultry, and other products.

Factor #2: Taxation

Score - Income taxation: 4-Stable (High tax rates)
Score - Corporate taxation: 3-Stable (Moderate tax rates)
Final Taxation Score: 4-Stable (High tax rates)

Colombia has an effective top income tax rate of 30 percent,[89] and the average income level is taxed at a rate of less than 5 percent. Many of these taxpayers are not required to fill out a tax return.[90] The government is cracking down on tax fraud, and more collections are being made than ever before. The top corporate tax rate is 35 per-

---

88 Office of the United States Trade Representative, *National Trade Estimate Report on Foreign Trade Barriers, 1996*, Document ID 1615, from National Trade Data Bank and Economic Bulletin Board—products of STAT–USA, U.S. Department of Commerce.

89 Colombia's top marginal income tax rate actually is 55 percent: a top tax rate of 30 percent plus a 25 percent tax penalty for making over a specific income. The 25 percent becomes a deduction, however, on the following year's taxes. Thus, for purposes of grading this factor, only the top rate of 30 percent was used.

90 For purposes of grading, the 5 percent figure was used.

cent, up from 30 percent in 1995. Colombia also has a 35 percent capital gains tax and a 16 percent value-added tax.

Factor #3: Government Intervention in the Economy
Score: 2- (Low level of government intervention)

Even with its costly war on drugs, Colombia's government has managed to reduce its role in the economy. Government consumes 14.1 percent of GDP, and this percentage has been increasing. According to the Economist Intelligence Unit, "the weight of the state in the economy has been growing steadily in recent years. Total public outlays are estimated at 46 percent of GDP in 1995, six percentage points above the level at the start of the decade. Mr. Samper's Social Leap assumes that this proportion will grow to 51 percent by 1998, as he takes a more interventionist approach to economic policy."[91] Nevertheless, Colombia has undertaken significant privatization. Since 1991, the state has privatized ports, railroads, and cellular telephone services, along with a number of chemical, agro-industrial, fishing, and gasoline companies and banks. These privatization programs, however, have stalled recently.

Factor #4: Monetary Policy
Score: 4-Stable (High level of inflation)

Colombia had an average inflation rate of 25.1 percent from 1985 to 1994. Since then, the inflation rate has remained stable at around 21 percent.

Factor #5: Capital Flows and Foreign Investment
Score: 2-Stable (Low barriers to foreign investment)

Colombia permits 100 percent foreign ownership in almost all sectors of its economy. The few exceptions are in national security and hazardous waste industries. Permission is needed for investments in the public service, water, waste, and transportation industries, or for large investments in mining and petroleum enterprises. A simple registration and licensing process is required for all investments.

Factor #6: Banking
Score: 2-Stable (Low restrictions on banking)

Foreign banks have complete access to credit and the entire Colombian financial system. Moreover, almost all credit now is directed by the private sector. "Foreign investors experience no discrimination in access to local credit," reports the U.S. Department of Commerce. "While the Colombian government still directs credit to some areas, notably agriculture, credit is for the most part allocated by the private financial market. Credit subsidies were phased out with the establishment of FINAGRO, a state-owned agricultural credit intermediary."[92] Colombia has yet to achieve a completely free banking system, however. Domestic banks may sell securities, insurance policies, and investment services.

---

91   Economist Intelligence Unit, *ILT Reports, Colombia,* 1996, p. 7.

92   U.S. Department of Commerce, *Country Commercial Guide,* 1996.

Factor #7: Wage and Price Controls
Score: 2-Stable (Low level of wage and price controls)

Colombia has one of the most free-market pricing policies in Latin America. With the exception of a few pharmaceutical, agricultural, and petroleum products, prices are set by the market. Colombia maintains a minimum wage, however.

Factor #8: Property Rights
Score: 3-Stable (Moderate protection of private property)

The biggest threat to private property in Colombia is the violence created by the drug cartels and the government's attempt to distribute wealth more equally. Private property generally is well-protected in Colombia, and the government is privatizing state-owned enterprises. Colombia's legal system, however, is not always efficient. According to the U.S. Department of Commerce, "The Colombian judicial system continues to be clogged and cumbersome, although its reform and streamlining are stated goals of the Samper administration."[93]

Factor #9: Regulation
Score: 3-Stable (Moderate level of regulation)

Colombia has a free-market economy, and the government tends to exercise minimal control of the private sector. Obtaining a business license is not difficult, there is a limited registration process, and the government tends to allow businesses to operate as they see fit. Colombia's growing environmental movement, however, is causing increased regulation of business, and corruption within the bureaucracy is growing.

Factor #10: Black Market
Score: 5-Stable (Very high black market activity)

The drug trade makes Colombia's black market very large. Moreover, there is a growing black market in pirated intellectual property, mainly because of lagging legal protection of intellectual property rights. "Colombia has made significant improvements in its intellectual property rights protection," reports the U.S. Trade Representative's Office, "but does not yet appear to provide adequate and effective protection.... [T]he U.S. motion picture industry estimates that video cassette piracy continues to represent 60 percent of the video market and unauthorized parallel importation of U.S. videos continues to be a significant problem. The industry estimates losses due to video piracy at $14.6 million. In addition, satellite signal and cable television piracy continue to be widespread, resulting in estimated losses of $30.4 million."[94]

---

93   *Ibid.*

94   Office of the United States Trade Representative, *National Trade Estimate Report on Foreign Trade Barriers, 1996.*

Summary

Colombia				Overall Score	3.10
Trade	4	Monetary Policy	4	Property Rights	3
Taxation	4	Foreign Investment	2	Regulation	3
Government Intervention	2	Banking	2	Black Market	5
		Wage and Prices	2		

CONGO

The Central African country of Congo became a French colony in 1910 and gained its independence in 1960. Congo's post-colonial history has been marked by one-party rule, political repression, and frequent military coups. In 1992, multi-party elections were held. These elections spawned riots and civil unrest, which continue to this day. With the military wielding considerable clout, little progress toward democratic reform has been made, and market reforms have been negligible. Since independence, the state has played a leading role in the economy, which is stagnating.

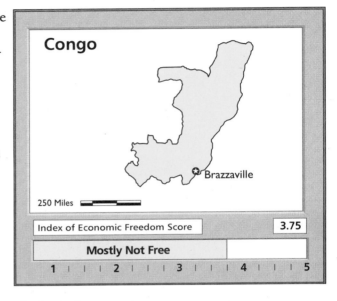

Index of Economic Freedom Score: 3.75

Mostly Not Free

1 2 3 4 5

Factor #1: Trade Policy

Score: 5-Stable (Very high level of protectionism)

Congo's current average tariff rate is unknown; in the early 1980s, it was 8.6 percent. Congo is a member of the Customs and Economic Union of Central Africa, however, and must set rates consistent with that union. Thus, assuming that it does so, Congo's tariffs would be 5 percent for essential goods, 15 percent for primary materials and manufacturing equipment, 35 percent for intermediary goods, and 50 percent for consumer goods.[95] The biggest non-tariff barriers to trade remain red tape, an inefficient customs service, and outright theft of imported goods by government officials.

Factor #2: Taxation

Score - Income taxation: 4-Stable (High tax rates)
Score - Corporate taxation: 4+ (High tax rates)
Final Taxation Score: 4.5+ (Very high tax rates)

Congo has a top income tax rate of 50 percent, and the average income level is taxed at a rate of 15 percent. The top corporate tax is 45 percent. Congo also has a 45 percent capital gains tax and a 16 percent to 20.5 percent goods and services tax.

Factor #3: Government Intervention in the Economy

Score: 3-Stable (Moderate level of government intervention)

Congo's government consumes 22.3 percent of GDP, and the state-owned sector is extremely large. A privatization effort has yielded few results.

---

95   Because most of the products that enter Congo do so under the 35 percent and 50 percent tariff rates, it is safe to assume that the average rate is above 30 percent.

Factor #4: Monetary Policy
Score: 1-Stable (Very low level of inflation)

Congo's average annual inflation rate from 1985 to 1994 was –0.3 percent. Inflation was running at an estimated 2 percent in 1995.

Factor #5: Capital Flows and Foreign Investment
Score: 4-Stable (High barriers to foreign investment)

Foreign investment is ruled by a government code that has yet to be implemented fully. Foreign investors face hostile government bureaucrats and labor conditions. Many labor unions remain under the influence of Marxist ideology, making it nearly impossible to do business. French vested interests also work against foreign investment. Consequently, new foreign investment is virtually nonexistent outside the petroleum and retail sectors. The government has established a "one-stop shop" in an attempt to lure foreign investment.

Factor #6: Banking
Score: 4-Stable (High level of restrictions on banking)

Banks remain under the control or influence of corrupt government officials, and hostile labor conditions limit the ability of foreign banks to operate. The Congolese government claims that it may sell state banks to foreign investors.

Factor #7: Wage and Price Controls
Score: 3-Stable (Moderate level of wage and price controls)

Prices are controlled through large government-owned companies, which also are subsidized by the government. There is a minimum wage.

Factor #8: Property Rights
Score: 4-Stable (Low level of protection of private property)

Government expropriation of property remains possible. An insufficient judicial and legal framework results in little government protection of private property. Although the courts are supposed to be independent of the government, most are not. According to the U.S. Department of Commerce, "Judicial independence is guaranteed by the 1992 constitution, but is a new concept and may sometimes be compromised, particularly in labor courts."[96]

Factor #9: Regulation
Score: 4-Stable (High level of regulation)

Government regulators are corrupt, often requiring bribes. Regulations, in addition to being burdensome, are enforced haphazardly. Labor laws favor militant unions at the expense of employers.

---

96   U.S. Department of Commerce, *Country Commercial Guide*, 1996.

Factor #10: Black Market

Score: 5-Stable (Very high level of black market activity)

Congo's black market is large. Corruption among customs officials creates a market for smuggling of all types of goods, and high tariffs encourage the smuggling of many foodstuffs. There is a considerable illegal arms trade in the Congo.

Summary

Congo					Overall Score	3.75
Trade	5	Monetary Policy	1		Property Rights	4
Taxation	4.5	Foreign Investment	4		Regulation	4
Government	3	Banking	4		Black Market	5
Intervention		Wage and Prices	3			

COSTA RICA

The Central American country of Costa Rica declared its independence from Spain in 1821. The United States remains Costa Rica's largest trading partner. Foreign aid has decreased drastically since the end of the Cold War, and trade between the United States and Costa Rica is growing. Costa Rica's economic growth is mainly the result of increased trade and economic reforms. Despite recent gains in reducing inflation, it is on the rise again, and some economic reforms have slowed.

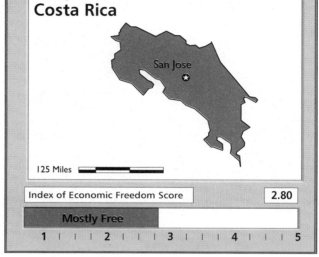

Factor #1: Trade Policy

Score: 4-Stable (High level of protectionism)

Although Costa Rica has been moving to open its borders, it remains a rather difficult market to penetrate. Costa Rica's average tariff rate is 11 percent, and customs procedures are cumbersome and plagued with inefficiency. Many importers are forced to hire a customs specialist just to get their products across the border. Costa Rica maintains significant non-tariff barriers.

Factor #2: Taxation

Score - Income taxation: 2-Stable (Low tax rates)
Score - Corporate taxation: 3-Stable (Moderate tax rates)
Final Taxation Score: 3-Stable (Moderate tax rates)

Costa Rica's top marginal income tax rate is 25 percent, and the tax on the average income is about 10 percent. The top corporate income tax rate is 30 percent. Costa Rica also has a 10 percent sales tax.

Factor #3: Government Intervention in the Economy

Score: 2-Stable (Low level of government intervention)

Government consumes about 17.1 percent of Costa Rica's GDP.

Factor #4: Monetary Policy

Score: 3-Stable (Moderate level of inflation)

Costa Rica had an inflation rate of 18.2 percent from 1985 to 1994. The rate for 1995 was 23.2 percent.

Factor #5: Capital Flows and Foreign Investment

Score: 2-Stable (Low barriers to foreign investment)

Costa Rica offers one of the best investment climates in Central America. There are no repatriation requirements, foreigners are allowed to take out all of their profits, and the government offers a widening group of foreign investment incentives, including tax holidays for some specific investments. Costa Rica does not discriminate against foreign investors, who are treated the same as local investors. Some restrictions remain on utilities and services, investments in which are barred.

Factor #6: Banking
Score: 3-Stable (Moderate restrictions on banking)

Foreigners are prevented from engaging in some banking services, such as checking and savings. Banking competition is generally free and open in Costa Rica, however, although banks are not permitted to sell insurance policies and other services.

Factor #7: Wage and Price Controls
Score: 2-Stable (Low level of wage and price controls)

Most wages and prices are set by the market. As a condition for loans from the International Monetary Fund, Costa Rica was forced to eliminate most of its price controls, except for those on a few basic foodstuffs. Costa Rica maintains a minimum wage.

Factor #8: Property Rights
Score: 3-Stable (Moderate level of protection of private property)

Private property is not entirely safe in Costa Rica. Expropriation remains a threat, and the owner rarely receives market value when property is taken. In many cases, the government offers no compensation. Some U.S. property rights claims date back 25 years. Domestic property owners could lose their land to increasing numbers of squatters who band together to expropriate property and are becoming increasingly violent. The legal system has been unable to deal with the situation.

Factor #9: Regulation
Score: 3-Stable (Moderate level of regulation)

There are few major barriers to opening a business in Costa Rica. Regulations are easily understood and, for the most part, equally applied. There is scant evidence of corruption or bribery. Some regulations (for example, regulations requiring environmental impact studies), however, pose a moderate threat to businesses. Moreover, the government requires private companies to grant vacations, holidays, overtime, and social insurance.

Factor #10: Black Market
Score: 3-Stable (Moderate level of black market activity)

Black market activity is relatively moderate in Costa Rica. Some construction, telephone installation, and transportation is performed in the black market. Intellectual property rights laws, although sufficient, are not adequately enforced. Thus, piracy in computer software, sound recordings, and video tapes remains a problem.

Summary

Costa Rica				Overall Score	2.80
Trade	4	Monetary Policy	3	Property Rights	3
Taxation	3	Foreign Investment	2	Regulation	3
Government Intervention	2	Banking	3	Black Market	3
		Wage and Prices	2		

CROATIA

The collapse of Yugoslavia in 1990–1991 led to the creation of four independent countries. Among these is Croatia, which has been involved in a civil war that erupted in 1991 and has ravaged the economy. Some 25 percent to 30 percent of the country's agricultural capacity has been decimated. Croatia's economy remains about half of its size in 1990. The ongoing instability in the region, with its flow of dispossessed refugees, continues to strain the country.

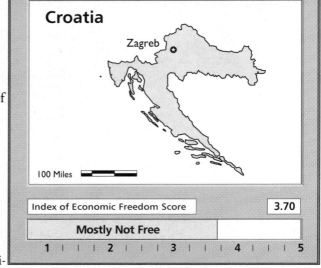

Factor #1: Trade Policy

Score: 3-Stable (Moderate level of protectionism)

Croatia has an average tariff rate of about 12.1 percent.[97] It also maintains such non-tariff barriers as strict testing and certification requirements for some foods, pharmaceuticals, and electronics.

Factor #2: Taxation

Score - Income taxation: 3-Stable (Moderate tax rates)
Score - Corporate taxation: 2-Stable (Low tax rates)
Final Taxation Score: 3-Stable (Moderate tax rates)

Croatia's top income tax rate is 35 percent, and the average taxpayer is in the 25 percent bracket. The top marginal corporate tax rate is 25 percent. Croatia also maintains a host of other taxes, such as a 2.5 percent to 20 percent goods and services tax and a sales tax.

Factor #3: Government Intervention in the Economy

Score: 5-Stable (Very high level of government intervention)

Government consumes about 45 percent of Croatia's GDP,[98] much of which is generated by state-owned and state-subsidized companies.

---

97   Based on total taxes on international trade as a percentage of total imports; from International Monetary Fund, *Government Financial Statistics 1995*.

98   This figure includes central government spending, spending on health and pension plans, and local government spending; from *Croatia* (London: Smith New Court, 1995).

Factor #4: Monetary Policy
Score: 5-Stable (Very high level of inflation)

Chronic inflation has plagued Croatia until very recently. In 1992, retail inflation alone was 669 percent; in 1993, it was 1,517 percent. In 1994, Croatia's inflation rate was 98 percent.

Factor #5: Capital Flows and Foreign Investment
Score: 3-Stable (Moderate barriers to foreign investment)

Croatia encourages foreign investment. It provides national treatment to foreign companies, making them equal with domestic firms under the law. Foreign investors are not allowed, however, to establish a fully owned company that involves military equipment, rail or air transport, insurance, publishing, or the mass media. The most formidable deterrents to foreign investment are political and civil unrest and an underdeveloped infrastructure.

Factor #6: Banking
Score: 3-Stable (Moderate restrictions on banking)

The banking system in Croatia is heavily regulated by the government. Permission from the government is required for foreign banks to open branches. Banks may not engage in such non-bank services as selling insurance. Moreover, the government continues to own many banks, either outright or through other state-owned companies, which are major shareholders in many banks.

Factor #7: Wage and Price Controls
Score: 4-Stable (High level of wage and price controls)

Wages and prices in Croatia are not fully set by the free market. Croatia continues to harbor a large public sector that controls prices and wages on many items. The government also extends large subsidies and price payments to farmers.

Factor #8: Property Rights
Score: 4- (Low level of protection of private property)

Private property has yet to become a protected right. Although property is generally free from expropriation, it is unclear whether this trend will continue. A significant increase in political or civil unrest, for example, could place property at risk of expropriation. Finally, Croatia's court system is cumbersome and inefficient. According to the U.S. Department of Commerce, "As Croatian courts face a tremendous backlog, partly due to lack of judges, settlement of commercial disputes is often a matter of years. In October 1995, there were more than a million cases pending in Croatian courts."[99]

Factor #9: Regulation
Score: 4-Stable (High level of regulation)

Croatia's bureaucracy, like the bureaucracies of many other post-communist regimes, remains entrenched. Privatization of public firms often is opposed by ex-party officials and bureaucrats. Corruption exists.

---

99   U.S. Department of Commerce, *Country Commercial Guide,* 1996.

Factor #10: Black Market
Score: 3+ (Moderate level of black market activity)

A black market exists, primarily in labor services. Some transportation and construction, for example, are provided mostly by the black market. Croatia has stamped out some black market activity, however, particularly in pirated intellectual property. A copyright law passed in 1993 provides stiff penalties for trafficking in pirated video and music recordings, as well as related materials. Over the past several years, Croatia has enforced these laws vigorously, partly to attract foreign investment. The Motion Picture Association of America recently said that Croatia's copyright laws should serve as a model for other countries.[100]

Summary

Croatia				Overall Score	3.70
Trade	3	Monetary Policy	5	Property Rights	4
Taxation	3	Foreign Investment	3	Regulation	4
Government Intervention	5	Banking	3	Black Market	3
		Wage and Prices	4		

---

100 State Department Report, 1996, p. 155.

CUBA

Cuba has one of the world's most repressed economies: a centralized, government-planned economy rife with corruption and graft. Despite recent news reports about Cuba's move toward a free market, there is a nearly complete lack of legal and private economic activity. Individual economic freedom is virtually nonexistent. Although some forms of foreign investment now are permitted, the Cuban constitution still outlaws foreign ownership of private property. In 1995, President Clinton signed the Helms–Burton Act, which seeks to protect American property stolen by the Castro regime in 1959. Cuba remains one of the world's poorest countries, primarily because of its lack of economic freedom.

Cuba

Havana

200 Miles

Index of Economic Freedom Score	5.00

Repressed

1   2   3   4   5

Factor #1: Trade Policy
Score: 5-Stable (Very high level of protectionism)

All imports into Cuba must be inspected and approved by Castro's government. In many cases, customs officials confiscate imports (especially scarce goods like electronics) for their own use; such corruption enjoys official sanction in Cuba. As a result, Cuba's trade barriers effectively bar most imports. Perhaps the biggest impediment to trade with Cuba is the country's obsession with protecting its borders; this makes it nearly impossible for merchant ships to bring imports into the country. According to the U.S. Department of State, "Entering Cuban territory, territorial waters or airspace without prior authorization from the Cuban government may result in arrest or other enforcement action by Cuban authorities for violation of Cuban law. Any vessel or aircraft that enters the 12-mile limit off Cuba would be inside Cuban territorial waters or airspace and thus subject to the jurisdiction of the Cuban government. If persons enter Cuban territorial waters or airspace without prior permission, they may place themselves and others at serious personal risk."[101]

Factor #2: Taxation
Score - Income taxation: 5-Stable (Very high tax rates)
Score - Corporate taxation: 5-Stable (Very high tax rates)
Final Taxation Score: 5-Stable (Very high tax rates)

Because the government controls Cuba's entire economy, it essentially confiscates the proceeds of all economic activity. The fruits of all economic activity are owned by the government, so the resulting rate of taxation approaches 100 percent.

---

101   U.S. Department of State Travel Advisory, 1996.

Factor #3: Government Intervention in the Economy
Score: 5-Stable (Very high level of government intervention)

Although Castro permits some private (albeit highly restricted) economic activity, the means of production and most of the profits gained remain entirely in the hands of the state. The Cuban government directly owns and runs most of the Cuban economy.

Factor #4: Monetary Policy
Score: 5-Stable (Very high level of inflation)

The Castro government claims that inflation does not exist in Cuba. This is a fiction. If price controls were lifted and the true value of the currency were measured, inflation would be extremely high. The official prices of goods may be low because they are controlled and subsidized by the state, but the tremendous scarcity of goods and services attests to their real value. In short, Cuba's currency is worthless. Nor is it convertible on the international market.

Factor #5: Capital Flows and Foreign Investment
Score: 5-Stable (Very high barriers to foreign investment)

Some foreign investment is permitted in Cuba. In September 1995, the government moved to allow foreigners, in exceptional cases, to control a majority share in some joint venture operations. To say that Cuba has liberalized its foreign investment code, however, is misleading. The Cuban Constitution still outlaws all foreign ownership of property and forbids any Cuban citizens from participating in joint ventures with foreigners. It also is still illegal to hire Cubans directly. Foreign employers must pay the wages due their employees directly to the Cuban government, and in hard currency. The Cuban government then pays the workers in Cuban pesos at a fraction of the value—sometimes less than 10 percent—of what the foreign business gives the government. Furthermore, although the new foreign investment law provides additional protection against expropriation, all arbitration must take place in corrupt, government-run ministries that afford the investor little protection. Although the Cuban government does not seek actively to prevent foreign investment, its constitution, economy, and corrupt legal and government institutions have the same effect. Moreover, foreigners are not physically safe in Cuba; according to the U.S. Department of Commerce, "Crimes against foreigners continue to increase. Foreigners are prime targets for purse snatchings, pickpocketing and thefts from hotel rooms, beaches, historic sites and other attractions."[102]

Factor #6: Banking
Score: 5-Stable (Very high level of restrictions on banking)

Banks in Cuba are owned and operated by the government and heavily influenced by the state-owned central bank. There is no free-market competition in this industry.

Factor #7: Wage and Price Controls
Score: 5-Stable (Very high level of wage and price controls)

Virtually all wages and prices are set by the Cuban government.

---

102   *Ibid.*

Factor #8: Property Rights
Score: 5-Stable (Very low level of protection of private property)

All private property is outlawed in Cuba. Although some individuals are allowed to operate self-employed businesses, the government can confiscate all earnings from these activities if the individuals are deemed "unduly wealthy." Moreover, corrupt government and police officials often confiscate the money arbitrarily, especially if it is in the form of hard currency. There is no enforcement of contract in Cuba. Many European and Canadian investors find that their investments can be renationalized and sold again to other uninformed investors. This has been particularly true in the hotel industry. Moreover, Cuba does not allow international arbitration of disputes. The Cuban court system is strongly influenced by the government, and corruption is rampant.

Factor #9: Regulation
Score: 5-Stable (Very high level of regulation)

The Cuban government regulates the entire economy by owning and operating the means of production. Moreover, corrupt government officials and police routinely require those who are engaged in the minuscule number of private-sector activities that are permitted to pay bribes or provide services free of charge.

Factor #10: Black Market
Score: 5-Stable (Very high level of black market activity)

Cuba's black market is larger than its official or legal economy. As might be expected in a command economy, even basic economic activities are performed in the black market. Thus, Cuba's black market involves the sale of basic foodstuffs like milk and bread, transportation services, and housing. Smuggling is big business in Cuba. In addition to its importance as a major hub for illegal drugs entering the United States, Cuba also has a substantial smuggling business in consumer goods.

Summary

Cuba					Overall Score	5.0
Trade	5	Monetary Policy	5	Property Rights		5
Taxation	5	Foreign Investment	5	Regulation		5
Government Intervention	5	Banking	5	Black Market		5
		Wage and Prices	5			

CYPRUS

The Mediterranean island of Cyprus gained its independence from the United Kingdom in 1960. Tensions between Greek Cypriots and the Turkish Cypriot minority led to intercommunal strife in 1963 and 1967. In 1974, Greek Cypriot military officers, supported by the military junta in Athens, staged a coup and sought unity with Greece. Turkey responded by dispatching troops to protect the Turkish minority. Today, the Cypriot government controls 59 percent of the island; the "Turkish Republic of Northern Cyprus," recognized only by Turkey, controls 37 percent, supported by 30,000 Turkish troops; and the United Nations, which is promoting negotiations to establish a federal, bicommunal republic, maintains peacekeeping forces in a buffer zone that comprises the remaining 4 percent.

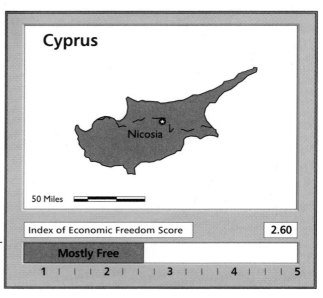

Index of Economic Freedom Score | 2.60

Mostly Free

1 · · · 2 · · · 3 · · · 4 · · · 5

Factor #1: Trade Policy

Score: 3-Stable (Moderate level of protectionism)

The average tariff rate in Cyprus is 8.3 percent. Non-tariff barriers include licensing requirements and strict inspections.

Factor #2: Taxation

Score - Income taxation: 5-Stable (Very high tax rates)
Score - Corporate taxation: 2-Stable (Low tax rates)
Final Taxation Score: 4-Stable (High tax rates)

Cyprus has a top income tax rate of 40 percent, with the average taxpayer in the 30 percent bracket. The top marginal corporate tax rate is 25 percent. Cyprus also has a 20 percent capital gains tax and an 8 percent value-added tax.

Factor #3: Government Intervention in the Economy

Score: 3-Stable (Moderate level of government intervention)

The government of Cyprus consumes 15.7 percent of GDP and continues to play a large role in many companies. For example, it both owns and operates the telecommunications industry.

Factor #4: Monetary Policy

Score: 1-Stable (Very low level of inflation)

The average annual rate of inflation in Cyprus from 1985 to 1994 was 4.1 percent. In 1995, the inflation rate was 4.7 percent to 5 percent.

Factor #5: Capital Flows and Foreign Investment
Score: 2-Stable (Low barriers to foreign investment)

Most of the few restrictions on foreign investment in Cyprus are imposed in areas vital to national security. The government requires an approval process for some investments; but, although this may cause some delays, there is little evidence that it serves as a barrier to investment. The government also is trying to streamline regulations governing foreign investment.

Factor #6: Banking
Score: 2-Stable (Low level of restrictions on banking)

The banking system in Cyprus is open and competitive. There are over 28 foreign banks.

Factor #7: Wage and Price Controls
Score: 3-Stable (Moderate level of wage and price controls)

Wages and prices in Cyprus are set mainly by the market. The government plays a large role in setting wages for state-owned companies, however, and also controls some prices, particularly in the state-owned telecommunications industry.

Factor #8: Property Rights
Score: 3-Stable (Moderate level of protection of private property)

Private property in Cyprus is protected from government expropriation. Although some legal enforcement is lax, expropriation is not likely.

Factor #9: Regulation
Score: 2-Stable (Low level of regulation)

Establishing a business in Cyprus is relatively easy. Regulations are applied evenly in most cases, although some (such as worker health and safety laws) are burdensome. Corruption is nearly nonexistent, but the bureaucracy often is inefficient and laden with red tape.

Factor #10: Black Market
Score: 3-Stable (Moderate level of black market activity)

There is some smuggling of pirated video and audio cassettes, as well as copied books and other materials.

Summary

Cyprus					Overall Score	2.60
Trade	3	Monetary Policy	1	Property Rights	3
Taxation	4	Foreign Investment	2	Regulation	2
Government Intervention	3	Banking	2	Black Market	3
		Wage and Prices	3		

THE CZECH REPUBLIC

The Czech Republic became an independent state in January 1993 after its separation from Slovakia. Since the breakup of the Warsaw Pact in 1989, the Czech Republic has pursued economic liberalization. It trades mainly with other countries of the former Soviet Union and with the European Union (EU); at least half of its foreign trade is with countries in the EU, especially Germany. One of the leading free-market reformers among Europe's formerly communist states, the Czech Republic recently re-elected Prime Minister Vaclav Klaus, who is responsible for much of the country's economic reform to date and remains dedicated to keeping the Czech Republic on the path to further reform. The Czech Republic has seen an increase in black market activity recently.

Czech Republic

Prague

125 Miles

| Index of Economic Freedom Score | 2.05 |

Mostly Free

1 | | | 2 | | | 3 | | | 4 | | | 5

Factor #1: Trade Policy
Score: 1-Stable (Very low level of protectionism)

The Czech Republic is one of the most open markets in Europe. The average tariff rate is about 4.5 percent, although tariffs on some products can run as high as 70 percent. There are, however, no other significant barriers to imports.

Factor #2: Taxation
Score - Income taxation: 2+ (Low tax rates)
Score - Corporate taxation: 4-Stable (High tax rates)
Final Taxation Score: 3.5+ (High tax rates)

The Czech Republic's top marginal income tax rate is 40 percent, down from 44 percent in 1995, and the tax on the average income level is 0 percent. The top marginal corporate income tax rate is 39 percent, down from 41 percent in 1995. The Czech Republic also has a 39 percent capital gains tax, a 22 percent value-added tax, and a real estate transfer tax.

Factor #3: Government Intervention in the Economy
Score: 2-Stable (Low level of government intervention)

Of all the countries that used to make up the Soviet bloc, the Czech Republic today has one of the freest economies. The government has been consuming about 21 percent of GDP since the first half of 1996.

Factor #4: Monetary Policy
Score: 2-Stable (Low level of inflation)

The Czech Republic has pursued an anti-inflationary monetary policy since 1992 and, according to the U.S. Department of State, has one of the world's most stable currencies.[103] The rate of inflation was 10 percent in 1992, 18 percent in 1993, 11 percent in 1994, and 9 percent in 1995, for an average of about 12 percent. In 1996, the inflation rate is expected to be about 10 percent.

Factor #5: Capital Flows and Foreign Investment
Score: 2-Stable (Low barriers to foreign investment)

With the exception of defense-related industries, all sectors of the Czech Republic's economy are open to foreign investment. The Czech Republic attracts the most foreign investment per capita of any country in Central and Eastern Europe.

Factor #6: Banking
Score: 1-Stable (Very low level of restrictions on banking)

Competition in the Czech banking system is increasing, and there are few, if any, barriers to opening either a foreign or domestic bank. Banks also are open to foreign participation; a foreign bank may establish a wholly owned bank, buy into an existing bank, or open a branch. Private Czech banks are allowed to sell securities and make some investments.

Factor #7: Wage and Price Controls
Score: 2-Stable (Low level of wage and price controls)

Most wages and prices are set by the market. Both the prices of many utilities and the rent paid on government-owned housing remain controlled, however. The Czech Republic maintains minimum wage standards.

Factor #8: Property Rights
Score: 2-Stable (High level of protection of private property)

Private property receives a high level of protection in the Czech Republic, and expropriation is highly unlikely. A system of law in which property receives total protection has yet to be created, however.

Factor #9: Regulation
Score: 1-Stable (Very low level of regulation)

The Czech Republic imposes few regulations on businesses, and most companies do not need a license to begin operations. The government is planning additional reductions in the level of its regulation of business activity.

Factor #10: Black Market
Score: 4- (High level of black market activity)

Some goods and services in the Czech Republic are still supplied on the black market. In addition, despite recent legislation to combat piracy of intellectual property, lax

---

103   State Department Report, 1996.

enforcement remains a problem. According to the U.S. Department of State, piracy accounts for as much as 35 percent to 40 percent of all prerecorded video cassettes, and 83 percent of all computer software, sold in the Czech Republic.[104]

Summary

Czech Republic		Overall Score	2.05

Czech Republic							
Trade	1	Monetary Policy	2	Property Rights	2
Taxation	3.5	Foreign Investment	2	Regulation	1
Government Intervention	2	Banking	1	Black Market	4
		Wage and Prices	2		

---

104   Ibid.

DENMARK

Denmark became a constitutional monarchy in 1849 and remained neutral during World War I. In World War II, it was invaded and occupied by Germany. After World War II, Denmark focused on rebuilding its industries. In 1992, the Danes voted to stay out of the European Union (EU). After the EU made changes in its social charter to meet Danish objections, Denmark voted to join in 1993.

Denmark

Copenhagen

125 Miles

| Index of Economic Freedom Score | 2.05 |

Mostly Free

1   2   3   4   5

Factor #1: Trade Policy

Score: 2-Stable (Low level of protectionism)

Although its average tariff rate is 3.6 percent, Denmark maintains trade restrictions common to other EU members (for example, in financial services, credit cards, insurance, and legal services). As EU standards are applied to all members, however, Denmark has led the fight within the EU to reduce non-tariff barriers to imports.

Factor #2: Taxation

Score - Income taxation: 5- (Very high tax rates)
Score - Corporate taxation: 3-Stable (Moderate tax rates)
Final Taxation Score: 4.5- (Very high tax rates)

Denmark's top income tax rate is 61 percent, and the average taxpayer pays 47 percent. The top marginal corporate tax rate is 34 percent. Denmark also has a 34 percent capital gains tax and a 25 percent value-added tax.

Factor #3: Government Intervention in the Economy

Score: 4-Stable (High level of government intervention)

The Danish government consumes about 26 percent of GDP. Although this figure is moderate, it probably understates the extent to which government consumes the country's economic output. Denmark's government, unlike those of many other countries, pays most of the unemployment benefits and other welfare bills. Although this is good for business, which does not have to pay, it is bad for the rest of the economy because it forces up tax rates. Denmark's public sector is a net debtor and continues to lose money each year.

Factor #4: Monetary Policy

Score: 1-Stable (Very low level of inflation)

Denmark's average rate of inflation from 1985 to 1994 was 2.9 percent. In 1995, the inflation rate was 2 percent, where it remains today.

Factor #5: Capital Flows and Foreign Investment
Score: 2-Stable (Low barriers to foreign investment)

There are few restrictions on investments in Denmark. Notable exceptions are the hydrocarbon exploration, arms production, aircraft, and maritime industries.

Factor #6: Banking
Score: 2-Stable (Low level of restrictions on banking)

The banking system in Denmark is open to foreign investment and largely independent of the government. Danish law allows banks to engage in securities and insurance services, but there are restrictions on real estate activities.

Factor #7: Wage and Price Controls
Score: 1-Stable (Very low level of wage and price controls)

Wages and prices in Denmark are set mainly by the market. There is no minimum wage.

Factor #8: Property Rights
Score: 1-Stable (Very high level of protection of private property)

Private property in Denmark is safe from government expropriation. The legal and judicial system is efficient.

Factor #9: Regulation
Score: 2-Stable (Low level of regulation)

Establishing a business in Denmark is a simple process. Regulations are applied evenly in most cases, although some regulations, such as safety and health standards, make it harder for businesses to keep their doors open.

Factor #10: Black Market
Score: 1-Stable (Very low level of black market activity)

The black market in Denmark is negligible.

Summary

Denmark					Overall Score	2.05
Trade	2	Monetary Policy	1		Property Rights	1
Taxation	4.5	Foreign Investment	2		Regulation	2
Government Intervention	4	Banking	2		Black Market	1
		Wage and Prices	1			

DJIBOUTI

Located in East Africa and bordering Somalia, Djibouti won its independence from France on June 27, 1977, although France still maintains a military presence in the country. During the 1980s, Djibouti focused mainly on maintaining political order and avoiding civil unrest. In 1991, crisis finally erupted and led to increased civil unrest and calls for multi-party democratic elections. Little progress has been made in developing sustainable levels of economic growth, and Djibouti remains in economic chaos.

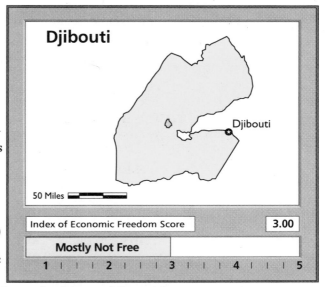

Index of Economic Freedom Score — 3.00

Mostly Not Free

1 | | | 2 | | | 3 | | | 4 | | | 5

Factor #1: Trade Policy

Score: 4-Stable (High level of protectionism)

The largest barriers to imports in Djibouti are corruption within the customs service, inadequate infrastructure to bring products into the country, and poor banking and financial services. Djibouti lies in the crucial maritime shipping lanes between the Mediterranean and the Indian Ocean. With its ports located so strategically, the regime feels some pressure to liberalize its trade laws.

Factor #2: Taxation

Score - Income taxation: 2-Stable (Low tax rates)
Score - Corporate taxation: 2-Stable (Low tax rates)
Final Taxation Score: 2-Stable (Low tax rates)

Djibouti's top income tax rate is 20 percent, as is its top corporate tax rate. Djibouti also has a 20 percent capital gains tax, in addition to other taxes.

Factor #3: Government Intervention in the Economy

Score: 3-Stable (Moderate level of government intervention)

The extent to which government consumes GDP in Djibouti is not known. Most of the country's GDP, however, is produced by the state.

Factor #4: Monetary Policy

Score: 1-Stable (Very low level of inflation)

Djibouti has maintained the value of its currency over a considerable period of time. The average annual rate of inflation from 1985 to 1994 was 4.4 percent. No data are available for 1995.

Factor #5: Capital Flows and Foreign Investment
Score: 3-Stable (Moderate barriers to foreign investment)

Djibouti is open to foreign investment. Investments must be reviewed, however, by the government. Some sectors are closed to investment, mainly in areas the government determines are vital to national security.

Factor #6: Banking
Score: 3-Stable (Moderate restrictions on banking)

The banking system is very open and competitive. According to the U.S. Department of Commerce, "Djibouti has one of the most liberal economic regimes in Africa, with almost unrestricted banking and commerce sectors."[105] The biggest problem is the lack of sufficient capital to finance economic expansion.

Factor #7: Wage and Price Controls
Score: 3-Stable (Moderate level of wage and price controls)

Wages and prices for most products are set mainly by the market. The government, however, controls prices on electricity and transportation services.

Factor #8: Property Rights
Score: 3-Stable (Moderate level of protection of private property)

Private property is a respected right in Djibouti, although the court systems are often overburdened, and enforcing contracts can be time-consuming and cumbersome.

Factor #9: Regulation
Score: 4-Stable (High level of regulation)

Government corruption is a burden on business, and bribes are often necessary. Health and safety regulations also add to the cost of doing business.

Factor #10: Black Market
Score: 4-Stable (High level of black market activity)

Much economic activity in Djibouti, especially the trade in pirated trademarks and computer software, occurs in the black market. Laws protecting intellectual property are not fully enforced.

Summary

Djibouti					Overall Score	3.00
Trade	4	Monetary Policy	1		Property Rights	3
Taxation	2	Foreign Investment	3		Regulation	4
Government Intervention	3	Banking	3		Black Market	4
		Wage and Prices	3			

105 National Trade Data Bank and Economic Bulletin Board—products of STAT–USA, U.S. Department of Commerce.

DOMINICAN REPUBLIC

The Dominican Republic won its independence from Spain in 1865. Since that time, this Caribbean island nation has developed a large agricultural industry, and the government has intervened quite often in this and other industries. In the 1980s the country suffered a major economic crisis as its socialist economic policies and bad weather ruined agricultural production. Since 1990, the government has been trying to reform the economy, but not much progress has been made.

Dominican Republic

Santo Domingo

125 Miles

| Index of Economic Freedom Score | 3.45 |

Mostly Not Free

1 2 3 4 5

Factor #1: Trade Policy

Score: 5-Stable (Very high level of protectionism)

The Dominican Republic maintains very high trade barriers. Its average tariff rate is 34 percent.[106] Non-tariff barriers include arbitrary customs clearance procedures and a burdensome licensing requirement for selected imports. According to the Office of the U.S. Trade Representative, "Many business people complain that bringing goods through Dominican Customs is a slow and arduous process. Arbitrary customs clearance procedures sometimes cause firms to have their merchandise held up for as long as a year. U.S. poultry exports to the Dominican Republic are further restricted by an array of non scientifically based sanitary measures."[107]

Factor #2: Taxation

Score - Income taxation: 2-Stable (Low tax rates)
Score - Corporate taxation: 2-Stable (Low tax rates)
Final Taxation Score: 2.5-Stable (Moderate tax rates)

The Dominican Republic's marginal top income tax rate is 25 percent. The tax on the average income level is 0 percent. The top corporate tax rate is 25 percent. The country also has a 25 percent capital gains tax and an 8 percent value-added tax.

Factor #3: Government Intervention in the Economy

Score: 2-Stable (Low level of government intervention)

The Dominican Republic's government consumes about 7 percent of GDP. The state-owned sector is extensive.

---

106 Based on total taxes on international trade as a percentage of total imports; from International Monetary Fund, *Government Financial Statistics 1995*.

107 Office of the U.S. Trade Representative, *National Trade Estimate Report on Foreign Trade Barriers*, 1996.

Factor #4: Monetary Policy
Score: 5-Stable (Very high level of inflation)

The Dominican Republic's annual rate of inflation from 1985 to 1994 was 28.8 percent. In 1995, the inflation rate fell to 9.5 percent.

Factor #5: Capital Flows and Foreign Investment
Score: 3-Stable (Moderate barriers to foreign investment)

Foreign investment is discouraged by government bureaucracy and corruption. Prohibitions on foreign investment exist in the following industries: communications, media, national defense, transportation, and public utilities. Foreigners need a presidential decree to own more than one-half acre of land. The Dominican Republic maintains repatriation requirements and prevents the reinvestment of some profits.

Factor #6: Banking
Score: 3-Stable (Moderate level of restrictions on banking)

Foreign banks are virtually shut out of the Dominican Republic. The two exceptions are Citibank and the Bank of Nova Scotia, which have been operating relatively freely in the Dominican Republic for decades. The government strictly controls the supply of credit. Foreign companies cannot obtain loans from local banks for a period longer than one year.

Factor #7: Wage and Price Controls
Score: 2-Stable (Low level of wage and price controls)

Most wages and prices are set by the market. The government combats inflation with sound monetary measures and price controls. The Dominican Republic has a minimum wage policy.

Factor #8: Property Rights
Score: 4-Stable (Low level of protection of private property)

Property rights are not respected and receive low levels of protection in the Dominican Republic. The court system is inefficient; corruption and bureaucratic red tape run high; and property can be expropriated by the government.

Factor #9: Regulation
Score: 4-Stable (High level of regulation)

Regulations are not applied evenly or honestly, and both corruption and red tape impose significant burdens on businesses. According to the U.S. Department of Commerce, "Dominican and foreign business leaders complain of judicial and administrative corruption, and some persons have charged that corruption affects the settlement of business disputes."[108]

---

108   U.S. Department of Commerce, *Country Commercial Guide,* 1996.

Factor #10: Black Market

Score: 4-Stable (High level of black market activity)

The Dominican Republic has a high level of black market activity, particularly in labor services. Competition for workers is so intense that many legal labor regulations are ignored. Moreover, there is a complete disregard for intellectual property protection. According to the U.S. Department of State, "In general, copyright laws are adequate, but enforcement is weak, resulting in widespread piracy. Although the Dominican Republic is a signatory to the Paris Convention and the Universal Copyright Convention, and in 1991 became a member of the World Intellectual Property Organization, the lack of a strong regulatory environment results in inadequate protection of intellectual property rights."[109]

Summary

Dominican Republic					Overall Score	3.45
Trade	5	Monetary Policy	5		Property Rights	4
Taxation	2.5	Foreign Investment	3		Regulation	4
Government Intervention	2	Banking	3		Black Market	4
		Wage and Prices	2			

---

109   State Department Report, 1996, p. 370.

ECUADOR

Originally a part of Gran Colombia, which also included Venezuela, Ecuador became independent from Spain in 1830. For the next century, Ecuador was plagued by instability and dictatorship. Today, its economy is based mainly on oil and bananas. During the oil boom of the late 1970s and early 1980s, Ecuador's government used its increased wealth to subsidize businesses and generally to raise the level of government consumption of the economy. As oil prices plummeted after 1981, however, Ecuador's oil-based economy began to decline. Since the early 1990s, Ecuador has been trying with mixed results to carry out reforms that would reduce the level of state intervention in the economy. A new president, Abdala Bucaram, was elected in July 1996.

| Index of Economic Freedom Score | 3.05 |
| Mostly Not Free | |

Factor #1: Trade Policy

Score: 3+ (Moderate level of protectionism)

Ecuador's average tariff rate is 9 percent.[110] Importers must obtain import licenses, and this can delay the movement of goods into the country. Ecuador's government has made progress in reforming its cumbersome customs procedures. According to the U.S. Department of State, "Customs procedures can be difficult, but they are not normally used to discriminate against U.S. products. The government is implementing a new customs reform law to reduce corruption and improve efficiency in the customs service, thereby eliminating a major constraint on trade."[111]

Factor #2: Taxation

Score - Income taxation: 2-Stable (Low tax rates)
Score - Corporate taxation: 2-Stable (Low tax rates)
Final Taxation Score: 2.5-Stable (Moderate tax rates)

Ecuador's top marginal income tax rate is 25 percent, and the rate that applies to the average income level is 0 percent. The top tax rate on corporate profits is 25 percent. Ecuador also has a 10 percent value-added tax.

---

110   Based on total taxes on international trade as a percentage of total imports; from International Monetary Fund, *Government Financial Statistics 1995.*

111   State Department Report, 1996, p. 375.

Factor #3: Government Intervention in the Economy
Score: 1-Stable (Very low level of government intervention)

Ecuador's government consumes only 7 percent of GDP. This may seem very low, considering that the government employs 25 percent of the workforce and many industries are dominated by state-owned firms; but the vast majority of firms are privately owned. The state-owned sector contributes less than 8 percent of GDP.

Factor #4: Monetary Policy
Score: 5-Stable (Very high level of inflation)

Ecuador's main monetary goal has been to stabilize inflation by controlling the money supply. From 1985 to 1994, the average annual rate of inflation was 47.5 percent. In 1995, the inflation rate was 22 percent.

Factor #5: Capital Flows and Foreign Investment
Score: 2-Stable (Low barriers to foreign investment)

Ecuador's government has been liberalizing its foreign investment policies since 1990. Most investors are free to invest in almost any industry, except for such so-called strategic industries as mining and enterprises owned by the state.

Factor #6: Banking
Score: 3-Stable (Moderate restrictions on banking)

Ecuador has 35 private banks—considerably more than many of its neighbors—and a large number of foreign banks. Domestically owned banks are relatively competitive with foreign banks; however, these privately owned banks must compete with state-owned development banks that provide a variety of subsidized loans to farmers, ranchers, and small businessmen.

Factor #7: Wage and Price Controls
Score: 3-Stable (Moderate level of wage and price controls)

Although there are fewer price controls today than several years ago, prices on such items as bananas, cocoa, coffee, and pharmaceuticals are still set by the government. Ecuador maintains a minimum wage policy.

Factor #8: Property Rights
Score: 3-Stable (Moderate level of protection of private property)

Ecuador's large disparities in wealth increase the chances that property may be redistributed to the poor. According to the U.S. Department of Commerce, "A cumbersome legal system and complex land reform legislation can make it somewhat difficult to enforce property and concession rights in the agriculture and mining sectors."[112] In 1994, however, the government passed a new agrarian law that enforces the rights of rural landowners. Corruption still plagues the legal framework, however, making it unnecessarily difficult to enforce property rights.

---

112   U.S. Department of Commerce, *Country Commercial Guide, 1996.*

Factor #9: Regulation

Score: 4-Stable (High level of regulation)

The Superintendency of Companies, the Superintendency of Banks and Insurance Companies, and the Ecuadorian Standards Institute are the main regulatory bodies in Ecuador. Corruption in these and other agencies causes them to enforce regulations haphazardly, imposing an additional burden on business.

Factor #10: Black Market

Score: 4-Stable (High level of black market activity)

Because of Ecuador's bureaucratic inefficiency and corruption, many entrepreneurs resort to the black market. The government has reduced many trade tariffs on items that were being sold as contraband. According to the U.S. Department of State, however, "Copyright infringement occurs and there is widespread local trade in pirated audio and video recordings, as well as computer software."[113]

Summary

Ecuador					Overall Score	3.05
Trade	3	Monetary Policy	5		Property Rights	3
Taxation	2.5	Foreign Investment	2		Regulation	4
Government Intervention	1	Banking	3		Black Market	4
		Wage and Prices	3			

---

113   State Department Report, 1996, p. 375.

EGYPT

gypt gained its independence from Great Britain in 1922. Today, the country is a social democracy ruled by President Hosni Mubarak. The government launched a desperately needed market liberalization program in 1991 and has attempted to remove the state from the market, but little progress has been made in privatizing Egypt's massive and inefficient public sector. Nor has much been done to reform and reduce the size of the bureaucracy. There has been some progress, however, in lowering extremely high tariffs and establishing more fiscal discipline. Egypt is the second-largest annual recipient of U.S. foreign aid.

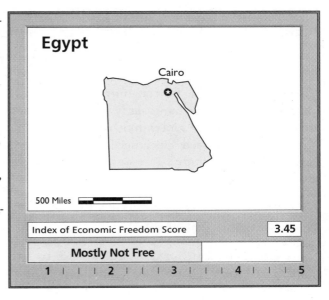

| Index of Economic Freedom Score | 3.45 |
| Mostly Not Free | |

Factor #1: Trade Policy

Score: 5-Stable (Very high level of protectionism)

Despite progress over the past several years in liberalizing its trade policy, Egypt remains one of the world's more heavily protected markets with an exceptionally high average tariff rate of 22 percent.[114] Import bans now apply only to textiles and apparels, although the government is considering eliminating them, and import licenses no longer are required. Nevertheless, 159 previously banned items have been placed on a "quality control" list that subjects them to discriminatory treatment.

Factor #2: Taxation

Score - Income taxation: 4-Stable (High tax rates)
Score - Corporate taxation: 4-Stable (High tax rates)
Final Taxation Score: 4.5-Stable (Very high tax rates)

In 1993, Egypt lowered its top income tax rate from 65 percent to 48 percent. The tax on the average income level is 20 percent, and corporate income is taxed at a rate of 40 percent. Egypt has a 40 percent capital gains tax, a sales tax, and a social insurance tax.

Factor #3: Government Intervention in the Economy

Score: 3-Stable (Moderate level of government intervention)

With plans for wide-scale privatization proceeding at a slow pace, a large and inefficient state sector still accounts for some 70 percent of industrial production. Over 300 enterprises remain in state hands. Government consumes 14 percent of Egypt's GDP.[115]

---

114 Based on total taxes on international trade as a percentage of total imports; from International Monetary Fund, *Government Financial Statistics 1995*.

115 World Bank, *World Development Report 1996*.

Factor #4: Monetary Policy
Score: 3-Stable (Moderate level of inflation)

Egypt's average annual rate of inflation from 1985 to 1994 was 16.4 percent. The estimate for 1995 is approximately 9.4 percent.

Factor #5: Capital Flows and Foreign Investment
Score: 3-Stable (Moderate barriers to foreign investment)

The Egyptian government has established business zones free of customs duties, sales taxes, and other taxes. Despite these improvements, however, a cumbersome bureaucracy continues to frustrate foreign investment. Foreign investors occasionally face official discrimination, particularly when their proposals threaten public-sector interests. In practice, 100 percent foreign ownership, even though legally permitted in most sectors, is rarely approved. It is possible that most foreigners, particularly non-Arabs, will find themselves excluded from Egypt's still-embryonic privatization process. Foreigners are prohibited from owning Egyptian agricultural land.

Factor #6: Banking
Score: 3-Stable (Moderate level of restrictions on banking)

Egypt's banking industry is dominated by four state-owned commercial banks. Twenty-one foreign banks operate branches in Egypt, however, and there are plans for further privatization of the banking sector, which has been undergoing liberalization. Existing foreign branch banks were granted permission in 1993 to operate in local currency, and bank lending ceilings were lifted in 1992. New banks, however, face formidable barriers to entry into the banking sector.

Factor #7: Wage and Price Controls
Score: 3-Stable (Moderate level of wage and price controls)

Price controls have been removed on most products, the notable exceptions being pharmaceutical products, sugar, edible oils, and cigarettes. Basic foods and transport are subsidized, although not as much as in recent years. The existence of a massive public sector limits the private sector's ability to set wages and prices. The government limits the amount of profit earned on some imported goods and also is involved in setting wages. There is a minimum wage.

Factor #8: Property Rights
Score: 3-Stable (Moderate level of protection of private property)

Egypt's commendable privatization effort is bogged down. Although private property is protected by the constitution, the Egyptian judiciary is inefficient. "In some instances," according to the U.S. Department of Commerce, "Government entities refuse for years to accept contractual requirements to arbitrate even if arbitration is explicitly written into the contract. Local lawyers insist, however, that the recalcitrant party cannot prevent indefinitely the initiation of arbitration. It requires time, sometimes numerous court proceedings which in many cases average five years to reach primary court decision, and sometimes numerous appeals to senior Government officials. Legal appeal procedures can extend court cases to 15 years or longer."[116]

---

116   U.S. Department of Commerce, *Country Commercial Guide*, 1996.

Factor #9: Regulation

Score: 4-Stable (High level of regulation)

Corruption is endemic in the Egyptian bureaucracy, which is massive and inefficient. Bribery is the norm. The business environment is overregulated, with managers spending an estimated 30 percent of their time handling bureaucratic requirements, and the labor market is heavily regulated. It is difficult, for example, to obtain government permission to lay off workers. Regulations also severely constrain the employment of foreigners. Some progress has been made in reducing the time it takes to start a business.

Factor #10: Black Market

Score: 3-Stable (Moderate level of black market activity)

With its long commitment to a command economy, and with economic reform proceeding at a slow pace, Egypt retains a large black market sector. Although most goods are available in shops, substantial trade restrictions encourage smuggling.

Summary

Egypt					Overall Score	3.45
Trade	5	Monetary Policy	3		Property Rights	3
Taxation	4.5	Foreign Investment	3		Regulation	4
Government Intervention	3	Banking	3		Black Market	3
		Wage and Prices	3			

EL SALVADOR

The Central American country of El Salvador suffered a terrible civil war in the 1980s. After peace was established in 1991, the economy slowly began to recover; but despite massive infusions of foreign aid, it grew by an average of only 2 percent per year from 1982 to 1989. Once El Salvador began to make market reforms, however, its economy began to grow steadily: 3.4 percent in 1990, 3.5 percent in 1991, 4.8 percent in 1992, 7.4 percent in 1993, 6 percent in 1994, and 5.5 percent in 1995. Under President Alfredo Cristiani, the government abolished price controls, slashed import tariffs, privatized most of the financial system, and followed a relatively tight monetary policy. Although some problems remain, El Salvador's economy is growing and shows signs of increasing prosperity. New President Armando Calderon Sol has maintained Cristiani's reforms. El Salvador recently slashed tariffs, eliminated non-tariff barriers, and reduced the government's consumption of economic output. It has retreated on some of its privatization plans, however, leaving some companies in government hands.

El Salvador

San Salvador

125 Miles

Index of Economic Freedom Score   2.55

Mostly Free

1   2   3   4   5

Factor #1: Trade Policy

Score: 3-Stable (Moderate level of protectionism)

El Salvador recently slashed tariff rates and probably will cut them more through 1999. It now has an average tariff rate of 5 percent. El Salvador also has removed many non-tariff barriers. It still maintains arbitrary sanitation requirements on poultry imports, however, as well as some non-tariff restrictions on selected agricultural imports.

Factor #2: Taxation

Score - Income taxation: 2-Stable (Low tax rates)
Score - Corporate taxation: 2-Stable (Low tax rates)
Final Taxation Score: 2.5-Stable (Moderate tax rates)

El Salvador's top marginal income tax rate is 30 percent,[117] and the tax rate for the average income level is 0 percent. The top corporate income tax rate is 25 percent. El Salvador also has a 13 percent value-added tax.

---

117   The effective tax rate may not exceed 25 percent of taxable income.

Factor #3: Government Intervention in the Economy
Score: 2-Stable (Moderate level of government intervention)

El Salvador's government consumes 8.2 percent of GDP, down from 14 percent in 1980. Although the sale of the last state-owned banking institutions has gone forward, privatization of the telecommunications industry and electricity has stalled.

Factor #4: Monetary Policy
Score: 3-Stable (Moderate level of inflation)

El Salvador had an average annual inflation rate of 16.2 percent from 1985 to 1994. In 1995, the inflation rate was 9.8 percent.

Factor #5: Capital Flows and Foreign Investment
Score: 2-Stable (Low barriers to foreign investment)

Foreign investors can invest in almost any enterprise except electricity and telecommunications, which remain in government hands. El Salvador provides tax incentives for some investments.

Factor #6: Banking
Score: 2-Stable (Low level of restrictions on banking)

Foreign banks are permitted to operate in El Salvador as if they were domestic banks. All restrictions on foreign banks have been removed, and most local and foreign banks are allowed to compete in offering a wide range of financial services.

Factor #7: Wage and Price Controls
Score: 2-Stable (Low level of wage and price controls)

The government has eliminated price controls on some 240 goods, although price controls remain on bus fares and utilities. El Salvador has a minimum wage.

Factor #8: Property Rights
Score: 3-Stable (Moderate level of protection of private property)

The government of El Salvador has undertaken a massive privatization program and is returning banks, hotels, and other enterprises to the private sector. Although private property is guaranteed by law, the country lacks efficient legal protection of property.

Factor #9: Regulation
Score: 3-Stable (Moderate level of regulation)

Because price controls have been abolished, the government maintains little regulatory control over most businesses. Corruption, however, remains a problem.

Factor #10: Black Market
Score: 3-Stable (Moderate level of black market activity)

Some labor, such as construction, is still provided by the black market. In addition, El Salvador's intellectual property laws suffer from a lack of enforcement and an inefficient bureaucracy.

Summary

El Salvador		Overall Score	2.55
Trade	3	Monetary Policy	3	Property Rights	3
Taxation	2.5	Foreign Investment	2	Regulation	3
Government Intervention	2	Banking	2	Black Market	3
		Wage and Prices	2		

ESTONIA

The Baltic country of Estonia was independent between 1918 and 1940, at which time it was forcibly annexed by the Soviet Union. It is the most Western-oriented country of the former Soviet Union, with a clear Scandinavian and Northern European orientation. It has associate membership in European Union and is applying for full membership. Of all the former Soviet republics, Estonia has been the most successful in reforming its economy. The government has undertaken a massive program of privatization, selling off many formerly state-owned enterprises, and has established its own national currency—the kroon—which is stable and convertible. The inflation rate has fallen dramatically, even though trade with the West has grown 500 percent since 1991.

Factor #1: Trade Policy

Score: 2-Stable (Low level of protection)

Estonia has an average tariff rate of approximately 5.5 percent[118] and maintains few if any non-tariff barriers to trade. The central impediments to imports are an insufficient and inefficient telephone system and other infrastructure-related problems.

Factor #2: Taxation

Score - Income taxation: 3-Stable (Moderate tax rates)
Score - Corporate taxation: 3-Stable (Moderate tax rates)
Final Taxation Score: 3.5-Stable (High tax rates)

Estonia has a flat income tax rate of 26 percent and a top corporate tax rate of 26 percent. It also has a 26 percent capital gains tax, an 18 percent value-added tax, a 20 percent social security tax, a 13 percent social insurance tax, and a 1 percent land tax.

Factor #3: Government Intervention in the Economy

Score: 2-Stable (Low level of government intervention)

Estonia's government consumes 20.6 percent of GDP, up from 16 percent a year ago.

---

118   This figure, which was derived by taking Estonia's taxes raised from international trade in 1993 and determining the percentage of total imports, probably understates the real average tariff rate.

Factor #4: Monetary Policy
Score: 4-Stable (High level of inflation)

Although historically high because of the 1992 monetary crisis in the former Soviet Union, Estonia's inflation has dropped dramatically in the past two years. In 1992, the annual rate of inflation was 1,009 percent. In 1993, it fell to about 26 percent; in 1994, it rose to 40 percent; and in 1995, it fell again to about 29 percent. Overall, the average rate of inflation since 1992 remains high.

Factor #5: Capital Flows and Foreign Investment
Score: 1-Stable (Very low barriers to foreign investment)

There are relatively few restrictions on foreign investors. Investments are permitted in all areas of industry, including some utilities, and all foreign investment ventures are treated the same as Estonian businesses. There are no repatriation requirements forcing investors to keep their capital in the country.

Factor #6: Banking
Score: 2-Stable (Low level of restrictions on banking)

Banks in Estonia have been made more accessible to foreign operation. Private banks are growing, and competition with state banks is increasing.

Factor #7: Wage and Price Controls
Score: 2-Stable (Low level of wage and price controls)

Price controls have been removed on 95 percent of Estonia's goods and services; the only remaining controls are on the prices of such items as electricity and energy-producing agents like shale. There is a minimum wage.

Factor #8: Property Rights
Score: 2-Stable (High level of protection of private property)

The chances of expropriation in Estonia are low, and the legal protection of private property is relatively high. The court system may be slightly inefficient at times.

Factor #9: Regulation
Score: 2-Stable (Low level of regulation)

Some regulations impose a burden on business. For example, increased attention to health, safety, and the environment, as well as testing and standards, inhibits some business creation. Obtaining a business license, however, is relatively easy and corruption-free.

Factor #10: Black Market
Score: 3-Stable (Moderate level of black market activity)

Because of reduced barriers to trade and a limited regulatory environment, the black market is shrinking, although many services like taxis still are supplied by the black market. In addition, according to the U.S. Department of State, "Widespread piracy has limited local demand for the legitimate products, especially video and audio tapes, and compact disks."[119] Moreover, there remains some smuggling of raw materials from the former Soviet Union.

Summary

Estonia				Overall Score	2.35
Trade	2	Monetary Policy	4	Property Rights	2
Taxation	3.5	Foreign Investment	1	Regulation	2
Government Intervention	2	Banking	2	Black Market	3
		Wage and Prices	2		

---

119   State Department Report, 1996, p. 170.

ETHIOPIA

thiopia was never colonized by a European power. Years of civil war and Marxist economic policies have devastated Ethiopia, the second most populous country in sub-Saharan Africa and one of the poorest. The Ethiopian People's Revolutionary Democratic Party seized power in 1991, having defeated the Marxist regime of Mengistu Haile Mariam. The transitional government of President Meles Zenawi adopted a new constitution in December 1995. Democratic elections were held in 1995, although they were boycotted by the major opposition parties. Zenawi's government favors a mixed economy and enjoys considerable support from foreign aid donors. Although the country suffers from poor agricultural production because of a recent drought, increased manufacturing output has buoyed the economy.

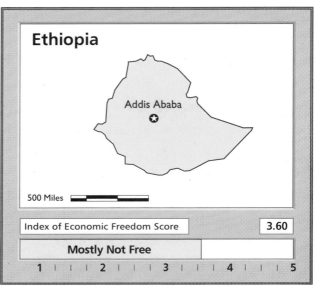

Ethiopia	
Index of Economic Freedom Score	3.60
Mostly Not Free	

Factor #1: Trade Policy

Score: 4+ (High level of protectionism)

Although Ethiopia has liberalized trade somewhat, partly by eliminating the negative list of imports and lowering its maximum tariff to 80 percent, the average tariff rate remains a high 13.5 percent.[120] The customs bureaucracy is cumbersome and inefficient, and delays in bringing goods into the country are not uncommon.

Factor #2: Taxation

Score - Income taxation: 5-Stable (Very high tax rates)
Score - Corporate taxation: 3-Stable (Moderate tax rates)
Total Taxation Score: 4-Stable (High tax rates)

Ethiopia recently has reduced taxes, but its top tax rates still remain over 50 percent, and the average income level is taxed at rates higher than 25 percent. The corporate tax rate is 50 percent.[121]

Factor #3: Government Intervention in the Economy

Score: 3-Stable (Moderate level of government intervention)

Ethiopia's government consumes 12 percent of GDP, which is considerably lower than 1990's 26.6 percent. The industrial sector is dominated by 15 public enterprises, and

---

120   Based on total taxes on international trade as a percentage of total imports; from International Monetary Fund, *Government Financial Statistics 1995.*

121   Tax information from *Foreign Tax and Trade Briefs,* Matthew Bender and Co., Inc., June 1994.

progress with planned privatization has been slow. State enterprises account for almost all of Ethiopia's manufacturing production.

Factor #4: Monetary Policy
Score: 2-Stable (Low level of inflation)

Ethiopia's inflation rate historically has been low. The average annual rate of inflation from 1985 through 1994 was only 5.6 percent, although this was artificially low because Ethiopia was a communist country until 1991. Ethiopia's inflation rate generally has increased over the last few years, rising to around 30 percent in 1994. In 1995, however, it was reduced to around 8 percent.

Factor #5: Capital Flows and Foreign Investment
Score: 4-Stable (High barriers to foreign investment)

President Zenawi's government has made modest progress in dismantling the hostile foreign investment climate created by the previous Marxist regime. Sectors remaining off-limits to private investment include the defense industry, large-scale electric power generation, and postal, telecommunications, financial, some export/import, and major transportation services. Ethiopians are granted priority for investment opportunities, and the bureaucratic decision-making process is slow. Other impediments to foreign investment include a $500,000 minimum investment requirement and regulations designed to encourage Ethiopian participation in management. Although foreign investors can enjoy some tax incentives, little foreign investment has materialized.

Factor #6: Banking
Score: 4-Stable (High level of restrictions on banking)

The financial sector, nationalized in 1975, recently was liberalized. Private investment in banking and insurance was permitted in 1994. The dominant Commercial Bank of Ethiopia and the Ethiopian Insurance Corporation, however, will remain under full state ownership; private investment is limited to newly established bank and insurance operations, of which a few were established last year, though they remain of marginal importance. Limits on banking and insurance ownership apply to individuals and families, and no foreign ownership of Ethiopian banks is permitted. Foreign banks may not operate in Ethiopia.

Factor #7: Wage and Price Controls
Score: 3-Stable (Moderate level of wage and price controls)

Official government-imposed price controls have been removed on all but a few products, although a slow and sometimes ineffective privatization program leaves large sections of the Ethiopian economy in government hands, often hindering price competition. State-owned retail and distribution companies, for example, reduce price and wage competition in these sectors because the government directly subsidizes their activities. Since many distribution companies are owned outright by the government, prices on all goods handled by these companies are negatively affected.

Factor #8: Property Rights
Score: 4-Stable (Low level of protection of private property)

The Mengistu regime nationalized most industries and vast tracts of agricultural land, and the current government's failure to address the status of rural land in an adequate fashion frustrates proposals for commercial agricultural development. Privatization of state farms is a long-term objective, but urban land will remain the property of the state, available to the private sector only through revocable long-term leases. Bureaucratic red tape and corruption further weaken property rights in Ethiopia. The judicial system remains weak and subject to political influence. Property may be expropriated legally with compensation.

Factor #9: Regulation
Score: 4-Stable (High level of regulation)

Impromptu police clearings of street stalls and other persecutions of merchants who threaten politically favored businesses are common. The business permit system is used to favor certain ethnic groups and is subject to some corruption. Businesses targeted for government crackdowns include schools teaching computer skills, foreign languages, and typing. Ethiopia's regulatory regime greatly impedes legitimate business activity.

Factor #10: Black Market
Score: 4-Stable (High level of black market activity)

Many legitimate economic activities, especially retailing, are driven underground by repressive authorities. There is considerable smuggling of coffee, khat, fruits and vegetables, cigarettes, alcohol, textiles, and electronics. Moreover, Ethiopia has no legal protection of many intellectual property products—for example, there are no trademark or patent laws—so piracy in these areas is rampant.

Summary

Ethiopia				Overall Score	3.60
Trade	4	Monetary Policy	2	Property Rights	4
Taxation	4	Foreign Investment	4	Regulation	4
Government Intervention	3	Banking	4	Black Market	4
		Wage and Prices	3		

FIJI

Fiji, a small island nation in the South Pacific Ocean, gained its independence from the United Kingdom in 1970 and shortly thereafter developed a democratic constitution. During the 1980s, however, there were several military coups. This political instability has prevented Fiji from adopting significant, long-lasting economic reform and achieving sustained economic growth, although the government has reduced taxes and cut its consumption of GDP recently.

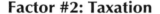

Fiji

Suva

125 Miles

| Index of Economic Freedom Score | 3.20 |

Mostly Not Free

1　　2　　3　　4　　5

Factor #1: Trade Policy

Score: 5-Stable (Very high level of protectionism)

Fiji has an average tariff rate of 13.7 percent.[122] It also has many non-tariff barriers. For example, special licenses are required for powdered milk, butter, potatoes, rice, coffee, canned fish, lubricants, transformer and circuit breaker oils, cleansing oils, and hydraulic brake oils.

Factor #2: Taxation

Score - Income taxation: 2-Stable (Low tax rates)
Score - Corporate taxation: 3-Stable (Moderate tax rates)
Final Taxation Score: 3-Stable (Moderate tax rates)

Fiji's top income tax rate is 35 percent, down from 40 percent in 1995, and the tax rate for the average income is 0 percent. The top corporate income tax rate is 35 percent. Fiji also has a 30 percent capital gains tax, a 10 percent value-added tax, and a 7 percent to 23 percent social contributions tax.

Factor #3: Government Intervention in the Economy

Score: 3- (Moderate level of government intervention)

Fiji's government consumes 16.6 percent of the country's GDP. The government continues to own many companies in various industries, however, including banking.

Factor #4: Monetary Policy

Score: 1-Stable (Very low level of inflation)

Fiji's average annual rate of inflation from 1985 to 1994 was 5.3 percent. In 1995, inflation was 2.2 percent.

122　Based on total taxes on international trade as a percentage of total imports; from International Monetary Fund, *Government Financial Statistics 1995.*

Factor #5: Capital Flows and Foreign Investment
Score: 3-Stable (Moderate barriers to foreign investment)

Among the many restrictions on foreign investment in Fiji, foreign investors are not permitted to buy into and gain a controlling share of any domestically owned business, and all investments must be approved by the government. Fiji does conform to an established foreign investment code, however.

Factor #6: Banking
Score: 3-Stable (Moderate level of restrictions on banking)

Fiji has few direct restrictions on banking. Although the government's direct ownership of banks inhibits competition, there also is a growing private banking industry.

Factor #7: Wage and Price Controls
Score: 3-Stable (Moderate level of wage and price controls)

Fiji maintains price controls on a select group of commodities and consumer goods. It also has a minimum wage.

Factor #8: Property Rights
Score: 3-Stable (Moderate level of protection of private property)

Property expropriation in Fiji remains a possibility. There is inadequate protection of property rights, and the dispute settlement process is not sufficient.

Factor #9: Regulation
Score: 4-Stable (High level of regulation)

Fiji's economy is heavily regulated, and many regulations impose a significant burden on business. For example, the Prices and Incomes Board monitors the pricing and wage policies of Fiji's businesses. If the government determines that a business's price and wage policies violate its own established policies, it can shut down any business that fails to comply.

Factor #10: Black Market
Score: 4-Stable (High level of black market activity)

Fiji's relatively closed market for imports creates a substantial black market in smuggled items. Moreover, there is rampant pirating of such intellectual property as video and sound recordings and motion pictures.

Summary

Fiji				Overall Score	3.20
Trade	5	Monetary Policy	1	Property Rights	3
Taxation	3	Foreign Investment	3	Regulation	4
Government Intervention	3	Banking	3	Black Market	4
		Wage and Prices	3		

FINLAND

Finland

Helsinki

250 Miles

Index of Economic Freedom Score	2.30

Mostly Free

1　　　2　　　3　　　4　　　5

Once a part of Sweden, Finland was an autonomous Grand Duchy under the Russian czar from 1809 to 1917 and later became an independent republic. During World War II, Finland fought both the Soviet Union and Germany; during the Cold War, however, it adopted a policy of neutrality between East and West. Finland has been ruled by a socialist coalition for most of the post–World War II period. During the 1990s, its economy was seriously weakened by the government's increasingly socialist economic policies. The economy shrank by 13 percent from 1990 to 1993, but recovered in 1994 as a result of economic liberalization. In 1995, Finland joined the European Union (EU). The Finnish economy continues to recover and may reach annual economic growth rates of 4 percent over the next several years. Recently, a privatization program has failed to redirect government ownership of many business activities, although Finland has made some progress in reducing regulations.

Factor #1: Trade Policy
Score: 2-Stable (Low level of protectionism)

Finland's average tariff rate is 3.6 percent, which is in line with the EU's average, and its trade restrictions are the same as those of other EU members. Non-tariff barriers include strict licensing and testing standards.

Factor #2: Taxation
Score - Income taxation: 4-Stable (High tax rates)
Score - Corporate taxation: 3-Stable (Moderate tax rates)
Final Taxation Score: 4-Stable (High tax rates)

Finland's top income tax rate is 39 percent; the average taxpayer is in the 21 percent bracket. The top marginal corporate tax rate is 28 percent, up from 25 percent in 1994. Finland also maintains many other taxes, including municipal taxes (which can raise the top income tax rate to 57 percent), a 28 percent capital gains tax, and a 22 percent value-added tax.

Factor #3: Government Intervention in the Economy
Score: 3- (Moderate level of government intervention)

Finland's government consumes about 21.7 percent of GDP, and the government's presence in the economy remains considerable. State-owned companies make up almost 19 percent of GDP. Moreover, much of Finland's privatization program is aimed not at eliminating government ownership and control, but only at reducing levels of ownership. Thus, the government owns shares in many Finnish companies. Finland's score was worse this year because of the failure of its privatization program to reduce government ownership of businesses.

Factor #4: Monetary Policy
Score: 1-Stable (Very low level of inflation)

Finland's rate of inflation averaged 4.2 percent from 1985 to 1994. In 1995, inflation was only about 1 percent.

Factor #5: Capital Flows and Foreign Investment
Score: 2-Stable (Low barriers to foreign investment)

Finland welcomes foreign investment, although there are some restrictions on investments in areas related to national security.

Factor #6: Banking
Score: 3-Stable (Moderate restrictions on banking)

The banking system in Finland remains under heavy government control, particularly in the savings industry. Many savings banks are on the verge of bankruptcy because of bad loans and the economic recession of 1990 to 1993. The government continues to own banks. Finland allows foreign bank competition, however, and Finnish banks may engage in some financial services, such as the buying and selling of securities.

Factor #7: Wage and Price Controls
Score: 3-Stable (Moderate level of wage and price controls)

Wages and prices in Finland are set by the market. Finland's government, however, can control prices through massive transfers of subsidies to such sectors as agriculture and manufacturing. The government also can control the prices of some pharmaceuticals through its medical reimbursement programs; drugs subject to government reimbursement must abide by pricing standards established by the government.

Factor #8: Property Rights
Score: 1- Stable (Very high level of protection of private property)

Private property is safe in Finland. The legal and judicial system is efficient, and there has been no government expropriation since the end of World War II.

Factor #9: Regulation
Score: 3+ (Moderate level of regulation)

Establishing a business in Finland is a simple process. Regulations are applied evenly in most cases, although increased regulation, primarily in financial services, is making it harder to acquire the capital needed to expand or to open new businesses. Moreover, Finland still maintains a plethora of onerous regulations in the form of health, safety, and employment requirements. According to the U.S. Department of State, "Finland's health and safety laws are among the strictest in the world."[123] Finland has made some recent progress in deregulating it economy, however, primarily to stimulate business activity.

---

123   State Department Report, 1996, pp. 171–175.

Factor #10: Black Market
Score: 1-Stable (Very low level of black market activity)

The black market in Finland is negligible. Finland has very strong laws protecting intellectual property, and the levels of piracy of computer software and prerecorded music and videos are among the lowest in the world.

Summary

Finland					Overall Score	2.30
Trade	2	Monetary Policy	1	Property Rights	1
Taxation	4	Foreign Investment	2	Regulation	3
Government Intervention	3	Banking	3	Black Market	1
		Wage and Prices	3		

FRANCE

France has the world's fourth-largest industrialized economy. Like much of the rest of Europe, however, France also has been in a state of recession for the past several years. Although essentially a free market, France has a history of centralized administrative control over many parts of the economy. Recently, attempts to privatize large sections of the economy have failed.

France

Paris

250 Miles

| Index of Economic Freedom Score | 2.50 |

Mostly Free

1   2   3   4   5

Factor #1: Trade Policy
Score: 2-Stable (Low level of protectionism)

Because it is a member of the European Union (EU), France's trade policy is the same as those of other EU members. Imports are subject to the common EU external tariff of 3.6 percent. Although economic integration has reduced some trade barriers, it has raised others. The industries particularly affected by raised barriers are electronics, audio-visual products, telecommunications equipment, medical and veterinary equipment, and agricultural products.

Factor #2: Taxation
Score - Income taxation: 5- (Very high tax rates)
Score - Corporate taxation: 4-Stable (High tax rates)
Final Taxation Score: 5- (Very High tax rates)

France has a top income tax rate of 57 percent; the tax rate on the average income is 35 percent. The corporate tax is 33 1/3 percent. France also maintains a capital gains tax of 19 percent to 33 1/3 percent, a value-added tax of 18.6 percent, a business activity tax of up to 20 percent, and a social contributions tax of 16 percent to 45 percent.

Factor #3: Government Intervention in the Economy
Score: 3- (Moderate level of government intervention)

Government consumes 19.8 percent of France's GDP. The French government has monopoly control over several parts of the economy—such as energy generation and supply, rail transportation, postal services, telecommunications, and tobacco production and distribution—and attempts to privatize some of these and other industries have failed. Moreover, many state-owned companies dominate various industrial sectors, skewing pricing and adding inefficiency to the entire French economy. Some of these companies are in such basic industries as iron and steel, aluminum, coal mining, aerospace, nuclear energy, and many forms of transportation (except trucking).

Factor #4: Monetary Policy
Score: 1-Stable (Very low level of inflation)

France had a 2.9 percent average annual rate of inflation from 1985 to 1994. In 1995, inflation was 1.7 percent.

Factor #5: Capital Flows and Foreign Investment
Score: 3-Stable (Moderate barriers to foreign investment)

Non-French investors must receive approval from the Ministry of Economics before buying a French business. The Ministry of Economics can block any foreign investment whenever it thinks a sale would violate the "national interest."

Factor #6: Banking
Score: 3-Stable (Moderate level of restrictions on banking)

The French government controls two of France's largest banks, the Banque Nationale de Paris and Credit Lyonnais. This control severely reduces the availability of credit. Nevertheless, foreign investors are finding it easier to invest in French financial services and to open banks.

Factor #7: Wage and Price Controls
Score: 3-Stable (Moderate level of wage and price controls)

France has a long history of legalized monopolies in such areas of the economy as telecommunications, public infrastructure, electricity, and rail transportation. In 1987, however, the French government removed price controls, and most prices are now set by the market. Products still under price controls are pharmaceuticals, books, tobacco, agricultural products, coal, and steel. France maintains a minimum wage, and some wages are controlled by the government.

Factor #8: Property Rights
Score: 2-Stable (High level of protection of private property)

Property rights are uniform throughout France, and enforcement is adequate. There are some impediments to acquiring property, however. The French Constitution, for example, states that any company defined as a national public service or natural monopoly must pass into state ownership. The constitution specifically allows the state to nationalize companies that fall into this category. Nevertheless, both in practice and by global standards, the level of property protection is high.

Factor #9: Regulation
Score: 2-Stable (Low level of regulation)

The reforms established by the EU have made it easier to open a business in France. Obtaining a business license is relatively easy, though some hurdles still must be overcome. For example, a company must obtain a registration number from the district commercial court, and a copy of the business's lease and other documentation must accompany the application. France has made some progress in streamlining this cumbersome process by incorporating all the registration requirements into one office.

Factor #10: Black Market
Score: 1-Stable (Very low level of black market activity)

The principal areas of black market activity in France are gambling and the buying and selling of illegal weapons, drugs, and stolen merchandise.

Summary

France			Overall Score	2.50
Trade	2	Monetary Policy 1	Property Rights	2
Taxation	5	Foreign Investment 3	Regulation	2
Government Intervention	3	Banking 3	Black Market	1
		Wage and Prices 3		

GABON

The Central African country of Gabon gained its independence from France in 1960. With a population of slightly over 1 million people, and enjoying generous deposits of oil and such other valuable minerals as uranium and manganese, it is one of the most prosperous countries in sub-Saharan Africa. Gabon is a member of the French Franc Zone and maintains close ties with its former colonizer. This relationship has provided Gabon with a measure of economic and political stability unusual in Africa. In 1990, French troops stationed in Gabon quelled riots against the regime of President Omar Bongo, who retains tight control of political activity and the media. Economic liberalization has been moving very slowly, and Gabon's economy remains dominated by the government and presidential cronies.

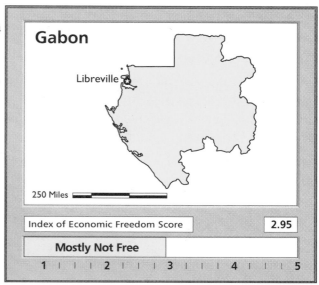

Factor #1: Trade Policy
Score: 5-Stable (Very high level of protectionism)

Gabon's average tariff rate is a high 30.7 percent,[124] and the tariff on electronics and vehicles is particularly high. In addition, there are quantitative import restrictions on sugar, vegetable oil, soap, mineral water, and cement; rice and wheat are subject to import licenses; there is customs fraud; and the customs process is slow and cumbersome. Import bans on mineral water, cement, soap, and other items recently have been lifted.

Factor #2: Taxation
Score - Income taxation: 5-Stable (Very high tax rates)
Score - Corporate taxation: 3-Stable (Moderate tax rates)
Final Taxation Score: 4.5-Stable (Very high tax rates)

The highest tax bracket in Gabon is 60.5 percent,[125] and the tax on the average income level is 15 percent. The corporate tax rate is 40 percent, and companies must pay 5 percent of their pre-tax profits into the Gabonese Investment Fund. Gabon also maintains a 40 percent capital gains tax and an 18 percent value-added tax, which was introduced in 1995 to replace various other taxes, including a business turnover tax. Small and medium businesses routinely receive tax holidays.

---

124   Based on 1993 figures.

125   Includes a 5.5 percent supplementary tax.

Factor #3: Government Intervention in the Economy
Score: 3-Stable (Moderate level of government intervention)

Government consumes 12.6 percent of Gabon's GDP, and the public sector remains bloated despite retrenchment efforts. Although some government-controlled enterprises have been liquidated, there has been little privatization of larger state-owned companies.

Factor #4: Monetary Policy
Score: 1-Stable (Very low level of inflation)

Gabon's average annual rate of inflation between 1985 and 1994 was 3.2 percent. Under the Franc Zone Mechanism, Gabon exercises only limited control over its monetary policies; instead, the Bank of France exerts tight control over Gabon's money supply. Inflation currently runs at some 10 percent.

Factor #5: Capital Flows and Foreign Investment
Score: 2-Stable (Low barriers to foreign investment)

A 1989 rewrite of the investment code liberalized conditions for foreign business. Government participation in investment is no longer required. A requirement that all private companies established in Gabon contribute 10 percent of their shares to the government was repealed in 1994. Foreign investors face only minimal restrictions in most areas, and the government has allowed foreign-owned operations to compete with local businesses. Very few areas are off-limits to foreign investors, but the government dominates the most lucrative sectors of the marketplace. Foreign investors encounter protracted delays in the investment approval process. There are no free trade zones in Gabon, but tax holidays for certain investors are available.

Factor #6: Banking
Score: 2-Stable (Low level of restrictions on banking)

Gabon has a sophisticated banking system—comprised primarily of competitive foreign banks—over which the government exercises little control. According to the U.S. Department of Commerce, "The local banking system, dominated by French and other foreign banks, is relatively sophisticated and offers most corporate banking services, or can procure them in Europe."[126]

Factor #7: Wage and Price Controls
Score: 3-Stable (Moderate level of wage and price controls)

Price controls are imposed on 17 goods and most services, including insurance and construction. A relatively high minimum wage has attracted many unskilled immigrants from neighboring African countries. The minimum wage for non-Gabonese is 80 percent of what Gabonese workers must be paid.

---

126   U.S. Department of Commerce, *Country Commercial Guide*, 1996.

Factor #8: Property Rights
Score: 3-Stable (Moderate level of protection of private property)

Expropriation of foreign property in Gabon is not likely. There have been charges, however, that government officials have used coercion to obtain control of successful businesses. Property also is threatened by ethnic clashes, by a lack of democratic progress, and by the growing resentment of foreign business. The courts are not entirely independent.

Factor #9: Regulation
Score: 3- Stable (Moderate level of regulation)

Although the bureaucracy is generally effective, lengthy delays in the processing of some business investments and expansions are common, corruption is present, and regulations make the business environment increasingly complicated. Moreover, the success of Gabonese enterprises depends largely on their political connections. A "Gabonization" program instituted in 1992 forces employers to decrease the number of foreigners in their workforce. This has led to inefficiency.

Factor #10: Black Market
Score: 3-Stable (Moderate level of black market activity)

The level of government control of and influence over economic activity in Gabon encourages black market activity, and the country's high tariffs on luxury goods and automobiles encourage smuggling.

Summary

Gabon				Overall Score	2.95
Trade	5	Monetary Policy	1	Property Rights	3
Taxation	4.5	Foreign Investment	2	Regulation	3
Government Intervention	3	Banking	2	Black Market	3
		Wage and Prices	3		

THE GAMBIA

The West African Republic of the Gambia gained its independence from the United Kingdom in 1965. Agriculture makes up 20 percent of the Gambia's GDP, with 12 percent of GDP produced by industry. After independence, the Gambia established a multi-party system with elections every five years. From then until 1994, when the government was overthrown by a military coup, the country was ruled continuously by President Dawda Kairaba Jawara, who was re-elected five times. Today, because of its deteriorating political and economic conditions, the Gambia remains on the travel advisory list of the U.S. Department of State.

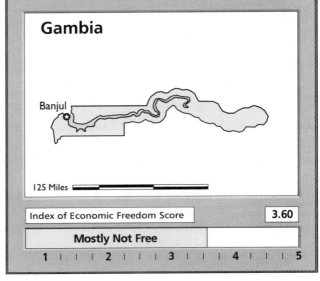

Gambia

Banjul

125 Miles

| Index of Economic Freedom Score | 3.60 |

Mostly Not Free

1 | | | 2 | | | 3 | | | 4 | | | 5

Factor #1: Trade Policy

Score: 4-Stable (High level of protectionism)

The Gambia's average tariff rate is 13.5 percent. Import bans apply mainly to over-the-counter medicines.

Factor #2: Taxation

Score - Income taxation: 4-Stable (High tax rates)
Score - Corporate taxation: 4-Stable (High tax rates)
Final Taxation Score: 4-Stable (High tax rates)

Total government revenues represent about 23 percent of the Gambia's GDP, higher than in most other countries in sub-Saharan Africa.[127]

Factor #3: Government Intervention in the Economy

Score: 3-Stable (Moderate level of government intervention)

The Gambia's government consumes about 18 percent of GDP, and most of the country's GDP is generated by the public sector. Many companies are government-owned.

Factor #4: Monetary Policy

Score: 2-Stable (Low level of inflation)

The Gambia had an average annual inflation rate of 10.9 percent from 1985 to 1994. Inflation rates are not available for 1995.

---

127   Tax information is not available for the Gambia.

Factor #5: Capital Flows and Foreign Investment
Score: 4-Stable (High barriers to foreign investment)

The Gambia provides equal treatment for domestic and foreign firms and actively seeks foreign investment. Investments, however, must be approved by the government on a case-by-case basis.

Factor #6: Banking
Score: 4-Stable (High level of restrictions on banking)

The banking system in the Gambia is both heavily controlled by the government and severely underdeveloped.

Factor #7: Wage and Price Controls
Score: 4-Stable (High level of wage and price controls)

Wages and prices in the Gambia sometimes are affected significantly by the large public sector, through heavy government subsidies that influence prices, and by import substitution policies.

Factor #8: Property Rights
Score: 2-Stable (High level of protection of private property)

The legal system in the Gambia is efficient, fair, and independent of the government. It also is overburdened at times with a backlog of unresolved cases, however, and judgments can take several years.

Factor #9: Regulation
Score: 4-Stable (High level of regulation)

Establishing a business in the Gambia is difficult because of corruption in the government bureaucracy. Bribery and embezzlement are prevalent among government officials responsible for collecting fees.

Factor #10: Black Market
Score: 5-Stable (Very high level of black market activity)

The Gambia's black market is large. Most of this activity occurs in smuggled consumer goods, labor, and pirated intellectual property.

Summary

Gambia				Overall Score	3.60
Trade	4	Monetary Policy	2	Property Rights	2
Taxation	4	Foreign Investment	4	Regulation	4
Government Intervention	3	Banking	4	Black Market	5
		Wage and Prices	4		

GEORGIA

A small state on the Black Sea, Georgia was independent from 1918 to 1921, at which time it was conquered by Soviet Russia. It has developed an agricultural sector, including citrus, as well as resorts, light industry, and some high-tech enterprises. Ethnic unrest and two civil wars since it gained independence in 1991 have hampered Georgia's progress toward a free market. The country has been plagued by hyperinflation and by an industrial and manufacturing decline. Although Georgia has privatized many state-owned industries, opened its market to imports and foreign investment, and established a commercial code, it is far from reaching a stabilized free-market economic system.

Georgia

Tbilisi

250 Miles

Index of Economic Freedom Score	3.85
Mostly Not Free	

1 | | | 2 | | | 3 | | | 4 | | | 5

Factor #1: Trade Policy

Score: 3-Stable (Moderate level of protectionism)

Georgia has an average tariff rate of about 8 percent. Although there are no import bans, some government licenses are required for particular goods like medical equipment. Georgia also maintains some non-tariff barriers in the form of import quotas.

Factor #2: Taxation

Score - Income taxation: 2-Stable (Low tax rates)
Score - Corporate taxation: 2-Stable (Low tax rates)
Final Taxation Score: 2.5-Stable (Moderate tax rates)

Georgia's top income tax rate is 20 percent, and the average taxpayer is in the 15 percent bracket. The top marginal corporate tax rate is 20 percent. Georgia also maintains several other taxes, such as a 20 percent value-added tax. Tax collection is hampered by an inefficient bureaucracy.

Factor #3: Government Intervention in the Economy

Score: 4-Stable (High level of government Intervention)

Georgia's government consumes over 30 percent of GDP; the state-owned sector, however, accounts for about 75 percent of the country's GDP.

Factor #4: Monetary Policy

Score: 5-Stable (Very high level of inflation)

Georgia suffers from chronic inflation, with prices increasing roughly 60 percent a month, for example, from 1993 to 1994. This is the result primarily of subsidies and loans to cover the costs of money-losing state-owned industries.

Factor #5: Capital Flows and Foreign Investment

Score: 3-Stable (Moderate barriers to foreign investment)

Georgia has few official restrictions on investments. Most industries are open to foreign investment, although there are problems in the form of a lack of legal protection, an inefficient and bloated bureaucracy, and the collapse of many state businesses. Laws concerning private ownership of land often are confusing and unclear.

Factor #6: Banking

Score: 4-Stable (High level of restrictions on banking)

The banking system in Georgia is in a complete shambles. The domestic banking system is heavily controlled by the government, and many government-owned banks are both inefficient and headed by officials who lack common business knowledge.

Factor #7: Wage and Price Controls

Score: 4-Stable (High level of wage and price controls)

Wages and prices in Georgia sometimes are set by the government. Government subsidies to state-owned industries cause goods to be sold at artificially low prices, and the government establishes prices for electricity, bread, and some municipal services.

Factor #8: Property Rights

Score: 4-Stable (Low level of protection of private property)

Both the lack of effective government control over parts of Georgia's territory and the existence of warlords in certain areas of the country hamper protection of private property. Georgia has yet to establish a fully functional court system and a legal environment conducive to the protection of private property. Expropriation is possible.

Factor #9: Regulation

Score: 4-Stable (High level of regulation)

Establishing a business in Georgia is often difficult, especially if the business competes directly with a state-owned company. Regulations are applied unevenly in most cases, and corruption often is present. The U.S. Department of Commerce has identified "the high level of crime and corruption" and "remnants of central planning and bureaucracy" as additional deterrents to business.[128]

Factor #10: Black Market

Score: 5-Stable (Very high level of black market activity)

Some estimates indicate that Georgia's black market is equal to its formal market. Such activities as pirated computer software, compact discs, and videos, as well as labor, are provided in the informal sector. Smuggling from neighboring Turkey, Russia, Armenia, and Azerbaijan is becoming more prevalent.

---

128   U.S. Department of Commerce, *Country Commercial Guide*, 1996.

Summary

Georgia				Overall Score	3.85
Trade	3	Monetary Policy	5	Property Rights	4
Taxation	2.5	Foreign Investment	3	Regulation	4
Government Intervention	4	Banking	4	Black Market	5
		Wage and Prices	4		

GERMANY

ermany is the largest economic power in the European Union (EU). Nevertheless, since reunification with East Germany, the Federal Republic has experienced a high unemployment rate of around 10 percent per year. To ease the pain of reunification, Germany increased social spending, which accounts for some 48 percent of total government expenditure.[129] Now, with unemployment having reached 10 percent, the government is considering several deregulatory and tax-cutting measures to stimulate the economy. At the same time, however, the pace of its privatization program has slowed.

| Germany |
| Berlin |
| 250 Miles |

| Index of Economic Freedom Score | 2.20 |
| Mostly Free | |
| 1   2   3   4   5 |

Factor #1: Trade Policy
Score: 2-Stable (Low level of protectionism)

Germany maintains an average tariff rate of about 5 percent. It also maintains some non-tariff barriers, however, such as overbearing consumer regulations on the labeling and testing of products. According to the U.S. Department of State, "Germany's regulations and bureaucratic procedures can prove a baffling maze, blunting the enthusiasm of U.S. exporters.... [G]overnment regulation does offer a degree of protection to German suppliers."[130] Nevertheless, by global standards, Germany's level of protectionism is low.

Factor #2: Taxation
Score - Income taxation: 5-Stable (Very high tax rates)
Score - Corporate taxation: 4-Stable (High tax rates)
Final Taxation Score: 5-Stable (Very high tax rates)

Germany's taxes remain among the highest in both the industrialized world and the EU. The top income tax bracket is 53 percent,[131] and the tax on the average income level is over 35 percent. The top corporate tax rate is 45 percent; but corporations also pay a 7.5 percent "surcharge," and municipality taxes on profits can increase the total tax rate to over 70 percent. Germany also has a 45 percent capital gains tax; a 15 percent value-added tax; and land, property, and real estate taxes.

---

129   See Lawrence T. Di Rita and Bryan T. Johnson, "An Agenda for Leadership: The G–7 Summit in Naples," Heritage Foundation *Talking Points*, July 5, 1994.

130   State Department Report, 1996, p. 188.

131   Some economists argue that the actual tax rates in Germany are much higher. Some middle-income Germans have reported paying well above 70 percent of their income. For purposes of the *Index*, however, the official, published top income tax rate of 53 percent is used.

Factor #3: Government Intervention in the Economy
Score: 3- (Moderate level of government intervention)

Germany's government consumed 19.6 percent of GDP in 1995. After reunification, the government extended its generous social welfare system to the former East Germany. It also expanded subsidies for private investment. These hefty expenditures have increased the government's role in the economy. The German government continues to be heavily involved in the economy, mainly through local and state government regulations. Despite recent attempts to privatize sections of the economy, little progress has been made. For example, the postal and telephone systems remain largely government-owned (although the telephone system is being privatized), and the government still owns portions of the automobile and transportation industries. Thus, because privatization has slowed and the government continues to own significant sectors of the economy, Germany's score is worse this year.

Factor #4: Monetary Policy
Score: 1-Stable (Very low level of inflation)

Germany's rate of inflation has been among the lowest in the world: an average of 2.9 percent annually from 1985 to 1994, as well as 1.8 percent in 1995 and about 1.6 percent during the first quarter of 1996.

Factor #5: Capital Flows and Foreign Investment
Score: 2-Stable (Low barriers to foreign investment)

Germany welcomes foreign investment and is one of the few countries that impose no permanent currency or administrative controls on foreign investments. It does restrict, however, investments in insurance, telecommunications, and other services. Some government regulations—such as those regulating monopolies and competition—also present barriers to investment.

Factor #6: Banking
Score: 2-Stable (Low level of restrictions on banking)

Germany is a world financial center and banking powerhouse. The U.S. Department of State reports that Germany's banking system is becoming more open to foreigners. Nevertheless, Germany still maintains some restrictions on foreign banks. All foreign banks, for example, must obtain a license to do business in Germany. This process can take up to four months, and the German bureaucracy can be cumbersome, acting as a barrier to banks that want to establish themselves quickly.

Factor #7: Wage and Price Controls
Score: 2-Stable (Low level of wage and price controls)

Germany's free enterprise system is based on market-set prices and wages. Although wages are set largely by the market, however, the government still maintains a Federal Cartel Office (FCO) to monitor prices on specific goods and services. With the exception of rents and some agricultural goods, there are virtually no price controls in Germany.

Factor #8: Property Rights
Score: 1-Stable (Very high level of protection of private property)

Germany's economy, based on the private ownership of property, is undergoing extensive privatization, especially in the former East Germany. The government is pursuing privatization of state-owned property, and the chances of expropriation are virtually nonexistent. Germany's court system provides a very high level of property protection; it is efficient and available for all types of dispute resolution.

Factor #9: Regulation
Score: 3-Stable (Moderate level of regulation)

Establishing a business in Germany is relatively easy, with few or no barriers to new business creation. All a new business must do is notify the local economic supervisory office, which supplies a certificate. There is no corruption, and regulations are applied evenly and consistently. Germany's employment, product safety, and environmental laws, however, impose some burdens on business. The government also regulates business by mandating certain social benefits, such as mandatory occupational safety and health insurance. The U.S. Department of State reports that Germany has a "regulatory system which discourages new entrants especially in the services sector."[132]

Factor #10: Black Market
Score: 1-Stable (Very low level of black market activity)

Black markets in Germany involve such illegal activities as drugs and guns. Prostitution is legal, as are some forms of gambling. Moreover, Germany's protection of intellectual property is among the best in the world, leaving only a negligible black market in pirated materials.

Summary

Germany					Overall Score	2.20
Trade	2	Monetary Policy	1	Property Rights	1
Taxation	5	Foreign Investment	2	Regulation	3
Government Intervention	3	Banking	2	Black Market	1
		Wage and Prices	2		

---

132 State Department Report, 1996, p. 187.

GHANA

The West African country of Ghana gained its independence from Great Britain in 1957, and Prime Minister Kwame Nkrumah quickly transformed Ghana into a one-party socialist state. In 1992, Flight Lieutenant J. J. Rawlings legalized political parties and won Ghana's presidential election (even though the fairness of the election has been questioned). Today, political tensions are rising because of concerns over the government's allegedly undemocratic practices. An economic liberalization program begun by Rawlings has improved what was a collapsing socialist economy. Annual growth has averaged around 4 percent since 1992, and the government recently has reduced tariffs. At the same time, however, the government also has lost fiscal discipline; the money supply has ballooned to pay for government wage increases and subsidies to inefficient state enterprises.

Ghana

Accra

250 Miles

| Index of Economic Freedom Score | 3.20 |

Mostly Not Free

1   2   3   4   5

Factor #1: Trade

Score: 4+ (High level of protectionism)

Ghana's average tariff rate is a high 12.5 percent.[133] Although most goods do not require licenses, handling and customs delays are frequent.

Factor #2: Taxation

Score - Income taxation: 2-Stable (Low tax rates)
Score - Corporate taxation: 3-Stable (Moderate tax rates)
Final Taxation Score: 3-Stable (Moderate tax rates)

Ghana has a progressive income tax system with a top bracket of 35 percent; the average taxpayer falls within the 5 percent bracket. Ghana taxes corporate profits at a top rate of 35 percent. In addition, Ghana has a 5 percent capital gains tax and a gift tax that ranges from 0 percent to 15 percent.

Factor #3: Government Intervention in the Economy

Score: 3-Stable (Moderate level of government intervention)

Government consumes 12 percent of Ghana's GDP,[134] and state-owned enterprises dominate many industrial sectors, including the petroleum, steel, diamond, timber marketing, retail, and construction industries. Ghana's public sector continues to be one

---

133   Based on total taxes on international trade as a percentage of total imports; from International Monetary Fund, *Government Financial Statistics 1995*.

134   World Bank, *World Development Report 1996*.

of the largest in sub-Saharan Africa. Organized labor generally opposes the government's privatization program, which has stalled.

Factor #4: Monetary Policy
Score: 4-Stable (High level of inflation)

Ghana's average rate of inflation from 1985 to 1994 was 28.4 percent. In 1995, inflation was 24.9 percent.

Factor #5: Capital Flows and Foreign Investment
Score: 3-Stable (Moderate barriers to foreign investment)

In 1992, the government of Ghana developed a new investment code that eased restrictions on private-sector investment. Some investment incentives exist, including exemptions from import duties on specified products. Despite these liberalizing measures, however, restrictions on foreign investment remain in place. Twenty economic activities are either closed to foreign investors or subject to a high minimum investment, and wholly owned foreign firms must meet a $200,000 investment minimum. An inefficient and corrupt bureaucracy creates considerable formal barriers to potential foreign investment.

Factor #6: Banking
Score: 3-Stable (Moderate level of restrictions on banking)

Five private commercial and investment banks are chartered in Ghana, and there is a considerable degree of banking competition. Interest rate controls have been abolished by the central bank, which otherwise maintains tight control over financial activities. There is a government monopoly on personal insurance. Several state-owned banks are being divested from government control. Ghana's central bank is influenced heavily by the government, however, and public-sector borrowing crowds out the private sector.

Factor #7: Wage and Price Controls
Score: 2-Stable (Low level of wage and price controls)

Although employers and workers generally are encouraged to negotiate wages and working conditions, Ghana also has a minimum wage. The government also maintains some food subsidies.

Factor #8: Property Rights
Score: 3-Stable (Moderate level of protection of private property)

Ghana's investment code guarantees private property against expropriation, which remains unlikely. Domestically owned property is less secure than foreign-owned property, however; during the past several years, there have been some cases of arbitrary seizure of domestic commercial property. There is no central land registry.

Factor #9: Regulation
Score: 4-Stable (High level of regulation)

Private-sector investors face a burdensome licensing process, and regulations require foreign firms to hire local employees. Businesses also face other problems, such as the need to gain bureaucratic approval for acquiring and selling land. Bureaucratic inertia and politically inspired administrative judgments reduce competition among domestic firms.

Factor #10: Black Market

Score: 2-Stable (Low level of black market activity)

The dismantling of price controls has reduced the number of Ghana's once-legion "economic criminals" and removed a large incentive to engage in black market activity. At the same time, however, a recently imposed increase in the tariff on used clothes has encouraged smuggling.

Summary

Ghana				Overall Score	3.20
Trade	5	Monetary Policy	4	Property Rights	3
Taxation	3	Foreign Investment	3	Regulation	4
Government Intervention	3	Banking	3	Black Market	2
		Wage and Prices	2		

GREECE

Greece won its independence from the Ottoman Empire in 1827 and established a monarchy in 1833. From 1941 until 1944, during World War II, Greece was occupied by Germany. In 1946, after the war, a Soviet-backed communist attempt to take over the country led to a civil war in which many lives were lost. Greece emerged from the civil war as a pro-Western democracy and joined the North Atlantic Treaty Organization in 1952. It also has been involved in a bitter standoff with Turkey over the island of Cyprus. Since joining the European Community in 1981, Greece has worked to bring its economy in line with those of the other European democracies. Four years of free-market economic reform undertaken by the conservative government of Prime Minister Constantine Mitsotakis came to an end in October 1993 when Mitsotakis lost his reelection bid to Andreas Papandreou, the Socialist leader who was Prime Minister from 1981 to 1989. Taxes recently have been increased.

Index of Economic Freedom Score — 2.85

Mostly Free

1 | | | 2 | | | 3 | | | 4 | | | 5

Factor #1: Trade Policy

Score: 2-Stable (Low level of protectionism)

Greece has a low average tariff rate of 3.6 percent. As a member of the European Union (EU), it must conform to EU trade standards and practices. In addition to common EU trade restrictions, Greece maintains nationality requirements on a variety of services such as those provided by lawyers, architects, and accountants. This severely restricts imported services.

Factor #2: Taxation

Score - Income taxation: 2-Stable (Low tax rates)
Score - Corporate taxation: 4- (high tax rates)
Final Taxation Score: 3.5- (High tax rates)

Greece's top income tax rate is 45 percent, and the average income level is taxed at 5 percent. The top corporate income tax is 40 percent. Greece also has a 35 percent capital gains tax and an 18 percent value-added tax.

Factor #3: Government Intervention in the Economy

Score: 3-Stable (Moderate level of government intervention)

Government consumption of GDP in Greece is 14.1 percent and falling. State-owned industries, however, make up a significant portion of the economy.

Factor #4: Monetary Policy
Score: 3-Stable (Moderate level of inflation)

Greece had an average annual inflation rate of 15.5 percent from 1985 to 1994. In 1995, the rate of inflation decreased to 9.3 percent.

Factor #5: Capital Flows and Foreign Investment
Score: 2-Stable (Low barriers to foreign investment)

Greece has an open foreign investment code that invites many investments. There are, however, some restrictions—especially with regard to banks—that prevent 100 percent foreign ownership.

Factor #6: Banking
Score: 4-Stable (High level of restrictions on banking)

Greece does not permit non-EU members to own more than 40 percent of its state-owned banks. The government still owns a significant number of banks.

Factor #7: Wage and Price Controls
Score: 3-Stable (Moderate level of wage and price controls)

Some prices, including those for bread, freight charges, motor vehicle insurance, pharmaceuticals, and telephone service, are set by the government. The government recently imposed price controls on fuel.

Factor #8: Property Rights
Score: 2-Stable (High level of protection of private property)

Property expropriation in Greece is unlikely. Property receives adequate protection from the courts.

Factor #9: Regulation
Factor Score: 3-Stable (Moderate level of regulation)

Greece is highly bureaucratic, and many government regulations are burdensome.

Factor #10: Black Market
Score: 3-Stable (Moderate level of black market activity)

Greece is a popular place for smuggling, especially in recorded music and videos.

Summary

Greece				Overall Score	2.85
Trade	2	Monetary Policy	3	Property Rights	2
Taxation	3.5	Foreign Investment	2	Regulation	3
Government Intervention	3	Banking	4	Black Market	3
		Wage and Prices	3		

GUATEMALA

The Central American country of Guatemala gained its independence from Spain in 1821, after which time it underwent decades of civil unrest and war. In 1985, a democratically elected government began to reform the economy by reducing the state's role in the country's economic life. This process has faltered in the 1990s, leaving the country with a reform-resistant legislature. In the resultant chaos, however, the private sector has managed to flourish. The government sector accounts for only 6 percent of GDP. In January 1996, Alvaro Arzu was elected president. Shortly after his inauguration, Arzu nominated several business leaders to cabinet-level and other government positions. His government is pursuing a new economic liberalization program. Although the government recently has increased taxes, it also has reduced its regulation of banking.

Guatemala

250 Miles

| Index of Economic Freedom Score | 2.80 |

Mostly Free

1   2   3   4   5

Factor #1: Trade Policy

Score: 3-Stable (Moderate level of protectionism)

Guatemala has an average tariff rate of 9 percent. Non-tariff barriers take the form of arbitrary application of customs procedures and red tape in the customs agency. In addition, there are some restrictions on poultry imports.

Factor #2: Taxation

Score - Income taxation: 3- (Moderate tax rates)
Score - Corporate taxation: 2-Stable (Low tax rates)
Final Taxation Score: 3- (Moderate tax rates)

Guatemala's top tax rate is 30 percent, up from 25 percent in 1995, and the average income level is taxed at 15 percent. The top corporate income tax is 30 percent. Guatemala also has a 15 percent capital gains tax, a 10 percent value-added tax, and a land tax.

Factor #3: Government Intervention in the Economy

Score: 1-Stable (Very low level of government intervention)

Government consumes 6 percent of Guatemala's GDP. The only remaining state-owned sectors to be privatized are the telecommunications, electricity, and railways industries.

Factor #4: Monetary Policy

Score: 3-Stable (Moderate level of inflation)

From 1985 to 1994, Guatemala's average annual inflation rate was 19.5 percent. In 1995, inflation was 8 percent.

Factor #5: Capital Flows and Foreign Investment
Score: 3-Stable (Moderate barriers to foreign investment)

Foreign investment in Guatemala is relatively welcome, although restrictions are imposed on investment in utilities and such domestic industries as fishing, mining, and forestry. Investments in banks, auditing, and insurance services also are subject to some restrictions.

Factor #6: Banking
Score: 2+ (Low level of restrictions on banking)

The government recently has liberalized the banking sector, allowing more foreign participation. Today, there are 31 foreign banks in Guatemala, up from 21 in 1993. According to the U.S. Department of Commerce, "Government intervention in the financial sector is limited to implementation of monetary policy and to prudential regulation of the banks, investment firms, bonded warehouses and exchange houses. Credit is not rationed or otherwise directed by the government...."[135]

Factor #7: Wage and Price Controls
Score: 3-Stable (Moderate level of wage and price controls)

Guatemala has a minimum wage law. The government imposes no official price controls, but does use "price bands" for some agricultural goods. A "price band" defines the price level of a given product; if the price rises above this level, the government may step in to impose a lower price. The effect, therefore, often is to control prices.

Factor #8: Property Rights
Score: 3-Stable (Moderate level of protection of private property)

Property is not subject to expropriation in Guatemala, and no property has been expropriated since the 1950s. There are restrictions on property ownership, however, particularly with respect to foreigners who wish to own property adjoining rivers or the ocean. Moreover, the criminal code often includes ineffective penalties on those who violate property rights, especially intellectual property rights.

Factor #9: Regulation
Score: 4-Stable (High level of regulation)

Guatemala's regulations are ambiguous, leaving their interpretation to capricious government bureaucrats who apply them arbitrarily. "Bureaucratic hurdles are common for both domestic and foreign companies wishing to operate in Guatemala." reports the U.S. Department of Commerce. "Not infrequently, companies are subject to ambiguous requirements, applied inconsistently by different government agencies. Regulations— where they exist—often contain few explicit criteria for the government decision maker, creating uncertainty. Public participation in the promulgation of regulations is rare and there is no consistent judicial review of administrative rule making."[136]

---

135   U.S. Department of Commerce, *Country Commercial Guide,* 1996.

136   *Ibid.*

Factor #10: Black Market
Score: 3-Stable (Moderate level of black market activity)

Guatemala provides no effective protection for intellectual property. As a result, there is much black market activity in this area. According to the U.S. Department of Commerce, "Guatemalan law does not provide for sufficient protection against counter-feiters nor does it afford adequate protection for internationally famous trademarks. The right to exclusive use of a trademark, for instance, is granted to whomever happens to file first to register the trademark. There is no requirement for use nor any cancellation process for nonusage. As a result, foreign firms whose trademark has been registered by another party in Guatemala have often had to pay royalties to that party."[137]

Summary

Guatemala		Overall Score	2.80

Guatemala				Overall Score	2.80
Trade	3	Monetary Policy	3	Property Rights	3
Taxation	3	Foreign Investment	3	Regulation	4
Government Intervention	1	Banking	2	Black Market	3
		Wage and Prices	3		

---

137 *Ibid.*

GUINEA

The West African country of Guinea was colonized by France in 1891 and became independent in 1958. After independence, the government took control of the economy and established a socialist state. With abundant natural resources, Guinea could have benefited from a free market; instead, its state-controlled economy stagnated. In 1990, a new constitution was adopted, allowing for limited political and economic reforms. Opposition parties were legalized in 1992, and a flawed presidential vote was held in 1993. Foreign aid donors have been disappointed with Guinea's slow progress in economic reform, although they continue to provide it with considerable amounts of aid. Private property in Guinea has received less legal protection recently than in past years.

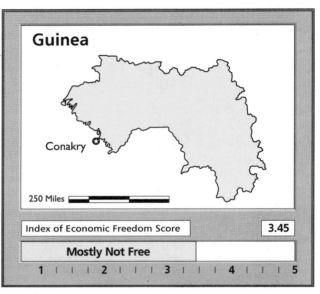

Guinea	
Conakry	
250 Miles	

Index of Economic Freedom Score	3.45
Mostly Not Free	

1   2   3   4   5

Factor #1: Trade Policy
Score: 5-Stable (Very high level of protectionism)

Guinea has a flat tariff rate of 33 percent for almost all imports.[138] Licenses are required for all "restricted goods," which include cement, rice, wheat flour, and other agricultural products. Some imports require special authorization from the central bank.

Factor #2: Taxation
Score - Income taxation: 5-Stable (Very high tax rates)
Score - Corporate taxation: 3-Stable (Moderate tax rates)
Final Taxation Score: 4.5-Stable (Very high tax rates)

Guinea's top income tax rate is 40 percent, and the average income level is taxed at 25 percent. The top corporate tax rate is 35 percent. Guinea also has a 35 percent capital gains tax.

Factor #3: Government Intervention in the Economy
Score: 2-Stable (Low level of government intervention)

Government consumes 9 percent of Guinea's GDP. In an attempt to decrease its swollen government, Guinea has been planning to privatize schools and to return doctors to the private sector by ending the state-supplied health care system. The pace of privatization has been slow, however, and Guinea still has a large state-owned sector.

---

138   U.S. Department of Commerce, *Country Commercial Guide, 1996.*

Factor #4: Monetary Policy
Score: 3-Stable (Moderate level of inflation)

From 1985 to 1994, Guinea's average annual rate of inflation was 18.5 percent. In 1995, the inflation rate was reduced to about 3.5 percent.

Factor #5: Capital Flows and Foreign Investment
Score: 3-Stable (Moderate barriers to foreign investment)

Guinea has been opening its economy to foreign investment since 1990 and has adopted an investment code based on a system used by the Ivory Coast, which allows investments in many industrial sectors. In 1992, the government allowed 100 percent private participation in the mining sector, and the telecommunications sector was opened partially to private participation. There is one wholly foreign-owned mining venture, and new investment is screened carefully.

Factor #6: Banking
Score: 2-Stable (Low level of restrictions on banking)

There are few restrictions on banks in Guinea. Most are in private hands as a result of a massive privatization of the banking industry in the late 1980s and early 1990s. Foreign banks are welcome, and six commercial banks currently are operating in the country. The government is considering legislation to tighten lending regulations, raise reserve requirements, and tighten borrower qualifications.

Factor #7: Wage and Price Controls
Score: 2-Stable (Low level of wage and price controls)

Price controls have been removed on most items, but remain on some foodstuffs. The Ministry of Trade reserves the right to introduce emergency price control measures. There is no minimum wage.

Factor #8: Property Rights
Score: 4- (Low level of protection of private property)

Property is not completely secure in Guinea. Government corruption, an inefficient judiciary, and poor law enforcement all prevent the full legal protection of property. Crime also remains a threat. In addition, the land tenure system established in 1992 has not been administered successfully, and the government has "reclaimed" properties acquired by Guineans through privatization. According to the U.S. Department of Commerce, "Expatriate business sources indicate that Guinea's court system does not guarantee fair and transparent administration of the law and offers little protection to expatriate business persons. Finally, corruption is rampant and has a negative impact on even the most straightforward business transactions."[139]

Factor #9: Regulation
Score: 4-Stable (High level of regulation)

Although the government has taken steps to remove its interference in private business, a huge bureaucracy remains an impediment to free enterprise. Registering a

---

139 *Ibid.*

business is relatively easy, but corruption exists, and the most straightforward business transaction can be problematic. An employer's right to hire and fire is severely constrained, and regulations are manipulated occasionally to advance the personal interests of the regulators. Hiring expatriate workers, however, is not as troublesome in Guinea as it is in many other African countries.

Factor #10: Black Market
Score: 5-Stable (Very high level of black market activity)

Guinea has a large black market, especially in luxury goods that face a 40 percent tariff rate. Disorder on Guinea's borders with Liberia and Sierra Leone encourages smuggling, there is little if any judicial protection of intellectual property, and piracy remains rampant. "Enforcement of protection of intellectual property rights...is left to the still reforming Guinean court system," reports the U.S. Department of Commerce. "We know of no intellectual property case yet treated by the court system. There are no specific mechanisms in place to protect proprietary information or trade secrets."[140]

Summary

Guinea				Overall Score	3.45
Trade	5	Monetary Policy	3	Property Rights	4
Taxation	4.5	Foreign Investment	3	Regulation	4
Government Intervention	2	Banking	2	Black Market	5
		Wage and Prices	2		

---

140 *Ibid.*

GUYANA

The South American country of Guyana won its independence from the United Kingdom in 1966. Since then, it has followed a mainly socialist economic course, and today is among the world's poorest countries. The government is controlled by the People's Progressive Party. Although Guyana's past economic policies seriously impeded economic growth, since 1992 the government has made sweeping reforms aimed at attracting foreign investment by relying on the free market. Recently, Guyana has reduced its government consumption of GDP by limiting the size of its public sector, reforming its banking industry, and cutting back on some black market activities. The country's privatization program has slowed, however, and Guyana's government has failed to sell off significant sectors of the economy.

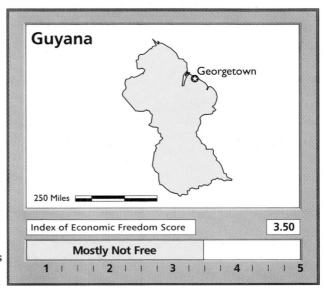

Guyana

Georgetown

250 Miles

| Index of Economic Freedom Score | 3.50 |

Mostly Not Free

1 2 3 4 5

Factor #1: Trade Policy
Score: 4-Stable (High level of protectionism)

Despite easing formal barriers to trade, Guyana's tariffs still range from 0 percent to 40 percent. Even though these rates will be reduced to 0 percent to 20 percent by 1998, government paperwork, corruption, and informal obstacles remain substantial barriers to trade. Import licenses are required for fruit, meat, and poultry.[141]

Factor #2: Taxation
Score - Income taxation: 3-Stable (Moderate tax rates)
Score - Corporate taxation: 4-Stable (High tax rates)
Final Taxation Score: 4-Stable (High tax rates)

Guyana's tax on income is a flat 33.3 percent, and its top corporate tax rate is 45 percent.[142] Guyana also has a 20 percent capital gains tax and a property tax.

Factor #3: Government intervention in the Economy
Score: 3- (Moderate level of government intervention)

Guyana's central government consumes about 12.8 percent of GDP. Its privatization program, however, has not met the expectations of investors. The government remains heavily involved in banking, certain utilities such as electrical and energy generation, transportation, and some agriculture.

141   The average tariff rate was not available.

142   This is the rate that applies to profits of commercial companies.

Factor #4: Monetary Policy
Score: 5-Stable (Very high level of inflation)

Guyana's average annual rate of inflation from 1985 to 1994 was 56.4 percent. In 1995, the inflation rate was 9 percent.

Factor #5: Capital Flows and Foreign Investment
Score: 3-Stable (Moderate barriers to foreign investment)

There are few restrictions on foreign investment in Guyana, although investors are concerned about civil unrest, crime, and corruption.

Factor #6: Banking
Score: 3-Stable (Moderate level of restrictions on banking)

Guyana's banking system is becoming more competitive. The government still owns portions of some banks, but plans are underway to divest its holdings.

Factor #7: Wage and Price Controls
Score: 2-Stable (Low level of wage and price controls)

Guyana maintains both a minimum wage and price controls on electricity rates.

Factor #8: Property Rights
Score: 3-Stable (Moderate level of protection of private property)

Private property is guaranteed and receives legal protection. Several Western firms are engaged in legal battles with the government over contracts, however, and the judicial system often is slow and inefficient.

Factor #9: Regulation
Score: 4-Stable (High level of regulation)

Some sectors, such as utilities and other state-owned industries, are highly regulated, and corruption often hinders the ability of companies in these sectors to do business. The U.S. Department of Commerce reports that "Attempts to reform bureaucratic procedures have not succeeded in limiting red tape: for example, businesses find that clearing shipments through customs is a long and tedious process."[143]

Factor #10: Black Market
Score: 4-Stable (High level of black market activity)

Guyana has a rather large black market, mainly because of trademark and copyright infringement and the massive pirating of video, audio recordings, and computer software. According to the U.S. Department of Commerce, "there is so far essentially no enforcement of laws regarding intellectual property rights. Although some local television operators have signed agreements with U.S. broadcast and cable firms for the right to air programs, the pirating of satellite signals still takes place with impunity. A U.S. fast food franchise which opened in April 1994 has also failed so far to prevent a local outlet from using its trademark name."[144]

---

143   U.S. Department of Commerce, *Country Commercial Guide,* 1996.

Summary

Guyana				Overall Score	3.50
Trade	4	Monetary Policy	5	Property Rights	3
Taxation	4	Foreign Investment	3	Regulation	4
Government Intervention	3	Banking	3	Black Market	4
		Wage and Prices	2		

144 *Ibid.*

HAITI

The Caribbean nation of Haiti has little economic freedom. President Rene Preval, elected in 1995 to replace Jean-Bertrand Aristide, is no advocate of free markets. Aristide remains the most powerful and influential political figure in Haitian politics. Following his ouster by military coup in September 1991, the country was isolated economically and subjected to an embargo by the United Nations. In October 1994, Aristide was returned to power by U.S. armed intervention; Preval was elected a year later, but Haiti's economy has not improved. A well-entrenched, corrupt bureaucracy continues to hinder the development of free and open markets, and political violence could destroy the economy. The Haitian government recently reduced some barriers to trade, investment, and banking; at the same time, however, the country's rate of inflation has increased.

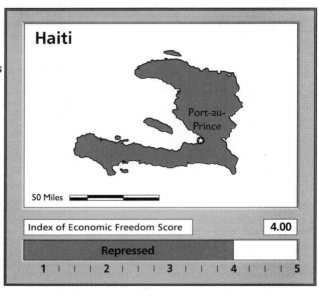

Factor #1: Trade Policy
Score: 4+ (High level of protectionism)

Haiti has slashed tariffs to an average of about 10 percent, but crime, corruption, and poor infrastructure make the Haitian market inaccessible to most imports.

Factor #2: Taxation

Score - Income taxation: 3-Stable (Moderate tax rates)
Score - Corporate taxation: 3-Stable (Moderate tax rates)
Final Taxation Score: 3-Stable (Moderate tax rates)

Haiti's top income tax rate is 30 percent, but the tax collection system is so poor that it is impossible to determine what rate applies to the average income. Tax evasion is massive, and direct taxes paid represent only 15 percent of total receipts.[145] The top corporate income tax rate is 35 percent.

Factor #3: Government Intervention in the Economy
Score: 3-Stable (Moderate level of government intervention)

Haiti's government consumes about 20 percent of economic output, and a significant portion of GDP is produced by the state-owned sector. Preval wants to privatize many large state-owned enterprises, but his plans are being resisted by Aristide.

---

145   For this factor, Haiti was graded only on its top income tax rate.

Factor #4: Monetary Policy
Score: 3- (Moderate level of inflation)

Haiti's average annual rate of inflation from 1985 to 1994 was 13.4 percent. In 1995, the inflation rate was about 24 percent.

Factor #5: Capital Flows and Foreign Investment
Score: 4+ (High barriers to foreign investment)

Haiti has opened its market to foreign investment, providing equal treatment to domestic and foreign firms. Its investment laws remain outdated, however, and are not always enforced by the corrupt bureaucracy. Bribes are sometimes solicited by bureaucrats.

Factor #6: Banking
Score: 4+ (High level of restrictions on banking)

Although Haiti has welcomed foreign banks, and recent changes allow them to engage in a variety of financial services, the banking system remains underdeveloped and in disarray. Only three private banks now operate in Haiti.

Factor #7: Wage and Price Controls
Score: 4-Stable (High level of wage and price controls)

Haiti's government controls prices on many items, including cement and gasoline. With most of the economy in a shambles, the government has sought to control prices on a variety of staples, such as certain foods. Haiti maintains a minimum wage. Under Aristide, the government established "communitarian" shops to provide basic goods. These shops, because they are subsidized by the government, depress prices for legitimate store operators and limit competition.

Factor #8: Property Rights
Score: 5-Stable (Very low level of protection of private property)

Private property enjoys little or no protection in Haiti. The judiciary is notoriously corrupt; and even though expropriation is unlikely, property remains subject to crime and thievery. Haiti's police force also is corrupt, and oppression of the country's people is routine.

Factor #9: Regulation
Score: 5-Stable (Very high level of regulation)

It was virtually impossible to open a business legally under past Haitian governments. Under Preval, however, there is growing tolerance for private business, although the bureaucracy remains corrupt.

Factor #10: Black Market
Score: 5-Stable (Very high level of black market activity)

Even before the embargo, price controls and other inefficient government policies created a large black market. At that time, the black market was around 40 percent of GDP. Today, it surpasses GDP.

Summary

Haiti				Overall Score	4.0
Trade	4	Monetary Policy	3	Property Rights	5
Taxation	3	Foreign Investment	4	Regulation	5
Government Intervention	3	Banking	4	Black Market	5
		Wage and Prices	4		

HONDURAS

onduras declared its independence from
Spain in 1821, when it joined with Costa
Rica, El Salvador, Guatemala, and Nicaragua to form the Federal Republic of Central America. It withdrew from that group of nations in 1838.
In the 1950s, the Honduran government introduced
agrarian reforms, such as returning many farms to
private owners. This became the basis for a market
system. The next several decades were characterized by military coups and civil unrest. "Despite
abundant natural resources and substantial U.S. and
multilateral economic assistance," reports the U.S.
Department of State, "Honduras remains one of the
poorest countries in the [Western] hemisphere."[146]
Recently, however, the government has managed
to reduce inflation.

Honduras

Tegucigalpa

200 Miles

| Index of Economic Freedom Score | 3.15 |

Mostly Not Free

1   2   3   4   5

Factor #1: Trade Policy

Score: 4-Stable (High level of protectionism)

Tariffs in Honduras range from 5 percent to 20 percent; the average tariff rate is
about 11 percent. Non-tariff barriers include strict labeling and sanitary requirements. According to the U.S. Department of State, "Honduras' customs administrative procedures
are burdensome. There are extensive documentary requirements and red tape involving
the payment of numerous import duties, customs surcharges, selective consumption
taxes, consular fees and warehouse levies."[147]

Factor #2: Taxation

Score - Income taxation: 2-Stable (Low tax rates)
Score - Corporate taxation: 4-Stable (High tax rates)
Final Taxation Score: 3.5-Stable (High tax rates)

The top income tax rate in Honduras is 40 percent, and no taxes are imposed on
the average level of income. The top corporate tax rate is 40.25 percent. Honduras also
has a 40.25 percent capital gains tax, a 7 percent sales tax, and various local taxes.[148]

---

146   State Department Report, 1996, p. 391.

147   *Ibid.*, p. 393.

148   Although Honduras recently reduced its top corporate tax rate from 40 percent to 35 percent,
the real top rate is based on a surcharge which brings the rate to 40.25 percent. For more
information, see *Worldwide Corporate Tax Guide and Directory*, Ernst & Young's International
Business Series (New York, N.Y.: Ernst & Young International, 1995), pp. 181–183.

Factor #3: Government Intervention in the Economy
Score: 2-Stable (Low level of government intervention)

The Honduran government consumes 10.6 percent of GDP and has achieved significant privatization of state-owned enterprises and services. For example, Honduras has allowed several privately owned companies to open energy generation plants, removing these utilities from state ownership and control. The government also is privatizing some transportation services and airport services.

Factor #4: Monetary Policy
Score: 2+ (Low level of inflation)

From 1985 to 1994, the average annual rate of inflation in Honduras was 12.4 percent. In 1994, the inflation rate was 21.4 percent.

Factor #5: Capital Flows and Foreign Investment
Score: 3-Stable (Moderate barriers to foreign investment)

Honduras maintains some restrictions on foreign investment. Special state authorization must be obtained for investments in air transport, forestry, telecommunications, and agriculture. The government also requires that a majority of certain companies must be owned by Hondurans.

Factor #6: Banking
Score: 3-Stable (Moderate level of restrictions on banking)

Foreigners must obtain government permission to engage in some types of banking services. Domestic banks are under the control of the government and the central bank, and are unduly influenced by Honduran business interests. According to the U.S. Department of Commerce, "Most [Honduran] banks are associated with powerful economic groups, and lend primarily to businesses owned by the group of which they are a part. The system has been criticized for permitting excessive amounts of unsecured lending to major stockholders or bank principals."[149]

Factor #7: Wage and Price Controls
Score: 3-Stable (Moderate level of wage and price controls)

After years of eliminating price controls, Honduras in 1993 imposed controls on the prices of a basket of 44 goods, including certain foodstuffs. The government still controls the prices of utilities, public transportation, fertilizer, cement, ground roasted coffee, and air fares. Honduras has a minimum wage.

Factor #8: Property Rights
Score: 3-Stable (Moderate level of protection of private property)

Expropriation remains possible in Honduras. The government does not fully protect property, corruption is a continuing problem, and those seeking legal recourse to protect their property frequently face an inefficient and ill-functioning court system. "Honduras' legal system does not function on precedent, lacks codified laws and does not offer the option of a jury trial," reports the U.S. Department of Commerce. "As a re-

---

149   U.S. Department of Commerce, *Country Commercial Guide, 1996.*

sult, international investors often find themselves caught up in a nasty web of contradictory laws and regulations. Occasionally, those who believe they have followed prescribed legal procedures find they do receive clear and timely adjudication of their cases.... The Honduran judiciary is weak and riddled with corruption, and often incapable of effectively protecting property rights"[150]

Factor #9: Regulation
Score: 4-Stable (High level of regulation)

The Honduran bureaucracy suffers from corruption and cronyism. Regulations are applied unequally and often haphazardly.

Factor #10: Black Market
Score: 4-Stable (High level of black market activity)

Because Honduras maintains significant barriers to trade, its black market is rather large. Almost 50 percent of the labor force is supplied by the black market. Moreover, although Honduras has passed laws protecting intellectual property rights, piracy in this area continues. According to the U.S. Department of State, "The piracy of books, music cassettes, records, video tapes, compact discs, cable TV and computer software is widespread in Honduras."[151]

Summary

Honduras				Overall Score	3.15
Trade	4	Monetary Policy	2	Property Rights	3
Taxation	3.5	Foreign Investment	3	Regulation	4
Government Intervention	2	Banking	3	Black Market	4
		Wage and Prices	3		

---

150 *Ibid.*

151 State Department Report, 1996, p. 394.

HONG KONG

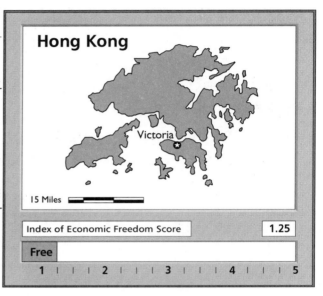

Hong Kong

Victoria

15 Miles

| Index of Economic Freedom Score | 1.25 |

Free

1　　2　　3　　4　　5

Hong Kong is a colony of the United Kingdom until July 1997, at which time it will become a "special administrative region" of the People's Republic of China. In the meantime, both the British and Hong Kong governments are attempting to solidify democracy and maintain Hong Kong's vast market economy. Hong Kong now has the world's freest economy. There is little government interference in the marketplace; taxes are low and predictable; increases in government spending are linked closely to economic growth; foreign trade is free; and regulations, in addition to being transparent, are applied both uniformly and consistently. This is the third year in a row that Hong Kong has ranked first in the *Index of Economic Freedom*.

Factor #1: Trade Policy

Score: 1-Stable (Very low level of protectionism)

Hong Kong levies no import tariffs and is a duty-free port.[152] There are, in fact, very few barriers to imports in Hong Kong, which is one of the world's most accessible markets. It also is a vital market for U.S. exports, consuming U.S. manufactured and agricultural goods at a higher rate per capita than most of the world's other economies.

Factor #2: Taxation

Score - Income taxation: 2-Stable (Low tax rates)
Score - Corporate taxation: 1-Stable (Very low tax rates)
Final Taxation Score: 1.5-Stable (Low tax rates)

The top marginal personal income tax rate in Hong Kong is 20 percent,[153] and the tax on the average income level is 2 percent. The corporate tax is a flat 16.5 percent.

Factor #3: Government Intervention in the Economy

Score: 1-Stable (Very low level of government intervention)

Although Hong Kong's government has been criticized for increased spending on social welfare, government spending as a percentage of GDP continues to decrease.[154]

152　There are some minor import duties on alcoholic beverages, tobacco, and cosmetics.

153　The maximum tax rate, however, is limited to the "standard rate" of 15 percent on the total taxable income above $155,454. Therefore, since the maximum tax rate on the highest level of income is 15 percent, this is used to grade Hong Kong's income tax score.

154　See "Biting the Invisible Hand," *Reason,* April 1996, p. 34.

Hong Kong's government consumes 6.4 percent of GDP, down from 8 percent in 1994.[155]

Factor #4: Monetary Policy
Score: 2-Stable (Low level of inflation)

The Hong Kong dollar has been linked to the U.S. dollar since 1983. Hong Kong's inflation rate has averaged 9 percent since 1985.

Factor #5: Capital Flows and Foreign Investment
Score: 1-Stable (Very low barriers to foreign investment)

The government of Hong Kong encourages foreign investment and has one of the most open borders, in terms of investment, in the world. There are no restrictions on foreign capital or investment, except in the media sector.

Factor #6: Banking
Score: 1-Stable (Very low level of restrictions on banking)

Hong Kong is a world banking center and one of the world's most stable banking environments. Banks are completely independent of the government.

Factor #7: Wage and Price Controls
Score: 2-Stable (Low level of wage and price controls)

Wages and prices are set almost completely by the market. There are, however, price controls on rent, public transport, and electricity. The government has the power to enforce "minimum wages" but has never done so.

Factor #8: Property Rights
Score: 1-Stable (Very high level of protection of private property)

Private property rights in Hong Kong are completely protected. The legal system to protect these rights is both highly efficient and effective.

Factor #9: Regulation
Score: 1-Stable (Very low level of regulation)

Hong Kong has a simple business licensing system. The regulations imposed on business are few, are not burdensome, and are applied uniformly.[156] In addition, Hong

---

155 "Hong Kong in Figures, 1996," Hong Kong government Internet site, *http://www.info.hk/cenststd/hkstat/hkinf/gdp/htm.*

156 Although Hong Kong lacks antitrust laws, this does not restrain individual economic freedom; it empowers consumers. With such open borders to investment and trade, "malevolent monopolies" are impossible to sustain because competition is maximized by the absence of barriers to new entrants. On the other hand, "altruistic monopolies" can benefit consumers by providing them with goods and services of the highest quality at the cheapest price; otherwise, competition from foreign investment or foreign trade will put them out of business. Rather than rely on government-imposed antitrust regulation, the government relies on a private-sector organization, the Hong Kong Consumer Council, which regularly issues reports on business practices. If collusion among businesses is suspected and competition is hindered as a result, the government may act to break up the companies, as it did in 1994 when it moved to

Kong has refused to implement such regulations as antitrust or antidumping laws. The absence of both maximizes competition from both domestic and foreign firms.

Factor #10: Black Market

Score: 1-Stable (Very low level of black market activity)

The black market in Hong Kong is virtually nonexistent. There is no significant smuggling problem, and black market activity in pirated intellectual property is negligible.[157]

Summary

Hong Kong				Overall Score	1.25
Trade	1	Monetary Policy	2	Property Rights	1
Taxation	1.5	Foreign Investment	1	Regulation	1
Government Intervention	1	Banking	1	Black Market	1
		Wage and Prices	2		

---

eliminate regulations on the banking industry to maximize competition.

157 Although some pirated intellectual property from the People's Republic of China (PRC) finds its way into Hong Kong, the government customs bureau is among the best in the world. As a result, most pirated material from the PRC is confiscated at the border and does not enter Hong Kong. What pirated material does exist in Hong Kong is minuscule compared to the size of the economy.

HUNGARY

Once part of the Austro–Hungarian Empire, Hungary was incorporated into the Soviet bloc after World War II. The government, which had practiced a type of reform communism, collapsed in 1989, and a democratically elected government introduced market reforms soon thereafter. Despite the socialist victory in the 1994 elections, Hungary's political climate is relatively stable. Hungary has an efficient intellectual property rights protection system, relatively weak labor unions, and a liberal foreign trade policy. It also has pursued an extensive privatization program.

Hungary

Budapest

125 Miles

| Index of Economic Freedom Score | 2.90 |

Mostly Free

1   2   3   4   5

Factor #1: Trade Policy

Score: 4-Stable (High level of protectionism)

Hungary's average tariff rate for countries enjoying most favored nation status is 13 percent; the rate for other countries is 17 percent. The government also maintains import quotas that mainly affect such consumer products as automobiles, clothing, leather footwear, and some foodstuffs. Other quotas, such as the quota on agricultural products, have been replaced with tariffs.

Factor #2: Taxation

Score - Income taxation: 5-Stable (Very high tax rates)
Score - Corporate taxation: 2-Stable (Low tax rates)
Final Taxation Score: 4-Stable (High tax rates)

Hungary's top income tax rate is 48 percent,[158] and the average income level is taxed at 40 percent. The top corporate income tax rate is 18 percent (the government cut corporate taxes in half in 1995). Hungary also has an 18 percent capital gains tax, a 12 percent to 25 percent value-added tax, and various local taxes.

Factor #3: Government Intervention in the Economy

Score: 3-Stable (Moderate level of government intervention)

Hungary's government consumes 13 percent of GDP; but the public sector also generates most of Hungary's GDP, and the government remains heavily involved in energy, telecommunications, transportation, pharmaceuticals, and other areas. Nevertheless, privatization continues.

---

158   Economist Intelligence Unit, *ILT Reports: Hungary, 1996.*

Factor #4: Monetary Policy
Score: 4-Stable (High level of inflation)

Hungary's annual rate of inflation was 28.2 percent in 1995, 18.8 percent in 1994, 22.5 percent in 1993, 23.0 percent in 1992, and 35 percent in 1991.[159] Thus, the average rate of inflation since the collapse of the communist regime has been about 25 percent.

Factor #5: Capital Flows and Foreign Investment
Score: 2-Stable (Low barriers to foreign investment)

Hungary is very open to foreign investment and is leading the way on foreign investment reform, attracting most American investment in the region. Although 100 percent ownership is guaranteed to foreign investors, the government sometimes opposes 100 percent foreign ownership of newly privatized businesses. After the foreign investor is located in Hungary, the law provides equal legal treatment for foreign and domestic firms.

Factor #6: Banking
Score: 2-Stable (Low level of restrictions on banking)

Privatization of Hungary's banking industry is progressing. The government may not own more than 25 percent of a bank. The banking system, however, still remains partly under government control. Of the 45 banks operating in Hungary in 1995, only 23 had at least some foreign ownership. Nevertheless, the banking market is becoming increasingly competitive, and banks are relatively free from burdensome government oversight.

Factor #7: Wage and Price Controls
Score: 2-Stable (Low level of wage and price controls)

Hungary has eliminated most price controls. According to the U.S. Department of State, however, "the state continues to control the prices for public transportation and utilities, such as gas, electricity, and water."[160] Hungary maintains a minimum wage.

Factor #8: Property Rights
Score: 2-Stable (High level of protection of private property)

There is little chance of property expropriation in Hungary. There have been no cases of government expropriation of foreign-owned assets since the 1950s, and private property is guaranteed by law. Although the Hungarian legal system can be corrupt, ineffective, and inefficient, the U.S. Department of Commerce reports that it also "protects and facilitates the acquisition and disposition of property rights."[161]

---

159   Based on consumer price inflation; see *Ibid.*

160   State Department Report, 1996, p. 197.

161   U.S. Department of Commerce, *Country Commercial Guide,* 1996.

Factor #9: Regulation
Score: 3-Stable (Moderate level of regulation)

Hungary has few regulations that burden business. A business license is required only for a few activities. New consumer protection and environmental laws, however, are becoming burdensome. Hungary's environmental law, for example, imposes a "green tax" on certain businesses engaged in manufacturing such products as tires and refrigerators.

Factor #10: Black Market
Score: 3-Stable (Moderate level of black market activity)

As Hungary moves closer to a free market, black market activities are decreasing. There is some infringement of intellectual property, and a significant black market exists in pirated materials, especially pharmaceuticals. By global standards, however, Hungary's black market is moderate.

Summary

Hungary					Overall Score	2.90
Trade	4	Monetary Policy	4	Property Rights	2
Taxation	4	Foreign Investment	2	Regulation	3
Government Intervention	3	Banking	2	Black Market	3
		Wage and Prices	2		

ICELAND

Situated in the North Atlantic Ocean, Iceland is the westernmost outpost of Europe. During the 1800s, Iceland was mainly an agricultural and fishing nation, and these industries provided substantial economic growth; by the 1900s, it had an established industrial base. Iceland won its independence from Denmark in 1944. An island nation about the size of Ireland, it has an advanced market economy and is a major export base for manufactured goods.

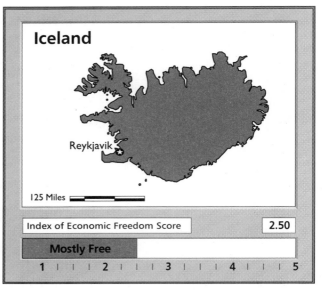

Factor #1: Trade Policy
Score: 2-Stable (Low level of protectionism)

Iceland has an average tariff rate of about 2.1 percent,[162] and continues to maintain non-tariff barriers in the form of quotas and licensing requirements.

Factor #2: Taxation
Score - Income taxation: 4-Stable (High tax rates)
Score - Corporate taxation: 3-Stable (Moderate tax rates)
Final Taxation Score: 4-Stable (High tax rates)

Iceland has a flat income tax rate of 41.94 percent and a top marginal corporate tax rate of 33 percent. It also has a 33 percent capital gains tax and a 24.5 percent value-added tax.

Factor #3: Government Intervention in the Economy
Score: 3-Stable (Moderate level of government intervention)

Iceland's government consumes about 22 percent of GDP, a substantial portion of which is produced by state-owned companies.

Factor #4: Monetary Policy
Score: 3-Stable (Moderate level of inflation)

Iceland maintained a stable inflation rate of 13.2 percent from 1985 to 1994. In 1995, the inflation rate was 1.7 percent.

---

162   Based on total government taxation of international transactions as a percentage of imports.

Factor #5: Capital Flows and Foreign Investment
Score: 2-Stable (Low barriers to foreign investment)

Iceland generally welcomes foreign investment, although the government still maintains some restrictions on foreign investment in fishing and primary fish processing, energy development, commercial banks, airlines, and industries considered vital to national security.

Factor #6: Banking
Score: 3-Stable (Moderate level of restrictions on banking)

Although Iceland's banking system is becoming more liberalized, there are some state-owned banks, and foreign banks are not permitted.

Factor #7: Wage and Price Controls
Score: 3-Stable (Moderate level of wage and price controls)

Wages and prices in Iceland are set by the market. The government has indirect control over many prices and wages, however, through its heavy involvement in the public sector.

Factor #8: Property Rights
Score: 1-Stable (Very high level of protection of private property)

Private property is safe from government confiscation. Iceland has an efficient and independent legal system.

Factor #9: Regulation
Score: 3-Stable (Moderate level of regulation)

Some of Iceland's economy remains heavily regulated—especially fishing, agriculture, and such service industries as telecommunications and the airlines. Strict environmental laws also can add to the cost of doing business.

Factor #10: Black Market
Score: 1-Stable (Very low level of black market activity)

Iceland has both a very small black market and very strong and efficient intellectual property rights laws. Piracy in these products is virtually nonexistent.

Summary

Iceland				Overall Score	2.50
Trade	2	Monetary Policy	3	Property Rights	1
Taxation	4	Foreign Investment	2	Regulation	3
Government Intervention	3	Banking	3	Black Market	1
		Wage and Prices	3		

INDIA

India gained its independence from the United Kingdom in 1947 and became a republic in 1950. For much of the following three decades, it pursued socialist economic policies—nationalizing industries, raising trade tariffs, subsidizing industries, and raising taxes—and the economy suffered as a result. In 1991, India began to liberalize its economy, accepting foreign investment and reducing barriers to trade. As a result, the economy has been growing. The mid-1995 reversal of a major foreign energy project by the local government in Maharashtra Province, however, demonstrates that positive central government reforms designed to increase foreign investment face significant nationalist opposition.

India

New Delhi

500 Miles

Index of Economic Freedom Score	3.70
Mostly Not Free	

1   2   3   4   5

Factor #1: Trade Policy

Score: 5-Stable (Very high level of protectionism)

India has an average tariff rate of 33.4 percent[163] and maintains a number of non-tariff barriers. The government, for example, requires import licenses for such products as electronics, agricultural goods, and pharmaceuticals.

Factor #2: Taxation

Score - Income taxation: 3+ (Moderate tax rates)
Score - Corporate taxation: 4-Stable (High tax rates)
Final Taxation Score: 4+ (High tax rates)

India's top income tax level is 40 percent, down from 44 percent in 1995, and the tax on the average income level is 0 percent. The top corporate tax rate is 40 percent. India also maintains a 30 percent capital gains tax and both interest and sales taxes.

Factor #3: Government Intervention in the Economy

Score: 3-Stable (Moderate level of government intervention)

India's government consumes 11 percent of GDP, a large portion of which is generated by state-owned enterprises, and the government's privatization program has slowed in recent years.

---

163   Based on total taxes on international trade as a percentage of total imports; from International Monetary Fund, *Government Financial Statistics 1995*.

Factor #4: Monetary Policy
Score: 2-Stable (Low level of inflation)

India had an average annual inflation rate of 9.7 percent from 1985 to 1993. In 1995, inflation reached 9 percent.

Factor #5: Capital Flows and Foreign Investment
Score: 3-Stable (Moderate barriers to foreign investment)

India recently has reduced some barriers to foreign investment. Foreign investors, however, cannot own 100 percent of an Indian concern without prior government approval, although there are a few instances in which approval is not granted. In 1995, the Indian government turned down a previously approved investment by a consortium of Enron Corporation, Bechtel Enterprises Inc., and General Electric Company's GE Capital unit to build a power generation plant. In January 1996, the government renegotiated the deal, once again allowing the investment to go forward.

Factor #6: Banking
Score: 4-Stable (High level of restrictions on banking)

The banking sector in India continues to be heavily controlled by the government. According to the U.S. Department of Commerce, "All large Indian banks are nationalized, and all Indian financial institutions are in the public sector."[164] The government currently has plans to permit only five licenses per year for foreign bank branches or extensions of current operations. Only 12 such licenses were granted from June 1993 to September 1994.

Factor #7: Wage and Price Controls
Score: 4-Stable (High level of wage and price controls)

Central and state governments still regulate the pricing of most essential products, including cereals, sugar, basic medicines, some energy, coal, and many industrial inputs. India has a minimum wage.

Factor #8: Property Rights
Score: 3-Stable (Moderate level of protection of private property)

The massive gap between rich and poor leads to government policies that redistribute wealth, mainly through direct property expropriation. India has an efficient court system, but property remains at risk in rural areas because of crime and corruption. The U.S. Department of Commerce reports that "Indian courts provide adequate safeguards for the enforcement of property and contractual rights. However, case backlogs frequently lead to long procedural delays."[165]

---

164   U.S. Department of Commerce, *Country Commercial Guide*, 1996.

165   *Ibid.*

Factor #9: Regulation

Score: 4-Stable (High level of regulation)

India's economy is heavily regulated. The large public sector must meet all kinds of burdensome requirements, including restrictive licensing requirements, in order to remain open for business. Some corruption remains present.

Factor #10: Black Market

Score: 5-Stable (Very high level of black market activity)

India's huge tariffs make smuggling foreign goods into the country very profitable. Many goods are smuggled in from Burma. According to the U.S. Department of Commerce, "Local shopkeepers act as contact points for heavier smuggled goods, mostly teak and rice, and for Burmese Gem stones."[166]

Summary

India				Overall Score	3.70
Trade	5	Monetary Policy	2	Property Rights	3
Taxation	4	Foreign Investment	3	Regulation	4
Government Intervention	3	Banking	4	Black Market	5
		Wage and Prices	4		

---

166 *Ibid.*

INDONESIA

An archipelago situated between Australia and Malaysia, Indonesia gained its independence from the Netherlands in 1945. Recently, it has made significant progress toward economic liberalization. Although Indonesia has received rather large sums of foreign aid from the international community, the most significant impact on its economic prosperity has come from such policy reforms as cutting taxes, lowering barriers to trade, and opening the economy to foreign investment.

Factor #1: Trade Policy

Score: 2-Stable (Low level of protectionism)

Indonesia's average tariff rate is 6 percent. There are strict licensing requirements on a number of products, including flour, sugar, and rice.

Factor #2: Taxation

Score - Income taxation: 3-Stable (Moderate tax rates)
Score - Corporate taxation: 3-Stable (Moderate tax rates)
Final Taxation Score: 3.5-Stable (High tax rates)

Indonesia's top income tax rate is 30 percent, and the average income level is taxed at 10 percent. The top corporate income tax rate is 30 percent. Indonesia also has a 10 percent value-added tax and a sales tax.

Factor #3: Government Intervention in the Economy

Score: 1-Stable (Very low level of government intervention)

Indonesia's government consumes 8.2 percent of GDP. According to the Economist Intelligence Unit, "The State continues to play a major role in Indonesian industry. But the government increasingly requires state firms to meet private-sector accounting and competitive standards. At the same time it is phasing out subsidies and a multitude of preferences, and making privatization a serious goal."[167] Thus, government consumption of Indonesia's $196 billion economy is minuscule.

Factor #4: Monetary Policy

Score: 2-Stable (Low level of inflation)

Indonesia's average annual rate of inflation from 1985 to 1994 was 8.9 percent. In 1995, the inflation rate was 9.4 percent.

---

167   Economist Intelligence Unit, *ILT Reports: Indonesia 1996.*

Factor #5: Capital Flows and Foreign Investment
Score: 2-Stable (Low barriers to foreign investment)

Indonesia recently reformed its foreign investment code. The government now allows 100 percent foreign ownership and has opened many sectors once closed to foreign investors, although foreign investment still is not permitted in some retail operations.

Factor #6: Banking
Score: 3-Stable (Moderate level of restrictions on banking)

Until the late 1980s, no foreign bank had been granted a license since 1969. Some changes have occurred to allow more foreign bank participation, but foreign banks remain highly regulated. In many cases, they can operate only through joint ventures with Indonesian banks. Moreover, 100 percent foreign-owned banks are not permitted. Domestic banks, however, have gained increased independence from the government.

Factor #7: Wage and Price Controls
Score: 3-Stable (Moderate level of wage and price controls)

Most prices are set by the market, though the prices of many products, including rice, sugar, soybeans, and rice, are controlled. "The government enforces a system of floor and ceiling prices for certain 'strategic' food products such as rice," reports the U.S. Department of State. "In some cases, business associations, with government subsidies are confined to a few goods such as fertilizers."[168] Indonesia has a minimum wage.

Factor #8: Property Rights
Score: 3-Stable (Moderate level of protection of private property)

Indonesia's legal framework is based on outdated Dutch Commercial Codes that have not been updated since colonial times. Court rulings can be arbitrary and inconsistent. According to the U.S. Department of Commerce, "Many foreign investors believe that the court system does not provide effective recourse for solving commercial disputes."[169]

Factor #9: Regulation
Score: 4-Stable (High level of regulation)

Indonesia's regulatory environment is characterized by bribery, kickbacks, and other corruption. Many regulations are applied arbitrarily, and bribes may be necessary to receive an "exemption" from a government regulation. According to the U.S. Department of Commerce, corruption continues at some Indonesian port facilities where bribes often are required to get some goods through customs.[170] Moreover, "Despite major improvements in its economic environment, Indonesia continues to have a reputation as a difficult place to do business. The regulatory and legal environment can be tangled, confusing and time-consuming. In recent years, considerable attention has focused on the costs of corruption and influence-peddling. Complaints arise from irregular

---

168   State Department Report, 1996, p. 56.

169   U.S. Department of Commerce, *Country Commercial Guide*, 1996.

170   See U.S. Department of Commerce, "Indonesia—Economic News—IMI960409, Market Research Reports," April 1996.

fees and/or commissions that companies are asked to pay to operate businesses in a timely manner. Red tape has been another major concern to foreign investors. Deregulation has been successful in removing barriers, creating more transparent trade and investment regimes, and alleviated, but not entirely eliminated, red tape."[171]

Factor #10: Black Market

Score: 5-Stable (Very high level of black market activity)

Indonesia has a very large black market, mainly in its labor and manufacturing sectors. According to the U.S. Department of Commerce, "The informal sector in Indonesia is significant, with some estimates placing two thirds of the labor force in the sector."[172] Another cause of black market activity is the lack of intellectual property protection. Indonesia recently was targeted by the United States for intellectual property rights violations; and although it has begun a swift crackdown on pirated copyrighted materials like video and audio tapes, pirated computer software remains rampant. Biotechnology products are not yet protected under Indonesian law, although they may be in the future.

Summary

Indonesia						Overall Score	2.85
Trade	2		Monetary Policy	2		Property Rights	3
Taxation	3.5		Foreign Investment	2		Regulation	4
Government Intervention	1		Banking	3		Black Market	5
			Wage and Prices	3			

---

171 *Ibid.*

172 See U.S. Department of Commerce, "Indonesia Labor Trends, 1992–94, Foreign Labor Trends," 1996, and Ministry of Manpower, Republic of Indonesia, "Manpower and Employment Situation in Indonesia, 1992," p. 77.

IRAN

Iran boasted of one of the most advanced economies in the Middle East before it was crippled by the 1979 Iranian revolution, the 1980–1988 Iran–Iraq war, and widespread economic mismanagement. Iran's radical Islamic leaders established an economic system that discouraged private enterprise and favored state-run enterprises. As a result, most of the economy was nationalized. Following the election of President Ali Akbar Rafsanjani in 1989, some economic reforms were pursued. A corrupt and intransigent bureaucracy allied with hardline Islamic militants in Iran's parliament, however, has hamstrung these proposed reforms.

Index of Economic Freedom Score	4.7

Repressed

1   2   3   4   5

Factor #1: Trade Policy

Score: 5-Stable- (Very high level of protectionism)

Iran controls imports by exorbitant tariff rates, import bans, licensing, and a customs service that confiscates many goods that cross the border. Many Western goods, especially ones representing Western culture, are banned from entering Iran. Iran is essentially closed to imports, except those that the government deems vital—mainly raw materials, food, and medicine.

Factor #2: Taxation

Score - Income taxation: 5-Stable (Very high tax rates)
Score - Corporate taxation: 5-Stable (Very high tax rates)
Final Taxation Score: 5-Stable (Very high tax rates)

Iran's top income tax rate is 54 percent, and the average taxpayer is in the 35 percent bracket. The top marginal corporate tax rate is 54 percent. Iran also maintains a host of other taxes, such as a 10 percent capital gains tax, a 3 percent municipality tax, and a social contributions tax.

Factor #3: Government Intervention in the Economy

Score: 5-Stable (Very high level of government intervention)

The government produces most of the GDP in Iran. The private sector is discouraged, and the state owns the banking, petroleum, transportation, utilities, and mining sectors, although the government plans to privatize portions of the banking sector.

Factor #4: Monetary Policy

Score: 4-Stable (High level of inflation)

Iran's average rate of inflation from 1985 to 1993 was 22 percent. In 1995, the inflation rate was about 30 percent.

Factor #5: Capital Flows and Foreign Investment
Score: 5-Stable (Very high barriers to foreign investment)

Although Iran has removed some restrictions on foreign investment, there is a general hostility to foreigners, especially non-Muslims. Foreign ownership is prohibited in banking, domestic trade, construction, and most defense-related industries.

Factor #6: Banking
Score: 5-Stable (Very high level of restrictions on banking)

The banking system in Iran is completely government-owned.

Factor #7: Wage and Price Controls
Score: 4-Stable (High level of wage and price controls)

Wages and prices in Iran are controlled through the large public sector.

Factor #8: Property Rights
Score: 5-Stable (Very low level of protection of private property)

Iran's legal and judicial system is corrupt and inefficient. The government has confiscated huge amounts of private property—particularly property owned by supporters of the former Shah, political dissidents, or Westerners—and recently outlawed private ownership of satellite dishes because people were using them to watch Western movies and television programs.

Factor #9: Regulation
Score: 4-Stable (High level of regulation)

Establishing a business in Iran is discouraged. Regulations are applied unevenly in most cases, and corruption is rampant.

Factor #10: Black Market
Score: 5-Stable (Very high level of black market activity)

Because the government actively manages the level of imports into Iran, and because it maintains import bans on many consumer goods, smuggling is rampant.

Summary

Iran					Overall Score	4.70
Trade	5	Monetary Policy	4		Property Rights	5
Taxation	5	Foreign Investment	5		Regulation	4
Government Intervention	5	Banking	5		Black Market	5
		Wage and Prices	4			

IRAQ

Iraq gained its independence from Great Britain in 1932. A military coup in 1958 replaced the Iraqi monarchy and ushered in a period of political instability. The Ba'ath socialist party, which came to power in a 1968 coup, nationalized large portions of the economy. Although Iraq's oil reserves are second only to Saudi Arabia's, its economy has been weakened by government mismanagement, the 1980–1988 war with Iran, the disastrous 1991 Persian Gulf War, and continuing United Nations economic sanctions. Iraq's government is dedicated to a socialist economic ideology and public ownership. Some private-sector initiatives are permitted, but the government regularly executes businessmen who charge excessive prices for scarce imported goods.

Index of Economic Freedom Score	4.90

Repressed

1 | | | 2 | | | 3 | | | 4 | | | 5

Factor #1: Trade Policy
Score: 5-Stable (Very high level of protectionism)

Customs officials apply tariff rates arbitrarily. Moreover, the government inspects and controls all imports, although there is considerable smuggling across most of Iraq's borders.

Factor #2: Taxation

Score - Income taxation: 5-Stable (Very high tax rates)
Score - Corporate taxation: 5-Stable (Very high tax rates)
Final Taxation Score: 5-Stable (Very high tax rates)

Taxes in Iraq generally take the form of confiscated property, much as in North Korea and Cuba. Farmers are permitted to grow their own crops, but much of the harvest is confiscated and rationed. Thus, Iraq has the equivalent of very high tax rates.

Factor #3: Government Intervention in the Economy
Score: 5-Stable (Very high level of government intervention)

Most of Iraq's economic output is produced by the government or performed in the black market, which the government is trying to restrict. There is little entrepreneurship; and where it does occur, it is often subject to government extortion.

Factor #4: Monetary Policy
Score: 5-Stable (Very high level of inflation)

Iraq's average rate of inflation from 1989 to 1993 was 53 percent. In 1994, the inflation rate was 60 percent. The rate for 1995 is not available; however, the U.S. Department of Commerce reports that "Rampant inflation has made it difficult for the average

Iraqi to turn to the open market to find the products now restricted under rationing. Reliable statistics are not available, but it is reported that the cost of basic food items has far outstripped salaries. Government troop movements to the Kuwaiti border in October 1995 led to a temporary doubling of food prices."[173]

Factor #5: Capital Flows and Foreign Investment
Score: 5-Stable (Very high barriers to foreign investment)

Even though Iraq has permitted some foreign investment, mainly in order to re-build from the damage of the Persian Gulf War, it discourages such investment in most areas. Moreover, contracts are not guaranteed, and there is little recourse available in the event their enforcement is needed. Investment is allowed only on a case-by-case basis.

Factor #6: Banking
Score: 5-Stable (Very high level of restrictions on banking)

Some private banks exist, but most are under the indirect and sometimes even direct control of the government. The banking system is virtually void of competition and in complete disarray.

Factor #7: Wage and Price Controls
Score: 5-Stable (Very high level of wage and price controls)

Rationing is the norm in Iraq. The government confiscates most durable goods from producers in order to ration them. The regime also does not allow private merchants to establish their own prices, and regularly executes businessman who try to set prices of which it disapproves.

Factor #8: Property Rights
Score: 5-Stable (Very low level of protection of private property)

Private property is not respected in Iraq. The legal and judicial system is corrupt and inefficient, and the state regularly confiscates private property. According to the U.S. Department of Commerce, "The seriousness of the economic situation is illustrated by the increasing number and severity of punishments for economic crimes. Apparent hoarding of crops has led the government to withhold seeds and fertilizer from farmers who fail to bring their crop to market. Farmers who fail to cultivate their land altogether have their land confiscated.... Merchants have been executed for hoarding and fixing prices."[174]

Factor #9: Regulation
Score: 4-Stable (High level of regulation)

Iraq executes government officials convicted of corruption. Its bureaucracy is large and inefficient, however, and corruption remains rampant, particularly among President Saddam Hussein's inner circle. Officially sanctioned extortion is increasing as

---

173   National Trade Data Bank and Economic Bulletin Board—products of STAT–USA, U.S. Department of Commerce.

174   *Ibid.*

the government seeks to force merchants to turn a large portion of their products over to the state.

Factor #10: Black Market

Score: 5-Stable (Very high level of black market activity)

Smuggling of all kinds of products is rampant in Iraq. According to the U.S. Department of Commerce, "Many consumer goods and basic necessities, including medicine, are available on the black market at highly inflated prices."[175] In an attempt to crack down on black market activity, the government has resorted to execution. "Capital punishment," reports the U.S. Department of Commerce, "has been decreed for those smuggling cars and trucks from the country and harsh penalties have been levied on currency traders and 'profiteers.'"[176]

Summary

Iraq					Overall Score	4.90
Trade	5	Monetary Policy	5		Property Rights	5
Taxation	5	Foreign Investment	5		Regulation	4
Government Intervention	5	Banking	5		Black Market	5
		Wage and Prices	5			

---

175   *Ibid.*

176   *Ibid.*

IRELAND

Ireland is a largely free market. Throughout most of its history, Ireland was an agricultural country. Since the mid-1950s, however, it has become increasingly industrialized. Today, mining, manufacturing, construction, and public utilities account for about 37 percent of gross domestic product; agriculture accounts for only 12 percent of GDP. In the late 1980s and early 1990s, Ireland became a base for the production of advanced consumer electronics products. Many high-tech companies, both foreign and domestic, now operate there.

| Index of Economic Freedom Score | 2.20 |

Mostly Free

1 | | | 2 | | | 3 | | | 4 | | | 5

Factor #1: Trade Policy

Score: 2-Stable (Low level of protectionism)

As part of the European Union (EU), Ireland has an average tariff rate of 3.6 percent. It also maintains some of the strictest plant and animal health standards in the EU, although there have been some recent attempts to remove some of these restrictions, which often present barriers to the importation of such items as meat and vegetables.

Factor #2: Taxation

Score - Income taxation: 5-Stable (Very high tax rates)
Score - Corporate taxation: 4-Stable (High tax rates)
Final Taxation Score: 5-Stable (Very high tax rates)

Ireland's top income tax rate is 48 percent, and the average income level is taxed at 27 percent. The top corporate income tax rate is 38 percent, down from 40 percent in 1995. Ireland also has a 40 percent capital gains tax and a 21 percent value-added tax. The government recently has instituted a top 10 percent corporate tax on some companies involved in manufacturing, international finance, data processing, and research and development. This lower tax rate is aimed at attracting high-tech companies to Ireland.

Factor #3: Government Intervention in the Economy

Score: 2-Stable (Low level of government intervention)

Ireland's government consumes about 16 percent of GDP. The government has sold most state-owned industries—including its iron and steel companies, which are some of the world's largest—and there are no prohibitions on private-sector involvement in any sector of the economy. State-owned industries are confined to such areas as the production of energy and the telecommunications industry.

Factor #4: Monetary Policy
Score: 1-Stable (Very low level of inflation)

Ireland's average annual rate of inflation from 1985 to 1994 was 2 percent. Inflation was around 2.5 percent in 1995 and around 3 percent during the first half of 1996.

Factor #5: Capital Flows and Foreign Investment
Score: 2-Stable (Low barriers to foreign investment)

Ireland welcomes foreign investment and offers such incentives as a guaranteed 10 percent maximum tax on investment profits for manufacturing companies. Foreigners may not invest in sugar production, however, the production of electricity, or air and rail transport companies.

Factor #6: Banking
Score: 2-Stable (Low level of restrictions on banking)

Ireland has a highly competitive and advanced banking and financial system. Foreign banks are welcome and treated equally with domestic banks.

Factor #7: Wage and Price Controls
Score: 2-Stable (Low level of wage and price controls)

Ireland has no price controls but does maintain a minimum wage.

Factor #8: Property Rights
Score: 1-Stable (Very high level of protection of private property)

Property expropriation is very unlikely in Ireland. Property receives sufficient protection from the court system.

Factor #9: Regulation
Score: 2-Stable (Low level of regulation)

Regulations are applied uniformly and are not substantially burdensome. Regulation in Ireland has been increasing, however. The environmental movement is putting a great strain on business, especially on manufacturing companies which must comply with stringent air quality laws. Some occupational health and safety laws also burden some businesses.

Factor #10: Black Market
Score: 3- (Moderate level of black market activity)

The level of black market activity in Ireland is moderate. Because of the conflict in Northern Ireland, an entire smuggling network was established to run guns and weapons to the Irish Republican Army. This network has grown over the years to include stolen items ranging from consumer electronics, like computers, to cigarettes and cigars.

Summary

Ireland				Overall Score	2.20
Trade	2	Monetary Policy	1	Property Rights	1
Taxation	5	Foreign Investment	2	Regulation	2
Government Intervention	2	Banking	2	Black Market	3
		Wage and Prices	2		

ISRAEL

Since becoming independent in 1948, Israel technically has been at war with most of its Arab neighbors. This has imposed a heavy defense burden that has been lightened only slightly by peace treaties with Egypt in 1979 and Jordan in 1994. Because of limited natural resources, Israel depends on imports of oil, grain, and raw materials. Israel usually posts current account deficits that are caused by large transfer payments from abroad, as well as by foreign loans and foreign aid. A free trade area formed with the United States in 1985 has increased trade between the two countries; but despite this agreement, and despite massive infusions of foreign aid (Israel is the foremost recipient of U.S. foreign assistance), the Israeli economy is mixed. Prime Minister Benjamin Netanyahu, elected in May 1996, has called both for economic liberalization and for a reduction in U.S. foreign aid to Israel.

Factor #1: Trade Policy
Score: 2-Stable (Low level of protectionism)

The average Israeli tariff rate is less than 2 percent. This figure, however, severely understates Israel's trade protectionism. Many imports from the United States come in at reduced rates because of the free trade area, but duties applied to less developed countries and others can be as high as 95 percent. In addition, Israel imposes such non-tariff barriers as import bans, strict product standards, and import quotas.

Factor #2: Taxation

Score - Income taxation: 5-Stable (Very high tax rates)
Score - Corporate taxation: 4-Stable (High tax rates)
Final Taxation Score: 5-Stable (Very high tax rates)

Israel's top income tax level is 50 percent, with the average income level taxed at a rate of 30 percent. The top corporate tax rate is over 36 percent. Israel also has a 36 percent capital gains tax and a 17 percent value-added tax.

Factor #3: Government Intervention in the Economy

Score: 4+ (High level of government intervention)

The Israeli government consumes 27.5 percent of GDP. This high level of spending is due mainly to military expenditures and social welfare programs. According to the Economist Intelligence Unit, "The state bureaucracy and the public sector continue to play a considerable role in the Israeli economy."[177] For example, the government continues to own large portions of manufacturing companies in pharmaceuticals, utilities, telecommunications, airlines, and shipyards.

Factor #4: Monetary Policy
Score: 3-Stable (Moderate level of inflation)

Israel's average annual rate of inflation from 1985 to 1994 was 18 percent. In 1995, consumer price inflation was 8.1 percent.

Factor #5: Capital Flows and Foreign Investment
Score: 1-Stable (Very low barriers to foreign investment)

There are no significant barriers to foreign investment in Israel. The government permits 100 percent foreign ownership of businesses and offers such investment incentives as tax holidays.

Factor #6: Banking
Score: 3-Stable (Moderate level of restrictions on banking)

The government of Israel continues to sell shares of state-owned banks, but these banks remain highly centralized. A significant portion of the industry is manipulated by the government through regulations and controls. Banks are restricted from investing in real estate, insurance, and some other business activities.

Factor #7: Wage and Price Controls
Score: 2-Stable (Low level of wage and price controls)

Although most price controls have been lifted, they remain in effect in a few areas, such as transportation. Israel has a minimum wage.

Factor #8: Property Rights
Score: 2-Stable (High level of protection of private property)

Expropriation of property in Israel is unlikely. Israel has a sophisticated legal system that provides extensive protection of private property. "Israel has a modern legal system based on mandate and British case law," reports the U.S. Department of Commerce. "Effective means exist for enforcing property and contractual rights. Courts are independent; there is no government interference in the court system."!178•

Factor #9: Regulation
Score: 2-Stable (Low level of regulation)

Despite the central government's large role in the economy, Israel has an efficient bureaucracy that encourages business. Regulations are applied evenly and are not significantly burdensome.

Factor #10: Black Market
Score: 4-Stable (High level of black market activity)

Israel's black market activity is shrinking, although the level of non-tariff barriers encourages fairly extensive smuggling of some consumer goods. Moreover, although most smuggling of consumer electronics equipment is diminishing, the black market in

---

177   Economist Intelligence Unit, *ILT Country Reports, Israel, 1996.*

178   U.S. Department of Commerce, *Country Commercial Guide,* 1996.

pirated videos and other forms of entertainment is substantial. According to the U.S. Department of State, "Cable, television, video, and software piracy is common in Israel. Israel currently has an antiquated copyright law which together with weak enforcement, has led to piracy in these industries."[179] In addition, illegal showings of pirated American movies, television programs, and black market versions of American music continue to flourish.

Summary

Israel				Overall Score	2.80
Trade	2	Monetary Policy	3	Property Rights	2
Taxation	5	Foreign Investment	1	Regulation	2
Government Intervention	4	Banking	3	Black Market	4
		Wage and Prices	2		

---

179   State Department Report, 1996, p. 470.

ITALY

I taly is the world's fifth-largest economy and a member of the G–7 group of advanced industrialized nations. Despite its relatively large economy, Italy has pursued state-interventionist economic policies that have created periods of deep economic recession and have restricted economic freedom. Moreover, Italy's continuing political turmoil has made it impossible to achieve successful economic reform quickly, although there has been some progress. For example, Italy recently has privatized many state-owned banks and has reduced price controls. Black market activity, however, is on the rise.

Italy	
Index of Economic Freedom Score	2.60
Mostly Free	

Factor #1: Trade Policy

Score: 3-Stable (Moderate level of protectionism)

As a member of the European Union (EU), Italy has an average tariff rate of 3.6 percent. Customs procedures, however, can be both strict and arbitrary, particularly with respect to agricultural goods, and this affects imports from all non-EU countries. "In Italy," reports the U.S. Department of State, "highly-fragmented, non-transparent government procurement practices and significant problems with corruption have created obstacles [to] imports...."[180]

Factor #2: Taxation

Score - Income taxation: 5-Stable (Very high tax rates)
Score - Corporate taxation: 4-Stable (High tax rates)
Final Taxation Score: 5-Stable (Very high tax rates)

Italy's top income tax rate is 51 percent, and the average income level is taxed at a rate of 27 percent. The top corporate income tax rate is 37 percent. Italy also has a 37 percent capital gains tax and a 19 percent value-added tax.[181]

Factor #3: Government Intervention in the Economy

Score: 3-Stable (Moderate level of government intervention)

Italy's government consumes about 17.3 percent of GDP and is responsible for about 40 percent of all economic output. According to the U.S. Department of State, "The state plays an active role in the economy, not only in the formulation of macroeconomic policy and regulations, but also through state ownership of a number of large

---

180 State Department Report, 1996.

181 It is important to point out that many Italians probably avoid paying taxes altogether.

industrial and financial concerns."[182] The government owns the telephone utility, Tele-com Italia, as well as companies in energy utilities and transportation.

Factor #4: Monetary Policy
Score: 2-Stable (Low level of inflation)

Italy's average annual rate of inflation from 1985 to 1994 was 6.2 percent. Inflation was 5.4 percent in 1995.

Factor #5: Capital Flows and Foreign Investment
Score: 2-Stable (Low barriers to foreign investment)

As part of the EU, Italy generally welcomes foreign investment, mainly because of its importance in bringing new technologies into Italy's ailing industries. There are, how-ever, a few restrictions and bans on foreign investment in domestic air transport, aircraft manufacturing, and state monopolies. In addition, industrial projects require a multitude of approvals and permits. Nevertheless, overall barriers to foreign investment are low by global standards.

Factor #6: Banking
Score: 2+ (Low level of restrictions on banking)

Banks face some government restrictions and regulations, although Italy recently has undergone some financial reform, including privatization of several large Italian banks.

Factor #7: Wage and Price Controls
Score: 2+ (Low level of wage and price controls)

Although few direct price controls exist, the government does affect prices through state-owned and state-subsidized industries for which pricing policies are not de-termined by market forces. The government also has abolished many of its price con-trols on pharmaceuticals and other products, however; and because many businesses have been privatized, it has much less control over prices than it had just a few years ago. Thus, Italy's wage and price controls today are low by global standards.

Factor #8: Property Rights
Score: 2-Stable (High level of protection of private property)

Property is safe from arbitrary government expropriation. Italy has an advanced le-gal system to protect property, although there are claims of corruption.

Factor #9: Regulation
Score: 3-Stable (Moderate level of regulation)

Despite recent government initiatives, put in place to eliminate regulations that can be cumbersome and open to corruption, Italy's political crisis has led to the return of corruption. Although it is easy to open businesses and bribes are no longer necessary, cumbersome workers' rights laws harm the competitiveness of many Italian companies.

---

182   State Department Report, 1996.

Factor #10: Black Market
Score: 2- (Low level of black market activity)

Italy's organized criminals are heavily involved in drugs and guns, but black market activity in smuggling, transportation services, and the construction industries is limited, and the government is making progress in stamping out some organized crime.[183] Italy recently has enacted severe penalties for engaging in the piracy of protected intellectual property. For example, pirated computer software represented some 86 percent of the market in 1992; today, it represents less than 50 percent. Pirated video sales represent some 40 percent of the market. Compared with the size of Italy's economy (the world's fifth-largest), these black market activities are negligible.

Summary

Italy				Overall Score	2.60
Trade	3	Monetary Policy	2	Property Rights	2
Taxation	5	Foreign Investment	2	Regulation	3
Government Intervention	3	Banking	2	Black Market	2
		Wage and Prices	2		

---

183 The methodology for this factor considers only black market activity that results from government restrictions on free enterprise. For a detailed explanation, see Chapter 4.

IVORY COAST

The West African country of Ivory Coast became a French colony in 1893. From 1904 to 1958, it was part of the Federation of French West Africa, a group of West African French colonies. It gained its independence from France in 1960, although its cultural, economic, and military ties to Paris remain very close. Until his death in 1993, President Felix Houphouet-Boigny ruled the country with little regard for democracy. His successor, Henri Konan Bedie, has made modest strides with political and economic reform, which foreign aid donors also have been pushing. The country has been in an economic slump since the mid-1980s, although the 1994 currency devaluation has helped the economy to some extent. Ivory Coast scores the same this year as last year, having reduced its government consumption of economic output while increasing its regulatory burden. In addition, private property has received less legal protection in recent times.

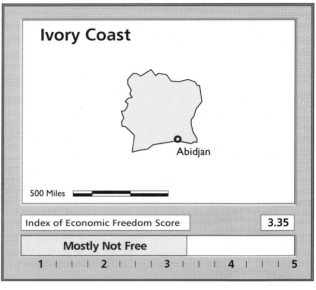

Ivory Coast

Abidjan

500 Miles

| Index of Economic Freedom Score | 3.35 |

Mostly Not Free

1   2   3   4   5

Factor #1: Trade Policy
Score: 5-Stable (Very high level of protectionism)

Ivory Coast has been reducing tariffs somewhat, although they remain high. The average tariff rate is 25.5 percent,[184] and there is a quota system for some goods. The government has a monopoly on rice imports, and other imports, including poultry products, are banned. There is extensive customs fraud.

Factor #2: Taxation
Score - Income taxation: 3-Stable (Moderate tax rates)
Score - Corporate taxation: 3-Stable (Moderate tax rates)
Final Taxation Score: 3.5-Stable (High tax rates)

Ivory Coast has moderately high taxes. The top income tax rate is 60 percent, and the average income is taxed at 10 percent. The top corporate income tax level is 35 percent. Ivory Coast also has a 35 percent capital gains tax, a 20 percent value-added tax, and a turnover tax of from 10 percent to 25 percent on services and interest provided by banks and financial companies.

---

184   Based on total taxes on international trade as a percentage of total imports; from International Monetary Fund, *Government Financial Statistics 1995.*

Factor #3: Government Intervention in the Economy
Score: 3-Stable (Moderate level of government intervention)

Government consumes 17 percent of Ivory Coast's GDP,[185] most of which is generated by a significant state-owned sector. The country also has a large civil service, and the government is enthusiastic about showpiece public works projects. There has been some progress in privatization, including the recent sale of the country's largest rubber producer to a Belgian company.

Factor #4: Monetary Policy
Score: 1-Stable (Very low level of inflation)

Ivory Coast's average annual rate of inflation from 1985 to 1994 was -5.2 percent. In 1994–1995, however, the inflation rate was about 25 percent.

Factor #5: Capital Flows and Foreign Investment
Score: 3-Stable (Moderate barriers to foreign investment)

Ivory Coast recently developed a foreign investment code. There is little discrimination between domestic and foreign investors; however, proposals for total foreign ownership of assets are not always approved, and some industries are off-limits to private investors. Foreign investors remain wary because of crime, corruption, an inefficient and abusive bureaucracy, and unstable legal protections.

Factor #6: Banking
Score: 3-Stable (Moderate level of restrictions on banking)

There are 10 commercial banks operating in Ivory Coast. As a member of the Communaute Financiere Africaine (CFA), a financial grouping of several African countries that base the values of their currency on the French franc, the government exercises only moderate control of banking institutions, although it still owns shares in some banks.

Factor #7: Wage and Price Controls
Score: 3-Stable (Moderate level of wage and price controls)

Ivory Coast's government has made some progress toward liberalizing prices. In 1994, however, price controls on 30 goods and services were imposed for three months in the wake of the CFA's devaluation of the franc.[186] In addition, state dominance of several sectors reduces price competition; the state both sets the producer price and engages in the marketing of coffee and cocoa exports; and there are price controls on wheat and rice. Ivory Coast maintains a minimum wage law.

Factor #8: Property Rights
Score: 4- (Low level of protection of private property)

The court system in Ivory Coast, although much more efficient than in the past, is still unable to protect private property adequately. According to the U.S. Department of

---

185 World Bank, *World Development Report 1996.*

186 The CFA franc is a form of common currency by which African member countries agree to peg their currencies to a set value of the French franc.

Commerce, "Enforcement of contract rights can be a time consuming and expensive process. Not all cases are decided quickly, and some do not appear to be judged on their legal or contractual merits. This has led to a widely-held view within the business community that there are elements within the judiciary which can be corrupted."[187] Moreover, even when corruption is not present, the courts often rule in favor of the employee, regardless of the merits of the case. As the U.S. Department of Commerce also notes, "The Ivorian courts have historically been viewed as favoring the employee in labor disputes."[188]

Factor #9: Regulation
Score: 4-Stable (High level of regulation)

The bureaucracy in Ivory Coast is cumbersome, corrupt, and subject to political manipulation. Companies sometimes find it difficult to complete the paperwork required to open a business. The government has tried, with very modest success, to reduce the bureaucratic barriers to business by making it easier for businesses to conform to government regulations, but the private sector remains highly regulated. Labor legislation is more onerous than in many developed countries, and foreign companies are under increasing informal pressure to use local labor. "The labor laws in force in Côte d'Ivoire are considerably more burdensome than those that an American employer may be accustomed to practicing in the United States," reports the U.S. Department of Commerce. "For example, expatriate labor contracts as well as all fixed term contracts must be registered with the labor authorities and approved before such employees can be hired. In addition, all employees accrue during the time with the company in question, certain statutory benefits and entitlements which may not be waived by contract."[189]

Factor #10: Black Market
Score: 4-Stable (High level of black market activity)

Ivory Coast's high trade barriers make the smuggling of many items, mainly consumer goods, a lucrative business. There is a growing black market in food aid, in addition to substantial black market activity in pirated intellectual property like videos and computer software. According to the U.S. Department of Commerce, "Though in theory prohibited, counterfeit clothing, textiles, footwear, watches, and audio and video tapes can be found, particularly among street vendors."[190]

---

187   U.S. Department of Commerce, *Country Commercial Guide*, 1996.

188   *Ibid.*

189   *Ibid.*

190   *Ibid.*

Summary

Ivory Coast			Overall Score	3.35
Trade	5	Monetary Policy	1	Property Rights	4
Taxation	3.5	Foreign Investment	3	Regulation	4
Government Intervention	3	Banking	3	Black Market	4
		Wage and Prices	3		

JAMAICA

The Caribbean island nation of Jamaica seldom has adopted a free-market approach to economic policy. During the 1970s and part of the 1980s, the Jamaican government was the primary player in the economy, entrepreneurship was not encouraged, and the country was on its way to developing a socialist economy. Until recently, the Jamaican economy was characterized by a high level of protectionism and government intervention. The government has opened the economy to foreign investments, however, and has reduced both taxes and tariffs. Although Jamaica's economy has grown slowly in the past, the prospects for future economic growth seem encouraging.

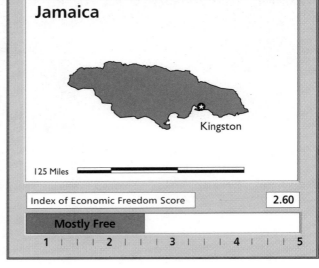

Jamaica

Kingston

125 Miles

| Index of Economic Freedom Score | 2.60 |

Mostly Free

1 | | | 2 | | | 3 | | | 4 | | | 5

Factor #1: Trade Policy
Score: 2+ (Low level of protectionism)

Jamaica's tariff rates range from 0 percent to 30 percent (to be reduced to 20 percent by 1998). The average tariff rate is about 9 percent. There are no significant non-tariff barriers.

Factor #2: Taxation
Score - Income taxation: 2-Stable (Low tax rates)
Score - Corporate taxation: 3-Stable (Moderate tax rates)
Final Taxation Score: 3-Stable (Moderate tax rates)

Jamaica's top marginal income tax rate is 25 percent; the average income level also is taxed at 25 percent. The top marginal corporate tax rate is 33.33 percent. Jamaica also has a consumption tax of up to 15 percent.

Factor #3: Government Intervention in the Economy
Score: 2-Stable (Low level of government intervention)

The Jamaican government consumes 14.1 percent of GDP, down from around 20 percent in 1980. In an effort to limit budget deficits and stimulate the private sector, Jamaica has undertaken an aggressive program of privatization—for example, by trying to privatize the railway system.

Factor #4: Monetary Policy
Score: 4-Stable (High level of inflation)

Jamaica's average annual rate of inflation from 1985 to 1994 was 28.3 percent. The inflation rate decreased to 20 percent in 1995.

Factor #5: Capital Flows and Foreign Investment
Score: 2-Stable (Low barriers to foreign investment)

Jamaica encourages foreign investment in nearly all areas. It also provides some incentives to investors who use Jamaican raw materials and supplies.

Factor #6: Banking
Score: 2-Stable (Low level of restrictions on banking)

Jamaica has a mixture of domestic and foreign banks. There are few direct restrictions on the formation of banks, and the government has reduced its control of the financial system.

Factor #7: Wage and Price Controls
Score: 3-Stable (Moderate level of wage and price controls)

Price controls remain on many items, including bus fares and kerosene. Jamaica has a minimum wage law.

Factor #8: Property Rights
Score: 2-Stable (High level of protection of private property)

The chance of expropriation in Jamaica is remote. Private property receives adequate protection.

Factor #9: Regulation
Score: 3-Stable (Moderate level of regulation)

Most regulations are only moderately burdensome. Bribery and corruption exist in government, but they are minimal.

Factor #10: Black Market
Score: 3-Stable (Moderate level of black market activity)

Smuggling is big business in Jamaica because prices remain high in many areas such as consumer electronics. Pirated broadcasts, video tapes, and recorded music are found frequently on the black market. The U.S. Department of State reports that McDonald's Corporation is suing a Jamaican restaurant for allegedly stealing its name and sign.[191]

Summary

Jamaica				Overall Score	2.60
Trade	2	Monetary Policy	4	Property Rights	2
Taxation	3	Foreign Investment	2	Regulation	3
Government Intervention	2	Banking	2	Black Market	3
		Wage and Prices	3		

191   State Department Report, 1996.

JAPAN

Japan has been one of the world's fastest-growing economies throughout the post–World War II era. With a democracy firmly in place by 1946 and an economy in ruins, Japan eliminated most elements of its formerly statist economy and adopted the basics of a free-market system. This helped propel it to the economic status it now enjoys. Japan's governmental system continues to impose controls on the economy, however, often informally but sometimes formally. Recently, the government's mismanagement of the economy has left Japan in a dismal economic recession. The economy has posted its third straight year of less than 1 percent growth. It seems at last to be recovering, posting an impressive gain of 13 percent for the first quarter of 1996. This improvement has been achieved mainly through government stimulus of the economy and reduced regulations.

Index of Economic Freedom Score   2.05

Mostly Free

Factor #1: Trade Policy
Score: 2-Stable (Low level of protectionism)

Many economists argue that Japan is very protectionist. Yet Japan's average tariff rate is among the world's lowest—less than 2 percent, which is less than that of even the United States. Tariffs have never been the problem in Japan, as they are in the United States and the European Union, but the country does remain plagued with non-tariff barriers. These include government red tape, government toleration of business collusion, exclusionary private business practices, a fragmented distribution system, and a relatively unapproachable government bureaucracy. Although these may prove to be impediments to some imports, Japan's market is more accessible than those of most other countries.[192] Therefore, by global standards, especially when compared with those of countries like Bangladesh, India, and Yemen, Japan's trade barriers are relatively low. Moreover, since 1994 Japan has achieved several agreements with other countries, both within the General Agreement on Tariffs and Trade and bilaterally with the United States, to reduce many non-tariffs barriers, including its import ban on rice.

192   Based on the criteria used in this survey, Japan's heavy use of non-tariff barriers moves its score one point higher, representing less economic freedom.

Factor #2: Taxation

Score - Income taxation: 4-Stable (High tax rates)
Score - Corporate taxation: 4-Stable (High tax rates)
Final Taxation Score: 4.5-Stable (Very high tax rates)

Japan's top income tax rate is 50 percent, and the tax on the average income level is 20 percent. The top marginal corporate tax rate is 37.5 percent. Japan also has prefectural and municipal taxes, an inhabitant's tax that is paid to the prefecture or municipality in which the company is located, a capital gains tax of 37.5 percent, and an enterprise tax of 6 percent to 12.84 percent.

Factor #3: Government Intervention in the Economy

Score: 1-Stable (Very low government intervention)

Government consumes 9.7 percent of Japan's GDP. The Japanese government has gone from periods of extensive subsidies to opening up its market for some products, such as rice. Moreover, government expenditures have been kept lower than those of other countries because the United States has provided for Japan's defense. Even though Japan's economic recovery is based partially on increased government spending, that spending is declining as a percentage of GDP.

Factor #4: Monetary Policy

Score: 1-Stable (Very low level of inflation)

Japan's annual rate of inflation averaged only 1.4 percent from 1985 to 1994. In 1995, the country had a negative inflation rate of about 0.1 percent. For 1996, the inflation rate is expected to be 0.2 percent.

Factor #5: Capital Flows and Foreign Investment

Score: 3-Stable (Moderate barriers to foreign investment)

Japan's foreign investment procedures were overhauled in the early 1990s, eliminating the need to notify the government in advance of investment in all areas except agriculture, aircraft, atomic energy, fisheries, forestry, leather goods, oil and gas production, and space development. The close relationship between government and private businesses, however, continues to impede foreign investment because some businesses and government agencies collude to make it too costly. The biggest barrier to investment in Japan is the high value of the yen.

Factor #6: Banking

Score: 3-Stable (Moderate level of restrictions on banking)

The banking industry is very competitive in Japan. The government places few restrictions on Japanese banks and their ability to engage in a variety of services. For example, banks are allowed to underwrite, deal, and broker all kinds of securities through subsidiaries. This allows them to be more competitive. Japan maintains significant regulations on banks, however; it is difficult, for example, for banks to liquidate bad loans by selling them off to buyers at a discount. Moreover, banks may not list a loan as "in default" until it has been in arrears for at least six months (compared to only three months in the United States). These and other regulations make it difficult for banks to diversify risk and recoup losses on bad loans. Finally, the Japanese government has imposed a host of new regulations to deal with a financial crisis, and has agreed to bail out many failing financial institutions.

Factor #7: Wage and Price Controls
Score: 2-Stable (Low level of wage and price controls)

With the exception of rice, there are no price controls in Japan. Wages are set mainly by the market, although Japan also has a minimum wage.

Factor #8: Property Rights
Score: 1-Stable (Very high level of protection of private property)

Japan has an efficient legal and court system capable of protecting property rights. Government expropriation of property is unlikely.

Factor #9: Regulation
Score: 2-Stable (Low level of regulation)

Although Japan's economy often is characterized as heavily regulated, most businesses enjoy a large amount of economic freedom. The process for opening a business in Japan has been made easier in the past several years. Moreover, even though some regulations may impose a burden on individuals, regulations on businesses are aimed at allowing them enough room to maximize profits. Therefore, many regulations on business either are not enforced or are not significantly burdensome. For example, Japan rarely enforces its anti-trust laws, allowing businesses to join forces without the threat of anti-monopoly litigation from competitors. Therefore, by global standards, Japan's level of regulation is low.

Factor #10: Black Market
Score: 1-Stable (Very low level of black market activity)

The Japanese government has undertaken an immense crackdown on such illegal activities as the buying and selling of guns and narcotics. Although Japan has very strong intellectual property protection, there still is some black market activity in pirated sound recording and computer software. As a result, the government has increased its prosecution of those who violate the intellectual property laws. These activities represent a minuscule portion of Japan's $4 trillion economy.

Summary

Japan					Overall Score	2.05
Trade	2	Monetary Policy	1	Property Rights	1
Taxation	4.5	Foreign Investment	3	Regulation	2
Government Intervention	1	Banking	3	Black Market	1
		Wage and Prices	2		

JORDAN

Ruled by the Hashemite monarchy, Jordan became an independent country in 1946. In 1988, King Hussein began a series of economic reforms to correct lagging growth rates. The king is attempting to reduce Jordan's budget deficit through controlled spending, reduced subsidies and tariffs, and lower taxes. The government still maintains, however, many policies that limit economic freedom and hinder economic growth, although it has reduced both income and corporate tax rates recently.

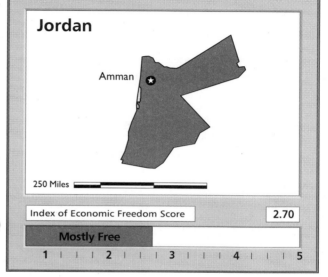

Jordan

Amman ⊛

250 Miles

| Index of Economic Freedom Score | 2.70 |

Mostly Free

1　　2　　3　　4　　5

Factor #1: Trade Policy

Score: 4-Stable (High level of protectionism)

Jordan's average tariff rate is 16 percent.[193] Taxes on items like automobiles are particularly high, ranging from 44 percent to 200 percent, and customs procedures are plagued by bureaucracy.

Factor #2: Taxation

Score - Income taxation: 3-Stable (Moderate tax rates)
Score - Corporate taxation: 3+ (Moderate high tax rates)
Final Taxation Score: 3+ (Moderate tax rates)

Jordan's top marginal income tax rate is 45 percent, down from 55 percent in 1995, and the average income level is taxed at a rate of 5 percent. The top corporate tax rate is 35 percent, down from 55 percent in 1996.

Factor #3: Government Intervention in the Economy

Score: 2-Stable (Low level of government intervention)

Jordan's government consumes 23.1 percent of GDP.

Factor #4: Monetary Policy

Score: 2-Stable (Low level of inflation)

Jordan's annual rate of inflation from 1985 to 1994 averaged 7.1 percent. In 1995, the inflation rate was 2.4 percent.

193　Based on IMF statistics for taxes on international transactions as a percentage of total imports; from International Monetary Fund, *Government Financial Statistics, 1995.*

Factor #5: Capital Flows and Foreign Investment
Score: 2-Stable (Low barriers to foreign investment)

Jordan maintains few restrictions on foreign investment. Industries deemed vital to national security, however, such as utilities, are not open to outside investors, and there are some ownership restrictions on trade and transportation industries.

Factor #6: Banking
Score: 2-Stable (Low level of restrictions on banking)

Foreigners are allowed to invest in Jordanian banks. The government maintains some control over banks through strict reserve requirements.

Factor #7: Wage and Price Controls
Score: 3-Stable (Moderate level of wage and price controls)

Jordan's government sets prices on such items as "non-strategic food commodities" and "non-food commodities." For example, it rations such goods as sugar, rice, and milk, and subsidizes prices of such basic foodstuffs as cereals, sugar, milk, and frozen meat. There is a minimum wage for specific trades.

Factor #8: Property Rights
Score: 2-Stable (High level of protection of private property)

Expropriation is unlikely in Jordan. Property receives adequate protection from legal institutions and the police force.

Factor #9: Regulation
Score: 3-Stable (Moderate level of regulation)

Jordan's regulatory environment is moderately bureaucratic and burdensome. Under Jordan's 1993 disabilities law, for example, many businesses are being forced to retrofit their buildings to accommodate the hearing, sight, and physically disabled. This expense is proving to be a substantial burden on many businesses.

Factor #10: Black Market
Score: 4-Stable (High level of black market activity)

Because levels of trade protectionism are so high, smuggling is a big business in Jordan. In particular, computer software and related items provide significant business to black marketeers. According to the U.S. Department of State, "The practice of pirating audio and video tapes for commercial purposes is widespread, with the government making no effort to intervene. Pirated books are sold in Jordan though few, if any, are published within the country."[194]

---

194   State Department Report, 1996, p. 476.

Summary

Jordan					Overall Score	2.70
Trade	4	Monetary Policy	2	Property Rights	2
Taxation	3	Foreign Investment	2	Regulation	3
Government Intervention	2	Banking	2	Black Market	4
		Wage and Prices	3		

KENYA

The East African country of Kenya gained its independence from Great Britain in 1963. A long period of one-party rule ended in 1991 with the legalization of opposition political parties. Political freedoms, however, remain fairly constricted, and the economy—once one of Africa's freest and prosperous—has deteriorated badly because of government corruption and mismanagement. Over the past several years, the government of President Daniel arap Moi frequently has been in conflict with Western donors and international financial institutions over Kenya's corruption and lack of economic reform. Kenya is plagued with serious ethnic conflict. Recently, the average tariff rate has increased, and customs delays have worsened. Kenya, however, also has opened up its banking sector to more competition.

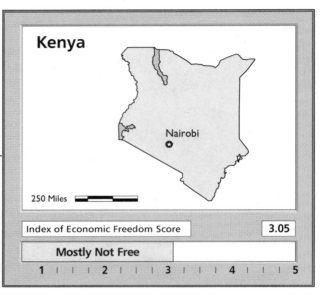

Kenya

Nairobi

250 Miles

| Index of Economic Freedom Score | 3.05 |

Mostly Not Free

1 2 3 4 5

Factor #1: Trade Policy
Score: 4- (High level of protectionism)

Kenya's average tariff rate is 13.5 percent. In 1993, import licenses were abolished for most goods. The customs system, however, is prone to corruption. According to the U.S. Department of State, "Customs procedures are overly detailed and rigidly implemented with resulting delays in clearing both imports and exports."[195] Some imports, including sugar, maize, wheat, and milk, are banned.

Factor #2: Taxation
Score - Income taxation: 3-Stable (Moderate tax rates)
Score - Corporate taxation: 3-Stable (Moderate tax rates)
Total Taxation Score: 3.5-Stable (High tax rates)

Kenya's top income tax rate is 35 percent, and the average income is taxed at approximately 10 percent. The top corporate income tax is 35 percent. Kenya also has a value-added tax that ranges from 18 percent to 40 percent.

Factor #3: Government Intervention in the Economy
Score: 3- Stable (Moderate level of government intervention)

Kenya's government consumes 17.5 percent of GDP. It also plans to privatize over 100 state-owned companies, though at least 31 will be kept under state control. To date, however, little progress has been made in privatization. There are fears in Kenya that

---

195   State Department Report, 1996, p. 17.

Asians will be the beneficiaries, and President Moi has complained that his government was being pressured to hand over state assets to "whites."

Factor #4: Monetary Policy
Score: 2-Stable (Low level of inflation)

Kenya's average annual rate of inflation between 1985 and 1994 was 11.7 percent. The inflation rate was approximately 28 percent in 1994.

Factor #5: Capital Flows and Foreign Investment
Score: 3-Stable (Moderate barriers to foreign investment)

Kenya permits complete foreign ownership of some enterprises, and most sectors are open to foreign participation. The government also has suggested that foreigners would be acceptable buyers of state-owned enterprises slated for privatization, although enterprises on the Kenyan Stock Exchange are limited to 40 percent foreign participation (which previously was 20 percent). Export Promotion Zones offering tax breaks have been established; but because investment proposals are approved on a case-by-case basis and the procedures for obtaining government approval are so burdensome, arbitrary, and often corrupt, foreign investment is declining. President Moi has been railing against foreign investment, and presidential approval is required for foreign acquisition of agricultural land. The government does not permit foreign investment in insurance or in government-sanctioned monopolies.

Factor #6: Banking
Score: 2+ (Low level of restrictions on banking)

Two state-controlled banks make loans to state industries. The National Bank of Kenya has been partially privatized. Lending levels to agriculture are mandated, and commercial banks are required to store a percentage of their deposits with the central bank. Kenya recently has deregulated the banking industry, however. The U.S. Department of Commerce reports that "NBFIs [non-bank financial institutions] recently have exhibited an ability to compete with commercial banks, particularly because of the less restrictive regulatory framework within which they operate. On paper, NBFIs operate as merchant or investment banks. In practice, they operate as commercial banks, taking deposits and making short-term loans."[196]

Factor #7: Wage and Price Controls
Score: 3-Stable (Moderate level of wage and price controls)

Price controls have been lifted in almost every sector of Kenya's economy. The pricing of petroleum products has been freed. Some agricultural products, however, including coffee, must be sold through monopolistic government marketing boards. Monopolies, many of them government-sanctioned, control approximately half of the Kenyan market, reducing price competition. Most wages are negotiated, although Kenya has a minimum wage.

---

196   U.S. Department of Commerce, *Country Commercial Guide*, 1996.

Factor #8: Property Rights
Score: 3-Stable (Moderate level of protection of private property)

Property in Kenya is constitutionally protected from compulsory state takeover. In the exceptional case of expropriation, owners receive compensation, albeit in local currency. In some cases, foreign investors have been deported and business licenses arbitrarily revoked. The independence of the judiciary is questionable. "At times," reports the U.S. Department of Commerce, "resolution of these [property] disputes is delayed either due to the influence of the person involved, or because authorities are reluctant to take action because of the perceived political importance of the individuals."[197]

Factor #9: Regulation
Score: 4-Stable (High level of regulation)

Companies are registered with relative ease, although some have found their operating licenses arbitrarily suspended. Businesses are required to file monthly reports on their activities, and it is difficult to terminate employees. To reduce unemployment, the government pressures firms to use labor-intensive methods of production instead of technology. As a result, companies often are over-staffed and face excessively high payroll demands. Moreover, although the government has made some progress in cracking down, corruption continues. According to the U.S. Department of Commerce, "Internal politics influences the Kenyan business climate. Corruption is a pervasive issue. Appointments to ministries, parastatals, and financial institutions based on political connections occur. Tenders have been awarded on the basis of political connections."[198]

Factor #10: Black Market
Score: 3-Stable (Moderate level of black market activity)

The government's monopoly on the distribution of some agricultural products in Kenya encourages illegal trading, and the heavy regulation placed on business likewise encourages "illegal" commerce in many items. There is significant piracy of stolen intellectual property. According to the U.S. Department of State, "Kenyan laws on intellectual property are less than adequate and enforcement of existing legislation is poor, resulting in widespread piracy."[199] Nevertheless, compared to the size of Kenya's $6.6 billion economy, these activities affect the economy only moderately.

Summary

Kenya				Overall Score	3.05
Trade	4	Monetary Policy	2	Property Rights	3
Taxation	3.5	Foreign Investment	3	Regulation	4
Government Intervention	3	Banking	2	Black Market	3
		Wage and Prices	3		

197 *Ibid.*

198 *Ibid.*

199 State Department Report, 1996, p. 18.

KOREA, DEMOCRATIC PEOPLE'S REPUBLIC OF (NORTH KOREA)

North Korea remains one of the world's most economically repressed countries. Its economy is still controlled by the central government, few entrepreneurial activities are legal, and there has been little economic growth in the past decade. Although some signs point toward eventual economic liberalization, there is scant evidence that North Korea is heading down the road of *perestroika*. North Korea is now facing a severe food shortage that will place increasing strains on its already weak economy.

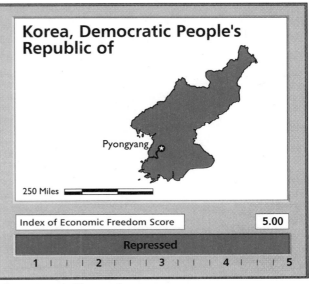

Korea, Democratic People's Republic of

Pyongyang

250 Miles

| Index of Economic Freedom Score | 5.00 |

Repressed

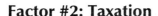

Factor #1: Trade Policy

Score: 5-Stable (Very high level of protectionism)

All imports into and exports from North Korea are controlled and inspected by the government. There is an effective ban on many imports from Western countries. North Korea is essentially closed to trade, except for items manufactured in and imported from South Korea.

Factor #2: Taxation

Score - Income taxation: 5-Stable (Very high tax rates)
Score - Corporate taxation: 5-Stable (Very high tax rates)
Final Taxation Score: 5-Stable (Very high tax rates)

As North Korea is a communist state, all property is owned by the government. Therefore, the government confiscates all economic output, resulting in real tax rates of 100 percent.

Factor #3: Government Intervention in the Economy

Score: 5-Stable (Very high level of government Intervention)

North Korea has a command economy in which the government owns most of the property and still sets production levels on most products. State-owned industries account for nearly all GDP.

Factor #4: Monetary Policy

Score: 5-Stable (Very high level of inflation)

As a communist state, North Korea does not officially admit to having inflation. This is, however, a fiction. The official prices of goods may be low because they are controlled and subsidized by the state, but the tremendous scarcity of goods and services attests to their real value. Moreover, the government covers its huge domestic debts simply by printing money. As a result, the currency is worth little and is not convertible on the international market.

Factor #5: Capital Flows and Foreign Investment
Score: 5-Stable (Very high barriers to foreign investment)

North Korea recently has claimed to recognize the importance of foreign investment, but foreign investors are not afforded equal treatment under North Korean law. The government must remain a majority owner, and investments are effectively banned in most industries.

Factor #6: Banking
Score: 5-Stable (Very high level of restrictions on banking)

The North Korean financial system is controlled by the government. Foreigners are barred from North Korean banking services.

Factor #7: Wage and Price Controls
Score: 5-Stable (Very high level of wage and price controls)

Wages and prices are determined by the North Korean government.

Factor #8: Property Rights
Score: 5-Stable (Very low level of protection of private property)

North Korea bans private property ownership.

Factor #9: Regulation
Score: 5-Stable (Very high level of regulation)

As North Korea's chief economic player, the government regulates the economy heavily.

Factor #10: Black Market
Score: 5-Stable (Very high level of black market activity)

North Korea has an immense black market. Many who engage in such activities have been imprisoned.

Summary

Korea, Democratic People's Republic of				Overall Score	5.00
Trade	5	Monetary Policy	5	Property Rights	5
Taxation	5	Foreign Investment	5	Regulation	5
Government Intervention	5	Banking	5	Black Market	5
		Wage and Prices	5		

KOREA, REPUBLIC OF (SOUTH KOREA)

Following the Korean War, economic liberalization became the standard in the Republic of Korea (ROK), while nationalization and collectivization were the norm in communist North Korea. Faced with a potential reduction in U.S. foreign aid in the 1960s, South Korea reformed its economy to attract foreign investment and develop its export industries. As a result, it has become one of the world's fastest-growing countries. The ROK recently cut taxes, although its average tariff is higher than in previous years.

Korea, Republic of

Seoul

125 Miles

| Index of Economic Freedom Score | 2.45 |

Mostly Free

1   2   3   4   5

Factor #1: Trade Policy

Score: 3- (Moderate level of protectionism)

The average tariff rate in South Korea is 7.9 percent, up from about 4 percent a year ago but down from 23.7 percent in 1980. This is due mainly to the Uruguay Round of the General Agreement on Tariffs and Trade (GATT), which permitted the government to remove some quotas on agricultural goods in exchange for tariffs. The ROK's non-tariff barriers remain stringent. According to the U.S. Department of State, "a variety of non-tariff barriers have emerged as obstacles to imports, including onerous and non-scientific food safety and plant quarantine requirements."[200] Moreover, "The typical trade barriers U.S. exporters experience today are rooted in the maze of regulations which greatly complicate the process of licensing, inspections, type approval, marking requirements and other standards affecting trade."[201]

Factor #2: Taxation

Score - Income taxation: 4+ (High tax rates)
Score - Corporate taxation: 4-Stable (High tax rates)
Total Taxation Score: 4.5+(Very high tax rates)

South Korea's top income tax rate is 45 percent, down from 48 percent in 1995, and the average income level is taxed at a rate of 18 percent. The top corporate income tax rate is 28 percent. The ROK also has a 10 percent "resident surtax" (which raises the effective rate to over 35 percent) and a 20 percent capital gains tax.

Factor #3: Government Intervention in the Economy

Score: 2-Stable (Low level of government intervention)

South Korea's government consumes 10 percent of GDP, down from 11 percent a year ago, and there has been little privatization. The government remains heavily in-

200   State Department Report, 1996, p. 69.

201   *Ibid.*

volved in such industries as banking, utilities, and services, as well as in some heavy manufacturing. According to the U.S. Department of State, "government intervention is extensive and costly in terms of economic efficiency."[202] Still, by global standards, South Korea's government intervention in the economy is low.

Factor #4: Monetary Policy
Score: 2-Stable (Low level of inflation)

South Korea's average inflation rate from 1985 to 1994 was 6.8 percent. Inflation fell to 4.5 percent in 1995.

Factor #5: Capital Flows and Foreign Investment
Score: 3-Stable (Moderate barriers to foreign investment)

The government of South Korea has relied on foreign investment to build its export economy. Foreign investments have been particularly useful in developing the ROK's high-tech industries, which are heavily involved in exports. Yet Korea's foreign investment code is subject to variable interpretation and is not always applied systematically. Foreign investors are not always treated the same as domestic firms, for example, and may encounter discriminatory lending practices when dealing with local financial institutions. Some restrictions remain on land ownership.

Factor #6: Banking
Score: 2-Stable (Low level of restrictions on banking)

Foreign banks were welcome in South Korea as early as 1967. Although the government occasionally tries to steer capital to small businesses, it also has been removed from direct ownership of banks since the early 1990s. Local banks are permitted to underwrite, deal, and broker all kinds of securities and to invest in some real estate ventures.

Factor #7: Wage and Price Controls
Score: 2-Stable (Low level of wage and price controls)

Most prices in South Korea are set by the market, although controls are imposed on the prices of beef, electric power, petroleum products, and transportation services. The government also maintains stockpiles of foodstuffs which it releases into the market to raise or lower prices. South Korea maintains a minimum wage law, but some companies are exempt.

Factor #8: Property Rights
Score: 1-Stable (Very high level of protection of private property)

Private property is secure in South Korea, and expropriation is very unlikely. The ROK has a stable, efficient legal system to protect private property.

Factor #9: Regulation
Score: 3-Stable (Moderate level of regulation)

Obtaining a business license in South Korea is a simple process. All businesses must be registered, but the process is efficient and not significantly burdensome. The

---

202   *Ibid.*, p. 68.

government sometimes fails to publish all of its regulations, however, and enforcement remains haphazard. Sometimes businesses find themselves in violation of regulations they did not know existed. In addition, South Korea enforces most labor standards only on domestic firms, leaving foreign firms vulnerable to such radical labor activities as arbitrary strikes. In some cases, these activities have forced the bankruptcy of foreign firms, which have fled the country without paying their employees. As a result, Korea requires that foreign firms deposit three months' wages in a special account.

Factor #10: Black Market

Score: 2-Stable (Low level of black market activity)

South Korea has a fairly small black market. A sizable number of employers, however, try to avoid the minimum wage laws. South Korea has stringent intellectual property laws, and recent government crackdowns on pirated material are beginning to take effect. Piracy of computer software, although still widespread, represents a small portion of the South Korean economy.

Summary

Korea, Republic of		Overall Score	2.45
Trade	3		
Taxation	4.5		
Government Intervention	2		

Monetary Policy	2
Foreign Investment	3
Banking	2
Wage and Prices	2

Property Rights	1
Regulation	3
Black Market	2

KUWAIT

Kuwait is a Persian Gulf emirate with a small and relatively open oil-rich economy. Kuwait has about 94 billion barrels of crude oil reserves, about 10 percent of total world reserves. This almost assures that it will remain affluent into the next century, absent external interference. Kuwait's economy has undergone several major shocks over the past two decades, including massive government intervention in the late 1970s, the collapse of the Kuwaiti securities market in 1982, the collapse of world oil prices in the mid-1980s, and invasion by Iraq in 1990. The Kuwaiti government continues to control oil production. Oil revenues are its chief source of income and allow it keep import tariffs and taxation to a minimum.

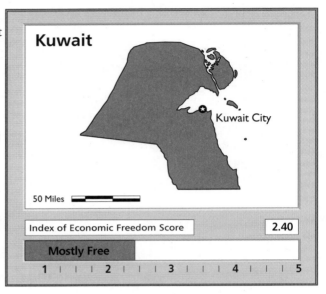

Factor #1: Trade Policy
Score: 2-Stable (Low level of protectionism)

Kuwait's average tariff rate is 4 percent. Government procurement policies generally cater to Kuwaiti firms, and there are non-tariff barriers in the form of strict standards on imports, especially food.

Factor #2: Taxation
Score - Income taxation: 1-Stable (Very low tax rates)
Score - Corporate taxation: 1-Stable (Very low tax rates)
Final Taxation Score: 1-Stable (Very low tax rates)

Kuwait has no income tax. Nor does it have either a corporate tax (except on some foreign firms) or any other significant taxes.

Factor #3: Government Intervention in the Economy
Score: 4-Stable (High level of government intervention)

The Kuwaiti government consumes about 36.7 percent of GDP. Most of the country's GDP is from oil production, nearly all of which is owned by the government.

Factor #4: Monetary Policy
Score: 2-Stable (Low level of inflation)

Kuwait's average rate of inflation from 1989 to 1994 was about 10.5 percent. In 1995, the inflation rate was about 3 percent.

Factor #5: Capital Flows and Foreign Investment
Score: 4-Stable (High barriers to foreign investment)

Kuwait is generally open to some types of foreign investment, but some significant restrictions still exist. "Foreign investment...is welcome in Kuwait," according to the U.S. Department of State, "but only in select sectors as minority partners and only on terms compatible with continued Kuwaiti control of all basic economic activities."[203] Moreover, although Kuwaiti firms pay no corporate tax, foreign firms must pay a corporate tax as high as 55 percent.

Factor #6: Banking
Score: 3-Stable (Moderate level of restrictions on banking)

Banking in Kuwait is competitive, and banks are relatively free from government control. But with the exception of investment banking, the banking system is closed to foreigners, although the government does plan to increase foreign participation.

Factor #7: Wage and Price Controls
Score: 3-Stable (Moderate level of wage and price controls)

Wages and prices in Kuwait are set mainly by the market. The government continues to offer subsidies to many businesses, however, thus distorting prices on some goods and services like food.

Factor #8: Property Rights
Score: 1-Stable (Very high level of protection of private property)

Private property is protected in Kuwait. The legal and judicial system is efficient.

Factor #9: Regulation
Score: 2-Stable (Low level of regulation)

Establishing a business in Kuwait is easy if the business does not compete directly with state-owned concerns. Regulations are applied evenly in most cases.

Factor #10: Black Market
Score: 2-Stable (Low level of black market activity)

The black market is confined mainly to pirated software, video and cassette recordings, and similar products. The government continues to combat violators.

Summary

Kuwait				Overall Score	2.40
Trade	2	Monetary Policy	2	Property Rights	1
Taxation	1	Foreign Investment	4	Regulation	2
Government Intervention	4	Banking	3	Black Market	2
		Wage and Prices	3		

---

203 State Department Report, 1996, p. 480.

LAOS

A constitutional monarchy before 1975, Laos now has one of the world's most repressed economies. Laos is a one-party communist state with a highly centralized, government-planned economy that is riddled with corruption and graft. The Clinton Administration recently has removed a U.S. restriction on foreign aid, paving the way for development assistance to the regime. With such a highly corrupt and restricted system, however, the Laotian government is likely to squander U.S. foreign aid and use it to maintain the country's centrally planned communist economy.

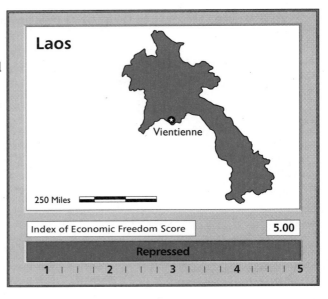

Laos

Vientienne

250 Miles

| Index of Economic Freedom Score | 5.00 |

Repressed

1　2　3　4　5

Factor #1: Trade Policy

Score: 5-Stable (Very high level of protectionism)

All imports into Laos are inspected by a corrupt customs service that arbitrarily applies customs levels and taxes imports. These officials sometimes simply confiscate imports at the border. With corruption sanctioned and supported by customs officials, Laos has trade barriers that effectively bar most imports.

Factor #2: Taxation

Score - Income taxation: 5-Stable (Very high tax rates)
Score - Corporate taxation: 5-Stable (Very high tax rates)
Final Taxation Score: 5-Stable (Very high tax rates)

Because of its total control of the economy, the Laotian government in essence is able to confiscate the proceeds of all economic activity; and since the government owns the fruits of almost all economic activity, the resulting rate of taxation approaches 100 percent.

Factor #3: Government Intervention in the Economy

Score: 5-Stable (Very high level of government intervention)

Laos permits some private economic activity in a restricted way, but both the means of production and most of the profits gained from them remain entirely in the hands of the state. The Laotian government directly owns and runs most of the economy, which is centered around agriculture.

Factor #4: Monetary Policy

Score: 5-Stable (Very high level of inflation)

The official average rate of inflation for Laos from 1985 to 1993 is 29.6 percent; the actual level, however, is much higher. Because the government maintains a centrally planned economy, demand usually exceeds supply for most items. In a market economy, this often results in inflation; in centrally planned economies, it results in shortages and rationing, as is the case with many goods and services in Laos.

Factor #5: Capital Flows and Foreign Investment
Score: 5-Stable (Very high barriers to foreign investment)

Laos permits some foreign investment, and the Laotian government allows 100 percent foreign ownership of investments in almost all areas of the economy. But to say that Laos is open to foreign investment is misleading. Corruption and arbitrary government confiscation of profits through a multitude of constantly changing fees, taxes, stipends, and other charges make it nearly impossible to conduct business. Bribes to government officials are practically mandatory when establishing a business in Laos, and foreigners often are subject to government surveillance. Property is confiscated and foreigners are expelled from the country on a regular basis. Although Laos does not seek actively to prevent foreign investment, its centralized, corrupt, and bureaucratic economy and one-party communist rule have the same effect. Moreover, travel within Laos often is life-threatening. The U.S. Department of State warns that "Persons traveling overland in some areas, particularly in the highlands, run the risk of ambush by insurgents or bandits."[204]

Factor #6: Banking
Score: 5-Stable (Very high level of restrictions on banking)

Banks in Laos are owned and operated by the government and heavily influenced by the state-owned central bank. There is no free-market competition in this industry.

Factor #7: Wage and Price Controls
Score: 5-Stable (Very high level of wage and price controls)

Virtually all wages and prices in Laos—particularly on such products as rice, sugar, cloth, and gasoline—are set by the government.

Factor #8: Property Rights
Score: 5-Stable (Very low level of protection of private property)

Individuals are free to accumulate some private property, such as a home or a piece of land, but all such property is subject to expropriation, pillaging by Vietnamese "security" forces that routinely enter Laos, extortion by corrupt local government officials, and destruction by criminal elements sanctioned by the government. Moreover, Laos has a corrupt, state-controlled legal system that rarely sides with private citizens against the government.

Factor #9: Regulation
Score: 5-Stable (Very high level of regulation)

The Laotian government regulates the entire economy by owning and operating the means of production.

---

204 U.S. Department of State Travel Advisory, 1996.

Factor #10: Black Market

Score: 5- (Very high level of black market activity)

The black market in Laos is larger than the official or legal economy. As might be expected in a command economy, even basic economic activity is performed in the black market.

Summary

Laos				Overall Score	5.0
Trade	5	Monetary Policy	5	Property Rights	5
Taxation	5	Foreign Investment	5	Regulation	5
Government Intervention	5	Banking	5	Black Market	5
		Wage and Prices	5		

LATVIA

Latvia was an independent republic from 1918 to 1940, at which time it was annexed by the Soviet Union. Since declaring its independence on August 21, 1991, Latvia has liberalized its economy and has made substantial progress in opening its borders to trade and investment, although some roadblocks remain. Latvia enjoys a highly trained labor force and is home to several high-tech enterprises, as well as major ports on the Baltic Sea. After a 50 percent drop in GDP from 1991 to 1993, the economy began to recover in 1994 and has stabilized since. Latvia, which is applying for membership in the European Union, recently has reduced some barriers to foreign investment and banking. It also has streamlined its court system.

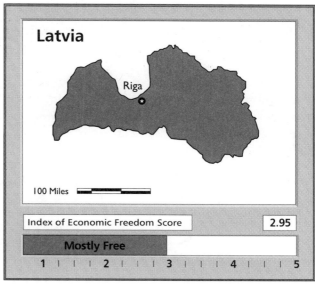

Index of Economic Freedom Score — 2.95

Mostly Free

1 2 3 4 5

Factor #1: Trade Policy

Score: 4-Stable (High level of protectionism)

Latvia's average tariff rate is 10 percent.[205] According to the U.S. Department of State, "Latvia requires a license for the import of grain, sugar, and alcohol to protect domestic production."[206] This is the principal non-tariff barrier to trade.

Factor #2: Taxation

Score - Income taxation: 2-Stable (Low tax rates)
Score - Corporate taxation: 2-Stable (Low tax rates)
Final Taxation Score: 2.5-Stable (Moderate tax rates)

Latvia has a flat income tax rate of 25 percent and a flat corporate tax rate of 25 percent. It also maintains an 18 percent value-added tax and a 37 percent social payments tax.

Factor #3: Government Intervention in the Economy

Score: 3- (Moderate level of government intervention)

Latvia's government consumes about 22 percent of GDP, almost 40 percent of which is still produced by the public sector.[207]

---

205 Constantine Michalopoulos and David Tarr, *Trade Performance and Policy in the New Independent States* (Washington, D.C.: The World Bank, 1996), p. 5.

206 State Department Report, 1996, p. 224.

207 Government of Latvia, *Latvia, Country Profile*, provided by Latvian embassy, Washington, D.C.

Factor #4: Monetary Policy
Score: 5-Stable (Very high level of inflation)

Latvia's rate of inflation was 25 percent in 1995, 35.9 percent in 1994, 109.2 percent in 1993, 951.2 percent in 1992, and 124.5 percent in 1991. Thus, even though Latvia has made tremendous progress in reducing inflation, the average annual rate since independence is over 200 percent.

Factor #5: Capital Flows and Foreign Investment
Score: 2+ (Low barriers to foreign investment)

There are few restrictions on investment in Latvia. Investors are permitted to invest in most industries but are restricted from acquiring majority shares in companies related to national defense. Investors now may own land in Latvia if there is an existing investment protection agreement between the two countries. Latvia's foreign investment code has been streamlined and updated.

Factor #6: Banking
Score: 2+ (Low level of restrictions on banking)

Latvia's banking sector underwent a significant transformation in 1995, with less competitive banks going out of business. Financial crisis in the banking industry in neighboring Russia also has caused collapse of some Latvian banks. Today, Latvia's banking system is beginning to stabilize; it is competitive and mostly free of onerous government regulation. "With the exception of the State Savings Bank (Krajbanka) system and Unibank (currently under privatization)," reports the U.S. Department of Commerce, "Latvia's commercial banking system is completely private. Since the first private commercial banks were established in the late 1980's, banking has grown exponentially in Latvia."[208] All foreign investments and foreign bank branches, however, must be approved by the Bank of Latvia.

Factor #7: Wage and Price Controls
Score: 2-Stable (Low level of wage and price controls)

Wages and prices in Latvia are set mainly by the private sector, although the government continues to set prices on some goods and services, such as electricity, government-controlled housing rents, and telecommunications.

Factor #8: Property Rights
Score: 2+ (High level of protection of private property)

Since independence, the government has not expropriated any property. The court system is becoming more efficient, and laws are being drafted to reflect Western standards more closely. There is no indication that the government unduly influences the legal process. According to the U.S. Department of Commerce, "Latvia is moving to re-organize its court system according to Western standards. In general, the Latvian judiciary is independent of improper government influences."[209] Some problems, however, with contract enforcement and judicial review continue.

---

208   U.S. Department of Commerce, *Country Commercial Guide,* 1996.

209   *Ibid.*

Factor #9: Regulation
Score: 3-Stable (Moderate level of regulation)

Establishing a business in Latvia is relatively easy, and many private businesses are opening in the country. There is some corruption, however, and some regulations are applied unevenly. "As in other countries to emerge from the old Soviet Bloc," reports the U.S. Department of Commerce, "government bureaucracy, corruption and organized crime are the most significant hurdles to U.S. trade and investment in Latvia."[210]

Factor #10: Black Market
Score: 4- (High level of black market activity)

The black market in Latvia involves mainly agricultural goods, transportation, and labor. The government estimates that black market activity is equivalent to one-third of the official economy, and significant trafficking in pirated video tapes and motion pictures persists. In addition, there is increasing black market activity in banking and the smuggling of commodities from Russia.

Summary

Latvia					Overall Score	2.95
Trade	4	Monetary Policy	5	Property Rights	3
Taxation	2.5	Foreign Investment	2	Regulation	2
Government Intervention	3	Banking	2	Black Market	4
		Wage and Prices	2		

---

210 *Ibid.*

LEBANON

In 1992, after 17 years of bloody civil war, Lebanon elected a new Prime Minister, Rafiq Hariri, who embarked on an ambitious reform plan aimed at stimulating the Lebanese economy. The war-torn nation suffers from a shattered infrastructure, outdated utilities, and crumbling buildings. This situation has provided great opportunities to businesses, which are rushing to rebuild the country. As a result, Lebanon is attempting to implement a more open foreign investment regime. Parts of the Lebanese economy are among the freest in the world; most restrictions on economic freedom are the result of civil war, the lack of the rule of law, and the intimidating presence of more than 30,000 Syrian troops, who engage extensively in car theft and smuggling operations.

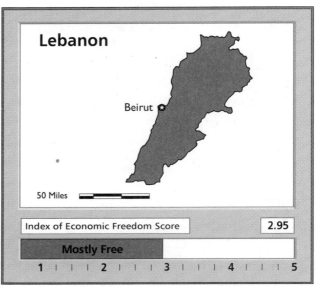

Factor #1: Trade Policy
Score: 2-Stable (Low level of protectionism)

The average tariff rate in Lebanon is less than 5 percent, and there are few non-tariff barriers, although the government does require import licenses for firearms and ammunition. Some corruption and inefficiency may exist within the customs service.

Factor #2: Taxation
Score - Income taxation: 2-Stable (Low tax rates)
Score - Corporate taxation: 2-Stable (Low tax rates)
Final Taxation Score: 2.5-Stable (Moderate tax rates)

Lebanon's top income tax rate is 10 percent, and the average taxpayer is in the 2 percent bracket. The top marginal corporate tax rate is 10 percent. Lebanon also has a 6 percent capital gains tax and a 12 percent social contributions tax.

Factor #3: Government Intervention in the Economy
Score: 2-Stable (Low level of government intervention)

The Lebanese government consumes about 11.6 percent of GDP, down from 15 percent a year ago. The government also has established a significant privatization program to reduce its role in the economy. "Lebanon enjoys a free-market economy and a strong laissez-faire commercial tradition," reports the U.S. Department of Commerce. "The government is seriously considering privatization of some public services. It has succeeded in awarding some contracts on a build/operate/transfer (BOT) basis. In 1994 it reduced the state's shares in three local medium and long term development banks to 30 percent in order to encourage private sector participation in economic reconstruction."[211]

Factor #4: Monetary Policy
Score: 5-Stable (Very High level of inflation)

Lebanon's average rate of inflation from 1990 to 1995 was about 50 percent.[212] In 1995, the inflation rate was reduced to about 12 percent.

Factor #5: Capital Flows and Foreign Investment
Score: 3-Stable (Moderate barriers to foreign investment)

According to the U.S. Department of Commerce, "Lebanon offers the most liberal investment climate in the Middle East."[213] It also, however, restricts the amount of real estate foreigners can own, still is lacking in the rule of law, and still needs an efficient investment approval regime. Thus, by global standards, the barriers to foreign investment in Lebanon are moderate.

Factor #6: Banking
Score: 2-Stable (Low level of restrictions on banking)

The banking system in Lebanon is highly competitive and saturated with private banks. There are over 70 commercial banks. Foreign banks, however, are not permitted to open wholly owned branches.

Factor #7: Wage and Price Controls
Score: 2-Stable (Low level of wage and price controls)

Wages and prices in Lebanon are set mainly by the market with very little government involvement. The government's consumer protection agency, however, can establish price controls.

Factor #8: Property Rights
Score: 3-Stable (Moderate level of protection of private property)

The largest threats to private property are the illegal activities and seizure of property by the Syrian army, the lack of an efficient legal system, and the inconsistent application of the rule of law. According to the U.S. Department of Commerce, "The legal system, modified after the French system, is being studied for modernization, and new laws tend to follow international patterns. Still, court cases are not settled rapidly because of shortage of judges and inadequate support structure."[214]

Factor #9: Regulation
Score: 3-Stable (Moderate level of regulation)

Establishing a business in Lebanon is easy, but corruption and crime can hinder normal business operations. The U.S. Department of Commerce reports that "The USG [U.S. government] continues to receive credible reports of corrupt activities by Syrian officials, particularly among Syrian military and intelligence units in the Bekaa Valley."[215]

---

211 U.S. Department of Commerce, *Country Commercial Guide,* 1996.

212 Average inflation rate figures from 1985 to 1993 are not available.

213 U.S. Department of Commerce, *Country Commercial Guide,* 1996.

214 *Ibid.*

Factor #10: Black Market

Score: 5-Stable (Very high level of black market activity)

Lebanon's black market includes extensive trading in such pirated intellectual property as trademarks, patents, and copyrights. Many services, such as transportation and construction, also are performed in the black market.

Summary

Lebanon				Overall Score	2.95
Trade	2	Monetary Policy	5	Property Rights	3
Taxation	2.5	Foreign Investment	3	Regulation	3
Government Intervention	2	Banking	2	Black Market	5
		Wage and Prices	2		

---

215 *Ibid.*

LESOTHO

The Southern African country of Lesotho, completely encircled by South Africa, gained its independence from the United Kingdom in 1966. During the 1970s and much of the 1980s, it adopted heavy restrictions on almost all economic activity. By 1990, the government began considering an economic reform program that remains in place today.

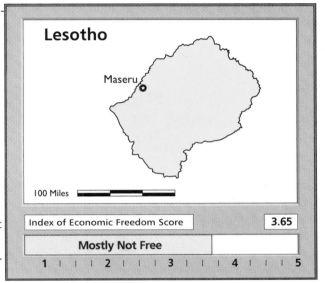

Lesotho

Maseru

100 Miles

Index of Economic Freedom Score	3.65
Mostly Not Free	

1 2 3 4 5

Factor #1: Trade Policy

Score: 4-Stable (High level of protectionism)

Lesotho's common average tariff rate is about 17.4 percent.[216] The newly established South African Customs Union, comprised of South Africa, Botswana, Lesotho, Namibia, and Swaziland, should reduce this rate over time.

Factor #2: Taxation

Score - Income taxation: 4-Stable (High tax rates)
Score - Corporate taxation: 4-Stable (High tax rates)
Final Taxation Score: 4.5-Stable (Very high tax rates)

Lesotho's top income tax rate is 40 percent, and the average taxpayer is in the 15 percent bracket. The top marginal corporate tax rate is 40 percent. Lesotho also has a 40 percent capital gains tax and a 10 percent general services tax.

Factor #3: Government Intervention in the Economy

Score: 3-Stable (Moderate level of government intervention)

Lesotho's government consumes about 18.1 percent of GDP,[217] and a significant portion of overall GDP is generated by the state-owned sector.

Factor #4: Monetary Policy

Score: 3-Stable (Moderate level of inflation)

Lesotho's average rate of inflation from 1985 to 1994 was 14.1 percent. In 1995, inflation was 8.3 percent.

---

216 Based on total taxes on international trade as a percentage of total imports for 1991; from International Monetary Fund, *Government Financial Statistics 1995*.

217 Based on the most recent data, a 1991 figure from the Economist Intelligence Unit.

Factor #5: Capital Flows and Foreign Investment
Score: 3-Stable (Moderate barriers to foreign investment)

Lesotho maintains some informal restrictions on investments in areas competing with domestic local investment. It has an established investment code but offers few incentives.

Factor #6: Banking
Score: 4-Stable (High level of restrictions on banking)

The banking system in Lesotho is heavily regulated by the government, which also owns one of the country's largest banks. According to the U.S. Department of Commerce, "Lesotho has a modern if heavily regulated banking sector. Three commercial banks, one a parastatal, have a wide variety of correspondent relationships with U.S. banks and can assist with trade financing arrangements."[218]

Factor #7: Wage and Price Controls
Score: 4-Stable (High level of wage and price controls)

Wages and prices in Lesotho are affected by the large state sector, which receives government subsidies. Lesotho continues to set some prices on utilities, as well as on some agricultural goods.

Factor #8: Property Rights
Score: 3-Stable (Moderate level of protection of private property)

Private property is guaranteed in Lesotho, and expropriation is unlikely. Foreigners, however, are not allowed to own land.

Factor #9: Regulation
Score: 4-Stable (High level of regulation)

Establishing a business in Lesotho can be difficult if it will compete directly with a state-owned company or government-sanctioned monopoly. There is some corruption.

Factor #10: Black Market
Score: 4-Stable (High level of black market activity)

Lesotho has a substantial black market, primarily in consumer goods.

Summary

Lesotho				Overall Score	3.65
Trade	4	Monetary Policy	3	Property Rights	3
Taxation	4.5	Foreign Investment	3	Regulation	4
Government Intervention	3	Banking	4	Black Market	4
		Wage and Prices	4		

218   U.S. Department of Commerce, *Country Commercial Guide,* 1996.

LIBYA

The North African country of Libya gained its independence from Italy in 1951. Libya's state-dominated socialist economy depends primarily on oil revenues, which contribute almost all export earnings and about one-third of GDP. In 1992, the United Nations imposed sanctions on Libya for its support of terrorist activities. Although Libyan dictator Muammar Qadhafi has hinted at mild economic reforms, he remains hostile to capitalism and dedicated to quasi-Marxist economic theories. Libya remains one of the world's most economically repressive countries.

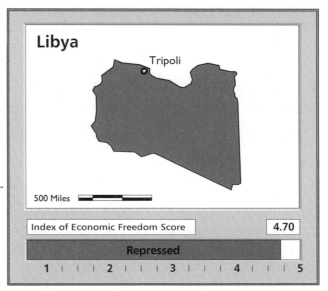

Factor #1: Trade Policy

Score: 5-Stable (Very high level of protectionism)

Libya's imports and exports are largely controlled by the government, and it remains difficult to move goods and services across the border. Libya also bans many imports, especially imports of goods like audio and video recordings that reflect Western culture.

Factor #2: Taxation

Score - Income taxation: 5-Stable (Very high tax rates)
Score - Corporate taxation: 5-Stable (Very high tax rates)
Final Taxation Score: 5-Stable (Very high tax rates)

Libya remains dedicated to redistribution of wealth and hostile to individual wealth. Its top income tax rate is 90 percent, and the average taxpayer is in the 35 percent bracket. The top marginal corporate tax rate is 60 percent. Libya also has a 60 percent capital gains tax and a *Jihad* (Holy War) tax of up to 4 percent of income.

Factor #3: Government Intervention in the Economy

Score: 5-Stable (Very high level of government intervention)

Government produces nearly all of Libya's GDP.

Factor #4: Monetary Policy

Score: 2-Stable (Low level of inflation)

Libya's average rate of inflation from 1990 to 1994 was 10 percent.[219]

---

219   Figures for the average rate of inflation from 1985 to 1993 are not available.

Factor #5: Capital Flows and Foreign Investment
Score: 5-Stable (Very high barriers to foreign investment)

Libya tolerates little foreign investment. When investment is allowed, it is on a case-by-case basis.

Factor #6: Banking
Score: 5-Stable (Very high level of restrictions on banking)

The banking system in Libya is completely government-owned.

Factor #7: Wage and Price Controls
Score: 5-Stable (Very high level of wage and price controls)

Wages and prices in Libya are set mainly by the government.

Factor #8: Property Rights
Score: 5-Stable (Very low level of protection of private property)

Private property is not legal in Libya, although there is growing tolerance of it as government officials often turn their backs when individuals do acquire property.

Factor #9: Regulation
Score: 5-Stable (Very high level of regulation)

Establishing a business in Libya is nearly impossible. Although there is growing tolerance for some small private stores and shops, the government often makes it very difficult for private businesses to operate.

Factor #10: Black Market
Score: 5-Stable (Very high level of black market activity)

The size of Libya's black market easily surpasses the size of its formal economy. Most consumer items must be smuggled into the country.

Summary

Libya				Overall Score	4.70
Trade	5	Monetary Policy	2	Property Rights	5
Taxation	5	Foreign Investment	5	Regulation	5
Government Intervention	5	Banking	5	Black Market	5
		Wage and Prices	5		

LITHUANIA

The Baltic country of Lithuania was independent from 1918 to 1940, at which time it was annexed by the Soviet Union. Lithuania has been undergoing intensive economic reform; the government, for example, has instituted a privatization program, selling off some formerly state-owned enterprises. The process of reform, however, is threatened by entrenched bureaucrats, former Communist Party officials, and large state-owned monopolies. Lithuania is applying for membership in the European Union. Like many of its European neighbors, it relies heavily on foreign aid from the World Bank, International Monetary Fund, European Bank for Reconstruction and Development, and U.S. Agency for International Development. Recently, Lithuania has reduced some barriers to trade and investments. It also has removed barriers to banking. Lithuanian voters recently elected a right-of-center coalition led by Vytautas Landsbergis, the father of Lithuanian resistance to Soviet rule.

Lithuania

Vilnius

100 Miles

Index of Economic Freedom Score — 3.10

Mostly Not Free

1 2 3 4 5

Factor #1: Trade Policy

Score: 2+ (Low level of protectionism)

Lithuania has reduced its average tariff to around 3 percent.[220] Customs procedures, however, are applied inconsistently. According to the U.S. Department of State, "U.S. exports are hindered by a weak economy, rigid bureaucratic system, and the absence of a solid infrastructure for trade, such as telecommunications and banking facilities."[221]

Factor #2: Taxation

Score - Income taxation: 2-Stable (Low tax rates)
Score - Corporate taxation: 3-Stable (Moderate tax rates)
Final Taxation Score: 3-Stable (Moderate tax rates)

Lithuania's top income tax rate is 33 percent, and the average taxpayer is in the 10 percent bracket. The top marginal corporate tax rate is 29 percent. Lithuania also has an 18 percent valued-added tax and a 30 percent social security tax.

---

220 Based on total taxes on international trade as a percentage of total imports; from International Monetary Fund, *Government Financial Statistics 1995*.

221 State Department Report, 1996, p. 227.

Factor #3: Government Intervention in the Economy
Score: 3-Stable (Moderate level of government intervention)

Lithuania's government consumes about 19.2 percent of GDP, and the country's large state-owned sector accounts for better than one-third of total GDP.

Factor #4: Monetary Policy
Score: 5-Stable (Very high level of inflation)

The rate of inflation in Lithuania was 35 percent in 1995, 45 percent in 1994, 189 percent in 1993, and 1,163 percent in 1992. Although Lithuania has made great progress in reducing inflation since 1992, the rate remains very high.

Factor #5: Capital Flows and Foreign Investment
Score: 2+ (Low barriers to foreign investment)

Lithuania has moved quickly to open its market to foreign investment, and this presents many opportunities. Foreign companies are accorded the same treatment as domestic firms. Investments in government-owned monopolies such as utilities, however, are not permitted.

Factor #6: Banking
Score: 3+ (Moderate level of restrictions on banking)

New legislation passed in June 1996 is aimed at creating more favorable conditions for banking in Lithuania, but has yet to have an impact. Thus, restrictions continue. There are few banking services, and businesses often find it difficult to obtain local financing. According to the U.S. Department of State, a major impediment to foreign investment in Lithuania is the "absence of an established infrastructure for trade, such as telecommunications and banking facilities."[222] Moreover, the government has passed a law requiring deposit insurance, and this regulation makes banks less competitive.

Factor #7: Wage and Price Controls
Score: 3-Stable (Moderate level of wage and price controls)

The Lithuanian government still sets some wages and prices. Price controls remain on natural gas, electricity, heating, timber, and postal services, for example, and prices for public utilities are set by state monopolies. Lithuania has a minimum wage.

Factor #8: Property Rights
Score: 3- (Moderate level of protection of private property)

A more efficient legal structure is providing better protection of private property in Lithuania. The court system, although sometimes slow, operates independently. The judiciary, however, has yet to transform itself into a market-oriented system, and enforcement of contracts remains very week.

---

222   *Ibid.*

Factor #9: Regulation
Score: 3-Stable (Moderate level of regulation)

Establishing a business in Lithuania is easy if the business does not compete directly with state-owned industries, and regulations are applied evenly in most cases. Nevertheless, Lithuania has passed many new health and safety regulations which, if enforced, will prove burdensome. These requirements, however, are in line with those of other European countries; by general European standards, Lithuania's level of regulation is moderate.

Factor #10: Black Market
Score: 4-Stable (High level of black market activity)

The black market in Lithuania mainly involves the sale of goods and services that compete with state-owned industries. Consumer goods also are sold on the black market. Although Lithuania maintains some intellectual property protection, the U.S. Department of State reports that "enforcement mechanisms and implementing regulations are poorly developed."[223] Thus, there is substantial black market activity in pirated computer software, compact discs, and prerecorded music and video tapes.

Summary

Lithuania					Overall Score	3.10
Trade	2	Monetary Policy	5	Property Rights	3
Taxation	3	Foreign Investment	2	Regulation	3
Government Intervention	3	Banking	3	Black Market	4
		Wage and Prices	3		

---

223 *Ibid.*

LUXEMBOURG

Luxembourg was recognized as a sovereign, independent state in 1839. Traditionally an agrarian society, throughout most of the 20th century it has grown into a manufacturing and services society and one of the world's richest and most highly industrialized countries. Luxembourg is a constitutional monarchy and a member of the European Union (EU) with a free, thriving economic system. Recently, government spending, particularly on infrastructure, has increased.

Luxembourg

25 Miles

Index of Economic Freedom Score | 2.05

Mostly Free

1 | | | 2 | | | 3 | | | 4 | | | 5

Factor #1: Trade Policy
Score: 2-Stable (Low level of protectionism)

Luxembourg has an average tariff rate of less than 3 percent and maintains non-tariff barriers common to all countries in the EU, including restrictions on telecommunications, television, and broadcasting, as well as quotas on agricultural products like bananas.

Factor #2: Taxation
Score - Income taxation: 5-Stable (Very high tax rates)
Score - Corporate taxation: 3-Stable (Moderate tax rates)
Final Taxation Score: 4.5-Stable (Very high tax rates)

Luxembourg's top income tax rate is 51.25 percent, and the average taxpayer is in the 36 percent bracket. The top marginal corporate tax rate is 33 percent. Luxembourg also has a 51.25 percent capital gains tax and a 15 percent value-added tax.

Factor #3: Government Intervention in the Economy
Score: 3- (Moderate level of government intervention)

The government of Luxembourg consumes about 13.5 percent of GDP and, despite recent attempts to privatize portions of the economy, remains entrenched in many sectors. According to the Economist Intelligence Unit, spending by the state on infrastructure projects continues to increase, raising government spending levels. Moreover, the government continues to own and operate the railways, as well as the mail and telephone service (known as the P&T). The government also is either the owner or a major shareholder in companies that provide banking, electricity, air transport, and financing services.

Factor #4: Monetary Policy
Score: 1-Stable (Very low level of inflation)

Luxembourg's average rate of inflation from 1985 to 1994 was 5.0 percent. In 1995, the inflation rate was 1.9 percent. For most of 1996, it was about 2 percent.

Factor #5: Capital Flows and Foreign Investment
Score: 2-Stable (Low barriers to foreign investment)

Luxembourg has a very open foreign investment regime. Foreign and domestic businesses receive equal treatment, and there are no local content requirements. The government restricts investments, however, that directly affect national security and investments in some utilities.

Factor #6: Banking
Score: 2-Stable (Low level of restrictions on banking)

With the exception of steel, the financial sector is probably Luxembourg's biggest and most important industry, employing over 14,000 people in a country whose total population is only about 390,000. In 1990, there were over 150 foreign banks in Luxembourg. The banking system is both highly competitive and subject to little government regulation, although banks are restricted in their ability to engage in some financial services, such as real estate.

Factor #7: Wage and Price Controls
Score: 2-Stable (Low level of wage and price controls)

Wages and prices in Luxembourg are set mainly by the market. Prices also are affected by government policies, such as subsidies to the state-owned sector and direct price controls on energy.

Factor #8: Property Rights
Score: 1-Stable (Very high level of protection of private property)

Private property is safe from government expropriation in Luxembourg. The legal and judicial system is advanced and efficient.

Factor #9: Regulation
Score: 2-Stable (Low level of regulation)

Establishing a business in Luxembourg is simple. Regulations are applied evenly in most cases, and businesses generally are free to operate with minimal government intrusion.

Factor #10: Black Market
Score: 1-Stable (Very low level of black market activity)

Luxembourg has almost no black market. Protection of intellectual property is strong, and there is little piracy.

Summary

Luxembourg		Overall Score	2.05

Trade	2	Monetary Policy	1	Property Rights	1
Taxation	4.5	Foreign Investment	2	Regulation	2
Government Intervention	3	Banking	2	Black Market	1
		Wage and Prices	2		

MADAGASCAR

Situated off the east coast of Africa, Madagascar is the world's fourth-largest island. It has a largely agrarian economy with rice as its largest crop. Much of its agricultural industry is state-owned, with some large plots of land held in private hands. Madagascar gained its independence from France in 1960 but enjoyed little economic growth during the rest of the decade. In 1970, the situation became worse as the government moved from a market-based economy to a command economy. In 1988, however, the government began to institute limited economic reforms, and the result was modest rates of economic growth. Democratic presidential elections in 1993 solidified Madagascar's political liberalization; its economic liberalization, however, has stalled in the face of populist political opposition, although some barriers to trade have been reduced recently. The combination of a wavering commitment to reform and a series of devastating cyclones in 1994 has left Madagascar with a relatively stagnant economy.

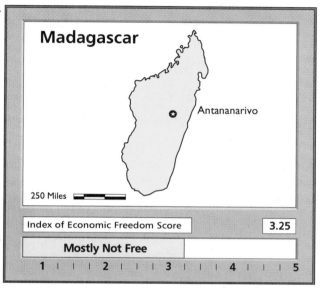

| Index of Economic Freedom Score | 3.25 |

Mostly Not Free

1   2   3   4   5

Factor #1: Trade Policy

Score: 4+ (High level of protectionism)

Madagascar's average tariff rate is 13.5 percent.[224] Non-tariff barriers include consumption taxes and other import taxes which significantly increase the price of imports. In addition the customs system is sometimes slow to admit imports.

Factor #2: Taxation

Score - Income taxation: 3-Stable (Moderate tax rates)
Score - Corporate taxation: 3-Stable (Moderate tax rates)
Total Taxation Score: 3.5- (High tax rates)

Madagascar's top income tax rate is 35 percent.[225] The top corporate income tax rate also is 35 percent. In addition, the government recently introduced both a 25 percent value-added tax and a 45 percent excess profits tax.

---

224   Based on total taxes on international trade as a percentage of total imports; from International Monetary Fund, *Government Financial Statistics 1995*.

225   It was not possible to determine the tax on the average income level. Therefore, Madagascar's score is based on its top income tax rate.

Factor #3: Government Intervention in the Economy
Score: 2-Stable (Low level of government intervention)

The government of Madagascar consumes 7 percent of GDP. Despite some progress in privatization, Madagascar maintains a large state-owned sector.

Factor #4: Monetary Policy
Score: 3-Stable (Moderate level of inflation)

Madagascar's average annual rate of inflation from 1985 to 1994 was 15.7 percent. In 1994, the inflation rate was around 40 percent.

Factor #5: Capital Flows and Foreign Investment
Score: 4-Stable (High barriers to foreign investment)

Madagascar has a free trade zone. Outside this zone, however, foreign investors are not treated as well as domestic investors. Restrictions exist on foreign investments in the banking and insurance, energy, water, hydrocarbon production, mining, and petroleum industries. Foreigners are not permitted to own land, and the bureaucratic process for establishing a new enterprise is time-consuming and not transparent. There are political considerations to be weighed, and foreign investors must demonstrate the social value of their investments.

Factor #6: Banking
Score: 4-Stable (High level of restrictions on banking)

Only five banks operate in Madagascar. Both private banking and foreign investment are limited, and the banking system remains under strict government control, particularly in such areas as credit extension. There are plans to begin privatizing two state-controlled commercial banks in mid-1997.

Factor #7: Wage and Price Controls
Score: 2-Stable (Low level of wage and price controls)

Most prices have been freed from government control. Administered prices for all agricultural goods except vanilla have been lifted, though there is a consumer subsidy for wheat flour. Madagascar has a minimum wage.

Factor #8: Property Rights
Score: 3-Stable (Moderate level of protection of private property)

Property expropriation is unlikely. The current government has slowly been settling expropriations claims dating back to the 1970s. Private property, however, receives little protection from a corrupt and inefficient legal system. According to the U.S. Department of Commerce, "Investors in Madagascar face a legal environment in which the security of private property and the enforcement of contracts is inadequately protected by the judicial system."[226]

---

226   U.S. Department of Commerce, *Country Commercial Guide,* 1996.

Factor #9: Regulation
Score: 3-Stable (Moderate level of regulation)

Madagascar's economy remains moderately regulated by the government. Obtaining business licenses and permits often involves bribery, and the bureaucracy tends to operate in a capricious manner. "Although foreign trade is now liberalized," reports the U.S. Department of Commerce, "a heavily bureaucratic regulatory system remains a burden for business people."[227]

Factor #10: Black Market
Score: 4-Stable (High level of black market activity)

Madagascar has a large black market because of high tariffs and government controls, although the removal of most price controls has reduced the size of the informal economy in recent years. Madagascar does not fully protect intellectual property rights. According to the U.S. Department of Commerce, "Major brand names and franchise rights are respected, but pirated copies of videotaped movies and music cassettes sell openly."[228]

Summary

Madagascar					Overall Score	3.25
Trade	4	Monetary Policy	3		Property Rights	3
Taxation	3.5	Foreign Investment	4		Regulation	3
Government Intervention	2	Banking	4		Black Market	4
		Wage and Prices	2			

---

227 *Ibid.*

228 *Ibid.*

MALAWI

Malawi is located in Central Africa and gained its independence from Great Britain in 1964. During the rest of the 1960s and into the 1970s, Malawi used increased agricultural production as an engine for economic growth. GDP more than doubled, with 3 percent annual growth rates. In the 1980s, however, as drought brought on an agricultural depression and refugees from the nearby Mozambique civil war flowed into the country, Malawi's economy sank into a deep recession. The government responded by restricting imports and spending more on social programs. This caused the budget deficit to balloon and pushed the country into a depression. As a result, the economy shrank nearly 8 percent and real per capita GDP dropped by 11 percent in 1992. Malawi has yet to recover from this depression.

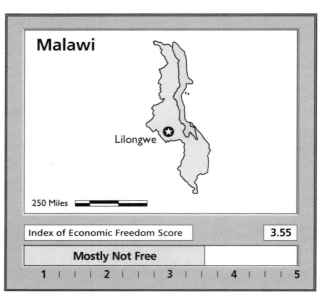

Malawi

Lilongwe

250 Miles

Index of Economic Freedom Score	3.55
Mostly Not Free	

1   2   3   4   5

Factor #1: Trade Policy
Score: 5- (Very high level of protectionism)

Malawi has an average tariff rate of 17.6 percent.[229] It also imposes non-tariff barriers, including strict import licenses on imports of fresh meat, gold, sugar, and military and hunting items.

Factor #2: Taxation
Score - Income taxation: 4-Stable (High tax rates)
Score - Corporate taxation: 4- (High tax rates)
Final Taxation Score: 4.5- (Very high tax rates)

The top income tax rate in Malawi is 35 percent, and the rate for the average income level is 0 percent. The top corporate tax rate is 38 percent. Malawi also levies municipal taxes, a border tax, and a capital gains tax.

Factor #3: Government Intervention in the Economy
Score: 3-Stable (Moderate level of government Intervention)

Malawi's government consumes 22.7 percent of GDP. In addition, Malawi has a large public sector that operates marketing boards for some agricultural products. These boards allow the government to confiscate crops, to pay lower than market value prices for them, and to export them at higher prices, keeping the profits.

---

229   Based on total taxes on international trade as a percentage of total imports; from International Monetary Fund, *Government Financial Statistics 1995*.

Factor #4: Monetary Policy
Score: 3-Stable (Moderate level of inflation)

Malawi's average annual rate of inflation from 1985 to 1994 was 18.8 percent. For the first half of 1995, the inflation rate was over 70 percent.

Factor #5: Capital Flows and Foreign Investment
Score: 3-Stable (Moderate barriers to foreign investment)

The government of Malawi encourages foreign investment only in industries that produce goods for export. Thus, it does not restrict foreign investments in the coffee, sugar, or tea industries. The government also requires that non-citizens obtain a labor license to work in Malawi, and these licenses are not granted if the government determines that Malawi citizens are capable of doing the work themselves.

Factor #6: Banking
Score: 3-Stable (Moderate level of restrictions on banking)

Only a few banks in Malawi are free from government ownership. Although the government freed interest rates in 1992, it still exercises a great deal of control over the financial system. Malawi plans to allow two foreign banks to open in the near future.

Factor #7: Wage and Price Controls
Score: 3-Stable (Moderate level of wage and price controls)

Price controls on almost all products have been lifted, although controls on the prices of some food items and energy remain in effect. Malawi maintains a minimum wage.

Factor #8: Property Rights
Score: 3-Stable (Moderate level of protection of private property)

Malawi has begun a huge privatization program aimed at selling its biggest state-owned enterprises. Despite plans to eliminate them, however, marketing boards still control the sale of such agricultural products as corn and fertilizer. The court system is only partially independent.

Factor #9: Regulation
Score: 4-Stable (High level of regulation)

The government of Malawi heavily regulates the sale of such agricultural products as corn and fertilizer. It also enforces health and safety regulations erratically, causing confusion among businesses. In addition, corruption is becoming more prevalent. "Malawi's business community and the public see corruption—particularly corruption in official circles—as a threat to legitimate competition and a critical drain on limited government coffers," reports the U.S. Department of Commerce. "The Government of Malawi's efforts at curbing corruption are in the early stages."[230]

---

230   U.S. Department of Commerce, *Country Commercial Guide*, 1996.

Factor #10: Black Market
Score: 4-Stable (High level of black market activity)

Because Malawi's government strictly controls the importation of food, there is a huge black market in such items as eggs and poultry, which often are imported illegally. Moreover, because the government provides insufficient legal protection of intellectual property rights, there is a rather large black market in pirated computer software and recorded music and videos.

Summary

Malawi					Overall Score	3.55
Trade	5	Monetary Policy	3		Property Rights	3
Taxation	4.5	Foreign Investment	3		Regulation	4
Government Intervention	3	Banking	3		Black Market	4
		Wage and Prices	3			

MALAYSIA

The Southeast Asian country of Malaysia gained its independence from Great Britain in 1957. In 1963, Singapore, Sarawak, and Sabah (North Borneo) joined the Federation of Malaya to form Malaysia. In 1964, Singapore withdrew to become an independent nation. Since then, Malaysia has undergone civil unrest and political instability. Thanks to economic reforms begun in the 1970s, it also has made great progress in developing a free market. More recently, however, the number of price controls has been growing (although many items are being removed from the list), and the government's increasing use of the Land Acquisition Law is infringing on private property rights. The average tariff rate also has been increased.

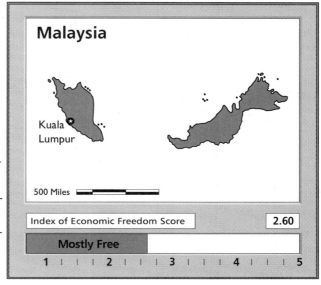

Factor #1: Trade Policy
Score: 5- (Very high level of protectionism)

Malaysia's average tariff rate is 15 percent, up from 9 percent a year ago.[231] Nontariff barriers include import bans, licensing requirements, and strict labeling requirements.

Factor #2: Taxation
Score - Income taxation: 2-Stable (Low tax rates)
Score - Corporate taxation: 3-Stable (Moderate tax rates)
Total Taxation Score: 3-Stable (Moderate tax rates)

Malaysia's top income tax rate is 32 percent, and the rate for the average income level is 0 percent. The top corporate tax is 30 percent. Malaysia also has a 15 percent sales tax.

Factor #3: Government Intervention in the Economy
Score: 2-Stable (Low level of government intervention)

The Malaysian government consumes 12.2 percent of GDP, down from 13.5 percent a year ago.

Factor #4: Monetary Policy
Score: 1- (Very low level of inflation)

The average annual rate of inflation in Malaysia from 1985 to 1994 was 3.1 percent. In 1995, the inflation rate was 3.4 percent.

231　From Economist Intelligence Unit, *ILT Reports, Malaysia*, May 1996.

Factor #5: Capital Flows and Foreign Investment
Score: 3-Stable (Moderate barriers to foreign investment)

Malaysia is relatively open to foreign investment. Most restrictions are on investments in utilities and industries considered essential to national security. Malaysia also restricts foreign participation in some services, however, such as law, architecture, and banking.

Factor #6: Banking
Score: 3-Stable (Moderate level of restrictions on banking)

Competition in Malaysia's banking industry is limited by government restrictions that prevent banks from providing a full range of financial services. The government also limits foreign participation in banking.

Factor #7: Wage and Price Controls
Score: 3-Stable (Moderate level of wage and price controls)

Most wages and prices in Malaysia are determined by the market, although the government has added price controls on key goods and maintains controls on the prices of fuel, public utilities, motor vehicles, rice, flour, sugar, and tobacco. Malaysia has a minimum wage.

Factor #8: Property Rights
Score: 2-Stable (High level of protection of private property)

Chances of property expropriation remain small. Protection of private property by the courts, however, is sometimes incomplete. In one recent case, for example, the government of Malaysia expropriated 6,520 acres from a private company and offered compensation equal to only 25 percent of the property's market value. According to some private-sector complaints, there is a "widening web of patronage and privilege between some influential politicians and private business groups."[232] This has created an incentive for the government to expropriate private property, provide less than market value for it, and then use government-owned development firms to develop it at a profit. This is an exception, however, to an otherwise high level of protection of private property.

Factor #9: Regulation
Score: 2-Stable (Low level of regulation)

Malaysia has eliminated most significantly burdensome regulations. Its regulatory regime is efficient and relatively free of corruption.

Factor #10: Black Market
Score: 2-Stable (Low level of black market activity)

Malaysia has a minimal black market. Most services are supplied legally, and there is little incentive to engage in the black market. There is a small and growing black market, however, in such pirated intellectual property as computer software and music and video tapes.

---

232   See Raphael Pura, "Property Firms' Suit Against Malaysian State Spotlights Controversial Land Acquisition Law," *Asian Wall Street Journal,* June 19, 1995, p. 1.

Summary

Malaysia			Overall Score	2.60
Trade	5	Monetary Policy	1	Property Rights	2
Taxation	3	Foreign Investment	3	Regulation	2
Government Intervention	2	Banking	3	Black Market	2
		Wage and Prices	3		

MALI

A vast and sparsely populated West African country, and also one of the world's poorest, Mali received its independence from France in 1960 and immediately adopted socialist economic policies under the leadership of President Modibo Keita. After years of state-dominated economic policy, Mali has begun to rely more on the market for everyday economic decisions. The economy has improved recently, with an estimated economic growth rate in the 3 percent range for 1994. In 1992, Mali held its first democratic national elections, which were contested by 21 political parties and judged to be free and fair. Mali's government has reduced its consumption of economic output and improved its banking regulations, protection of property rights, and business regulations.

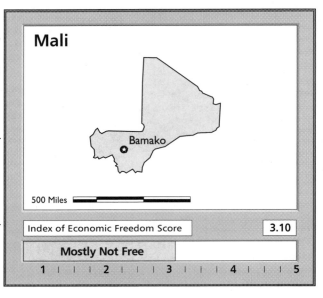

| Mali |
| Bamako |
| 500 Miles |

| Index of Economic Freedom Score | 3.10 |
| Mostly Not Free |
| 1   2   3   4   5 |

Factor #1: Trade Policy
Score: 3-Stable (Moderate level of protectionism)

Mali's average tariff rate is about 10 percent. However, the government uses a complex system of "fiscal duties" ranging from 5 percent to 30 percent.[233] Most import barriers have been lifted, although import licenses are still required. Import taxes on many goods were lowered or eliminated in 1994.

Factor #2: Taxation
Score - Income taxation: 4-Stable (High tax rates)
Score - Corporate taxation: 5-Stable (Very high tax rates)
Final Taxation Score: 5-Stable (Very high tax rates)

Mali has top income and corporate tax rates of over 50 percent.[234] It also has a capital gains tax and a turnover tax.

Factor #3: Government Intervention in the Economy
Score: 3-Stable (Moderate level of government intervention)

Mali's government consumes 12 percent of GDP. The state sector is dominant, but several state enterprises have been liquidated or privatized over the past few years.

---

233 Mali's average tariff rate does not include fiscal duties, which increase the rate to between 10 percent and 15 percent.

234 According to the U.S. Department of State, total taxation on income and corporate profits in Mali is over 50 percent. It was not possible to obtain the tax rate on the average income level. Therefore, Mali's score is based only on the top rate.

Factor #4: Monetary Policy
Score: 1-Stable (Very low level of inflation)

Mali's average annual rate of inflation from 1985 to 1994 was 3.4 percent. Inflation currently is running at 28 percent, due in large part to the 1994 devaluation of the CFA franc.

Factor #5: Capital Flows and Foreign Investment
Score: 2-Stable (Low barriers to foreign investment)

The government of Mali has an established investment code and permits investments in almost all areas. Foreign investors are offered some incentives and face few restrictions. Because of its poor economic state, however, Mali has received very little foreign investment to date, although there has been some upturn recently.

Factor #6: Banking
Score: 3-Stable (Moderate level of restrictions on banking)

Among the biggest impediments to efficient banking in Mali are corrupt government bureaucrats, collusion by some banks to maintain high interest rates, and a generally chaotic financial system. Some restrictions, however, have been liberalized. Six commercial banks are either privately owned or controlled by a majority of private-sector owners, and are now permitted to invest in foreign capital markets.

Factor #7: Wage and Price Controls
Score: 3-Stable (Moderate level of wage and price controls)

Most price controls have been removed, although prices continue to be influenced by the government's large public sector. Mali has a minimum wage.

Factor #8: Property Rights
Score: 3-Stable (Moderate level of protection of private property)

Property is at risk in Mali because of high crime rates and an inefficient (although generally fair) court system. Some property has been destroyed because of separatist strife in the North. Government expropriation is not likely under the current regime.

Factor #9: Regulation
Score: 3-Stable (Moderate level of regulation)

Regulations are applied sporadically, and government corruption increases the risk of doing business. According to the U.S. Department of Commerce, "The rule of law is generally respected, although petty corruption is a problem."[235] In addition to simplifying its business registration procedures, Mali has liberalized its commerce and labor codes over the past few years.

---

235   U.S. Department of Commerce, *Country Commercial Guide,* 1996.

Factor #10: Black Market
Score: 5-Stable (Very high level of black market activity)

Mali has a large black market in smuggled consumer electronics equipment like video cassette recorders. In addition, auto parts are stolen from operating cars to be re-sold by black marketeers, and cattle rustling is a growing problem.

Summary

Mali				Overall Score	3.10
Trade	3	Monetary Policy	1	Property Rights	3
Taxation	5	Foreign Investment	2	Regulation	3
Government Intervention	3	Banking	3	Black Market	5
		Wage and Prices	3		

MALTA

Located in the Mediterranean Sea, the island nation of Malta gained its independence from Great Britain in 1964. During the 1970s, socialist experiments left many of Malta's businesses bankrupt. Rather than let these businesses fail, the government intervened and nationalized them, causing the budget to become bloated. Today, Malta has made progress toward free-market reform by reducing some taxes, maintaining a tight money supply, and welcoming most foreign investment. It also has managed to reduce black market activity by cracking down on smuggling.

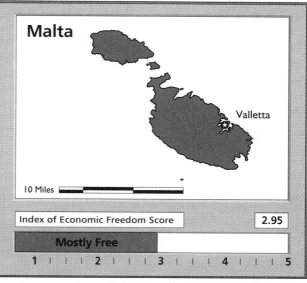

Factor #1: Trade Policy

Score: 4-Stable (High level of protectionism)

Malta's average tariff rate is 11.2 percent. Some import licenses are required, especially for health and environmental products.

Factor #2: Taxation

Score - Income taxation: 3-Stable (Moderate tax rates)
Score - Corporate taxation: 3-Stable (Moderate tax rates)
Total Taxation Score: 3.5-Stable (High tax rates)

Malta's top marginal income tax rate is 35 percent, and citizens making the average income pay a tax of 20 percent. The top corporate tax rate is 35 percent. Malta also has a 35 percent capital gains tax, a 2 percent to 7 percent stamp duty (tax on the transfer of property), and a 15 percent value-added tax.

Factor #3: Government Intervention in the Economy

Score: 2-Stable (Low level of government intervention)

Malta's government consumes 21.1 percent of GDP.

Factor #4: Monetary Policy

Score: 1-Stable (Very low level of inflation)

The average annual rate of inflation in Malta from 1985 to 1994 was 2.9 percent. In 1995, the inflation rate was 4.7 percent.

Factor #5: Capital Flows and Foreign Investment

Score: 2-Stable (Low barriers to foreign investment)

With the exception of utilities, almost all companies are open to foreign investment in Malta. There are few restrictions.

Factor #6: Banking
Score: 3-Stable (Moderate level of restrictions on banking)

Most domestic banks are now private, with only a few still owned by the government, and there is competition to attract customers. Foreign banks are increasing their presence in Malta.

Factor #7: Wage and Price Controls
Score: 4-Stable (High level of wage and price controls)

Malta's Department of Trade is responsible for pricing most items sold in Malta. There also is a minimum wage.

Factor #8: Property Rights
Score: 3-Stable (Moderate level of protection of private property)

Property expropriation is possible. Enforcement of property rights laws by Malta's court system is relatively weak.

Factor #9: Regulation
Score: 3-Stable (Moderate level of regulation)

There are no consumer safety regulations in Malta, although the government plans to introduce them. Environmental regulations are stringently enforced and carry large fines. Opening a business in Malta is difficult, and licenses must be granted by many bureaucracies, including the police.

Factor #10: Black Market
Score: 4+ (High level of black market activity)

Malta is a major center for smuggling, and its location makes it a preferred base for black market activity. The government recently has cracked down on smuggling and other black market activities, however, thereby reducing them to some extent.

Summary

Malta				Overall Score	2.95
Trade	4	Monetary Policy	1	Property Rights	3
Taxation	3.5	Foreign Investment	2	Regulation	3
Government Intervention	2	Banking	3	Black Market	4
		Wage and Prices	4		

MAURITANIA

The West African country of Mauritania gained its independence from France in 1960. Virtually all of its territory is desert, with the western border on the Atlantic Ocean. The largest industries are mining and fishing. During most of the 1980s, the government pursued a highly interventionist policy toward the economy. In the 1990s, it has been struggling to adopt a series of economic reforms. Mauritania recently has reduced its government spending; however, it also has increased its trade barriers and remains a major recipient of World Bank and other foreign aid funds.

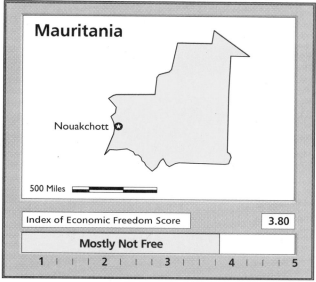

Factor #1: Trade Policy

Score: 5- (Very High level of protectionism)

Mauritania's average tariff rate is 20.3 percent.[236] Trade restrictions include strict labeling and inspection requirements, as well as a sometimes corrupt and inefficient customs agency.

Factor #2: Taxation

Score - Income taxation: 4-Stable (High tax rates)
Score - Corporate taxation: 4-Stable (High tax rates)
Final Taxation Score: 4-Stable (High tax rates)

Mauritania's tax score is based on total government revenues as a percentage of GDP (over 25 percent, compared to about 13 percent in Japan, which has a top income tax rate of 50 percent).[237]

Factor #3: Government Intervention in the Economy

Score: 3+ (Moderate level of government intervention)

Government consumes about 10 percent of GDP in Mauritania. Additionally, although much of the economy has been privatized, the government still owns some companies, including companies that produce electricity and water.

---

236 Based on total taxes on international trade as a percentage of total imports; from International Monetary Fund, *Government Financial Statistics 1995*.

237 Tax information for Mauritania is not available. Therefore, for purposes of grading Mauritania's taxation levels, total government revenues as a percentage of GDP were used.

Factor #4: Monetary Policy
Score: 2-Stable (Low level of inflation)

Mauritania's average rate of inflation from 1985 to 1994 was 7.2 percent. In 1995, inflation was about 4 percent to 5 percent.

Factor #5: Capital Flows and Foreign Investment
Score: 3+ (Moderate barriers to foreign investment)

Mauritania has passed new laws to attract foreign investors. Foreign and domestic firms generally enjoy equal treatment, and there are few legal barriers. Overall, despite some problems—such as government corruption, the lack of infrastructure, and a very poor population—the government's new investment code has been successful in opening the Mauritanian economy to foreign investment.

Factor #6: Banking
Score: 5-Stable (Very high level of restrictions on banking)

Some reforms are being introduced, but the banking system is still chaotic. Most banks are controlled strictly by the government.

Factor #7: Wage and Price Controls
Score: 4-Stable (High level of wage and price controls)

Wages and prices in Mauritania are controlled through subsidies to businesses, as well as to state-owned utilities like electricity.

Factor #8: Property Rights
Score: 4-Stable (Low level of protection of private property)

Private property is not safe in Mauritania. The legal and judicial system is chaotic and sometimes corrupt. According to the U.S. Department of Commerce, "Mauritania's banks, for example, have had difficulty getting local courts to enforce a bank's right under loan agreements to seize pledged assets from local merchants."[238]

Factor #9: Regulation
Score: 4-Stable (High level of regulation)

Establishing a business in Mauritania is getting easier. Regulations, although cumbersome, are applied fairly evenly in most cases. Mauritania's corrupt government bureaucracy, however, often imposes arbitrary requirements on businesses.

Factor #10: Black Market
Score: 4-Stable (High level of black market activity)

Mauritania's large informal market is confined mainly to consumer goods and entertainment products, especially computer software.

---

238   U.S. Department of Commerce, *Country Commercial Guide,* 1996.

Summary

Mauritania					Overall Score	3.80
Trade	5	Monetary Policy	2	Property Rights	4
Taxation	4	Foreign Investment	3	Regulation	4
Government Intervention	3	Banking	5	Black Market	4
		Wage and Prices	4		

MEXICO

After decades of socialist economic policies and limited economic freedom, Mexico has made some strides toward liberalizing its market, although (as in many other countries trying to reform their economies) many of the benefits of the free market are just beginning to take effect. Efforts to integrate Mexico's economy with those of the U.S. and Canada through the North American Free Trade Agreement (NAFTA) also promote economic liberalization. Despite the NAFTA, however, Mexico still imposes limits on economic freedom, especially with respect to trade with non-NAFTA members. In addition, Mexico has not reformed its political system as rapidly as it has reformed its economy. The lack of political openness and economic freedom was the reason the Mexican peso collapsed in December 1994, causing an economic recession from which Mexico has yet to recover. The recent infusion of U.S. capital is likely to do little to help, and the Clinton Administration's $50 billion bailout of Mexico only will postpone economic reforms. Mexico recently eliminated some price controls, but its privatization program has stalled, and many sectors remain government-owned.

| Index of Economic Freedom Score | 3.35 |

Mostly Not Free

1 2 3 4 5

Factor #1: Trade Policy

Score: 3-Stable (Moderate level of protectionism)

Mexico's average tariff rate is 11 percent.[239] Mexico also maintains import licenses for 198 different products, including beans, cars and trucks, corn, dairy products, firearms, and poultry. As a result of the NAFTA, tariffs on U.S. goods will drop to insignificant levels, although barriers will remain for non-NAFTA members.

Factor #2: Taxation

Score - Income taxation: 3-Stable (Moderate tax rates)
Score - Corporate taxation: 3-Stable (Moderate tax rates)
Total Taxation Score: 3.5-Stable (High tax rates)

Mexico's top marginal tax rate is 35 percent, and the rate for the average income level is 17 percent. The top corporate tax rate is 34 percent. Mexico also has a 15 percent value-added tax, a 34 percent capital gains tax, a state tax on salaries, and a resident tax.

---

239 Economist Intelligence Unit, *ILT Reports*, September 1995, updated March 1996.

Factor #3: Government Intervention in the Economy
Score: 3- (Moderate level of government intervention)

Mexico's government consumes 12 percent of GDP. The recent economic crisis has caused Mexico's privatization program to slow in some sectors as the government continues to backtrack on economic reform. For example, most port facilities, railroads, electricity plants, and petrochemical manufacturers remain state-owned.

Factor #4: Monetary Policy
Score: 5-Stable (Very high level of inflation)

Although Mexico has made great strides in containing inflation since 1988, its overall record in this area has been poor. From 1985 to 1994, the average rate of inflation in Mexico was 39.9 percent; in 1995, the inflation rate was 52 percent; and for 1996, it is expected to be from 25 percent to 28 percent—assuming the government does not relax its monetary and fiscal policies.

Factor #5: Capital Flows and Foreign Investment
Score: 2-Stable (Low barriers to foreign investment)

Mexico has reformed its foreign investment code to attract more investors, allowing for more equal treatment of foreign and domestic firms. Investors from non-NAFTA countries, however, may not own majority shares in many service industries such as banking.

Factor #6: Banking
Score: 4-Stable (High level of restrictions on banking)

Since the collapse of the Mexican peso on December 20, 1994, the government has allowed 100 percent foreign ownership of banks. The economic situation has led the government to bail out many private banks, effectively acquiring control of many institutions, and domestic banks are prohibited from investing in real estate and industrial firms. There is some corruption involved in the dispensing of loans to state-owned companies.

Factor #7: Wage and Price Controls
Score: 3+ (Moderate level of wage and price controls)

In 1994, 60 product areas were subject to price controls; in 1995, the number was reduced to 28. Some controls—such as those on milk and other foodstuffs—remain in effect, however. Mexico maintains a minimum wage with incremental cost-of-living increases.

Factor #8: Property Rights
Score: 3-Stable (Moderate level of protection of private property)

Private property is guaranteed by the Mexican Constitution, and legal protection of private property will increase as more state-owned property is privatized. Considering current levels of corruption and government-sanctioned cronyism, as well as a growing illegal drug trade, however, private property also faces increased risk.

Factor #9: Regulation
Score: 4-Stable (High level of regulation)

Opening a business remains a complicated task. Each business must obtain a license or some other form of certification from numerous government agencies, including the Public Registry of Commerce, the Bureau of Statistics, federal and local tax authorities, the Mexican Social Security Institute, and the National Housing Fund. In addition, some localities require each business to belong to a local chamber of commerce and trade association. Moreover, additional licenses may be required from the Ministry of Health and other agencies. Although Mexico is attempting to end corruption, its current regulatory environment remains an obstacle to business creation. The U.S. Department of Commerce reports that "official corruption, including drug-related corruption, remains a deep-rooted and persistent problem, particularly at middle and lower levels of Mexican government."[240]

Factor #10: Black Market
Score: 3-Stable (Moderate level of black market activity)

A black market in transportation services such as taxis and busing is prevalent in many Mexican cities, and black market labor is often available to businesses wanting to skirt minimum wage laws. Some estimates put black market labor in Mexico City at over 40 percent. Mexico is still plagued by black market activity in the construction industry, and there continues to be some piracy in such intellectual property as computer software.

Summary

Mexico					Overall Score	3.35
Trade	3	Monetary Policy	5	Property Rights	3
Taxation	3.5	Foreign Investment	2	Regulation	4
Government Intervention	3	Banking	4	Black Market	3
		Wage and Prices	3		

---

240   U.S. Department of Commerce, *Country Commercial Guide,* 1996.

MOLDOVA

Located in Eastern Europe, Moldova gained its independence from the Soviet Union in 1991. Moldova had been a large food-producing region within the Soviet Union. Since independence, the economy has shrunk, unemployment has grown, and inflation has skyrocketed. The government has made some progress, however, in stabilizing the economy and laying the groundwork for the creation of market infrastructure.

Factor #1: Trade Policy

Score: 3-Stable (Moderate level of protectionism)

Moldova has an average tariff rate of around 5 percent. It also maintains non-tariff barriers to trade in several areas. For example, the government imposes quotas on imports of unprocessed leather, energy products, and cereals.

Factor #2: Taxation

Score - Income taxation: 3+ (Moderate tax rates)
Score - Corporate taxation: 3-Stable (Moderate tax rates)
Total Taxation Score: 3.5-Stable (High tax rates)

Moldova's top income tax rate is 50 percent, and the average income level is taxed at 10 percent.[241] Moldova also has a 30 percent corporate tax and a 20 percent value-added tax.

Factor #3: Government Intervention in the Economy

Score: 3-Stable (Moderate level of government intervention)

Moldova's government consumes 21 percent of GDP.[242] The private sector accounts for less than 50 percent of the country's total GDP.

Factor #4: Monetary Policy

Score: 5-Stable (Very high level of inflation)

The government of Moldova has achieved substantial progress in reducing the hyperinflation of 1992, caused by the collapse of the ruble. The rate of inflation was 23.8 percent in 1995, down from 108 percent in 1994, 837 percent in 1993, and 1,276 percent in 1992. Thus, the average rate of inflation in Moldova from 1991 to 1995 is still very high.

---

241   State Department Report, 1996, p. 233.

242   World Bank, *World Development Report 1996*.

Factor #5: Capital Flows and Foreign Investment
Score: 3-Stable (Moderate barriers to foreign investment)

. Although Moldova has moved to develop foreign investment and commercial codes, foreigners may not own land. According to the U.S. Department of State, "Barriers to foreign trade and investments in Moldova include the improving but still somewhat underdeveloped banking, insurance, legal, and travel services."[243]

Factor #6: Banking
Score: 3-Stable (Moderate level of restrictions on banking)

Moldova's banking system is becoming more competitive and less subject to government control. There now are 26 private foreign banks operating in Moldova. Nevertheless, the banking industry remains underdeveloped, according to the U.S. Department of State (see Factor #5).

Factor #7: Wage and Price Controls
Score: 3-Stable (Moderate level of wage and price controls)

Most prices in Moldova are set by the market. The government, however, still controls the prices of goods produced by some state-run monopolies. Moldova has a minimum wage.

Factor #8: Property Rights
Score: 3-Stable (Moderate level of protection of private property)

Moldova has passed laws guaranteeing private property and strengthening its judiciary. According to the U.S. Department of Commerce, "The independence of Moldova's judiciary has increased since the 1991 dissolution of the Soviet Union, partly due to provisions for tenure designed to increase judicial independence. A series of reforms approved in 1995 have begun to be implemented, including creation of a court to deal with constitutional issues and a system of appeals courts."[244] These reforms have yet to take effect, however, and the enforcement of property rights can be cumbersome. Foreign investors are not permitted to own land.

Factor #9: Regulation
Score: 3-Stable (Moderate level of regulation)

Moldova is establishing a regulatory regime that will stress environmental protection and consumer safety. Existing government regulations, in addition to being burdensome, are applied haphazardly. State planning, however, has been reduced.

Factor #10: Black Market
Score: 4-Stable (High level of black market activity)

"At this time," reports the U.S. Department of State, "piracy of copyright materials is widespread (cable television, audio and video cassettes, computer software, and

---

243 State Department Report, 1996, p. 234.

244 National Trade Data Bank and Economic Bulletin Board—products of STAT–USA, U.S. Department of Commerce.

books)."[245] The result is massive theft and the smuggling of pirated products, although these activities are decreasing relative to the overall size of Moldova's economy.

Summary

Moldova					Overall Score	3.35
Trade	3	Monetary Policy	5	Property Rights	3
Taxation	3.5	Foreign Investment	3	Regulation	3
Government Intervention	3	Banking	3	Black Market	4
		Wage and Prices	3		

245　State Department Report, 1996, p. 234.

MONGOLIA

Located in Central Asia between Russia and China, Mongolia regained its independence in 1921. Its economy remained closely linked with that of the Soviet Union, however, and it copied the Soviet model of central economic planning. After the collapse of the Soviet Union in 1991, Mongolia embarked on a program of economic liberalization; and although much remains to be done, there also has been significant progress. Democratic elections were held in June 1996, and the new government has agreed to accelerate the process of economic reform.

Index of Economic Freedom Score	3.30
Mostly Not Free	

1 | | | 2 | | | 3 | | | 4 | | | 5

Factor #1: Trade Policy

Score: 3+ (Moderate level of protectionism)

Mongolia's average tariff rate is 8.2 percent.[246] Archaic customs procedures, however, present significant non-tariff barriers to international trade. Imports can sit at the border for lengthy periods before being approved for entry into the country.

Factor #2: Taxation

Score - Income taxation: 4+ (High tax rates)
Score - Corporate taxation: 4+ (High tax rates)
Total Taxation Score: 4+ (High tax rates)

Mongolia has a top income tax rate of 40 percent and a top corporate tax rate of 40 percent. It also has a 10 percent sales tax.

Factor #3: Government Intervention in the Economy

Score: 3+ (High level of government intervention)

Mongolia's government consumes 14 percent of GDP. Although the government has undertaken a substantial privatization program, a significant state-owned sector still generates almost 50 percent of GNP.

Factor #4: Monetary Policy

Score: 5-Stable (Very high level of inflation)

Mongolia's rate of inflation averaged 45.7 percent during the 1985–1994 period. No figure is available for 1995.

---

246   Based on total taxes on international trade as a percentage of total imports; from International Monetary Fund, *Government Financial Statistics 1995*.

Factor #5: Capital Flows and Foreign Investment
Score: 3-Stable (Moderate barriers to foreign investment)

Mongolia recently passed legislation to protect private property and foreign investments from government expropriation. New laws also provide equal treatment for Mongolian and foreign companies, and restrictions on currencies and profits have been removed. Although no industry is formally restricted, the government maintains a list of industries in which foreign investment is discouraged; examples include state-owned enterprises, liquor, securities, mining, animal skins, pharmaceuticals, and chemicals. Foreigners still may not own land.

Factor #6: Banking
Score: 3-Stable (Moderate level of restrictions on banking)

Although some progress has been made in deregulating Mongolia's banks, they remain under government control. Mongolia's banking system remains underdeveloped.

Factor #7: Wage and Price Controls
Score: 3-Stable (Moderate level of wage and price controls)

Mongolia controls prices through a complex system of government procurement. For example, the government often will buy a significant amount of a particular product in order to control the supply, thereby affecting the price. There has been notable progress in liberalizing prices, however, because the government has allowed the market to play a more prominent role. Mongolia has a minimum wage.

Factor #8: Property Rights
Score: 3- (Moderate level of protection of private property)

Expropriation of existing private property is unlikely in Mongolia. The government has instituted new laws to protect property owners. Enforcement of laws protecting private property, however, is inefficient, and the state still holds significant amounts of land that stand little chance of being privatized in the near future.

Factor #9: Regulation
Score: 3-Stable (Moderate level of regulation)

The growing private sector in Mongolia, especially newly privatized companies, is still subject to significant government control. Although few official regulations exist, corruption and government meddling in the private sector hinder the operation of private business.

Factor #10: Black Market
Score: 3-Stable (Moderate level of black market activity)

Mongolia's government buys many goods through its complex procurement program. This distorts prices for food commodities. The result is a black market in these and other government-regulated goods. There also is a moderate level of smuggling.

Mongolia				Overall Score	3.30
Trade	3	Monetary Policy	5	Property Rights	3
Taxation	4	Foreign Investment	3	Regulation	3
Government Intervention	3	Banking	3	Black Market	3
		Wage and Prices	3		

MOROCCO

The North African country of Morocco gained its independence from France in 1956. A constitutional monarchy, the government of King Hassan II recently has imposed free-market reforms on the country's mixed economy. The economy has experienced slow but steady growth in recent years, despite a drought in 1995. Morocco, which aspires to become a major manufacturing base, serving markets in both Europe and Africa, is undergoing modest political liberalization along with economic modernization. Its expensive military effort to retain control over the disputed Western Sahara, however, has been a financial drain and a diplomatic headache. Recent attempts to privatize much of the economy remain unfulfilled.

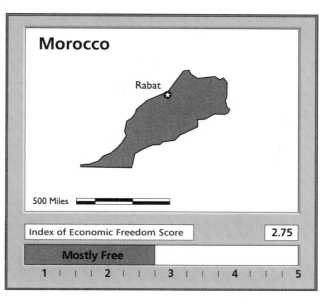

| Index of Economic Freedom Score | 2.75 |

Mostly Free

1 | | | 2 | | | 3 | | | 4 | | | 5

Factor #1: Trade Policy
Score: 4-Stable (High level of protectionism)

Morocco will be increasing its average tariff rate as it replaces import quotas, which have been used to protect many items, with tariffs. The average tariff is around 13 percent, and there is a 10 percent to 15 percent surtax on imports. Cereals, vegetable oils, sugar, and bananas are still protected by non-tariff barriers. Overall, the level of protectionism remains high.

Factor #2: Taxation
Score - Income taxation: 3+ (Moderate tax rates)
Score - Corporate taxation: 3-Stable (Moderate tax rates)
Total Taxation Score: 3.5+ (High tax rates)

Morocco's highest income tax rate is 46 percent, and the average income is taxed at a rate of 0 percent. The corporation tax rate is fixed at 35 percent of profits. A value-added tax is payable at rates of 7 percent or 20 percent on sales and 7 percent on banking activities. Morocco also has a capital gains tax of 35 percent.

Factor #3: Government Intervention in the Economy
Score: 3- (Moderate level of government intervention)

The Moroccan government consumes 18.2 percent of GDP. Under an ambitious privatization program begun in 1992, over 100 government-owned enterprises worth over $2 billion were to be sold by 1995. This goal still has not been met, though there has been steady progress. The government sold some 27 operations, including eight hotels, in 1994. Privatization slowed in 1995 but rebounded in 1996. The Moroccan government still owns substantial portions of the economy, mainly in some financial institutions, steel, and fertilizer companies.

Factor #4: Monetary Policy
Score: 1-Stable (Very low level of inflation)

Morocco's average annual rate of inflation between 1985 and 1994 was 5.1 percent. In 1995, the inflation rate was about 6.2 percent.

Factor #5: Capital Flows and Foreign Investment
Score: 2-Stable (Low barriers to foreign investment)

Foreign-owned and locally owned investments are treated the same by the Moroccan government, which also permits 100 percent foreign ownership. Tax holidays are granted, and there is a tax-free zone at Tangier. Neither foreigners nor Moroccans may invest in industries competing with the state energy and water monopoly, rail and transportation services, or the mining and processing of phosphates, although the government plans to open the energy sector to private investment. Although some foreign investors face a maze of regulations, foreign investment in Morocco has been increasing over the past several years.

Factor #6: Banking
Score: 3-Stable (Moderate level of restrictions on banking)

Foreign banks are relatively free to operate in Morocco. They also are permitted to possess controlling interests in Moroccan banks. Local banks are expanding their activities to include capital market activity. Although the government has privatized one major bank and plans to privatize another, it still owns several other financial and credit institutions. According to the U.S. Department of Commerce, "The banking system is still used by the government...as a way to channel domestic savings to finance government debt, and the banks are required to hold a part of their assets in bonds paying below market interest rates."[247]

Factor #7: Wage and Price Controls
Score: 3-Stable (Moderate level of wage and price controls)

Most price controls have been eliminated, although they remain on bread, cereal, milk, sugar, and other basics. These products also are subsidized by the state. Although wage and salary increases are negotiated freely between the Moroccan government and businesses, there is a minimum wage. When the Central Commission for Prices and Wages records an increase of at least 5 percent in the cost of living, the government can raise all wages and prices by decree.

Factor #8: Property Rights
Score: 2-Stable (High level of protection of private property)

Morocco's constitution prohibits the expropriation of private property except in special cases prescribed by law. There have been no expropriations since the early 1970s, and there are no outstanding cases of expropriation or nationalization of investments. The judicial system is efficient, but enforcement is sometimes weak.

---

247   U.S. Department of Commerce, *Country Commercial Guides,* 1996.

Factor #9: Regulation
Score: 3-Stable (Moderate level of regulation)

Although establishing a business is fairly straightforward, foreign businesses face complicated procedures and corruption. Government procedures are not always transparent, and routine business permits can be difficult to obtain, particularly from local authorities. Labor legislation makes it difficult to fire workers.

Factor #10: Black Market
Score: 3-Stable (Moderate level of black market activity)

The black market accounts for an estimated 20 percent of Morocco's GDP. There is considerable smuggling of consumer goods, as well as a lively contraband trade. Because Morocco's laws governing intellectual property do not cover computer software, black market activity in this area is on the rise. Trademark violations, mainly in the clothing industry, also constitute a growing problem.

Summary

Morocco					Overall Score	2.75
Trade	4	Monetary Policy	1		Property Rights	2
Taxation	3.5	Foreign Investment	2		Regulation	3
Government Intervention	3	Banking	3		Black Market	3
		Wage and Prices	3			

MOZAMBIQUE

Located in southern Africa, Mozambique is the world's poorest country, according to the World Bank. A conflict to win independence from Portugal began in 1964, and by 1974, Portugal was fighting independence movements in Angola and Guinea Bissau as well as in Mozambique. Mozambique received its independence in 1974; just two years later, however, it was engulfed by a bloody civil war that lasted until 1992. In the aftermath of United Nations–supervised multi-party elections, Mozambique has been reasonably successful in trying to build a democratic government and forge national reconciliation. The economy, one of the most heavily aid-dependent in the world, is moving away from the Marxism that led to its ruin. Over the past year, Mozambique has lowered its personal income tax and eliminated many price controls. It recently has reduced barriers to trade but also has increased both taxes and the level of government regulation.

Index of Economic Freedom Score: 4.00

Repressed

1 2 3 4 5

Factor #1: Trade Policy

Score: 3+ (Moderate level of protectionism)

Mozambique's tariff rates range from 5 percent to 35 percent, and the average tariff is 5.7 percent. There has been some trade liberalization, including a moderate lowering of tariffs and simplification of licensing procedures. The customs service, however, remains riddled with corruption, and the government is considering its privatization. A few imports, including imports of used automobiles, are prohibited.

Factor #2: Taxation

Score - Income taxation: 3- (Moderate tax rates)
Score - Corporate taxation: 4-Stable (High tax rates)
Total Taxation Score: 4- (High tax rates)

Mozambique adjusted personal income taxes in 1995. The highest bracket is now 30 percent, up from 15 percent in 1995, and the tax on the average income is 15 percent. The top corporate income tax rate is 45 percent. Mozambique also has a 45 percent capital gains tax and a 5 percent to 150 percent consumption tax.

Factor #3: Government Intervention in the Economy

Score: 3-Stable (Moderate level of government intervention)

Mozambique's government consumes 20 percent of GDP. Mozambique has progressed with privatization; some 350 small enterprises have been privatized, including a beer brewery and cement factory that were sold to South African and Portuguese concerns, and there are plans for additional privatizations. In the meantime, public enterprises will continue to account for a considerable amount of formal sector economic output.

Factor #4: Monetary Policy

Score: 5-Stable (Very high level of inflation)

Mozambique's average rate of inflation from 1985 to 1994 was 53.2 percent. In 1994, the inflation rate was about 60 percent.

Factor #5: Capital Flows and Foreign Investment

Score: 4-Stable (High barriers to foreign investment)

A recent change in the investment law has improved the climate for foreign investors. Mozambique has established a one-stop shop for foreign investment approval, and the government may soon grant land concessions to South African farmers. At the same time, however, feasibility study requirements and a corrupt government bureaucracy both frustrate foreign investment, especially by small-scale investors. Infrastructure and a few other areas are off-limits to private investment. Free trade zones were established in 1993, but their terms are not comparatively attractive.

Factor #6: Banking

Score: 4-Stable (High level of restrictions on banking)

Banking in Mozambique is dominated by state banks, although the system is being liberalized. Three private banks now operate in the capital; interest rates recently were freed; and the government is beginning to privatize both the Commercial Bank of Mozambique, which accounts for some 70 percent of banking assets, and the Popular Development Bank. There still are only four private banks, however, and they remain at a disadvantage in trying to compete with the many state-owned banks, in which corruption is a problem.

Factor #7: Wage and Price Controls

Score: 3-Stable (Moderate level of wage and price controls)

Price controls on several products were lifted in 1994. Remaining price controls apply to wheat, flour, bread, rents, fuels, utilities, newspapers, transportation, and a few other services. Mozambique has a minimum wage.

Factor #8: Property Rights

Score: 4-Stable (Low level of protection of private property)

Although some progress in bolstering property rights has been made lately, the land tenure and property rights regime remains fairly chaotic. Technically, all land still belongs to the state, and the vast majority of housing is state-owned, though some progress has been made with residential privatization. The government recently announced that it will not make restitution for pre-independence property claims. Mozambique's underdeveloped court system is unable to protect private property adequately.

Factor #9: Regulation

Score: 5- (Very high level of regulation)

Mozambique's regulatory environment is characterized by rising bureaucratic corruption. Registering a company is a cumbersome and secretive process, and there is considerable red tape. According to the U.S. Department of Commerce, "government bureaucracy, corruption at all levels, and unevenly applied customs duties frustrate many foreign business persons."[248]

Factor #10: Black Market
Score: 5-Stable (Very high level of black market activity)

Mozambique is a center for drug trafficking and money laundering, and international crime organizations use it as a clearinghouse for black market trade between Asia and Europe. It is estimated that, because of high tariffs and corruption in the customs service, 70 percent of Mozambique's consumer goods are smuggled into the country.

Summary

Mozambique				Overall Score	4.00
Trade	3	Monetary Policy	5	Property Rights	4
Taxation	4	Foreign Investment	4	Regulation	5
Government Intervention	3	Banking	4	Black Market	5
		Wage and Prices	3		

---

248   U.S. Department of Commerce, *Country Commercial Guide,* 1996.

MYANMAR

The Southeast Asian country of Myanmar, formerly known as Burma, gained its independence from the United Kingdom in 1948. A fragile parliamentary democracy arose but was overthrown by the military in 1962. The country then proceeded into a self-imposed state of isolation and declared itself a "Socialist Republic" in 1974. In 1988, an economic crisis led to some opening for foreign investment, particularly in energy and tourism (although tight controls over other sectors have kept foreign investment far below that of neighboring countries), and a new military government began to introduce some free-market and democratic reforms. These were put on hold in 1990, however, after opposition parties won national elections. Myanmar currently is seeking to join the Association of South East Asian Nations.

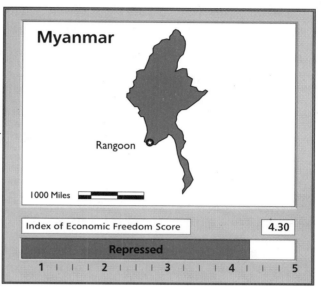

| Index of Economic Freedom Score | 4.30 |

Repressed

1 | | | 2 | | | 3 | | | 4 | | | 5

Factor #1: Trade Policy
Score: 5-Stable (Very high level of protectionism)

The average tariff rate in Myanmar is over 15 percent, primarily because of a scaled tariff schedule that includes rates as high as 30 percent for machinery, spare parts, and other regularly imported items. Non-tariff barriers include corrupt border officials, strict inspection requirements, and import bans.

Factor #2: Taxation
Score - Income taxation: 2-Stable (Low tax rates)
Score - Corporate taxation: 3-Stable (Moderate tax rates)
Final Taxation Score: 3-Stable (Moderate tax rates)

Myanmar's top income tax rate is 30 percent, but the average taxpayer is in the 3 percent bracket. The top marginal corporate tax rate is 30 percent. Myanmar also has a turnover tax ranging between 5 percent and 25 percent.

Factor #3: Government Intervention in the Economy
Score: 5-Stable (Very high level of government intervention)

The government of Myanmar is privatizing several companies, but the economy remains largely state-controlled, with most GDP generated by government sources. "Although the government has allowed the private sector to engage in most economic activities," reports the U.S. Department of Commerce, "it has retained its monopoly in postal and telecommunications services, broadcasting and television services, manufacturing of products related to security and defense, rice exports and electricity generation.

The government also does not allow foreign investment in banking, insurance and conservation of forests and plantation on a commercial scale."[249]

Factor #4: Monetary Policy
Score: 4-Stable (High level of inflation)

Myanmar's average annual rate of inflation from 1985 to 1994 was 25.1 percent. In 1995, the inflation rate was 31 percent.

Factor #5: Capital Flows and Foreign Investment
Score: 4-Stable (High barriers to foreign investment)

Investment in Myanmar is heavily restricted. Although the government has moved to open some sectors of the economy to foreign investment, most of the economy remains closed. Moreover, foreign investors face both a massive bureaucracy and extensive government corruption. Investments are approved only if they are deemed to benefit Myanmar, and only on a case-by-case basis.

Factor #6: Banking
Score: 4-Stable (High level of restrictions on banking)

The banking system in Myanmar is almost entirely government-controlled. There is little competition, although the private banking industry is growing.

Factor #7: Wage and Price Controls
Score: 4-Stable (High level of wage and price controls)

In many industries (such as public utilities and some agricultural goods), wages and prices are set primarily by the government. Prices, however, are becoming more liberalized.

Factor #8: Property Rights
Score: 4-Stable (Low level of protection of private property)

Private property owned by foreigners as a result of foreign investment is exempt from expropriation, but the property of citizens may still be confiscated. Government corruption makes it difficult to seek legal protection for property. The Burmese judiciary is both inefficient and subject to extensive government influence. According to the U.S. Department of Commerce, "Although Burma is in the process of revising its legislation in line with the needs of a market economy, laws and regulations governing property and contractual rights are outdated—many were enacted during colonial rule—and consequently are ineffective. The Government readily and thoroughly interferes in any case deemed politically sensitive, which could include business disputes involving state agencies or members of the military elite."[250]

---

249   U.S. Department of Commerce, *Country Commercial Guide,* 1996.

250   *Ibid.*

Factor #9: Regulation
Score: 5-Stable (Very high level of regulation)

Establishing a business in Myanmar can be time-consuming and costly. Bureaucrats are corrupt and often seek bribes, and regulations can be applied unevenly and inconsistently.

Factor #10: Black Market
Score: 5-Stable (Very high level of black market activity)

Myanmar's black market, mainly in consumer goods and pirated intellectual property from Western counties, continues to grow. "There is no effective protection of patents, copyrights, trademarks or any other intellectual property in Burma," reports the U.S. Department of Commerce. "A Patents and Design Act was introduced in 1945, but never brought into force.... Pirating of books, software, designs, etc. is rampant.... Civil action can be taken against misuse of a trademark, but is cumbersome and costly. Burma does not belong to any international conventions on patents, trademarks or copyrights."[251]

Summary

Myanmar				Overall Score	4.30
Trade	5	Monetary Policy	4	Property Rights	4
Taxation	3	Foreign Investment	4	Regulation	5
Government Intervention	5	Banking	4	Black Market	5
		Wage and Prices	4		

---

251 *Ibid.*

NAMIBIA

The southern African country of Namibia was a German colony before World War I and later became a colony of South Africa. It gained its independence in 1990 but remains closely linked to South Africa. Since becoming independent, Namibia has focused on creating a stable free-market system. The government has achieved substantial fiscal discipline and is opening the Namibian market to trade and investment.

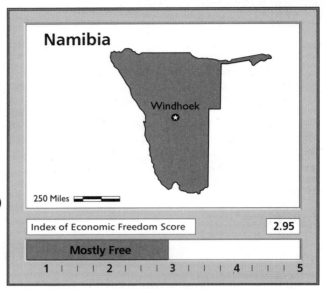

Index of Economic Freedom Score: **2.95**

Mostly Free

1 2 3 4 5

Factor #1: Trade Policy
Score: 4-Stable (High level of protectionism)

Namibia's average tariff rate is 24.4 percent. Namibia belongs to the Southern African Development Community, a regional trade arrangement among several southern African countries. Although Namibia strongly advocates free trade, its membership in the SADC forces it to abide by a common external tariff, which is very high. It also must maintain non-tariff barriers, including a requirement for letters of credit for all imports and strict labeling standards.

Factor #2: Taxation
Score - Income taxation: 3-Stable (Moderate tax rates)
Score - Corporate taxation: 3-Stable (Moderate tax rates)
Final Taxation Score: 3.5-Stable (High tax rates)

Namibia's top income tax rate is 35 percent, and the rate for the average income level is 0 percent. The top corporate tax rate is 35 percent. Namibia also imposes an 8 percent sales tax.

Factor #3: Government Intervention in the Economy
Score: 4-Stable (High level of government intervention)

Government consumes about 31 percent of Namibia's GDP, and the public sector of the economy is substantial.

Factor #4: Monetary Policy
Score: 2-Stable (Low level of inflation)

Namibia's average annual rate of inflation from 1985 to 1994 was 10.7 percent. In 1995, the inflation rate was 9.9 percent.

Factor #5: Capital Flows and Foreign Investment
Score: 2-Stable (Low barriers to foreign investment)

Namibia provides equal treatment for domestic and foreign firms and actively seeks foreign investment. It has a modern investment code which provides significant protection and incentives for investment.

Factor #6: Banking
Score: 2-Stable (Low level of restrictions on banking)

The banking system in Namibia is entirely private, with minimal government intrusion or regulation. There is no deposit insurance, but commercial banks are regulated by a central bank.

Factor #7: Wage and Price Controls
Score: 3-Stable (Moderate level of wage and price controls)

Wages and prices in Namibia are set mainly by the government. Petroleum prices are controlled, however, and a growing "buy Namibian" movement impedes competition and raises prices on some domestically produced goods and services.

Factor #8: Property Rights
Score: 2-Stable (High level of protection of private property)

The Namibian legal system is efficient, fair, and independent of the government. According to the U.S. Department of Commerce, "The Foreign Investment Act protects the investor from expropriation. It also guarantees settlement of any disputes by international arbitration. The local court system provides an effective means to enforce property and contractual rights."[252] Nevertheless, there is a shortage of lawyers, and Namibian courts often are backlogged.

Factor #9: Regulation
Score: 4-Stable (High level of regulation)

Although Namibia has passed new anti-corruption legislation, according to the Economist Intelligence Unit, "The ruling South West Africa People's Organization (Swapo) will continue to encounter unprecedented criticism over past civil rights abuses and current corruption levels."[253]

Factor #10: Black Market
Score: 3-Stable (Moderate level of black market activity)

Black market activity in Namibia is moderate and confined mainly to goods smuggled in from South Africa. The smuggling of gold and diamonds is a particular problem.

---

252 U.S. Department of Commerce, *Country Commercial Guide,* 1996.

253 Economist Intelligence Unit, *EIU Country Reports,* 1996.

Summary

Namibia				Overall Score	2.95
Trade	4	Monetary Policy	2	Property Rights	2
Taxation	3.5	Foreign Investment	2	Regulation	4
Government Intervention	4	Banking	2	Black Market	3
		Wage and Prices	2		

NEPAL

From 1846 to 1951, Nepal was ruled by hereditary leaders loyal to British colonial power. In 1992, following significant unrest, the conflict between parliamentary and royalist government was settled in favor of a constitutional monarchy with a multi-party parliament. In late 1994, communists gained a parliamentary plurality. Nepal's economy is mainly agricultural, and tight government controls have contributed to making the country one of the poorest in the world. Nevertheless, there are indications that the Nepalese government supports aggressive economic reform; for example, a substantial program of privatization is in place. This process has only begun, and much remains to be done.

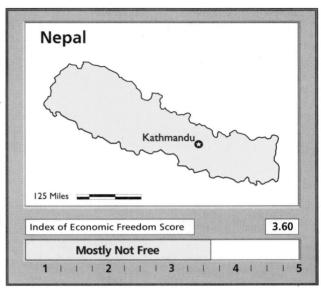

Index of Economic Freedom Score	3.60

Mostly Not Free

1 2 3 4 5

Factor #1: Trade Policy

Score: 4- (High level of protectionism)

Nepal's average tariff rate is about 11 percent.[254] According to the U.S. Department of Commerce, "Although tariffs have been reduced and customs procedures have been simplified, extended delay at the border is not uncommon. A further difficulty is the high degree of corruption among customs officials reflected in arbitrary valuation procedures."[255] Nepal bans imports of beef.

Factor #2: Taxation

Score - Income taxation: 3-Stable (Moderate tax rates)
Score - Corporate taxation: 3-Stable (Moderate tax rates)
Final Taxation Score: 3-Stable (Moderate tax rates)

Nepal's top income tax rate is 35 percent, and government revenues equal about 14 percent of GDP.[256]

---

254 Based on total taxes on international trade as a percentage of total imports; from International Monetary Fund, *Government Financial Statistics 1995.*

255 U.S. Department of Commerce, *Nepal,* National Trade Data Bank, 1995.

256 Nepal's tax rates are unavailable. Therefore, Nepal was graded solely on total government revenues as a percentage of GDP.

Factor #3: Government Intervention in the Economy
Score: 3-Stable (Moderate level of government intervention)

Government consumes about 9 percent of Nepal's GDP,[257] and the public sector is large. The government still owns significant portions of the national airlines, telecommunications companies, and energy companies.

Factor #4: Monetary Policy
Score: 2-Stable (Low level of inflation)

Nepal's average annual rate of inflation from 1985 to 1994 was 12 percent. In 1995, the inflation rate was 8.2 percent.

Factor #5: Capital Flows and Foreign Investment
Score: 4-Stable (High barriers to foreign investment)

Nepal has opened some of its market to foreign investment, but many investments are permitted only in the form of joint ventures, either with government-owned firms or with private companies. Bureaucratic red tape and government corruption often postpone, prolong, or terminate foreign investment initiatives.

Factor #6: Banking
Score: 4-Stable (High level of restrictions on banking)

Since 1984, Nepal has opened its banking system to foreign competition. Yet only a few banks have opened, primarily because the government prefers foreign banks to open branches through joint ventures with domestic banks. Foreign competition therefore is limited. The government owns significant shares of most banks in Nepal, although it does plan to privatize the 100-percent state-owned Rastriya Banija Bank over the next three years.

Factor #7: Wage and Price Controls
Score: 4-Stable (High level of wage and price controls)

Nepal controls most wages and prices through its large government-owned sector and the substantial subsidies it provides to these companies.

Factor #8: Property Rights
Score: 3+ (Moderate level of protection of private property)

The main threats to private property in Nepal are crime and government corruption. Despite recent judicial reform, protection of private property by the legal and judicial system is insufficient. According to the U.S. Department of Commerce, "There is an effective means of enforcing property rights as all such transactions must be registered and property holdings cannot be transferred without following procedures. Even so, property disputes account for half of the current backlog in Nepal's court system and such cases can take years to be settled."[258] By global standards, however, Nepal's judiciary provides a moderate level of protection for private property.

---

257   World Bank, *World Development Report 1996.*

258   U.S. Department of Commerce, *Country Commercial Guide,* 1996.

Factor #9: Regulation
Score: 4-Stable (High level of regulation)

Establishing a business in Nepal is difficult if the business competes with a state-owned company. Rather than create new competition for existing state-owned companies, the government attempts to redirect private investment to companies that are being privatized. In some cases, regulations are applied haphazardly by corrupt government bureaucracies.

Factor #10: Black Market
Score: 5-Stable (Very high level of black market activity)

The black market in Nepal is substantial, especially in consumer goods, labor, construction, and pirated intellectual property from Western countries. Nepal does not protect computer software and semiconductor designs adequately, and much piracy occurs in these areas.

Summary

Nepal				Overall Score	3.60
Trade	4	Monetary Policy	2	Property Rights	3
Taxation	3	Foreign Investment	4	Regulation	4
Government Intervention	3	Banking	4	Black Market	5
		Wage and Prices	4		

THE NETHERLANDS

The Netherlands declared its independence from Spain in 1579, although true independence did not come until several years later. The Netherlands gained prominence as it sought to expand its colonial influence throughout the East Indies. During the 17th and 18th centuries, it became a driving force in global trade and the establishment of overseas colonies. In the 19th century, Napoleon transformed the country into the Kingdom of Holland until independence was restored in 1815. The rest of the 19th century saw the development of parliamentary democracy. During World War II, Germany invaded the Netherlands, disrupting much of its political and economic progress. Since the end of the war, however, the country has re-established a stable government and built a solid economic system. The Netherlands maintains a large social welfare program that is funded by taxes that are among the highest in he world. Economic freedom in other areas, however, such as banking and monetary policy, is far greater than in most other countries.

Factor #1: Trade Policy

Score: 2-Stable (Low level of protectionism)

According to the U.S. Department of State, "Dutch trade and investment policy is among the most open in the world."[259] But although the average tariff rate in the Netherlands is 3.6 percent, the government also maintains trade restrictions common to all members of the European Union (EU), such as restrictions on foreign participation in telecommunications systems like broadcasting.

Factor #2: Taxation

Score - Income taxation: 5- (Very high tax rates)
Score - Corporate taxation: 4- (High tax rates)
Final Taxation Score: 5- (Very high tax rates)

The Netherlands has a top income tax rate of 60 percent, and the average taxpayer is in the 6.15 percent bracket.[260] The top marginal corporate tax rate is 37 percent. The Netherlands also has several other taxes, including a 35 percent capital gains tax and a 17.5 percent value-added tax.

---

259   State Department Report, 1996, p. 236.

260   This rate may increase to 37.65 percent, however, due to a national insurance tax that can be levied on top of the lowest tax bracket. Therefore, the income tax score for the Netherlands is based on this higher rate.

Factor #3: Government Intervention in the Economy
Score: 3- (Moderate level of government intervention)

In 1994, the government of the Netherlands undertook a massive reduction in spending and made substantial progress in slashing its budget deficit, now about 3.3 percent of GDP. According to the U.S. Department of State, "Budget cuts are getting into areas which were regarded as untouchable: development aid, social security, defense, education."[261] The Dutch government consumes about 15 percent of GDP and plays a relatively moderate role in the economy. It subsidizes private-sector research and development programs, provides funds to help some companies restructure, dominates the energy sector, and plays a large role in aviation, chemicals, steel, telecommunications, and transportation.

Factor #4: Monetary Policy
Score: 1-Stable (Very low level of inflation)

The average rate of inflation in the Netherlands from 1985 to 1994 was 1.6 percent. In 1995, the inflation rate was about 2 percent, as it has been for most of 1996.

Factor #5: Capital Flows and Foreign Investment
Score: 2-Stable (Low barriers to foreign investment)

There are few restrictions on investments in the Netherlands. Most investment restrictions occur in defense-related industries such as the manufacturing of weapons.

Factor #6: Banking
Score: 1-Stable (Very low level of restrictions on banking)

The Netherlands has been one of Europe's financial and banking centers for centuries, and its banking system operates freely, with almost no government restriction or regulation. Banks established in the Netherlands may engage in a variety of financial services, such as buying, selling, and holding securities, insurance policies, and real estate. There are few investment restrictions imposed on banks, and most financial institutions are not subject to supervision by the Central Bank. There are over 80 foreign banks operating in the Netherlands today.

Factor #7: Wage and Price Controls
Score: 2-Stable (Low level of wage and price controls)

Wages and prices in the Netherlands are set mainly by the market. There is a minimum wage. Cartels, especially in the utilities area, traditionally have been sanctioned by the government; but the country's entrance into the EU has forced the government to crack down on cartels, and most are now being eliminated.

Factor #8: Property Rights
Score: 1-Stable (Very high level of protection of private property)

Private property in the Netherlands is safe from expropriation. The legal and judicial system is advanced and efficient.

---

261   State Department Report, 1996, pp. 225–226.

Factor #9: Regulation
Score: 2-Stable (Low level of regulation)

Establishing a business in the Netherlands is a simple procedure. Regulations are applied evenly in most cases.

Factor #10: Black Market
Score: 1-Stable (Very low level of black market activity)

Because little is illegal in the Netherlands (both prostitution and drugs, for example, are legal), there is little incentive to engage in black market activity. Sales of pirated intellectual property are minuscule.

Summary

Netherlands					Overall Score	2.00
Trade	2	Monetary Policy	1	Property Rights	1
Taxation	5	Foreign Investment	2	Regulation	2
Government Intervention	3	Banking	1	Black Market	1
		Wage and Prices	2		

NEW ZEALAND

New Zealand joined the British Empire in 1840, became a self-governing dominion within the British Empire in 1907, and achieved full independence in 1932. For five decades prior to 1984, both Labor and National Party governments pursued an economic policy of "insulationism," under which high tariffs, import licensing, foreign exchange controls, high tax rates, strict regulations, and government provision of many commercial activities all stifled economic growth. After Labor's victory in the 1984 election, the government of Prime Minister David Lange reversed course and launched what the Organization for Economic Cooperation and Development called the most comprehensive economic liberalization program ever undertaken in a developed country. Following the National Party's triumph in the 1990

election, the government of Prime Minister Jim Bolger expanded on Labor's economic liberalization program by deregulating the labor market, balancing the budget, and cutting income tax rates. A new election was held October 12, 1996, in which none of the five major parties won a majority. As of this writing, the shape of the new government is undetermined.

Factor #1: Trade Policy
Score: 2-Stable (Low level of protectionism)

New Zealand's average tariff rate is about 3.2 percent. In 1994, New Zealand announced plans to eliminate all tariffs by 2004; all import licensing and other quantitative restrictions were abolished in 1992. New Zealand has a comprehensive free trade and investment agreement with Australia. Most non-tariff barriers to imports have been abolished; however, New Zealand does still maintain minor non-tariff barriers in the form of business-run marketing boards, private associations that can impede imports, mainly in the agricultural sector.

Factor #2: Taxation
Score - Income taxation: 3-Stable (Moderate tax rates)
Score - Corporate taxation: 3-Stable (Moderate tax rates)
Final Taxation Score: 3.5-Stable (High tax rates)

The top income tax rate in New Zealand is 33 percent, and the average income level is taxed at a rate of 21.5 percent. Other taxes include a 33 percent flat rate company tax, a 12.5 percent goods and services tax, a 49 percent fringe benefits tax, and a risk-based 1 percent to 8 percent levy on gross salaries and wages to pay for accident compensation insurance. New Zealand has no capital gains or estate taxes.

Factor #3: Government Intervention in the Economy
Score: 2-Stable (Low level of government intervention)

The government of New Zealand consumes about 14.9 percent of GDP. During the 1970s and early 1980s, New Zealand had a large state-owned sector that received government subsidies. Recent privatization efforts have reduced the size of this sector, and remaining state-owned companies have been "corporatized," meaning they must operate in the same way commercial companies operate. The government has eliminated all subsidies to these businesses.

Factor #4: Monetary Policy
Score: 1-Stable (Very low level of inflation)

New Zealand's average rate of inflation from 1985 to 1994 was 4.7 percent. In 1995, the inflation rate was 4 percent. For most of 1996, it has been below 4 percent.

Factor #5: Capital Flows and Foreign Investment
Score: 2-Stable (Low barriers to foreign investment)

Government approval is required for certain large direct investments and the purchase of commercial fishing assets and rural land. New Zealand actively encourages direct foreign investment, however, and approval is routine.

Factor #6: Banking
Score: 1-Stable (Very low level of restrictions on banking)

New Zealand's banking system is deregulated, and foreign banks are welcome. The Reserve Bank of New Zealand is limited to prudential supervision. The government does not impose deposit insurance on financial institutions; instead, banks provide full disclosure of their financial condition to the public.

Factor #7: Wage and Price Controls
Score: 2-Stable (Low level of wage and price controls)

Wages and prices in New Zealand are determined largely by the market. New Zealand enforces a relatively low minimum wage for most adult workers.

Factor #8: Property Rights
Score: 1-Stable (Very high level of protection of private property)

Private property is a fundamental right in New Zealand. The legal and judicial system is efficient and provides adequate protection of private property. Government expropriation is very unlikely.

Factor #9: Regulation
Score: 2-Stable (Low level of regulation)

Establishing a business in New Zealand is easy, and regulations are applied evenly and consistently. Environmental and safety regulations, however, can be burdensome.

Factor #10: Black Market
Score: 1-Stable (Very low level of black market activity)

The black market in New Zealand is negligible, confined to the sale of goods and services considered harmful to society, such as guns and drugs. There is virtually no black market in smuggling or pirated intellectual property.

Summary

New Zealand					Overall Score	1.75
Trade	2	Monetary Policy	1	Property Rights	1
Taxation	3.5	Foreign Investment	2	Regulation	2
Government Intervention	2	Banking	1	Black Market	1
		Wage and Prices	2		

NICARAGUA

The Central American country of Nicaragua became an independent state in 1838. In 1979, under the Sandinista regime, Nicaragua became a socialist economy; and despite infusions of foreign aid, there was little economic growth. In 1990, Nicaragua held a democratic election in which the victor, Violeta Chamorro, promised economic reform. Progress is occurring slowly, however. The Sandinistas, who still hold key posts in the military and police, have blocked reforms, especially the privatization of state-owned enterprises and other nationalized sectors of the economy. Nicaragua held new elections in October 1996, which resulted in Arnoldo Aleman succeeding Chamorro. The Sandinistas currently are disputing the results of the elections.

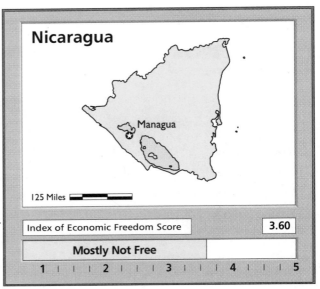

Nicaragua

Managua

125 Miles

| Index of Economic Freedom Score | 3.60 |

Mostly Not Free

1　　　2　　　3　　　4　　　5

Factor #1: Trade Policy
Score: 5-Stable (Very high level of protectionism)

According to the U.S. Department of State, Nicaragua's average nominal protection of goods in 1995 was 14.5 percent, in addition to which the government maintains significant non-tariff barriers: "Importers commonly complain of steep 'secondary' customs costs including custom declaration form charges and consular fees. In addition, importers are required to utilize the services of licensed customs agents, adding yet another layer of costs. Importers also complain that some competitors either smuggle in goods or under-declare their values in order to avoid tariffs and thus offer the goods on the market at reduced costs."[262] Although Nicaragua is becoming more open to trade than in the past, its level of protectionism is very high when measured against global standards.

Factor #2: Taxation
Score - Income taxation: 2-Stable (Low tax rates)
Score - Corporate taxation: 3-Stable (Moderate tax rates)
Total Taxation Score: 3-Stable (Moderate tax rates)

Nicaragua's top marginal income tax rate is 30 percent, with the average income taxed at a rate of 0 percent. The top corporate tax rate also is 30 percent. Nicaragua also has a 15 percent general sales tax, a consumption tax, and a municipality tax.

262　State Department Report, 1996, p. 410.

Factor #3: Government Intervention in the Economy
Score: 2-Stable (Low level of government intervention)

Government consumes 14 percent of Nicaragua's GDP. Nicaragua has privatized much of its economy, and most of the country's GDP is produced by the private sector.

Factor #4: Monetary Policy
Score: 5-Stable (Very high level of inflation)

Nicaragua's average annual rate of inflation from 1985 to 1994 was 1,850 percent. In 1995, the inflation rate was around 7.8 percent.

Factor #5: Capital Flows and Foreign Investment
Score: 2-Stable (Low barriers to foreign investment)

Nicaragua has liberalized its foreign investment code to allow for 100 percent foreign ownership. Most industries are open to investment.

Factor #6: Banking
Score: 3-Stable (Moderate level of restrictions on banking)

Despite some progress in ending state control, some of Nicaragua's banks remain in government hands. Three of the 14 commercial banks now operating in Nicaragua are owned by the government.

Factor #7: Wage and Price Controls
Score: 3-Stable (Moderate level of wage and price controls)

Almost all price controls have been lifted. The government of Nicaragua, however, still maintains a significant amount of control over some prices. It sets prices on petroleum products, public utilities, sugar, and locally produced soft drinks and beer. The government also affects free market pricing by purchasing "emergency stores" of such important basic foods as sugar, beans, and grain.

Factor #8: Property Rights
Score: 4-Stable (Low level of protection of private property)

Private property is not safe in Nicaragua. Property can be confiscated by armed criminals and corrupt local governments, the court system is ill-equipped to deal with claims of property confiscation, and local law enforcement remains inadequate. According to the U.S. Department of Commerce, "The legal system is inefficient and highly politicized; enforcement of judicial determinations is inconsistent."[263]

Factor #9: Regulation
Score: 4-Stable (High level of regulation)

Government regulation remains a serious problem in Nicaragua. Among other difficulties, environmental impact studies required of businesses can prevent both the expansion of existing businesses and the formation of new ones, regulations are applied haphazardly, and corruption persists.

---

263   U.S. Department of Commerce, *Country Commercial Guide*, 1996.

Factor #10: Black Market
Score: 5-Stable (Very high level of black market activity)

Nicaragua has a large black market in several goods, including pharmaceuticals and agricultural products, and there is rampant piracy of goods from Canada, the United States, and Latin America. With 40 percent unemployment rates, large numbers of people engage in black market activity. "Pirated videos are readily available in video rental stores nationwide, as are pirated audio cassettes," reports the U.S. Department of Commerce. "In addition, cable television operators are known to intercept and retransmit U.S. satellite signals—a practice which continues despite a trend of negotiating contracts with U.S. sports and news satellite programmers, and the first legal sales of HBO Ole/Cinemax concession to four Nicaraguan cable companies."[264]

Summary

Nicaragua		Overall Score	3.60
Trade	5	Monetary Policy	5	Property Rights	4
Taxation	3	Foreign Investment	2	Regulation	4
Government Intervention	2	Banking	3	Black Market	5
		Wage and Prices	3		

---

264 *Ibid.*

NIGER

The West Central African country of Niger gained its independence from France in 1960. Its economy is primarily agricultural and greatly affected by weather conditions. Only 12 percent of the land is arable. Niger's economy has shrunk 4.2 percent every year since 1980; at the same time, its population has continued to grow. Niger remains plagued by a large public sector, a bloated bureaucracy, corruption, and a massive black market.

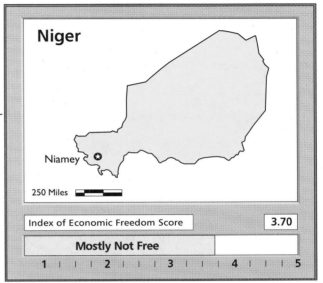

Index of Economic Freedom Score	3.70
Mostly Not Free	

1 | | | 2 | | | 3 | | | 4 | | | 5

Factor #1: Trade Policy

Score: 5- (Very high level of protectionism)

Niger's average tariff rate is 18.3 percent; the normal tariff rate is 5 percent, but additional tariffs on luxury and other items are as high as 60 percent. Niger also maintains some non-tariff barriers, mainly in the form of import bans and import substitution policies.

Factor #2: Taxation

Score - Income taxation: 3-Stable (Moderate tax rates)
Score - Corporate taxation: 4-Stable (High tax rates)
Final Taxation Score: 4-Stable (High tax rates)

Niger's top income tax rate is 60 percent, and the average taxpayer is in the 2 percent bracket. The top marginal corporate tax rate is 45 percent. Niger also has a value-added tax and a capital gains tax.

Factor #3: Government Intervention in the Economy

Score: 3-Stable (Moderate level of government intervention)

Government consumes about 17 percent of Niger's GDP, and most of total GDP is generated by the public sector.

Factor #4: Monetary Policy

Score: 1-Stable (Very low level of inflation)

Niger's average annual rate of inflation from 1985 to 1994 was 0.2 percent. In 1995, the inflation rate was 11 percent.

Factor #5: Capital Flows and Foreign Investment

Score: 4-Stable (High barriers to foreign investment)

Niger provides equal treatment for domestic and foreign firms. There are, however, some restrictions: a strict investment review process, a hostile government-owned sector, and corruption. In addition, a cumbersome bureaucracy often delays investments.

Factor #6: Banking
Score: 4-Stable (High level of restrictions on banking)

The banking system in Niger is subject to heavy government control, although recent efforts to increase private investment have shown some progress.

Factor #7: Wage and Price Controls
Score: 4-Stable (High level of wage and price controls)

Wages and prices are affected by Niger's large public sector, import substitution policies, and government subsidies.

Factor #8: Property Rights
Score: 3+ (Moderate level of protection of private property)

Private property in Niger is subject to government expropriation, although there are few recent examples of nationalization. Niger's government is attempting to privatize many government-owned enterprises, and the legal and judicial system is becoming more efficient. According to the U.S. Department of Commerce, "Niger has an independent court system which respects and protects property and commercial rights."[265]

Factor #9: Regulation
Score: 4-Stable (High level of regulation)

Establishing a business in Niger is difficult. The government bureaucracy is both massive and corrupt, bribery is sometimes present, and there is embezzlement by government officials responsible for collecting fees. Regulations often are applied haphazardly.

Factor #10: Black Market
Score: 5-Stable (Very high level of black market activity)

The World Bank estimates that the black market in Niger is both larger than the formal market and growing. According to the U.S. Department of Commerce, "The greatest barriers to investment are the small scale of the economy, limited buying power, low rates of capital accumulation, and the fact that an estimated two thirds of GDP is generated by informal manufacturing and trading."[266]

Summary

Niger				Overall Score	3.70
Trade	5	Monetary Policy	1	Property Rights	3
Taxation	4	Foreign Investment	4	Regulation	4
Government Intervention	3	Banking	4	Black Market	5
		Wage and Prices	4		

265 U.S. Department of Commerce, *Country Commercial Guide,* 1996.

266 *Ibid.*

NIGERIA

The West African country of Nigeria gained its independence from Great Britain in 1960. Nigeria is rich in natural resources, including oil, coal, natural gas, and fertile soil, and has the largest population in Africa. It also is in political crisis, with the military-dominated regime of General Sani Abacha resisting demands for democratic change. There have been increasing calls for international sanctions on Nigeria, although this is opposed by the Europeans. Nigeria is a growing center for both the narcotics trade and international crime. In 1996, the execution of human rights activists brought international outrage. Nigeria's mixed economy has been in decline; per capita income has fallen from $1,000 to less than $300 in the last decade as the country has accumulated a massive $37 billion international debt. Mismanagement and corruption have derailed the government's economic reform program, established in 1986, although the government has reduced taxes recently.

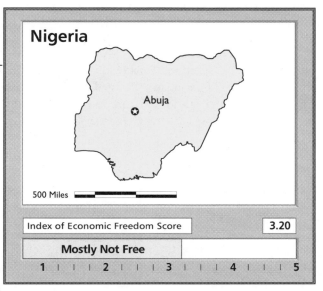

Nigeria

Abuja

500 Miles

Index of Economic Freedom Score: 3.20

Mostly Not Free

1   2   3   4   5

Factor #1: Trade Policy
Score: 5-Stable (Very high level of protectionism)

Despite 1995 reductions on many goods, Nigeria's average import duty is 18.3 percent, and all goods are subject to additional administrative surcharges totaling 6 percent. The list of banned imports (which includes maize, eggs, processed wood, textiles, and used vehicles) is substantial, although the ban on wheat imports was lifted recently. In addition, the customs process is burdensome, and there is talk of international sanctions because of Nigeria's poor human rights record.

Factor #2: Taxation
Score - Income taxation: 2+ (Low tax rates)
Score - Corporate taxation: 3-Stable (Moderate tax rates)
Total Taxation Score: 3+ (Moderate tax rates)

Nigeria's top income tax rate was lowered from 35 percent to 30 percent in 1995, and lowered again to 25 percent in 1996. The rate for the average taxpayer is 0 percent, and the corporate tax rate is 35 percent. In 1994, the government introduced a 5 percent value-added tax, applicable to 17 categories of goods and 24 services. Nigeria also has a capital gains tax.

Factor #3: Government Intervention in the Economy
Score: 2-Stable (Low level of government intervention)

The Nigerian government consumes 10 percent of GDP. The privatization drive has bogged down, and government-controlled companies, many of which are unprofitable, dominate many basic manufacturing industries.

Factor #4: Monetary Policy
Score: 4-Stable (High level of inflation)

Nigeria's average annual rate of inflation from 1985 to 1994 was 29.6 percent. The inflation rate was 58 percent in 1995 and remains about the same in 1996.

Factor #5: Capital Flows and Foreign Investment
Score: 2-Stable (Low barriers to foreign investment)

Foreign investment reforms in 1995 featured the scrapping of laws mandating the employment of Nigerians. As a result, foreigners now can own 100 percent of any Nigerian enterprise. The ministry charged with approving foreign investment, however, often acts arbitrarily, and there are long delays in the project approval process. Nigeria recently has been able to attract little significant foreign investment outside of the oil and gas sectors.

Factor #6: Banking
Score: 4-Stable (High level of restrictions on banking)

More than 100 domestic and foreign banks now operate branches in Nigeria. The banking sector is doing poorly, however. Although 60 percent Nigerian ownership is no longer required in foreign ventures, licensing refusals are common, and the government has taken control of four large commercial banks that recently had been privatized. The Central Bank, which is controlled directly by the president, fixes the discount rate, mandates lending to the agricultural and manufacturing sectors, and in general heavily regulates and controls the country's other banks. Private banks recently have been forced to purchase government securities.

Factor #7: Wage and Price Controls
Score: 2-Stable (Low level of wage and price controls)

Price controls were abolished in 1987, although some products, including petroleum, are subsidized. Wages are determined by negotiations between employers and unions, and the government has the final word on wage increases. Nigeria has a minimum wage.

Factor #8: Property Rights
Score: 3-Stable (Moderate level of protection of private property)

There is strong resistance to privatization efforts among Nigeria's labor unions, and the enforcement of laws protecting property remains lax. According to the U.S. Department of Commerce, "Disputes are resolved by the courts following local and common law cases. The administration of justice is adversarial in nature. The court system is hierarchical, with the Supreme Court the court of last resort. Generally, jurisdiction of the courts cannot be curtailed by agreement, but courts have the statutory duty to stay proceedings of an action which is the subject of an arbitration agreement."[267]

---

267   U.S. Department of Commerce, *Country Commercial Guide,* 1996.

Factor #9: Regulation
Score: 4-Stable (High level of regulation)

The process for establishing a business in Nigeria recently has been streamlined, although problems remain. Foreign investors must deal with bureaucratic delays, rampant corruption, and a complex web of restrictions and regulations. The U.S. Department of Commerce reports that "Nigeria offers potential investors a low-cost labor pool, abundant natural resources, and the largest domestic market in sub-Saharan Africa. However, these advantages must be weighed against Nigeria's autocratic military government, inadequate and poorly maintained infrastructure, increasing labor problems, complicated, confusing and inconsistent regulatory environment, the importance of personal ties in doing business and endemic corruption."[268] It can take several years just to acquire building permits.

Factor #10: Black Market
Score: 3-Stable (Moderate level of black market activity)

High tariffs and bans on textile and agricultural imports provide incentives for smuggling in Nigeria. Government monopolies on sugar and fertilizer distribution also encourage illegal trade, and a high duty on cigarettes and luxury goods likewise makes smuggling in these areas very lucrative. The black market in pirated computer software is substantial.

Summary

Nigeria					Overall Score	3.20
Trade	5	Monetary Policy	4		Property Rights	3
Taxation	3	Foreign Investment	2		Regulation	4
Government Intervention	2	Banking	4		Black Market	3
		Wage and Prices	2			

---

268 From *Nigeria—1996 Investment Climate Report—IMI960530*, National Trade Data Bank and Economic Bulletin Board—products of STAT–USA, U.S. Department of Commerce, May 30, 1996.

NORWAY

Norway

250 Miles

Oslo

Index of Economic Freedom Score | 2.45

Mostly Free

1 | | | | 2 | | | 3 | | | 4 | | | 5

Norway won its independence from Sweden in 1905. It remained neutral in World War I and throughout World War II until Germany invaded the country in 1940. Before the war, Norway had an established socialized economy with generous social welfare programs. When the government was restored in 1945, new elections resulted in a powerful victory for the Labor Party, which remained in power for the next 20 years, during which Norway consolidated its social welfare state. During the late 1950s, however, it also began to pursue free trade with its neighbors. Norway became a member of the European Free Trade Association in 1959. It has not become a full member of the European Union (EU) yet. Norway remains, however, closely linked to the EU through the European Economic Area, which provides for favorable access to the EU market for most Norwegian products.

Factor #1: Trade Policy

Score: 3-Stable (Moderate level of protectionism)

Norway maintains an average tariff of about 8 percent,[269] in addition to such non-tariff barriers as quotas and other restrictions on agricultural imports.

Factor #2: Taxation

Score - Income taxation: 5-Stable (Very high tax rates)
Score - Corporate taxation: 3-Stable (Moderate tax rates)
Final Taxation Score: 4.5-Stable (Very high tax rates)

Norway's top income tax rate of 41.7 percent, and the average taxpayer is taxed at a rate greater than 28 percent. The top marginal corporate tax rate is 28 percent. Norway also has a 28 percent capital gains tax and a 23 percent value-added tax.

Factor #3: Government Intervention in the Economy

Score: 3-Stable (Moderate level of government intervention)

Government consumes about 21.9 percent of Norway's GDP, and almost half of overall GDP is produced by government-owned industries.

---

269   Based on total government taxation of international transactions as a percentage of imports.

Factor #4: Monetary Policy

Score: 1-Stable (Very low level of inflation)

From 1985 to 1994, Norway maintained a stable 3 percent rate of inflation. In 1995, the inflation rate was 2.4 percent.

Factor #5: Capital Flows and Foreign Investment

Score: 2-Stable (Low barriers to foreign investment)

Although Norway generally welcomes foreign investment, the government still maintains some restrictions on investments in telecommunications, public utilities, and industries considered vital to national security.

Factor #6: Banking

Score: 3-Stable (Moderate level of restrictions on banking)

Norway's banking system is becoming more liberalized. Non-European banks are permitted to establish subsidiaries (not branches, however), and Norwegian banks may engage in a variety of financial services, including the buying and selling of securities, insurance policies, real estate, and other investments. According to the U.S. Department of State, "While there has been substantial banking reform, competition in this sector still remains distorted due to government ownership of the two largest commercial banks, and the existence of specialized state banks which offer subsidized loans in certain sectors and geographic locations."[270]

Factor #7: Wage and Price Controls

Score: 3-Stable (Moderate level of wage and price controls)

Wages and prices in Norway are set by the market. The government has indirect control over many prices and wages, however, through the country's large public sector. Large agricultural subsidies also continue to affect prices.

Factor #8: Property Rights

Score: 1-Stable (Very high level of protection of private property)

Private property is safe from government confiscation. Norway has an efficient legal system.

Factor #9: Regulation

Score: 3-Stable (Moderate level of regulation)

Some of Norway's economy remains heavily regulated. This is particularly true in agriculture and in service industries like telecommunications and transportation. The government, however, also is reducing expenditures and privatizing some businesses.

Factor #10: Black Market

Score: 1-Stable (Very low level of black market activity)

Norway has a very small black market. Because it also has very strong and efficient intellectual property rights laws, piracy in these products is virtually nonexistent.

---

270   State Department Report, 1996, p. 242.

Summary

Norway		Overall Score	2.45

Trade	3	Monetary Policy	1	Property Rights	1
Taxation	4.5	Foreign Investment	2	Regulation	3
Government Intervention	3	Banking	3	Black Market	1
		Wage and Prices	3		

OMAN

Oman is located on the Arabian Peninsula, on the eastern border of Saudi Arabia. Its coastal regions were dominated by the Portuguese from 1507 until 1650. In the 19th century, Oman's ruling sultans cultivated close relations with Great Britain to offset outside Arab and Persian interference. Today, Oman is an absolute monarchy. Its economy depends heavily on oil revenues, which account for 85 percent of export earnings and about 40 percent of GDP. It was not until 1991 that Oman began to introduce free-market reforms. Recently, government spending as a percentage of economic output has decreased.

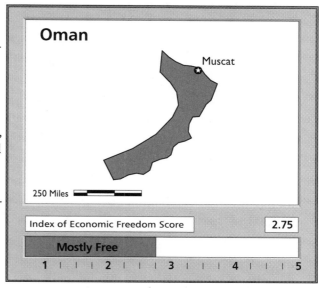

Index of Economic Freedom Score — 2.75
Mostly Free
1   2   3   4   5

Factor #1: Trade Policy

Score: 3-Stable (Moderate level of protectionism)

Oman has a flat 4 percent tariff rate and higher rates for other imports. The average tariff rate is about 6 percent. The government also imposes non-tariff barriers in the form of import licenses, which are required for all imports. According to the U.S. Department of State, "Oman's customs procedures are complex, and there are complaints of sudden changes in the enforcement of regulations. Processing of shipments at Omani ports and airports can add significantly to the amount of time that it takes to get goods to the market or inputs to a project."[271]

Factor #2: Taxation

Score - Income taxation: 1-Stable (Low tax rates)
Score - Corporate taxation: 5-Stable (Very high tax rates)
Total Taxation Score: 3.5-Stable (High tax rates)

Income taxes are not imposed on individuals, but the top corporate tax rate is 50 percent.[272] Oman also has a 50 percent capital gains tax, a training levy taken from non-Omani employees, and a social contributions tax.

Factor #3: Government Intervention in the Economy

Score: 4+ (High level of government intervention)

Oman's government consumes 30.6 percent of GDP. It also owns nearly all of the country's oil production.

---

271   State Department Report, 1996, p. 491.

272   This rate applies to foreign-owned corporations.

Factor #4: Monetary Policy
Score: 1-Stable (Very low level of inflation)

Oman's average annual rate of inflation from 1985 to 1994 was 0.1 percent. In 1995, the inflation rate was about 1 percent.

Factor #5: Capital Flows and Foreign Investment
Score: 3-Stable (Moderate barriers to foreign investment)

With few exceptions, companies in Oman must be fully owned by Omanis. Foreign investment is allowed only through joint ventures and joint-stock companies. There are some tax incentives for investments.

Factor #6: Banking
Score: 4-Stable (High level of restrictions on banking)

Although Oman has a thriving banking sector, competition is limited because foreigners are not permitted to open new banks.

Factor #7: Wage and Price Controls
Score: 3-Stable (Moderate level of wage and price controls)

There are few official price controls in Oman, but the government is the main consumer of goods and services, and its purchases therefore affect prices. Oman has a minimum wage law.

Factor #8: Property Rights
Score: 2-Stable (High level of protection of private property)

Property expropriation is not likely. However, although Oman's court system is efficient and private property is well protected, property does not always receive total legal protection.

Factor #9: Regulation
Score: 2-Stable (Low level of regulation)

Oman's relatively straightforward regulations are applied consistently in most cases.

Factor #10: Black Market
Score: 2-Stable (Low level of black market activity)

Oman has a negligible black market. Although there exists some traffic in pirated intellectual property (primarily sound and video recordings), Oman strictly enforces its laws, and black market activity in this area remains small.

Summary

Oman					Overall Score	2.75
Trade	3	Monetary Policy	1	Property Rights	2
Taxation	3.5	Foreign Investment	3	Regulation	2
Government Intervention	4	Banking	4	Black Market	2
		Wage and Prices	3		

PAKISTAN

The South Asian country of Pakistan gained its independence following the partition of the Indian subcontinent and the end of British rule in 1947. Since then, it has remained poor and has received huge amounts of foreign aid, much of which has been squandered. In 1990, the government of Prime Minister Nawaz Sharif undertook a program of economic liberalization to increase foreign and domestic private investment, but the pace of economic reform slowed after Benazir Bhutto became Prime Minister in 1993. Karachi, Pakistan's business center, has been destabilized in recent years by terrorist attacks and political violence between warring religious and ethnic factions. Pakistan recently has cut corporate tax rates, and black market activity is decreasing. Privatization has slowed, however, and the government continues to own several commercial banks. Bhutto's government collapsed in November 1996 when President Farooq Leghari dissolved it. New elections are scheduled for February 1997.

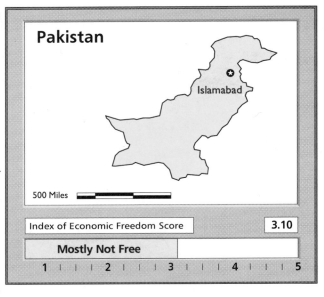

Factor #1: Trade Policy
Score: 5-Stable (Very high level of protectionism)

Pakistan has an average tariff rate of 27.5 percent and maintains non-tariff barriers in the form of import licenses and fees.

Factor #2: Taxation
Score - Income taxation: 3-Stable (Moderate tax rates)
Score - Corporate taxation: 4+ (High tax rates)
Total Taxation Score: 4-Stable (High tax rates)

Pakistan's top income tax rate is 35 percent, and the average income is taxed at a rate of about 10 percent. The top corporate income tax rate is 43 percent. Pakistan also has a 46 percent capital gains tax, a sales tax, state and local taxes, and a capital value tax that is added to certain properties like factories and automobiles.

Factor #3: Government Intervention in the Economy
Score: 3- (Moderate level of government intervention)

The Pakistani government consumes 12 percent of GDP, up from 11 percent in 1980. Although the government is proceeding with a significant privatization program, it continues to own many financial institutions, as well as companies in the energy and utilities, transportation, and marketing sectors.

Factor #4: Monetary Policy
Score: 2-Stable (Low level of inflation)

Pakistan's average annual rate of inflation from 1985 to 1994 was 8.8 percent. In 1995, the inflation rate rose to 13.2 percent.

Factor #5: Capital Flows and Foreign Investment
Score: 2-Stable (Low barriers to foreign investment)

There are no restrictions on the amount of foreign investment in Pakistani industries. The government offers some incentives to foreign investors, such as certain types of tax incentives for specific investments.

Factor #6: Banking
Score: 3- (Moderate level of restrictions on banking)

Banks in Pakistan are becoming more accessible to foreigners. Local banks are permitted to engage in securities and investments, but not insurance and real estate ventures. Foreign banks are subject to higher taxes than domestic banks. Moreover, despite recent attempts to privatize more banks, the government continues to own several banking institutions.

Factor #7: Wage and Price Controls
Score: 3-Stable (Moderate level of wage and price controls)

Pakistan maintains price controls on many products. Prices are set generally on products (such as automobiles) that are manufactured by state-operated firms, on petroleum, and on electricity. Pakistan has a minimum wage.

Factor #8: Property Rights
Score: 2-Stable (High level of protection of private property)

Property is protected in most cases, and expropriation is unlikely. Pakistan's courts, however, do not always enforce property rights.

Factor #9: Regulation
Score: 4-Stable (High level of regulation)

Pakistan's economy is heavily regulated. For example, such laws as the Environmental Protection Ordinance of 1983, the Industrial Relations Ordinance of 1974, and the Factories Act burden Pakistani businesses. Corruption also remains a problem. "As in many developing countries," reports the U.S. Department of Commerce, "corruption is an unwelcome, but ubiquitous, part of the business milieu in Pakistan. Recent anecdotal reports suggest that this problem continues and that, rather than serving to facilitate transactions, the phenomenon may be having a sclerotic impact on the economy."!273•

Factor #10: Black Market
Score: 3+ (Moderate level of black market activity)

Smuggling is encouraged by the extremely high tariffs on many consumer goods, and Pakistan has a substantial black market in such items as consumer electronics and re-

---

273   U.S. Department of Commerce, *Country Commercial Guide,* 1996.

corded music, although the size of the black market is shrinking. According to the U.S. Department of State, "Pakistani laws on protecting intellectual property rights (IPR) are generally adequate, but enforcement is weak, resulting in widespread piracy, especially of copyrighted materials."[274] When compared with Pakistan's almost $60 billion economy, however, these activities are moderate.

Summary

Pakistan					Overall Score	3.10
Trade	5	Monetary Policy	2		Property Rights	2
Taxation	4	Foreign Investment	2		Regulation	4
Government Intervention	3	Banking	3		Black Market	3
		Wage and Prices	3			

---

274   State Department Report, 1996, p. 528.

PANAMA

Panama gained its independence from Spain in 1821, and from Colombia in 1903. Panama, site of the U.S.-built Panama Canal, held democratic elections on May 8, 1994. President Ernesto Perez Balladares advocates a strong policy of economic liberalization. Panama's use of the U.S. dollar restricts the government's ability to inflate the currency to cover government spending, and is a major reason why Panama's inflation rate is less than 3 percent. Privatization recently has stalled, however, leaving many businesses and utilities in government hands.

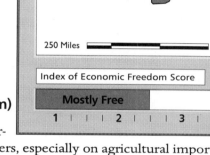

Panama

Panama City

250 Miles

| Index of Economic Freedom Score | 2.50 |

Mostly Free

1   2   3   4   5

Factor #1: Trade Policy

Score: 4-Stable (High level of protectionism)

In addition to an average tariff rate of 10 percent, Panama maintains significant non-tariff barriers, especially on agricultural imports. The government imposes import quotas on 48 agricultural products such as beef, corn, dairy products, and soybeans.

Factor #2: Taxation

Score - Income taxation: 2-Stable (Low tax rates)
Score - Corporate taxation: 3-Stable (Moderate tax rates)
Total Taxation Score: 3-Stable (Moderate tax rates)

Panama's top marginal tax rate is 30 percent, with the average income level taxed at a rate of 0 percent. The top corporate tax rate is 30 percent, down from 35 percent in 1995. Panama also has a 30 percent capital gains tax.

Factor #3: Government Intervention in the Economy

Score: 3- (Moderate level of government intervention)

Panama's government consumes about 16.7 percent of GDP. It also owns all telephone, electricity, and water systems, as well as some manufacturing companies.

Factor #4: Monetary Policy

Score: 1-Stable (Very low level of inflation)

Panama has made its most significant progress in its monetary policy, removing the government almost completely from supplying currency. The average annual rate of inflation between 1985 and 1994 was 1.5 percent, primarily because Panama uses the U.S. dollar as its currency. This restricts the government from printing money to cover deficit spending and has allowed Panama to maintain fairly low inflation rates. In 1995, the inflation rate was only 1.2 percent.

Factor #5: Capital Flows and Foreign Investment
Score: 2-Stable (Low barriers to foreign investment)

Most sectors of the Panamanian economy are open to foreign investment, although there are a few restrictions on sectors deemed "national interest" industries. The mining industry, for example, may not be bought by foreign investors.

Factor #6: Banking
Score: 1-Stable (Very low level of restrictions on banking)

Domestic competition in banking is relatively high, and major banks from all over the world operate in Panama. Domestic banks may sell securities and real estate, and may make some investments, but are not permitted to sell insurance. There are few restrictions on opening banks in Panama.

Factor #7: Wage and Price Controls
Score: 2-Stable (Low level of wage and price controls)

Most wages and prices in Panama are set by the market, although the government controls the prices of a few basic foodstuffs, industrial products, medicines, public transportation, and rent. Panama also imposes minimum wages.

Factor #8: Property Rights
Score: 3-Stable (Moderate level of protection of private property)

Property rights are constitutionally protected. The Panamanian legal system, however, is not always able to deal with threats to property rights. In addition, the privatization of state-owned industries has slowed, and expropriation remains a possibility.

Factor #9: Regulation
Score: 3-Stable (Moderate level of regulation)

Opening a business in Panama is a relatively easy process that requires obtaining a license from the Ministry of Commerce and Industry. Bureaucratic red tape, however, remains burdensome.

Factor #10: Black Market
Score: 3-Stable (Moderate level of black market activity)

Panama has a large black market in pirated computer software and prerecorded sound and video tapes. According the U.S. Department of State, it continues to be a haven for black marketeers in these and other pirated intellectual properties.[275]

---

275   State Department Report, 1996, p. 416.

Summary

Panama				Overall Score	2.50
Trade	4	Monetary Policy	1	Property Rights	3
Taxation	3	Foreign Investment	2	Regulation	3
Government Intervention	3	Banking	1	Black Market	3
		Wage and Prices	2		

PAPUA NEW GUINEA

The Pacific island of Papua New Guinea (PNG) gained its independence from Australia in 1975. Its parliamentary democracy is raucous but weak, beset by corruption, costly and overlapping local governments, and the expense of fighting a secessionist movement on the island of Bougainville. Papua New Guinea enjoys high economic growth, due largely to projects associated with its mining, logging, and oil industries; it also relies heavily on foreign aid. In 1994, faced with a chronic budget deficit that threatened bankruptcy, the government began to cut some trade restrictions while raising taxes and fees.

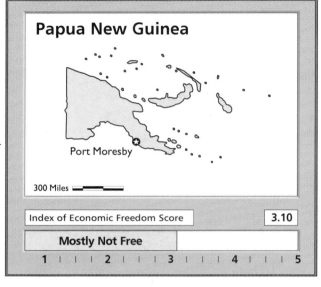

Factor #1: Trade Policy

Score: 5-Stable (Very high level of protectionism)

The average tariff rate in Papua New Guinea is 21.7 percent.[276] Non-tariff barriers include an inefficient bureaucracy and local government requirements.

Factor #2: Taxation

Score - Income taxation: 3-Stable (Moderate tax rates)
Score - Corporate taxation: 2-Stable (Low tax rates)
Final Taxation Score: 3-Stable (Moderate tax rates)

Papua New Guinea's top income tax rate is 35 percent, and the average taxpayer is in the 10 percent bracket. The top marginal corporate tax rate is 25 percent. Papua New Guinea also maintains a sales tax of varying rates.

Factor #3: Government Intervention in the Economy

Score: 3-Stable (Moderate level of government intervention)

Government consumes about 22.4 percent of GDP in Papua New Guinea. It also owns substantial portions of the economy, especially in the mining sector.

Factor #4: Monetary Policy

Score: 1-Stable (Very low level of inflation)

Papua New Guinea's average annual rate of inflation from 1985 to 1994 was 4.1 percent. In 1994, the inflation rate was 17.3 percent.

---

276 Based on total taxes on international trade as a percentage of total imports; from International Monetary Fund, *Government Financial Statistics 1995*.

Factor #5: Capital Flows and Foreign Investment
Score: 3-Stable (Moderate barriers to foreign investment)

The PNG government is opening more sectors to foreign investment, but some barriers still exist. Not all foreign companies are treated the same as domestic firms, several industrial sectors like mining are closed to foreign investment, and hostility to foreign investment in the lower levels of the bureaucracy can create delays in obtaining necessary documents and meeting licensing requirements. "Though the government favors investment," reports the U.S. Department of Commerce, "many investors trying to enter the market remain frustrated with the process. Potential investors often experience difficulties and delay in obtaining necessary clearances from a cumbersome bureaucracy. Large developments are inevitably contentious and quickly become political issues, necessitating cabinet decisions. Without consensus at this level, the investor faces additional delay. Several reports in the Australian and local media have charged corruption on the part of decision-makers. Some companies have reported delays in receiving investment approvals which they believe were attributable to their refusal to pay bribes."!277•

Factor #6: Banking
Score: 4-Stable (High level of restrictions on banking)

The government exercises a great deal of influence over the banking system in Papua New Guinea. Banks are not completely free to engage in all types of financial services.

Factor #7: Wage and Price Controls
Score: 3-Stable (Moderate level of wage and price controls)

Wages and prices in Papua New Guinea are set by both the private and public sectors. The government sets prices on some goods and services, such as certain foodstuffs and agricultural goods.

Factor #8: Property Rights
Score: 3-Stable (Moderate level of protection of private property)

Private property is safe from government expropriation, and the legal and judicial system is efficient. According to the U.S. Department of Commerce, "PNG has a Western legal system inherited primarily from Australia. The Courts, which are insulated from Government interference, provide a meaningful forum in which to enforce property and contractual rights, though the country does not have a written commercial code. The insolvency act is the source of bankruptcy law and controls the dissolution of failed corporations."!278 •The lack of a commercial code, however, sometimes makes enforcing property claims costly and ineffective.

Factor #9: Regulation
Score: 3-Stable (Moderate level of regulation)

Establishing a business in Papua New Guinea is sometimes difficult, especially if it requires extensive contact with the lower levels of bureaucracy and the local govern-

---

277   U.S. Department of Commerce, *Country Commercial Guide*, 1996.

278   *Ibid.*

ment. "At the lower levels," according to Political Risk Services, "bureaucratic difficulties and inordinate delay are sometimes encountered. Corruption is also a significant problem, particularly at the lower levels of the central government bureaucracy and in local and provincial government."[279]

Factor #10: Black Market
Score: 3-Stable (Moderate level of black market activity)

The black market in Papua New Guinea is confined mainly to illegal and smuggled goods, as well as pirated video and audio cassettes.

Summary

Papua New Guinea				Overall Score	3.10
Trade	5	Monetary Policy	1	Property Rights	3
Taxation	3	Foreign Investment	3	Regulation	3
Government Intervention	3	Banking	4	Black Market	3
		Wage and Prices	3		

---

279   Political Risk Services, "Papua New Guinea," 1995, p. 3.

PARAGUAY

The South American country of Paraguay gained its independence from Spain in 1811 but did not have its first free democratic election until May 1993. The current government of Juan Carlos Wasmosy is attempting to control government spending, reduce customs duties and inflation, and attract foreign investment. Although economic liberalization policies have pushed Paraguay ahead of many of its neighbors in Latin America, the country still is plagued by corruption and a repressive police force. Paraguay's privatization program has slowed recently, causing its score with respect to the level of government intervention in its economy to worsen.

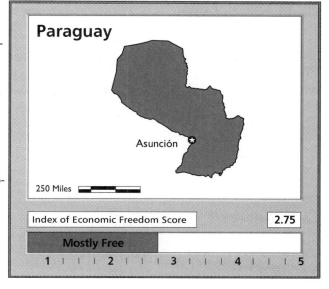

Factor #1: Trade Policy

Score: 2-Stable (Low level of protectionism)

Paraguay's average tariff rate is 8 percent. Although there are no major non-tariff barriers to trade, there are barriers to some agricultural imports, such as poultry.

Factor #2: Taxation

Score - Income taxation: 1-Stable (Very low tax rates)
Score - Corporate taxation: 3-Stable (Moderate tax rates)
Total Taxation Score: 2.5-Stable (Moderate tax rates)

Paraguay imposes no taxes on income derived from personal work, services provided, or professional services rendered. The top corporate tax rate is 30 percent. Paraguay also has a 30 percent capital gains tax and a 10 percent value-added tax.

Factor #3: Government Intervention in the Economy

Score: 2- (Low level of government intervention)

Government consumes almost 7 percent of Paraguay's GDP, up from 6 percent in 1990. Paraguay has a successful privatization program that involves selling off its airlines and other companies. Recent moves by the legislature have slowed the process, however, and many large firms remain government-owned.

Factor #4: Monetary Policy

Score: 4-Stable (High level of inflation)

Paraguay's average annual rate of inflation from 1985 to 1994 was 26.1 percent. In 1995, the inflation rate was 10.5 percent.

Factor #5: Capital Flows and Foreign Investment
Score: 1-Stable (Very low barriers to foreign investment)

There are few restrictions on foreign investment in Paraguay. Foreign and domestic companies are treated equally, and full repatriation of capital and profits is guaranteed by law. Some exceptions include bans on investments in the cement industry and such public utilities as electricity, telephones, and water. There is a 95 percent corporate income tax exemption for five years following most investments, and the tax rate for reinvested profits is fixed at 10 percent instead of the usual corporate tax rate of 30 percent.

Factor #6: Banking
Score: 2-Stable (Low level of restrictions on banking)

Of the 24 commercial banks in Paraguay, 12 are domestic and 12 are branches of foreign banks. Banks may engage in most financial activities, including the selling of stocks, bonds, and other securities.

Factor #7: Wage and Price Controls
Score: 3-Stable (Moderate level of wage and price controls)

Paraguay's government controls the prices of utilities, petroleum products, pharmaceuticals, and bus fares. Paraguay also has a minimum wage.

Factor #8: Property Rights
Score: 3-Stable (Moderate level of protection of private property)

Expropriation of private property is possible in Paraguay. The government remains committed to privatization, but the legislature has stalled the process and could act to reverse it.

Factor #9: Regulation
Score: 3-Stable (Moderate level of regulation)

Paraguay's government owns and operates several industries, including public utilities and industries involved in manufacturing cement and steel. These industries are tightly regulated by government officials who oversee production levels and pricing. Additional environmental, consumer, labor, financial, and other regulations also are burdensome. Another problem is bureaucratic corruption; according to the U.S. Department of State, "Key problems remain such as combating corruption (a recent financial scandal indicated its pervasive nature in both the public and private sector)...."[280] Obtaining a business license, however, is relatively easy.

Factor #10: Black Market
Score: 5-Stable (Very high level of black market activity)

Although most import restrictions have been removed, smuggling of illegal agricultural goods and products is lucrative. As much as 57 percent of Paraguay's labor force is supplied by the black market in Asunción. According the U.S. Department of State, the black market in Paraguay is growing.[281] This is indicated by the black market in pirated

---

280   State Department Report, 1996, p. 419.

281   *Ibid.*

intellectual property; pirated audio and video products alone cost the United States over $100 million in losses each year. In addition, some 50 U.S. companies are trying to win back their trademarks in Paraguay, where many businesses copy trademarked products and sell them on the black market.[282]

Summary

Paraguay				Overall Score	2.75
Trade	2	Monetary Policy	4	Property Rights	3
Taxation	2.5	Foreign Investment	1	Regulation	3
Government Intervention	2	Banking	2	Black Market	5
		Wage and Prices	3		

---

282   *Ibid.*

PERU

The South American country of Peru declared its independence from Spain in 1821. Since then, it has been ruled by a succession of military governments. During the 1980s, Peru was among the world's most socialist and inefficient economies. The 1990 election of Alberto Fujimori as president, however, resulted in a wave of economic reforms. Although far from achieving full liberalization, Peru has made great strides toward a free market. The government has reduced trade barriers significantly, state-owned enterprises continue to be privatized, and inflation is dropping.

Peru

Lima

500 Miles

Index of Economic Freedom Score	2.90

Mostly Free

1 | | | 2 | | | 3 | | | 4 | | | 5

Factor #1: Trade Policy

Score: 3+ (Moderate level of protectionism)

Peru has an average tariff rate of 13.2 percent[283] and maintains few, if any, substantial non-tariff barriers. "Almost all barriers to U.S. exports and direct investment have been eliminated over the past five years," according to the U.S. Department of State. "There are no qualitative or quantitative ceilings on imports. Import licenses have been abolished for all products except firearms, munitions, and explosives; chemical precursors (used in cocaine production); and ammonium nitrate fertilizer, which has been used as a blast enhancer for terrorist car bombs."[284]

Factor #2: Taxation

Score - Income taxation: 2-Stable (Low tax rates)
Score - Corporate taxation: 3-Stable (Moderate tax rates)
Total Taxation Score: 3-Stable (Moderate tax rates)

Peru's top income tax rate is 30 percent, and the average income is taxed at a rate of 0 percent. The corporate tax rate is a flat 30 percent. Peru also has a 30 percent capital gains tax and a sales tax.

Factor #3: Government Intervention in the Economy

Score: 1-Stable (Very low level of government intervention)

The Peruvian government consumes only 7 percent of GDP. President Fujimori has been successful in expanding the private sector while privatizing the public sector; the only areas in which the state has the primary role are education, mining, defense,

---

283 Based on taxes on international trade as a percentage of imports; from International Monetary Fund, *Government Financial Statistics 1995.*

284 State Department Report, 1996, p. 425.

362

and telecommunications. Many utilities are being privatized, or at least opened to private investment. Overall, the private sector accounts for most of Peru's GDP.

Factor #4: Monetary Policy
Score: 5-Stable (Very high level of inflation)

Peru's average annual rate of inflation from 1985 to 1994 was 495.3 percent, down from an average of 615.6 percent from 1985 to 1993. This decline is due primarily to progress in controlling inflation since the early 1990s. In 1995, the rate of inflation fell to 11.2 percent. Overall, however, levels of inflation in Peru historically have been very high.

Factor #5: Capital Flows and Foreign Investment
Score: 2-Stable (Low barriers to foreign investment)

The few restrictions the government of Peru places on foreign investments apply mainly to industries defined as vital to the national defense.

Factor #6: Banking
Score: 2-Stable (Low level of restrictions on banking)

There are few restrictions on foreign banks in Peru. All banks may sell securities, real estate, and insurance policies and make some investments, although they also are restricted in their ability to invest in industrial firms. According to the U.S. Department of State, "The Peruvian banking system has been cleaned up significantly with the liquidation of insolvent government sectoral development banks, as well as most savings and loans and cooperatives.... Peruvian law allows banks freely to take deposits and make loans in both foreign and domestic currency."[285]

Factor #7: Wage and Price Controls
Score: 2-Stable (Low level of wage and price controls)

Most wages and prices in Peru are set by the market. The U.S. Department of State reports that "Price controls, direct subsidies and restrictions on foreign investment have been eliminated."[286] Peru maintains a minumum wage.

Factor #8: Property Rights
Score: 3-Stable (Moderate level of protection of private property)

By global standards, private property is moderately well protected in Peru; but the court system is corrupt, and it is difficult to get a fair hearing. According to the U.S. Department of Commerce, "Enforcement of property and contractual rights has generally been effective, although the Peruvian legal system is slow and corruption is endemic. Improving the efficiency and transparency of the judicial system is a high priority of the Fujimori government, although a majority of judges and prosecutors appointed by the Fujimori administration since the April 5, 1992, coup remain in temporary status. Some problems with government interference in the court system still occur."[287]

---

285   U.S. Department of Commerce, *Country Commercial Guide,* 1996.

286   State Department Report, 1996, p. 424.

287   U.S. Department of Commerce, *Country Commercial Guide,* 1996.

Factor #9: Regulation

Score: 4-Stable (High level of regulation)

Even though the government has made significant progress in stamping out corruption, Peru remains plagued by a corrupt and inefficient bureaucracy. Obtaining a business license, although made easier in recent years, still may require bribes and can take a great deal of time. In addition, environmental regulations, which have been imposed only recently, are extremely burdensome.

Factor #10: Black Market

Score: 4-Stable (High level of black market activity)

Despite Peru's tremendous progress in reducing many black market operations (for example, in transportation), much of its labor force still operates in the informal sector. "Out of an estimated economically active population of 8 million," reports the U.S. Department of Commerce, "only about 7 percent belong to unions. Roughly two-thirds are employed in the informal sector, beyond government regulation and supervision."[288] Peru also has a rampant black market in the sale of pirated items from the United States and Europe. According to the U.S. Department of State, "Counterfeiting of trademarks is prevalent. Enforcement has improved in recent years at the administrative level, but at times the local courts have failed to back enforcement efforts in clear-cut cases. Some U.S. companies have spent years in fruitless litigation attempting to secure protection for their trademarks in Peru. Copyrights are widely disregarded, but enforcement is improving. Textbooks and books on technical subjects are rampantly copied, and illegal copies of audio cassettes are widely available. Pirated computer software accounts for more than 80 percent of the market."[289]

Summary

Peru					Overall Score	2.90
Trade	3	Monetary Policy	5		Property Rights	3
Taxation	3	Foreign Investment	2		Regulation	4
Government Intervention	1	Banking	2		Black Market	4
		Wage and Prices	2			

---

288   *Ibid.*

289   State Department Report, 1996, p. 426.

THE PHILIPPINES

The Philippines became a U.S. colony in 1900. During World War II, the country was conquered by the Japanese, who remained in control until driven off by U.S. forces in 1945. On July 4, 1946, the Philippines became the independent Republic of the Philippines. The many battles fought in the Philippines during World War II destroyed much of the country's infrastructure, and the United States played a major role in reconstruction after the end of the war. Nationalist economic policies pursued during the late 1950s and early 1960s laid the groundwork for both protectionism and government interventionism. Successive administrations were plagued by ineffectiveness and corruption. Today, under the leadership of President Fidel V. Ramos, the Philippines is well on its way to establishing a solid record of economic reform. In addition to dismantling some monopolies, opening banking to greater foreign competition, and reducing the level of regulation, the government recently has managed to cut tariffs, reduce its consumption of economic output, and achieve lower levels of inflation.

Factor #1: Trade Policy
Score: 5-Stable (Very high level of protectionism)

Despite a recent law passed to reduce the tariff rate to 5 percent over the next several years, the Philippines had an average tariff rate of 15.88 percent in 1996.[290] Republic Act 8179, passed in March 1996, eliminates all quantitative import restrictions on agricultural products (except rice) and replaces them with tariffs. The government also maintains significant non-tariff barriers to imports of rice, meat, and other products.

Factor #2: Taxation
Score - Income taxation: 2-Stable (Low tax rates)
Score - Corporate taxation: 3-Stable (Moderate tax rates)
Final Taxation Score: 3-Stable (Moderate tax rates)

The top income tax rate in the Philippines is 35 percent, with the average income level taxed at a rate of 7 percent. The top corporate tax is 35 percent. The Philippines also has a 35 percent capital gains tax and a 10 percent value-added tax.

---

290   State Department Report, 1996, p. 89.

Factor #3: Government Intervention in the Economy
Score: 1-Stable (Very low level of government intervention)

The government of the Philippines consumes 10 percent of GDP. Most state-owned companies are confined to utilities, and the government has made significant progress in privatizing other state-owned industries. The nation's largest state-owned bank, for example, was privatized in June 1996.

Factor #4: Monetary Policy
Score: 2-Stable (Low level of inflation)

The average annual rate of inflation in the Philippines from 1985 to 1994 was 9.9 percent. In 1994, the inflation rate was 7.1 percent; in 1995, it was 8.1 percent.

Factor #5: Capital Flows and Foreign Investment
Score: 3-Stable (Moderate barriers to foreign investment)

The Philippines maintains some barriers to foreign investment. For example, foreigners may not invest in advertising, the mass media, or public utilities, among other areas.

Factor #6: Banking
Score: 3-Stable (Moderate level of restrictions on banking)

Although the government recently privatized the Philippines National Bank, the country's largest state-owned financial institution, it also continues to own shares in the bank. According to the U.S. Department of State, "A new law, signed in May 1994, relaxed restrictions in place since 1948. A foreign investor can enter either on a wholly owned branch basis or own up to 60 percent (up from 30 percent) of an existing domestic bank or new locally incorporated banking subsidiary."[291] The new law allows foreign banks to establish only branches, not wholly owned subsidiaries, and restricts them to no more than six branches each.

Factor #7: Wage and Price Controls
Score: 2-Stable (Low level of wage and price controls)

Although the Philippine government controls the prices of automobiles, petroleum products, electricity, water, and related utilities, most wages and prices are set by the market. The Philippines also has a minimum wage.

Factor #8: Property Rights
Score: 2-Stable (High level of protection of private property)

The expropriation of private property in the Philippines is unlikely. According to the U.S. Department of Commerce, "The Philippine judicial system can be easily accessed and the courts are known to intervene in commercial and regulatory issues. The judicial system is independent from the executive and legislative bodies and, for the most part, avoids interference from these branches."[292]

---

291 *Ibid.*

292 U.S. Department of Commerce, *Country Commercial Guide*, 1996.

Factor #9: Regulation

Score: 3+ (Moderate level of regulation)

The Philippine government has eliminated some significantly burdensome regulations. Nevertheless, its regulatory regime is inconsistent, and regulations are applied haphazardly.

Factor #10: Black Market

Score: 4-Stable (High level of black market activity)

Even with an increase in the number of duty-free shops and a decline in smuggling, a substantial black market trade in pirated items exists in the Philippines. "Piracy of computer software is a serious problem," reports the Office of the U.S. Trade Representative.[293] According to the U.S. Department of State, "About 98 percent of all computer software is pirated. Computer shops routinely load software on machines as a free 'bonus' to entice sales. The Philippine government and related organizations such as state-run universities are reportedly the largest users of illegal software in the country.... [T]rademark counterfeiting is widespread. Many well-known international trademarks are copied, including denim jeans, designer shirts, and personal beauty and health products."[294]

Summary

The Philippines					Overall Score	2.80
Trade	5	Monetary Policy	2	Property Rights	2
Taxation	3	Foreign Investment	3	Regulation	3
Government Intervention	1	Banking	3	Black Market	4
		Wage and Prices	2		

---

293   Office of the United States Trade Representative, *1995 National Trade Estimate*, pp. 264–265.

294   State Department Report, 1996, pp. 92–93.

POLAND

Once a member of the Soviet-dominated Warsaw Pact, Poland has progressed economically since the fall of the Iron Curtain. A six-party coalition, led by Prime Minister Hanna Suchocka, collapsed in September 1993 and was replaced by a two-party alliance of the former Communist Party and the Agrarian Party in 1994 and again in 1995. The current government of Alexsander Kwasniewski is committed to continuing economic reform.

Factor #1: Trade Policy

Score: 4-Stable (High level of protectionism)

Poland has an average tariff rate of 17.7 percent, up from 14 percent a year ago.[295] Non-tariff barriers (which, in practice, rarely hinder imports) include strict product standards and labeling requirements.

Factor #2: Taxation

Score - Income taxation: 2-Stable (Low tax rates)
Score - Corporate taxation: 4-Stable (High tax rates)
Final Taxation Score: 3.5-Stable (High tax rates)

Poland's top income tax rate is 45 percent, and the average income level is taxed at a rate of 0 percent. The top corporate tax rate is 40 percent. Poland also has a 40 percent capital gains tax and a 22 percent value-added tax.

Factor #3: Government Intervention in the Economy

Score: 3-Stable (Moderate level of government intervention)

The Polish government consumes around 19 percent of GDP.[296] Almost 50 percent of industrial production is generated by the state-owned sector of the economy.

Factor #4: Monetary Policy

Score: 5-Stable (Very high level of inflation)

Poland's average annual rate of inflation between 1990 and 1994 was 147.9 percent. In 1994, the inflation rate fell to 22 percent; in 1995, it was 23 percent. Despite this obvious progress, however, the rate of inflation in Poland remains very high by global standards.

295   Based on total taxes on international trade as a percentage of total imports; from International Monetary Fund, *Government Financial Statistics 1995*.

296   World Bank, *World Development Report 1996*.

Factor #5: Capital Flows and Foreign Investment
Score: 2-Stable (Low barriers to foreign investment)

Domestic and foreign firms receive equal treatment under Poland's investment laws, and recent economic reforms are attracting increased foreign investment.

Factor #6: Banking
Score: 3-Stable (Moderate level of restrictions on banking)

Poland's banking system, although becoming more private, is still influenced by the government. Interest rates are not always set by market standards and may be driven by government budgetary concerns. This makes it more difficult for Poland's banks to provide affordable credit to needy businesses.

Factor #7: Wage and Price Controls
Score: 3-Stable (Moderate level of wage and price controls)

Firms must gain permission from the government to raise prices on certain products (fuel, transportation, and rent), and obtaining this permission may take as long as three months. Poland has a minimum wage law.

Factor #8: Property Rights
Score: 2-Stable (High level of protection of private property)

Private property is a constitutional right in Poland. Therefore, even though property is not always protected adequately by the courts and legal system, expropriation is unlikely. Some property expropriated previously by the communist regime, however, has yet to be returned to its original owners.

Factor #9: Regulation
Score: 3-Stable (Moderate level of regulation)

Despite some efforts at liberalization, Poland's regulatory regime remains an obstacle to the creation of new businesses. Some corruption persists, for example, and labor, health, and safety regulations are applied randomly. This creates uncertainty for businesses.

Factor #10: Black Market
Score: 3-Stable (Moderate level of black market activity)

By global standards, Poland's black market is moderate. It also is shrinking. Although some labor, transportation, construction, and other services once were supplied routinely on the black market, an increasingly free market is reducing black market activity. In general, Poland also has made significant progress in protecting intellectual property, although the black market trade in computer software is growing; the U.S. Department of Commerce reports that as much as 90 percent of all computer software in Poland is pirated.[297]

---

297 U.S. Department of Commerce, *Country Commercial Guide,* 1996.

Summary

Poland				Overall Score	3.15
Trade	4	Monetary Policy	5	Property Rights	2
Taxation	3.5	Foreign Investment	2	Regulation	3
Government Intervention	3	Banking	3	Black Market	3
		Wage and Prices	3		

PORTUGAL

Although Portugal's economy grew at an average annual rate of 5.3 percent from 1965 to 1980, it collapsed in the 1980s because of the government's socialist economic policies. The revised Portuguese Constitution of 1982 called for the public ownership of land, natural resources, and the principal means of production. Today, Portugal remains burdened by a cumbersome bureaucracy, although it recently has managed to reduce inflation.

Factor #1: Trade Policy

Score: 2-Stable (Low level of protectionism)

As a member of the European Union (EU), Portugal has an average tariff rate of 3.6 percent. It also requires import certificates for agricultural products, however, and these can act as a barrier to foreign agricultural imports.

Factor #2: Taxation

Score - Income taxation: 5-Stable (Very high tax rates)
Score - Corporate taxation: 4-Stable (High tax rates)
Final Taxation Score: 5-Stable (Very high tax rates)

Portugal's top income tax rate is 40 percent, and the average income level is taxed at a rate of 25 percent. The top corporate tax rate is 36 percent. Portugal also has a 36 percent capital gains tax, a 4 percent to 30 percent value-added tax, a 20 percent real estate tax, and a 50 percent inheritance tax.

Factor #3: Government Intervention in the Economy

Score: 3-Stable (Moderate level of government intervention)

The Portuguese government consumes 18.6 percent of GDP and, although it has begun an ambitious privatization program, continues to maintain major stakes in banking and in the production of alcohol, cement, chemicals, food, glass, and electricity. Portugal is undergoing what is known as "partial privatization," with private managers hired to run companies that continue under government ownership.

Factor #4: Monetary Policy

Score: 2-Stable (Low level of inflation)

Portugal's average annual rate of inflation from 1985 to 1994 was 11.9 percent. In 1995, the inflation rate was 4 percent.

Factor #5: Capital Flows and Foreign Investment
Score: 2-Stable (Low barriers to foreign investment)

Portugal has opened most of its industries to foreign investment. As a member of the EU, it treats foreign and domestic companies equally. Foreign investments are not permitted, however, in postal carriers or in such public utilities as sewage treatment, transportation, and water services. Foreign investors may face some government opposition when investing in state-owned businesses that are being privatized.

Factor #6: Banking
Score: 3-Stable (Moderate level of restrictions on banking)

As 100 percent owner of some of Portugal's large banks, including the Caixa Geral de Deposito and the Banco Fomento Exterior SA, the government plays a large role in controlling the lending practices of private banks. Moreover, because they are subsidized by the government, the state-owned banks enjoy an unfair competitive advantage against unsubsidized private banks.

Factor #7: Wage and Price Controls
Score: 2-Stable (Low level of wage and price controls)

Portugal's government eliminated almost all price controls in 1993, although the prices of electricity, water, and pharmaceutical products remain controlled. Portugal has a minimum wage.

Factor #8: Property Rights
Score: 2-Stable (High level of protection of private property)

Portugal is privatizing some of its bloated state-owned sector, and citizens are increasing their purchases of shares in state-owned companies. This provides an expanding base of private property. Portugal has a relatively efficient legal system that adequately protects property in most cases. Expropriation is unlikely.

Factor #9: Regulation
Score: 3-Stable (Moderate level of regulation)

Despite some liberalization, Portugal still maintains significant regulation. Its 1987 environmental protection law, for example, is the most stringent in the EU. As a result of this law, both new businesses and proposed business expansion projects must undergo cumbersome environmental impact reviews by various government bureaucracies—a hurdle that often proves to be too high for some businesses.

Factor #10: Black Market
Score: 2-Stable (Low level of black market activity)

Portugal's black market is confined to such scarce goods as auto parts and pharmaceutical products. These scarcities are created by government-imposed price controls and trade quotas. Despite Portugal's strong protection of intellectual property with stiff fines, there also is a small black market in such pirated items as pre-recorded music and video tapes.

Summary

Portugal				Overall Score	2.60
Trade	2	Monetary Policy	2	Property Rights	2
Taxation	5	Foreign Investment	2	Regulation	3
Government Intervention	3	Banking	3	Black Market	2
		Wage and Prices	2		

ROMANIA

Romania's transition to democracy and free markets has been troubled and at times even violent. After the killing of former communist strongman Nicolae Ceausescu in 1989, Romania was ruled by former communists who were only lukewarm about democracy and free markets. Since then, it has made significant progress in passing laws on taxation, foreign investment, and privatization. It also has reduced some barriers to trade. At the same time, however, the country's large state-owned sector continues to resist further reform. Anti-communist Emil Constantinescu was elected president in November 1996.

Romania	
Index of Economic Freedom Score	**3.40**
Mostly Not Free	

1   2   3   4   5

Factor #1: Trade Policy
Score: 2+ (Low level of protectionism)

Romania has an average tariff rate of 6 percent.[298] According to the U.S. Department of State, "There are no known laws that directly prejudice foreign trade or business operations [in Romania]."[299]

Factor #2: Taxation
Score - Income taxation: 5-Stable (Very high tax rates)
Score - Corporate taxation: 4-Stable (High tax rates)
Final Taxation Score: 5-Stable (Very high tax rates)

Romania's top income tax rate is 60 percent, and the average income is taxed at a rate of 40 percent. The top corporate income tax rate is 38 percent. Romania also has a 38 percent capital gains tax and an 18 percent value-added tax.

Factor #3: Government Intervention in the Economy
Score: 3+ (Moderately high level of government intervention)

The Romanian government consumes 13 percent of GDP, with the public sector of the economy producing more than 65 percent of GDP overall. Private firms and individuals make up only 5 percent of industrial output, 25 percent of construction, and 40 percent of services.

---

298   Based on total taxes on international trade as a percentage of total imports; from International Monetary Fund, *Government Financial Statistics 1995*.

299   State Department Report, 1996, p. 251.

Factor #4: Monetary Policy
Score: 5-Stable (Very high level of inflation)

Romania's rate of inflation was 295 percent in 1993, 61 percent in 1994, and 29 percent in 1995.

Factor #5: Capital Flows and Foreign Investment
Score: 2-Stable (Low barriers to foreign investment)

Romania maintains a fairly free market in foreign investment. Most barriers to foreign investment are the result of bureaucratic red tape and inefficiency.

Factor #6: Banking
Score: 3-Stable (Moderate level of restrictions on banking)

Although more private banks are opening in Romania, the banking environment has yet to mature. Banks are subject to strict government control. According to the U.S. Department of Commerce, "The system remains concentrated as four of the five state banks control 90% of the loans to the commercial sector."[300] Over the past six years, however, the number of banks in Romania has grown fourfold, thereby increasing competition.

Factor #7: Wage and Price Controls
Score: 2-Stable (Low level of wage and price controls)

Prices in Romania are set mainly by the market. Exceptions include pharmaceutical products, public transportation services, and residential heat and energy supply. Romania has minimum wage laws.

Factor #8: Property Rights
Score: 4-Stable (Low level of protection of private property)

Romania has yet to establish a system of property protection, and the legal system remains unable to arbitrate property rights disputes. "Property and contractual rights are recognized," reports the U.S. Department of Commerce, but "enforcement is not always effective, as suggested by specific cases brought to public attention by the media. The media also has often exposed cases of Government interference in the court system."[301] Nevertheless, expropriation remains unlikely.

Factor #9: Regulation
Score: 4-Stable (High level of regulation)

Regulations in Romania remain subject to haphazard application. Romania recently has made some progress in streamlining its bureaucracy, making it easier for businesses to obtain licenses, but the bureaucracy continues to be both cumbersome and inefficient.

---

300   U.S. Department of Commerce, *Country Commercial Guide,* 1996.

301   *Ibid.*

Factor #10: Black Market
Score: 4-Stable (High level of black market activity)

Most of Romania's economic activity is performed in the black market because the country's legal economy still cannot provide many basic consumer needs. Many food items, for example, can be bought on the black market but are scarce at stores. Moreover, although Romania has laws protecting intellectual property rights, enforcement is not taken seriously. According to the U.S. Department of State, "Pirated copies of audio and video cassette recordings are inexpensive and sold openly."[302]

Summary

Romania				Overall Score	3.40
Trade	2	Monetary Policy	5	Property Rights	4
Taxation	5	Foreign Investment	2	Regulation	4
Government Intervention	3	Banking	3	Black Market	4
		Wage and Prices	2		

---

302   State Department Report, 1996, p. 257.

RUSSIA

The largest of the former Soviet republics, Russia has struggled for several years to introduce democratic political institutions and a free-market economy. Progress has been slow. Privatization has been disorderly, and there is widespread criminality. The banking and investment systems are in disarray, and millions of investors have been defrauded. Capital continues to leak to the West at a rate of $1.5 billion per month. The result has been economic stagnation, civil unrest, coup attempts, and political polarization. At the same time, however, the orderly 1995 parliamentary and 1996 presidential elections indicate that reforms have begun to take root. Having rejected both the Communists and the ultranationalists, Russia's voters generally continue to support economic reform.

Russia

Moscow

1000 Miles

| Index of Economic Freedom Score | 3.65 |

Mostly Not Free

1   2   3   4   5

Factor #1: Trade Policy
Score: 5- (Very high level of protectionism)

Tariff rates in Russia range from 5 percent to 30 percent, with an average rate of 17 percent.[303] Tariffs on luxury items, however, can be as high as 150 percent, and duty rates change rapidly and arbitrarily. Russia also maintains many Soviet-era non-tariff restrictions, such as safety standards, licensing and testing, and other requirements. Corruption is a problem in the customs services, and bribes sometimes are necessary to bring goods into the country. The U.S. Department of Commerce reports that "customs regulations change frequently, often without sufficient prior notice, are subject to arbitrary application and can be quite burdensome."[304] The Office of the U.S. Trade Representative similarly reports that "Crime and corruption in commercial transactions are growing problems."[305]

---

303   Based on total taxes on international trade as a percentage of total imports; from International Monetary Fund, *Government Financial Statistics 1995.*

304   State Department Report, 1996, p. 262.

305   Office of the U.S. Trade Representative, *National Trade Estimate on Foreign Trade Barriers 1996;* from U.S. Department of Commerce, National Trade Data Bank.

Factor #2: Taxation

Score - Income taxation: 3-Stable (Moderate tax rates)
Score - Corporate taxation: 3+ (Moderate tax rates)
Final Taxation Score: 3.5+ (High tax rates)

Russia's top income tax rate is 30 percent, and the average income level is taxed at a rate of 12 percent. The top corporate income tax rate (including both federal and regional taxes) is 35 percent. Russia also has a 35 percent capital gains tax, a 20 percent value-added tax, and a social payments tax.[306]

Factor #3: Government Intervention in the Economy

Score: 4-Stable (High level of government intervention)

Russia's government officially consumes 21 percent of GDP.[307] State-owned enterprises still account for most industrial production, however, and there are indications that the government may renationalize previously privatized companies. According to the Economist Intelligence Unit, "Interior Minister Anatoly Kukilov caused an uproar in February when he called for the partial renationalization of key Russian enterprises, including gas monopoly *Gazprom*, oil concerns *LUKoil* and *Yukos*, *Promstroibank*, and car and truck manufacturers, *Zil*, *AvtoVAZ*, and *KamAZ*."[308] The government also heavily subsides many money-losing industries such as coal-mining, ferrous and non-ferrous metals, and agriculture.

Factor #4: Monetary Policy

Score: 5-Stable (Very high level of inflation)

In 1992, Russia's annual rate of inflation exceeded 1,300 percent. In 1993, it was down to 843 percent; in 1994, it was 203 percent; and in 1995, it was 133 percent.[309] Despite significant progress in reducing inflation from its extremely high 1992 levels, however, Russia's average inflation rate remains very high.

Factor #5: Capital Flows and Foreign Investment

Score: 3- (Moderate barriers to foreign investment)

A 1991 Russian law permits foreigners to acquire newly privatized firms and to establish wholly owned companies. By global standards, there are few legal restrictions on foreign investment; exceptions include investments in securities and insurance firms. The biggest barriers to foreign investment are legal uncertainty, crime, and political instability. "While the policy of the Russian government is to encourage foreign investment," reports the U.S. Department of Commerce, "it has had difficulties in creating a stable and attractive investment climate. Economic and political uncertainty serve as dis-

---

306   Russia has many overlapping, contradictory, and arbitrarily applied taxes. It also has varying and sometimes rapidly changing municipal and local taxes that could raise overall rates to more than 100 percent. For purposes of methodological consistency, however, only those taxes that are reported in the Ernst & Young Worldwide Corporate Tax Guide and Directory are used here. The arbitrary application of many taxes is taken into account in the regulation factor.

307   World Bank, *World Development Report 1996.*

308   Economist Intelligence Unit, *ILT Reports*, April 1996, p. 2.

309   Based on the Consumer Price Index; from State Department Report, 1996, p. 259.

incentives to companies looking for investment opportunities. Although there are no significant legal barriers to doing business in Russia, the absence of sufficiently developed civil, commercial and criminal codes is a major constraint. In addition, a confusing tax system, and a rise in violent 'mafia' instigated crime have become a problem for foreign (and Russian) business. Bureaucratic requirements can be confusing and burdensome to investors and bureaucratic discretion may be capricious in awarding tenders or development rights to companies."[310]

Factor #6: Banking
Score: 2+ (Low level of restrictions on banking)

Many of Russia's state-owned banks have been privatized, and there is fierce competition in the commercial banking market. Foreign banks now operate in Russia, although they are allowed to offer only a limited range of services and most maintain only representative offices. The environment is becoming more competitive with only limited government influence. According to the U.S. Department of Commerce, "The Russian commercial banking system is only five years old, but it has advanced rapidly since its inception. There are currently over 2500 banks making up the banking system...."[311]

Factor #7: Wage and Price Controls
Score: 3-Stable (Moderate level of wage and price controls)

Some 90 percent of all prices in Russia are set by free enterprise, with 5 percent fixed by the state and another 5 percent subject to government limits on the amount of profitability. Price controls remain on fuel, energy, grain, public transportation, and municipally owned housing rent.[312] Because the government controls much of the economy through its ownership of the public sector, however, it also exercises a high level of indirect control over wages and prices. Russia maintains a minimum wage.

Factor #8: Property Rights
Score: 3- (Moderate level of protection of private property)

Although private property is guaranteed in the Russian Constitution adopted in 1993, protection remains significantly lacking. The Russian court system works poorly, and no clear and concise method for the settlement of property disputes has been developed. Moreover, protection of private property receives different levels of police attention in different localities, and both corruption and organized crime remain significant threats. According to the U.S. Department of Commerce, "Russia has a body of conflicting, overlapping and rapidly changing laws, decrees and regulations which has resulted in an ad hoc and unpredictable approach to doing business. Independent dispute resolution in Russia is difficult to obtain; the judicial system is poorly developed. Regional and local courts are not accustomed to adjudicating either commercial or international matters, and they (as well as courts in Moscow) are often subject to political pressure."[313]

---

310   U.S. Department of Commerce, *Country Commercial Guide,* 1996.

311   *Ibid.*

312   Economist Intelligence Unit, *ILT Reports,* April 1996, p. 25.

313   U.S. Department of Commerce, *Country Commercial Guide,* 1996.

Factor #9: Regulation
Score: 4- (High level of regulation)

Russia is experiencing a wave of dynamic entrepreneurial spirit. Small businesses are sprouting by the hundreds in cities like Moscow, and many are growing around the larger cities as well. These businesses are easy to establish and subject to little regulation. The Russian government, however, has yet to extend similar treatment to larger enterprises. Some regulations are arbitrary and unevenly enforced, and corruption in the bureaucracy remains a serious problem. In addition, Russia's inefficient bureaucracy is getting worse, with the result that some 85 different taxes are applied—often arbitrarily—to businesses and individuals. Businesses frequently complain about the unpredictability of these taxes.

Factor #10: Black Market
Score: 4-Stable (High level of black market activity)

Despite recent moves to establish a free market, Russia's black market is massive (although it has shrunk considerably since 1991). Russia has not enforced its intellectual property laws, and piracy is rampant. "While the Russian government has successfully passed good laws on protection of intellectual property," reports the U.S. Department of Commerce, "enforcement of those laws has been a low priority.... Until these measures become reality...there is widespread marketing of pirated U.S. (and other) video-cassettes, recordings, books, computer software, clothes and toys. Losses to manufacturers, authors and others are estimated to be in the hundreds of millions of dollars."[314] Russian organized crime has moved from such traditional activities as prostitution, drugs, and illegal arms sales to money-laundering, commodity smuggling, and bank fraud.

Summary

Russia						Overall Score	3.65
Trade	5	Monetary Policy	5		Property Rights	3
Taxation	3.5	Foreign Investment	3		Regulation	4
Government Intervention	4	Banking	2		Black Market	4
		Wage and Prices	3			

314　*Ibid.*

RWANDA

After winning its independence from a Belgian-administered United Nations trusteeship in 1992, Rwanda almost immediately became a major recipient of foreign aid. Proponents of foreign aid often hold up Rwanda as an example of what can happen if aid is cut, but the fact is that Rwanda received its first foreign aid dollars from the United States in the mid-1960s and has been a major recipient of foreign aid ever since. Moreover, during the 1960s and 1970s, Rwanda did nothing to establish the basis for a free market. As a result, Rwanda today has one of Africa's poorest economies and remains one of the most economically repressed countries in the world. In FY 1997, the United States will spend another $59 million in foreign aid to Rwanda, which continues to be plagued by civil unrest, political instability, and ethnic warfare.

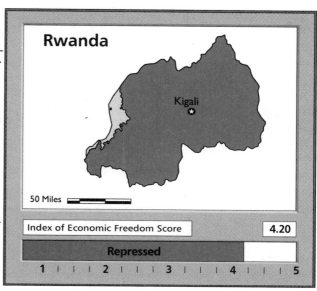

| Index of Economic Freedom Score | 4.20 |

Repressed

1 2 3 4 5

Factor #1: Trade Policy
Score: 5-Stable (Very high level of protectionism)

Import duties in Rwanda range from 10 percent to 60 percent. "Since the changes of government in July 1995," reports the U.S. Department of Commerce, "the government of Rwanda has streamlined the import licensing process and revised many import duties downward. Further reductions in duties are under consideration."[315] Rwanda's borders are virtually closed to all commerce, however, mainly because of civil unrest. According to the U.S. Department of State, "Border areas in particular have been the site of low-key insurgent outbreaks. Further, poor communication, transportation, and health services continue to make travel in Rwanda difficult and potentially hazardous."[316]

Factor #2: Taxation

Score - Income taxation: 5-Stable (Very high tax rates)
Score - Corporate taxation: 5-Stable (Very high tax rates)
Final Taxation Score: 5-Stable (Very high tax rates)

Rwanda's central government is beginning to establish official taxation guidelines and collection services. Taxation most often takes the form of private property confiscation by corrupt bureaucrats, however.

---

315   U.S. Department of Commerce, "Market Research Reports," 1996.

316   U.S. Department of State Travel Advisory, 1996.

Factor #3: Government Intervention in the Economy
Score: 4-Stable (Very high level of government intervention)

In 1993 (the most recent year for which a figure is available), Rwanda's government consumed 22 percent of GDP. Today, there is little economic activity in Rwanda that does not occur in the public sector; most private-sector economic activity occurs in the black market.

Factor #4: Monetary Policy
Score: 1-Stable (Very low level of inflation)

Rwanda has managed to maintain the value of its currency over time, chiefly because the government, faced with a lack of printing presses and the ongoing need to deal with civil unrest, has been unable to inflate the currency. Rwanda's average annual rate of inflation from 1985 to 1994 was 3.7 percent. There are no available figures for 1995.

Factor #5: Capital Flows and Foreign Investment
Score: 4-Stable (High barriers to foreign investment)

Rwanda remains in economic ruins, with no clear protection of foreign investment. The biggest threats to investment continue to be armed bandits, rampant street crime, and the lack of individual freedom of movement. The government, however, is attempting to limit criminal activity, establish an up-to-date investment code, and reform its legal institutions to protect contracts.

Factor #6: Banking
Score: 5-Stable (Very high level of restrictions on banking)

The banking system in Rwanda has collapsed, forcing banks operate in primitive conditions. According to the U.S. Department of State, "The Rwandan franc is freely exchangeable for hard currencies in Bureaux de Change and banks. Several Kigali Banks can efficiently handle wire transfers from U.S. Banks. Banks outside Kigali are slowly reopening."[317]

Factor #7: Wage and Price Controls
Score: 3-Stable (Moderate level of wage and price controls)

Wages and prices in Rwanda are set mainly by the market through barter. The government is not powerful enough to enforce laws that set prices.

Factor #8: Property Rights
Score: 5-Stable (Very low level of protection of private property)

Private property is virtually nonexistent in Rwanda. Property is subject to frequent confiscation by warring clans and corrupt government officials.

Factor #9: Regulation
Score: 5-Stable (Very high level of regulation)

The official government in Rwanda has yet to fully establish a regulatory regime for the country. Most business regulations are chaotic and subject to change depending

---

317 *Ibid.*

on which ministry is in charge of implementing them, in addition to which the jurisdictions of the government's various ministries often overlap.

Factor #10: Black Market

Score: 5-Stable (Very high level of black market activity)

Most economic activity in Rwanda occurs in the black market.

Summary

Rwanda					Overall Score	4.20
Trade	5	Monetary Policy	1	Property Rights	5
Taxation	5	Foreign Investment	4	Regulation	5
Government Intervention	4	Banking	5	Black Market	5
		Wage and Prices	3		

SAUDI ARABIA

S audi Arabia takes its name from the Saud family, which rose to prominence in central Arabia in about 1750. Throughout the next 150 years, Saudi Arabia vied with Egypt, the Ottoman Turks, and rival Arab dynasties for control of the Arabian peninsula. The modern Saudi state was formed in 1902 under King Abdul Aziz Al-Saud, who enlarged his holdings until uniting them as the Kingdom of Saudi Arabia in 1932. Oil was discovered in the 1930s, and large-scale production began after World War II. Saudi Arabia today has the world's largest oil reserves and is the world's largest oil exporter. It also has a developing economy with a large government sector. Regulations favor Saudi businesses and often discriminate against foreigners.

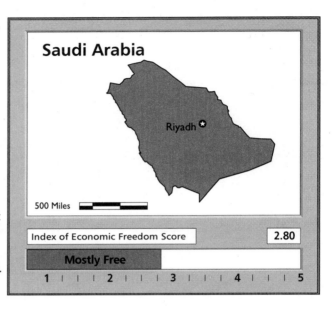

Saudi Arabia

Riyadh ⊙

500 Miles

| Index of Economic Freedom Score | 2.80 |

Mostly Free

1   2   3   4   5

Factor #1: Trade Policy
Score: 4-Stable (High level of protectionism)

The average tariff rate in Saudi Arabia is about 13 percent. Non-tariff barriers include strict labeling and certification requirements. According to the U.S. Department of State, "Saudi customs rules require that incoming goods be accompanied by documents certified by an approved Arab–U.S. Chamber of Commerce and the Saudi Embassy or Consulate in the United States. The latter requirement slows shipping, adds man-hours and fees, and ultimately increases the cost of the product to Saudi customers."[318]

Factor #2: Taxation
Score - Income taxation: 3-Stable (Moderate tax rates)
Score - Corporate taxation: 4-Stable (High tax rates)
Final Taxation Score: 4-Stable (High tax rates)

Saudi Arabia's top income tax rate is 30 percent, and the average taxpayer is in the 10 percent bracket. The top marginal corporate tax rate is 45 percent. The Saudi government also imposes several other taxes, including a 45 percent capital gains tax.

Factor #3: Government Intervention in the Economy
Score: 4+ (High level of government intervention)

The government of Saudi Arabia consumes 27 percent of GDP; it also generates most of the country's GDP. According to the Economist Intelligence Unit, "Although the government emphasises its basic commitment to free enterprise, it maintains a monopoly role in the oil sector and a virtual monopoly in infrastructure development and the provision of most utilities and communications services."[319]

---

318   State Department Report, 1996, p. 495.

Factor #4: Monetary Policy
Score: 1-Stable (Very low level of inflation)

Saudi Arabia's average rate of inflation from 1985 to 1994 was 2.7 percent. In 1995, the inflation rate was 4.9 percent.

Factor #5: Capital Flows and Foreign Investment
Score: 4-Stable (High barriers to foreign investment)

Although Saudi Arabia imposes few restrictions on foreign investments and allows 100 percent foreign ownership, complete foreign ownership is uncommon in practice. All investments must be reviewed and accepted by the government. "It is extremely rare for the government to award a license to any 100 percent-foreign-owned operation," reports the Economist Intelligence Unit. "Furthermore, oversupply in many industrial, service and commercial sectors has led the authorities to increase scrutiny of new foreign investment proposals."[320] According to the U.S. Department of State, "Foreigners may not invest at all in joint ventures engaged solely in advertising, trading, distribution or marketing. Real estate ownership is restricted to wholly-owned Saudi entities or citizens of the GCC [Gulf Cooperation Council]."[321]

Factor #6: Banking
Score: 3-Stable (Moderate level of restrictions on banking)

The banking system in Saudi Arabia is competitive, and the country has more than 24 commercial banks. A recent budgetary crisis, however, forced the government to finance its debt through Saudi banks; the government has resisted seeking financing from foreign banks because that would require it to release data on Saudi Arabia's financial status. The increased government pressure on commercial banks for more loans to meet this crisis has hindered the free operation of these banks.

Factor #7: Wage and Price Controls
Score: 3-Stable (Moderate level of wage and price controls)

Wages and prices in Saudi Arabia are set mainly by the market, although some prices on basic utilities are set by the government, which also subsidizes agriculture and some other enterprises. There is no minimum wage.

Factor #8: Property Rights
Score: 1-Stable (Very high level of protection of private property)

Private property is safe from expropriation in Saudi Arabia. The legal and judicial system is both sound and efficient.

---

319   Economist Intelligence Unit, "Saudi Arabia," *ILT Reports*, April 1996, p. 8.

320   Economist Intelligence Unit, "Saudi Arabia," *ILT Reports*, July 1995, p. 8.

321   State Department Report, 1996, p. 495.

Factor #9: Regulation
Score: 2-Stable (Low level of regulation)

Establishing a business in Saudi Arabia is a simple process. The activities of the country's growing environmental movement, however, could lead to increased regulation.

Factor #10: Black Market
Score: 2-Stable (Low level of black market activity)

The black market in Saudi Arabia is relatively small. Although the Saudi government has been very successful in stamping out pirated video tapes and related copyrighted material, there remains a black market in pirated computer software and sound recordings. According to the U.S. Department of State, "piracy of software among retailers and end-users is widespread, and enforcement efforts are sporadic. Further, the sound recordings market is dominated by pirated products. Most of the pirated sound recordings are produced locally."[322] Compared with the overall size of the Saudi economy (now about $126 billion a year), these activities are minuscule.

Summary

Saudi Arabia				Overall Score	2.80
Trade	4	Monetary Policy	1	Property Rights	1
Taxation	4	Foreign Investment	4	Regulation	2
Government Intervention	4	Banking	3	Black Market	2
		Wage and Prices	3		

---

322   *Ibid.*, p. 496.

SENEGAL

The West African country of Senegal gained its independence from France in 1960. A small, semi-arid country with limited natural resources, Senegal's economy depends on imports. Its largest industries are fishing, mining, and chemicals. Since 1990, Senegal has experienced a severe economic downturn. As a result, the government has sought to reduce spending and reform the country's economy.

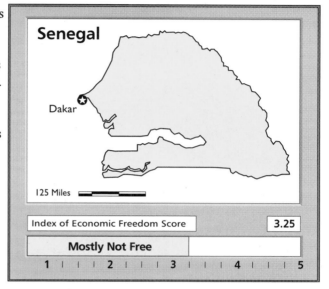

Senegal

Dakar

125 Miles

| Index of Economic Freedom Score | 3.25 |

Mostly Not Free

1   2   3   4   5

Factor #1: Trade Policy

Score: 5-Stable (Very High level of protectionism)

Senegal has an average tariff rate of 23.6 percent.[323] It also maintains trade restrictions in the form of import bans, import licenses, and strict documentation requirements.

Factor #2: Taxation

Score - Income taxation: 5- (Very high tax rates)
Score - Corporate taxation: 3-Stable (Moderate tax rates)
Final Taxation Score: 4.5-Stable (Very High tax rates)

Senegal's top income tax rate is 78 percent,[324] and the average taxpayer is in the 18 percent bracket. The top marginal corporate tax rate is 35 percent. Senegal also has a 35 percent capital gains tax and a 10 percent to 20 percent turnover tax.

Factor #3: Government Intervention in the Economy

Score: 3+ (Moderate level of government intervention)

The government of Senegal consumes about 12 percent of GDP.[325] It also remains heavily involved in agriculture (although the number of private firms is increasing) and continues to control railroads, electrical production, telecommunications, and postal services.

---

323   Based on total taxes on international trade as a percentage of total imports; from International Monetary Fund, *Government Financial Statistics 1995*.

324   Includes a top rate of 50 percent and a mandatory proportional tax of 28 percent.

325   World Bank, *World Development Report 1996*.

Factor #4: Monetary Policy
Score: 1-Stable (Very low level of inflation)

Senegal's average rate of inflation from 1985 to 1994 was 2.9 percent. In 1995, however, the inflation rate was 8 percent.

Factor #5: Capital Flows and Foreign Investment
Score: 3-Stable (Moderate barriers to foreign investment)

Senegal does not allow foreign investment in the food and fishing industries, although 100 percent ownership is permitted in most other areas. Foreign and domestic firms are treated equally. Industries such as railroads, electricity, telecommunications, and postal services remain under state control.

Factor #6: Banking
Score: 3-Stable (Moderate level of restrictions on banking)

Senegal's banking system is dominated by French banks. There is a moderate level of competition, and borrowing capital can be expensive. There is no stock market.

Factor #7: Wage and Price Controls
Score: 4-Stable (High level of wage and price controls)

Wages and prices in Senegal are set both by the market and by the large state-owned sector. The government continues to set prices on some goods and services, such as agricultural products and electricity.

Factor #8: Property Rights
Score: 2-Stable (High level of protection of private property)

Private property in Senegal is protected by an efficient legal system, and expropriation is unlikely.

Factor #9: Regulation
Score: 4-Stable (High level of regulation)

Establishing a business in Senegal can be onerous if the business competes with a state-owned sector. In addition, government-sanctioned monopolies often bribe government officials to keep out new entrants.

Factor #10: Black Market
Score: 3-Stable (Moderate level of black market activity)

Black market activity in Senegal is confined mainly to labor, construction, and transportation.

Summary

Senegal				Overall Score	3.25
Trade	5	Monetary Policy	1	Property Rights	2
Taxation	4.5	Foreign Investment	3	Regulation	4
Government Intervention	3	Banking	3	Black Market	3
		Wage and Prices	4		

SIERRA LEONE

The West African country of Sierra Leone gained its independence from France in 1961. During the next ten years, its economy grew by 4 percent a year. During the 1970s, however, this growth came to an end when the economy was devastated by the oil crisis. For the past 15 years, the government has made halfhearted efforts to reform the economy, but recovery has remained elusive. In 1996, Sierra Leone experienced both an increase in armed banditry and a continuation of its ongoing civil and political unrest.

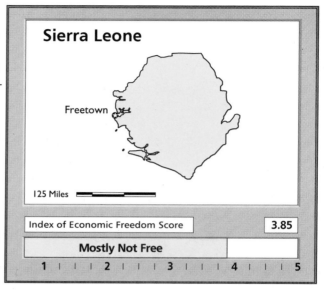

Factor #1: Trade Policy

Score: 4-Stable (High level of protectionism)

The average tariff rate in Sierra Leone is about 34.4 percent.[326] Non-tariff barriers take the form of excessive government red tape.

Factor #2: Taxation

Score - Income taxation: 3-Stable (Moderate tax rates)
Score - Corporate taxation: 5-Stable (Very high tax rates)
Final Taxation Score: 4.5-Stable (Very high tax rates)

Sierra Leone's top income tax rate is 50 percent, with the average income taxed at a rate of 5 percent. The corporate income tax rate is a flat 47.2 percent. Sierra Leone also imposes property taxes and a goods and services tax.

Factor #3: Government Intervention in the Economy

Score: 3-Stable (Moderate level of government intervention)

The government of Sierra Leone consumes 12 percent of GDP, and the large state-owned sector produces more than 30 percent of GDP.

Factor #4: Monetary Policy

Score: 5-Stable (Very high level of inflation)

Sierra Leone's average annual rate of inflation from 1985 to 1994 was 67.8 percent. In 1995, the inflation rate was 35 percent.

---

326 Based on total taxes on international trade as a percentage of total imports; from International Monetary Fund, *Government Financial Statistics 1995*.

Factor #5: Capital Flows and Foreign Investment
Score: 3-Stable (Moderate barriers to foreign investment)

All investments in Sierra Leone must be approved by the government, which has established an investment code. Foreigners are not permitted to invest either in "local industries," such as cement block manufacturing or granite and sandstone excavation, or in the manufacture of certain durable consumer goods.

Factor #6: Banking
Score: 4-Stable (High level of restrictions on banking)

Sierra Leone's banking system is in disarray. Banks are heavily regulated, and the government sets interest rates for commercial banks.

Factor #7: Wage and Price Controls
Score: 3-Stable (Moderate level of wage and price controls)

Some price controls are imposed on certain foodstuffs in Sierra Leone. Prices also are influenced by the state-owned industries, which are subsidized by the government. Sierra Leone does not maintain a minimum wage.

Factor #8: Property Rights
Score: 4- (Low level of protection of private property)

Although private property is permitted in Sierra Leone, it also can be expropriated. An inefficient legal and law enforcement environment provides little protection. The U.S. Department of State has issued a warning on travel to Sierra Leone, mainly because of crime and corruption: "Petty crime and theft of wallets and passports are common. Requests for payments at military roadblocks are common. Robberies and burglaries of residences also occur."[327]

Factor #9: Regulation
Score: 3-Stable (Moderate level of regulation)

Regulations in Sierra Leone are applied haphazardly, making compliance difficult. For example, the less than uniform enforcement of health and safety standards creates an environment of uncertainty among businesses. Nevertheless, bribes are not necessary. Regulations thus are only moderately burdensome overall.

Factor #10: Black Market
Score: 5-Stable (Very high level of black market activity)

The level of black market activity in Sierra Leone is nearly as high as the level of legal activity. High tariffs encourage smugglers to sell many products on the black market, and some products like coffee and rice are sold at much lower prices than in state-owned stores.

---

327 From U.S. Department of State, "Sierra Leone—Travel Conditions—IMI960208 Market Research Reports," 1996.

Summary

Sierra Leone				Overall Score	3.85
Trade	4	Monetary Policy	5	Property Rights	4
Taxation	4.5	Foreign Investment	3	Regulation	3
Government Intervention	3	Banking	4	Black Market	5
		Wage and Prices	3		

SINGAPORE

Singapore won its independence from Malaysia on August 9, 1965. Since then, economic liberalization gradually has moved it into the industrialized world. From 1965 to 1990, Singapore enjoyed average annual growth rates of about 6.5 percent; today, it is one of the richest countries in Asia. Singapore has made remarkable progress by maintaining an open trade and investment environment; a corruption-free, pro-business regulatory system; political stability; an efficient, strike-free labor force; and tax incentives for foreign investors.

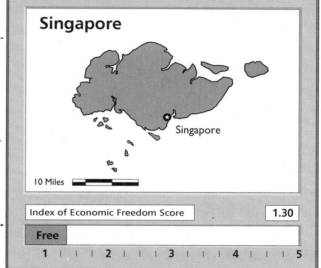

Factor #1: Trade Policy

Score: 1-Stable (Very low level of protectionism)

Singapore has an exceptionally low average tariff rate of from 0.3 to 0.5 percent; nearly 99 percent of all imports enter duty-free. The government maintains straightforward labeling requirements, no import quotas, and no non-tariff barriers to foreign trade. Import licenses are not required, and customs procedures are minimal. The code regulating product standards is not an impediment to trade.

Factor #2: Taxation

Score - Income taxation: 2-Stable (Low tax rates)
Score - Corporate taxation: 3-Stable (Moderate tax rates)
Final Taxation Score: 3-Stable (Moderate tax rates)

Singapore's top income tax rate is 30 percent, and the average income is taxed at 8 percent. There are no taxes on capital gains. The corporate tax rate is a flat 27 percent, which the government plans to reduce to 25 percent within the next few years. Singapore also has a 3 percent value-added tax, as well as a mandatory retirement fund to which employees and employers must contribute.

Factor #3: Government Intervention in the Economy

Score: 1-Stable (Very low level of government intervention)

In 1995, the government of Singapore consumed 8.5 percent of GDP, down from 9 percent in 1994. Although some critics of Singapore's economic reforms claim that the government is heavily involved in the private sector, most businesses are privately owned, and direct government control of corporations is negligible.[328]

---

328 Most direct government involvement in business is restricted to shipping, real estate, construction, air transportation, and some financial services. Many of these government-owned companies have joint ventures with private firms. According to the Economist Intelligence Unit, "Few GLCs (government-linked companies) compete in sectors involving MNCs (multinational corporations) though they are involved in joint ventures." Economist

Factor #4: Monetary Policy

Score: 1-Stable (Very low level of inflation)

Singapore's average annual rate of inflation from 1985 to 1994 was 3.9 percent. In 1995, the inflation rate was 1.7 percent; for most of 1996, it was below 2 percent.

Factor #5: Capital Flows and Foreign Investment

Score: 1-Stable (Very low barriers to foreign investment)

Investment laws in Singapore are clear and fair, and pose few problems for businesses. Foreign and domestic businesses are treated equally under the investment laws, and there are no production or local content requirements. According to the Economist Intelligence Unit, "Restrictions on equity, licensing and joint ventures are negligible."[329]

Factor #6: Banking

Score: 2-Stable (Low level of restrictions on banking)

Foreign banks in Singapore are restricted as to the number of branches and automatic teller machines they may operate. This is mainly the result of bank overcrowding. A nation of just under 3 million people, Singapore has over 120 foreign banks—more than the number of domestic banks. All banks may participate in securities exchanges, sell insurance policies, engage in some real estate ventures, and invest in industrial firms. It also is easy to form new banks.

Factor #7: Wage and Price Controls

Score: 1-Stable (Very low level of wage and price controls)

Almost all wages and prices in Singapore are set by the free market. Only a few items, such as steel reinforcement bars and cement, are subject to price controls. Singapore has no minimum wage.

Factor #8: Property Rights

Score: 1-Stable (Very high level of protection of private property)

Singapore has a solid history of private property protection, and there is no threat of expropriation. The court system is highly efficient and strongly protects private property.

Factor #9: Regulation

Score: 1-Stable (Very low level of regulation)

Obtaining a business license in Singapore is easy. Government regulations are straightforward, and corruption is nonexistent. Occupational safety and health regulations are not burdensome, and there are no antitrust regulations. The government does not tolerate price gouging, however, and will act to eliminate such practices whenever they are found to exist.

Intelligence Unit, "Singapore," *ILT Reports,* June 1995, p. 6.

329   *Ibid.,* p. 7.

Factor #10: Black Market

Score: 1-Stable (Very low level of black market activity)

The black market in Singapore is very small. Smuggling and black market activities in pirated intellectual property are negligible.

Summary

Singapore				Overall Score	1.30
Trade	1	Monetary Policy	1	Property Rights	1
Taxation	3	Foreign Investment	1	Regulation	1
Government Intervention	1	Banking	2	Black Market	1
		Wage and Prices	1		

THE SLOVAK REPUBLIC

Slovakia's split from the Czech Republic in 1993 left much of its banking, experienced personnel, data analysis capability, and competitive industry across the border. In addition to struggling to transform its centrally controlled economy into a market-based economy, the Slovak Republic has had to create a stable democratic government. Reform has been slower in Slovakia than in the Czech Republic, but the government has made significant progress in reducing inflation.

Slovak Republic	
Index of Economic Freedom Score	3.05
Mostly Not Free	

Factor #1: Trade Policy
Score: 2-Stable (Low level of protectionism)

Slovakia has an average tariff rate of about 6 percent.[330] Import licensing requirements, according to the U.S. Department of State, are not burdensome: "For most of the approximately 100 groups of items in the 'general' category, obtaining a license is a formality."[331]

Factor #2: Taxation
Score - Income taxation: 4-Stable (High tax rates)
Score - Corporate taxation: 4-Stable (High tax rates)
Final Taxation Score: 4.5-Stable (Very high tax rates)

Slovakia's top marginal income tax rate is 42 percent, with the average taxpayer subject to a rate of about 20 percent. The top corporate income tax rate is 40 percent. Slovakia also has a 40 percent capital gains tax, a 23 percent value-added tax, and a 38 percent social contributions tax.

Factor #3: Government Intervention in the Economy
Score: 3-Stable (Moderate level of government intervention)

The Slovak government consumes 23.1 percent of GDP. Although the private sector is the largest part of the economy, some 35 percent of GDP still is produced by the state. Slovakia has undergone significant privatization. Most smaller state-owned enterprises have been sold off, and many of the larger ones are being sold off.

---

330   State Department Report, 1996, p. 270.

331   *Ibid.*, p. 269.

Factor #4: Monetary Policy
Score: 3-Stable (Moderate level of inflation)

Since becoming an independent country, the Slovak Republic has had inflation rates of 10 percent in 1992, 23 percent in 1993, 13 percent in 1994, and 10 percent in 1995.[332] The average rate of inflation from 1992 to 1995 was about 14 percent.

Factor #5: Capital Flows and Foreign Investment
Score: 3-Stable (Moderate barriers to foreign investment)

Although foreign citizens may not own land in Slovakia, there are few restrictions on foreign direct investment. Slovakia provides equal treatment to foreign and domestic firms and has a well-established foreign investment code. Nevertheless, political instability caused by the populist government of Prime Minister Vladimir Meciar has made Slovakia less attractive to investors than the neighboring Czech Republic and Poland.

Factor #6: Banking
Score: 3-Stable (Moderate level of restrictions on banking)

Permission from the central bank is required to open banks, although this has become simply a formality. Of the 29 banks operating in Slovakia at the end of 1994, 10 were branches of foreign banks. Slovakia's banking system has yet to become completely independent of government coercion and control.

Factor #7: Wage and Price Controls
Score: 3-Stable (Moderate level of wage and price controls)

Almost 96 percent of Slovakia's price controls have been removed, although controls on the prices of some products (for example, food, fuel, electricity, and heat) remain in effect. In 1994, the government imposed some restrictions on wages in certain money-losing state-owned industries. The Slovak Republic has a minimum wage.

Factor #8: Property Rights
Score: 3- (Moderate level of protection of private property)

Expropriation is unlikely in the Slovak Republic, which has developed a moderately efficient and independent legal system. Decisions can be slow, however, and this often lessens the total protection of private property. According to the U.S. Department of Commerce, "Property and contractual rights are enforced within the legal structure, but decisions may take years, thus limiting the attractiveness of the system for dispute settlement."[333] This is not uncommon in countries moving from communist economic systems to more open markets.

Factor #9: Regulation
Score: 3-Stable (Moderate level of regulation)

Slovakia has reduced its level of regulation, and most businesses do not need a license. Because the remaining state-owned sector is controlled mainly by political allies

---

332   Based on consumer price inflation.

333   U.S. Department of Commerce, *Country Commercial Guide,* 1996.

of the government, private firms may find themselves subjected to regulations that state-run firms are able to avoid.

Factor #10: Black Market

Score: 3-Stable (Moderate level of black market activity)

The Slovak Republic's black market remains fairly large. About 15 percent of the working public is employed in the informal sector.[334]

Summary

Slovak Republic		Overall Score	3.05

Slovak Republic			Monetary Policy	3	Property Rights	3
Trade	2		Monetary Policy	3	Property Rights	3
Taxation	4.5		Foreign Investment	3	Regulation	3
Government Intervention	3		Banking	3	Black Market	3
			Wage and Prices	3		

---

334 Economist Intelligence Unit, *EIU Country Profile, 1995–96.*

SLOVENIA

Since the breakup of Yugoslavia, Slovenia has pursued an economic liberalization policy aimed at promoting international trade, attracting private investment, and privatizing the state-owned sector. The government also has made substantial progress in curbing inflation. Yet the path to progress has been slow, and many hurdles still exist. Slovenia recently opened its borders to foreign investment, cut taxes, and improved its protection of private property. The government, however, also has increased its control of some industries.

Slovenia

Ljubljana

50 Miles

| Index of Economic Freedom Score | 3.10 |

Mostly Not Free

1   2   3   4   5

Factor #1: Trade Policy

Score: 4-Stable (High level of protectionism)

Slovenia has an average tariff rate of 13 percent. The government also maintains non-tariff barriers in the form of quotas in textiles.

Factor #2: Taxation

Score - Income taxation: 5-Stable (Very high tax rates)
Score - Corporate taxation: 2+ (Low tax rates)
Final Taxation Score: 4+ (High tax rates)

Slovenia's top income tax rate is 50 percent, up from 45 percent in 1995, and the average taxpayer is in the 35 percent bracket. The top marginal corporate tax rate is 25 percent, down from 30 percent in 1995. Slovenia also has a 20 percent sales tax, among other additional taxes.

Factor #3: Government Intervention in the Economy

Score: 3- (Moderate level of government intervention)

The government of Slovenia consumes about 21.7 percent of GDP, and the state sector accounts for a significant portion of GDP overall. The government remains heavily involved in the banking, transportation, and utility sectors of the economy.

Factor #4: Monetary Policy

Score: 3-Stable (Moderate level of inflation)

In 1994, Slovenia's rate of inflation was 19.8 percent.

Factor #5: Capital Flows and Foreign Investment

Score: 3+ (Moderate barriers to foreign investment)

Slovenia allows foreign investment in most industries except for rail and air transportation, telecommunications, insurance, publishing, and the mass media, although it does require that the managing director of the business be a Slovenian national. With foreign investment continuing to increase, this does not appear to be a major barrier. The government does not permit foreign investors to own land.

Factor #6: Banking
Score: 2-Stable (Low level of restrictions on banking)

Most government control of the banking sector has been ended. As a result, more foreign banks are opening branches in Slovenia.

Factor #7: Wage and Price Controls
Score: 3-Stable (Moderate level of wage and price controls)

Wages and prices in Slovenia are driven by the market, although price controls continue on such items as electricity, gas, and telecommunications. Slovenia has a minimum wage.

Factor #8: Property Rights
Score: 3+ (Moderate level of protection of private property)

Private property is guaranteed by Slovenia's Constitution. The court system is becoming increasingly independent, but it also can be slow and moderately inefficient.

Factor #9: Regulation
Score: 3-Stable (Moderate level of regulation)

Establishing a business in Slovenia is becoming easier, and the number of private businesses is growing. An entrenched bureaucracy and corruption, however, continue to hinder the rapid growth of a free market.

Factor #10: Black Market
Score: 3+ (Moderate level of black market activity)

Slovenia has a large black market, primarily because of high tariffs. Black market activity also results from the government's control of the transportation industry. Nevertheless, according to the U.S. Department of State, Slovenia has made significant progress in protecting intellectual property, and piracy has been curtailed severely.

Summary

Slovenia				Overall Score	3.10
Trade	4	Monetary Policy	3	Property Rights	3
Taxation	4	Foreign Investment	3	Regulation	3
Government Intervention	3	Banking	2	Black Market	3
		Wage and Prices	3		

SOMALIA

Modern Somalia came about in 1960, when British Somalia joined with the former Italian and United Nations–controlled Northern Somalia. During the Cold War, Somalia was of geostrategic interest to both the Soviet Union and the Western superpowers. Today, it has a primarily agricultural economy, most of which has been destroyed by civil war. Since the fall of the central government in 1991, Somalia has been in the grasp of bands of repressive "clan militias." Somalia remains one of the world's poorest countries; massive transfers of food aid, foreign aid, and loans and grants from the United States, Europe, and Japan have done little to bring it out of the depths of poverty, the main cause of which is the lack of either economic freedom or the rule of law. There are some indications, however, that the northern part of Somalia is attempting to establish the basis for a free market.

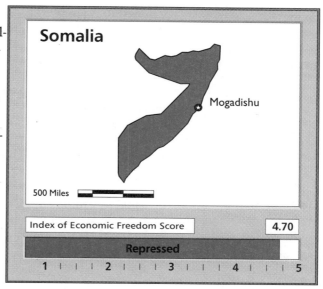

Factor #1: Trade Policy

Score: 5-Stable (Very high level of protectionism)

Tariff rates play a very minor role in restricting imports and exports in Somalia. The biggest impediment is the tendency of corrupt customs officials to confiscate goods for personal gain. In addition, Somalia's "clan militias" have destroyed what was left of a centralized customs service, although the government is trying to restore order. The U.S. Department of State warns that "looting, banditry, and all forms of violent crime are common."[335] This greatly impairs the movement of goods across Somalia's borders.

Factor #2: Taxation

Score - Income taxation: 5-Stable (Very high tax rates)
Score - Corporate taxation: 5-Stable (Very high tax rates)
Final Taxation Score: 5-Stable (Very high tax rates)

Little is left of Somalia's centralized government. Instead, the country is run primarily by warlords who operate a primitive feudal system. Taxation often takes the form of crop and private property confiscation, and it is not uncommon for citizens to find themselves taxed by more than one group.

---

335   U.S. Department of State Travel Advisory, July 3, 1996.

Factor #3: Government Intervention in the Economy
Score: 5-Stable (Very high level of government intervention)

Somalia has no official government and very little economic output. The entire economic system is in ruins. The level of crime, banditry and looting—much of it carried out by warring clans and militias—makes it nearly impossible to conduct business activity.

Factor #4: Monetary Policy
Score: 5-Stable (Very high level of inflation)

Somalia's average annual rate of inflation from 1985 to 1993 was 75.4 percent. No data for 1994 or 1995 are available.

Factor #5: Capital Flows and Foreign Investment
Score: 4-Stable (High barriers to foreign investment)

Somalia remains in economic ruins, with no clear protection of foreign investment. The biggest threat to foreign investment is the continued violence. According to the U.S. Department of State, "Sporadic fighting among local militias continues in parts of the country. Kidnappings and other threats to foreigners occur unpredictably in virtually all regions."[336]

Factor #6: Banking
Score: 5-Stable (Very high level of restrictions on banking)

The banking system in Somalia has collapsed, and banks operate in primitive conditions. Most lending is performed unofficially among family members and friends, some of whom reside in other countries.

Factor #7: Wage and Price Controls
Score: 3-Stable (Moderate level of wage and price controls)

Wages and prices in Somalia are set mainly by the market through barter. The government is not powerful enough to enforce laws that set prices. It is not uncommon, however, for militias to confiscate goods, particularly food, from their producers in order to distribute them freely to their supporters. Thus, prices often are affected by looting and theft.

Factor #8: Property Rights
Score: 5-Stable (Very low level of protection of private property)

Private property is virtually nonexistent in Somalia, and property often is confiscated by the clans and by corrupt government officials. According to the U.S. Department of State, "There is no national government in Somalia to offer security or police protection for travelers."[337]

---

336 *Ibid.*

337 *Ibid.*

Factor #9: Regulation
Score: 5-Stable (Very high level of regulation)

Establishing a business in Somalia is nearly impossible. Meeting official requirements is beyond the ability of most entrepreneurs, so they simply operate in the black market. Corruption is rampant.

Factor #10: Black Market
Score: 5-Stable (Very high level of black market activity)

Most of the economic activity in Somalia occurs in the black market.

Summary

Somalia				Overall Score	4.70
Trade	5	Monetary Policy	5	Property Rights	5
Taxation	5	Foreign Investment	4	Regulation	5
Government Intervention	5	Banking	5	Black Market	5
		Wage and Prices	3		

SOUTH AFRICA

South Africa's transition from apartheid to non-racial democracy has gone well; the level of national reconciliation has been impressive. A key to the country's future stability will be the revival of its long-depressed economy. South Africa enjoys many economic assets, including a modern industrial sector, a well-developed infrastructure, and abundant natural resources. The government over the years has maintained a great deal of control over the economy. Recently, however, some badly needed economic liberalization has been undertaken; but even though fiscal discipline has been maintained, the government will continue to be tempted to overspend on social programs and engage in other state interventions in an effort to improve the lives of previously disenfranchised black South Africans. After several dismal years, the South African economy is growing at a respectable pace, although the country continues to suffer from political violence.

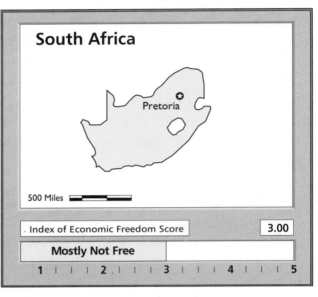

Factor #1: Trade Policy

Score: 5-Stable (Very high level of protectionism)

South Africa has an average tariff rate of 15 percent,[338] down from an average of 21 percent in 1993.[339] According to the U.S. Department of State, "Under terms of the Import and Export Control Act of 1963, South Africa's Minister of Trade and Industry may act in the national interest to prohibit, ration, or otherwise regulate imports. In recent years, the list of restricted goods requiring import permits has been reduced, but still includes such goods as foodstuffs, clothing, fabrics, footwear, wood and paper products, refined petroleum products and chemicals."[340]

Factor #2: Taxation

Score - Income taxation: 4-Stable (High tax rates)
Score - Corporate taxation: 3-Stable (Moderate tax rates)
Final Taxation Score: 4-Stable (High tax rates)

South Africa has a progressive tax system, with the highest income level taxed at a rate of 45 percent and the average income level taxed at a rate of 17 percent. The corpo-

---

338 Based on total tax revenues on international transactions as a percentage of imports; from International Monetary Fund, *Government Financial Statistics, 1995.*

339 Economist Intelligence Unit, *ILT Reports, South Africa, 1996,* February 1996, p. 27.

340 State Department Report, 1996, p. 28.

rate tax is 35 percent. South Africa also has a 14 percent value-added tax, a financial services tax, and regional taxes.

Factor #3: Government Intervention in the Economy
Score: 3-Stable (Moderate level of government intervention)

The South African government consumes 21 percent of GDP, and six state-owned companies rank among the country's 25 largest firms. State assets include South Africa's railways, national airline, broadcasting services, and electric utilities. The government currently is studying the possible "reconstruction" of state enterprises.

Factor #4: Monetary Policy
Score: 3-Stable (Moderate level of inflation)

South Africa's average annual rate of inflation from 1985 to 1994 was 14.2 percent. In 1995, the inflation rate was 8.7 percent.

Factor #5: Capital Flows and Foreign Investment
Score: 2-Stable (Low barriers to foreign investment)

No government approval is required for foreign investment, and foreign investors are subject to the same laws as domestic investors. In addition, there are no requirements for South African participation in management, only a few areas of the economy are reserved for South Africans, and foreign investors are free to acquire land. On the negative side, foreign-controlled firms are subject to domestic borrowing restrictions, and foreign investment incentives are nonexistent. High corporate taxes, political and criminal violence, and low labor productivity also are harming South Africa's attempt to attract foreign investment.

Factor #6: Banking
Score: 3-Stable (Moderate level of restrictions on banking)

South Africa has a world-class financial sector. Legal restrictions that discriminate against foreign-owned financial institutions have been eliminated, and over 30 foreign banks now operate in South Africa. The banking and insurance industries, however, are tightly controlled by the Reserve Bank, with which interest-free reserve balances must be deposited. Exchange controls preclude international investment by South African financial institutions. Licenses for new banks and insurance companies are not readily granted. The new government also may pressure banks into investing in its Reconstruction and Development Program, which is designed to promote the economic advancement of black South Africans.

Factor #7: Wage and Price Controls
Score: 2-Stable (Low level of wage and price controls)

Price controls, once pervasive, now exist only on coal, gasoline, and some utilities. There is no national minimum wage, but labor legislation currently under consideration could lead to the *de facto* imposition of wage controls.

Factor #8: Property Rights
Score: 3-Stable (Moderate level of protection of private property)

No private-sector company, whether South African or foreign-controlled, ever has been nationalized. The judiciary is both professional and effective. There is a danger, however, that the government's redistributionist policies, including its land reform program, may weaken private property rights. It also is possible that the protection of private property clause in the interim constitution will not be included in the new constitution. Squatters and crime pose additional problems, and the state may assume control of tribal-controlled communal land.

Factor #9: Regulation
Score: 2-Stable (Low level of regulation)

Regulation of economic activity is minimal in South Africa. It takes only four to ten days to incorporate a business, and most businesses can be started with a minimum of formalities. Licenses, required for certain activities, can be obtained with relative ease. There has been a blossoming of once-banned street vendors. The establishment of an affirmative action directorate within the Labor Ministry is a sign that increased political pressure to practice more affirmative action in the hiring and firing of personnel can be expected.

Factor #10: Black Market
Score: 3-Stable (Moderate level of black market activity)

Legal restrictions which prevented black South Africans from owning businesses, obtaining skilled jobs, or living in major urban centers were lifted in 1991. This will reduce black market activity. There still is significant informal activity in retail textiles and pirated intellectual property, however. Piracy, for example, accounts for as much as 70 percent of the trade in computer software.

Summary

South Africa				Overall Score	3.00
Trade	5	Monetary Policy	3	Property Rights	3
Taxation	4	Foreign Investment	2	Regulation	2
Government Intervention	3	Banking	3	Black Market	3
		Wage and Prices	2		

SPAIN

Spain's economy has long been dominated by the state. As a result, it lags behind those of most of Spain's European neighbors. Spain's accession into the European Union (EU) in 1986, however, has forced the government to open its economy, remove oppressive government-run bureaucracies from many economic decisions, and expand the free market. In 1992, after several years of economic growth that began in 1986, Spain entered a deep recession that largely has continued until the present time. This recession was mainly the result of renewed government intervention in the economy. Spain's new president, Jose Maria Aznar, elected in 1996, is dedicated to continued economic reform.

Index of Economic Freedom Score: 2.60

Mostly Free

1 2 3 4 5

Factor #1: Trade Policy
Score: 2-Stable (Low level of protectionism)

Spain has an average tariff rate of about 3.6 percent. It also maintains restrictive customs procedures, strict labeling and testing requirements, and many other non-tariff barriers.

Factor #2: Taxation
Score - Income taxation: 5-Stable (Very high tax rates)
Score - Corporate taxation: 3-Stable (Moderate tax rates)
Final Taxation Score: 5-Stable (Very high tax rates)

Spain's top income tax rate is 56 percent, and the average income level is taxed at a rate of 24.5 percent. The top corporate rate is 35 percent. Spain also has a 35 percent capital gains tax and a 4 percent to 16 percent value-added tax.

Factor #3: Government Intervention in the Economy
Score: 2-Stable (Low level of government intervention)

The government of Spain consumes 17 percent of GDP, and state ownership of industry remains extensive.

Factor #4: Monetary Policy
Score: 2-Stable (Low level of inflation)

Spain's average annual rate of inflation from 1985 to 1994 was 6.6 percent. In 1995, the inflation rate fell to 4.7 percent.

Factor #5: Capital Flows and Foreign Investment
Score: 2-Stable (Low barriers to foreign investment)

Membership in the EU has forced Madrid to remove most restrictions on foreign investment. Some restrictions remain in such areas as telecommunications.

Factor #6: Banking
Score: 3-Stable (Moderate level of restrictions on banking)

Integration into the EU has made Spain's banking system more competitive, forcing it to accept banks from other EU countries. These banks, however, also face cumbersome regulations, and non-EU banks are subject to increasing discrimination.

Factor #7: Wage and Price Controls
Score: 3-Stable (Moderate level of wage and price controls)

Price controls are imposed on electricity, telephone services, rail transport, postal service, and some pharmaceutical products. Spain maintains a minimum wage.

Factor #8: Property Rights
Score: 2-Stable (High level of protection of private property)

Property in Spain is safe from government expropriation. Spain's legal system effectively protects private property, although levels of corruption are higher than in most other EU countries.

Factor #9: Regulation
Score: 3-Stable (Moderate level of regulation)

The Spanish government maintains many regulations on businesses. These include labor and environmental laws, in addition to regulations dealing with fringe benefits. All are moderately burdensome.

Factor #10: Black Market
Score: 2+ (Low level of black market activity)

Spain's black market is confined mainly to pirated computer software, prerecorded music and video tapes, and illegal local cable transmissions of copyrighted movies. The government takes intellectual property infringement very seriously and has moved to enforce new laws.

Summary

Spain				Overall Score	2.60
Trade	2	Monetary Policy	2	Property Rights	2
Taxation	5	Foreign Investment	2	Regulation	3
Government Intervention	2	Banking	3	Black Market	2
		Wage and Prices	3		

SRI LANKA

S ri Lanka, an island off the southern shore of India, declared its independence from Great Britain in 1948. The country adopted a new constitution in 1972, creating a republic, and began a series of economic reforms in 1977. Since 1983, it has endured civil unrest and (most recently) civil war, all of which is a serious drain on the economy. Despite domestic turmoil, however, a new economic restructuring plan has helped fuel substantial economic growth. The government has focused on reducing trade barriers, privatizing businesses, and expanding the role of the private sector. Sri Lanka recently has reduced both trade barriers and tax levels, in addition to cracking down on government corruption.

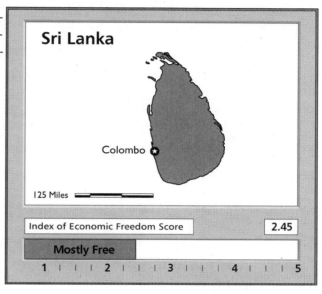

Factor #1: Trade Policy
Score: 3+ (Moderate level of protectionism)

Sri Lanka has a three-tiered system of 10 percent, 25 percent, and 30 percent tariffs on various imports. For some items, such as automobiles, the rates range from 50 percent to 100 percent. The government also imposes a 4.5 percent defense levy; an excise tax on selected consumer and nonessential goods; and a 10 percent export-development access surcharge, which applies to a few items subject to an import duty of 45 percent or more. All of these tariffs bring Sri Lanka's average tariff rate to 12 percent. However, there are no significant non-tariff barriers.

Factor #2: Taxation
Score - Income taxation: 3-Stable (Moderate tax rates)
Score - Corporate taxation: 3-Stable (Moderate tax rates)
Final Taxation Score: 3.5-Stable (High tax rates)

Sri Lanka's top marginal income tax rate is 35 percent, with the average income level taxed at a 10 percent rate. The top corporate income tax rate is 35 percent. Sri Lanka also has a 1 percent to 20 percent turnover tax and a social contributions tax.

Factor #3: Government Intervention in the Economy
Score: 2- (Low level of government intervention)

The government of Sri Lanka consumes 9.7 percent of GDP, up from 8.5 percent in 1980. It also owns some sectors of the economy. For example, although 9 of the 23 state-owned agricultural plantations have been privatized, the other 14 remain in state hands because privatization has been halted. The government also owns the telecommunications company (now undergoing privatization), some banks, the Independent Television Network, the National Paper Corporation, the National Salt Corporation, and a textile import and trading corporation.[341] Some of these enterprises may be candidates for privatization in the future.

Factor #4: Monetary Policy
Score: 2-Stable (Low level of inflation)

Sri Lanka's average annual rate of inflation between 1985 and 1994 was 11 percent. In 1995, the inflation rate was 4.8 percent.

Factor #5: Capital Flows and Foreign Investment
Score: 3-Stable (Moderate barriers to foreign investment)

Sri Lanka generally welcomes foreign investment. Its well-defined and accessible foreign investment code treats foreign and domestic firms equally. Equity restrictions of up to 40 percent apply to some businesses, however, and foreign investment in non-bank moneylending, pawn shops, retail trade outlets with capital investments of less than $1 million, some personal services, and coastal fishing is prohibited.

Factor #6: Banking
Score: 2-Stable (Low level of restrictions on banking)

Sri Lanka has over 20 commercial banks, most of them foreign-owned. The banking sector includes both private and state-owned banks, and competition has caused the industry to become increasingly efficient.

Factor #7: Wage and Price Controls
Score: 1-Stable (Very low level of wage and price controls)

Most wages and prices in Sri Lanka are determined by the market. There are some controls, however, on the prices of such items as foodstuffs and some energy products. A minimum wage is established by wage boards for specific sectors. Wages in other areas are determined by the market.

Factor #8: Property Rights
Score: 3-Stable (Moderate level of protection of private property)

Sri Lanka has an efficient and functional court system that is free from government influence. Since economic liberalization began in 1977, the government has not expropriated any foreign assets. Nevertheless, ethnic conflict and political violence still represent a threat; fighting in the eastern part of the country, for example, has forced citizens to abandon their homes and businesses.[342]

Factor #9: Regulation
Score: 2+ (Low level of regulation)

Sri Lanka's bureaucracy is both efficient and stable, and the government has imposed a review board to examine complaints of corruption. There are some regulations on employee leave, health, and safety standards.

---

341   Economist Intelligence Unit, *EIU Country Report: Sri Lanka, 2nd Quarter 1996.*

342   *Ibid.*

Factor #10: Black Market

Score: 3+ (Moderate level of black market activity)

Although Sri Lanka generally has strong and efficient intellectual property rights laws, there is a growing black market in pirated computer software, prerecorded music and video tapes, and compact disks. According to the U.S. Department of Commerce, "At present, copyright protection is not extended to computer programs, databases, and semiconductor layout designs. Under the U.S.–Sri Lanka bilateral agreement, however, U.S. software producers receive copyright protection in Sri Lanka."[343]

Summary

Sri Lanka				Overall Score	2.45
Trade	3	Monetary Policy	2	Property Rights	3
Taxation	3.5	Foreign Investment	3	Regulation	2
Government Intervention	2	Banking	2	Black Market	3
		Wage and Prices	1		

---

343 U.S. Department of Commerce, *Country Commercial Guide*, 1996.

SUDAN

The sub-Saharan African country of Sudan gained its independence from Great Britain in 1956. It is Africa's largest country, but President Omar Hassan al-Bashir's Islamic fundamentalist regime, which seized power in a 1989 coup, is authoritarian and increasingly isolated internationally. In 1993, the U.S. Department of State declared Sudan to be a supporter of terrorism. The country's ruling National Islamic Front tolerates no political opposition and is engaged in an expensive and brutal civil war with southern Sudanese separatists. Although the government has implemented modest economic liberalizations, the economy is unfree and continues to deteriorate. In addition, both government regulation and restrictions on banking have been increased recently. Sudan's economic mismanagement and radical politics also have left it with few remaining foreign aid donors.

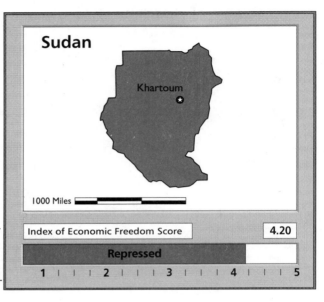

| Index of Economic Freedom Score | 4.20 |

Factor #1: Trade Policy
Score: 5-Stable (Very high level of protectionism)

Sudan's average tariff rate is 24 percent.[344] Import and export licenses were eliminated recently, though the importation of some 30 items is banned. Corruption within the customs service is rampant.

Factor #2: Taxation
Score - Income taxation: 5-Stable (Very high tax rates)
Score - Corporate taxation: 5-Stable (Very high tax rates)
Final Taxation Score: 5-Stable (Very high tax rates)

Sudan has top income and corporate tax rates of 60 percent.[345]

Factor #3: Government Intervention in the Economy
Score: 3-Stable (Moderate level of government intervention)

The government of Sudan consumes about 17 percent of GDP, and the state-owned sector generates a large portion of GDP overall.

---

344 This figure is for 1992–1993 and includes a defense tax; from United States Department of State, Bureau of African Affairs, Office of Economic Policy.

345 The most recent reliable information is based on 1989 tax data from World Bank sources. There is not enough information to determine the tax rate on the average income level; thus, Sudan was graded on its top tax rate.

Factor #4: Monetary Policy
Score: 5-Stable (Very high level of inflation)

Sudan's average annual rate of inflation from 1985 to 1994 was 55.3 percent. In 1995, the inflation rate was over 100 percent.

Factor #5: Capital Flows and Foreign Investment
Score: 4-Stable (High barriers to foreign investment)

Sudan's Islamic government is very sensitive to outside interference in its affairs, and this creates an inhospitable foreign investment environment. Foreign investment is approved on a case-by-case basis, foreign investment is not permitted in wholesale or retail companies or in the production of cotton, and bureaucratic procedures designed to encourage the employment of domestic laborers are cumbersome. There is no tax discrimination against foreign investment, however, although foreigners often find it nearly impossible to move about the country. According to the U.S. Department of State, "Travelers must obtain police permission before moving to another location in Sudan and must register with police within 24 hours of arrival at the new location. These regulations are strictly enforced. Even with proper documentation, travelers in Sudan have been subjected to delays and detentions by Sudan's security forces, especially when traveling outside Khartoum.... [D]isruptions of water and electricity are frequent, [and] telecommunications are slow and often impossible."[346]

Factor #6: Banking
Score: 4- (High level of restrictions on banking)

The new regime has moved to "Islamicize" Sudan's state-controlled banking system. This has increased government control over economic enterprises. There also is little freedom to exchange currency. According to the U.S. Department of Commerce, "Visitors who exchange money at other than an authorized banking institution risk arrest and loss of funds through unscrupulous black marketeers."[347]

Factor #7: Wage and Price Controls
Score: 4-Stable (High level of wage and price controls)

Although Sudan has liberalized some prices, price controls on foodstuffs remain in effect, and many goods are subsidized. The government regulates public and private salaries. Sudan has a minimum wage.

Factor #8: Property Rights
Score: 4-Stable (Low level of protection of private property)

There is little respect for private property in Sudan. The judiciary is not independent, the wanton destruction of private property by government troops is widespread in southern Sudan, and petty crime and thievery are common.

---

346 U.S. Department of State Travel Advisory, 1996.

347 U.S. Department of Commerce, *Country Commercial Guide*, 1996.

Factor #9: Regulation
Score: 4- (High level of government regulation)

Bureaucratic inefficiency makes business activity difficult. As with many developing countries, however, the regulatory burden is heavy and inefficient. Businesses often find it difficult to obtain licenses to operate. Business owners often may be harassed by corrupt bureaucrats. The government has cracked down on corruption, although it remains a problem.

Factor #10: Black Market
Score: 4-Stable (High level of black market activity)

Rationing has led to a black market in several items, including petroleum and sugar, and the ban on some imports encourages smuggling. The U.S. State Department reports that a slave trade exists in Sudan.[348]

Summary

Sudan						Overall Score	4.20
Trade	5	Monetary Policy	5		Property Rights	4
Taxation	5	Foreign Investment	4		Regulation	4
Government Intervention	3	Banking	4		Black Market	4
		Wage and Prices	4			

---

348   National Trade Data Bank and Economic Bulletin Board—products of STAT–USA, U.S. Department of Commerce, Washington, D.C., 1996.

SURINAME

Suriname gained its independence from the Netherlands in 1975. Throughout most of the 1980s, Suriname underwent political strife, and relations with the Netherlands deteriorated. In 1982, the Netherlands suspended cash development grants to Suriname because of political violence; this aid was reinstated in 1988. Most aid to Suriname has been squandered and has served as a primary obstacle to economic reform. Both inflation and government regulation have increased recently.

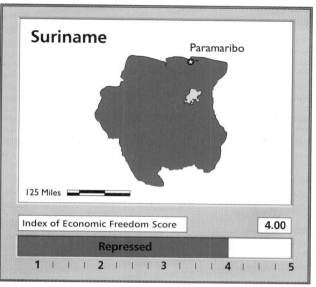

Suriname

Paramaribo

125 Miles

| Index of Economic Freedom Score | 4.00 |

Repressed

1　　2　　3　　4　　5

Factor #1: Trade Policy

Score: 5-Stable (Very high level of protectionism)

Average tariff rates in Suriname fluctuate between 30 percent and 40 percent. The government currently is planning a three-tiered tariff system that would incorporate three broad tariff classifications and rates. Other trade restrictions include strict import licensing and import bans.

Factor #2: Taxation

Score - Income taxation: 4- (High tax rates)
Score - Corporate taxation: 5- (Very high tax rates)
Final Taxation Score: 5- (Very high tax rates)

Suriname's top income tax rate is 60 percent, up from 55 percent in 1995, and the average taxpayer is in the 15 percent bracket. The top marginal corporate tax rate is 50 percent, up from 45 percent in 1995. Suriname also has a 50 percent capital gains tax.

Factor #3: Government Intervention in the Economy

Score: 3+ (Moderate level of government intervention)

The government of Suriname consumes about 18 percent of GDP, and the state sector generates a substantial amount of GDP overall.

Factor #4: Monetary Policy

Score: 5- (Very high level of inflation)

Suriname's average rate of inflation from 1985 to 1994 was 31.7 percent. In 1995, the inflation rate was 45 percent.

Factor #5: Capital Flows and Foreign Investment

Score: 3-Stable (Moderate barriers to foreign investment)

Suriname is quickly developing a sound foreign investment climate. Because the foreign investment environment still is being developed, investors are dealt with by the appropriate ministry on an *ad hoc* basis.[349]

Factor #6: Banking
Score: 4-Stable (High level of restrictions on banking)

The banking system in Suriname is in total disarray. The U.S. Department of Commerce characterizes it as "underdeveloped."[350]

Factor #7: Wage and Price Controls
Score: 3-Stable (Moderate level of wage and price controls)

Wages and prices in Suriname are set by both the market and the government. The large state-owned sector continues to influence the setting of prices.

Factor #8: Property Rights
Score: 3-Stable (Moderate level of protection of private property)

Private property is guaranteed by Suriname's Constitution and protected by law. The time involved in getting a dispute resolved in the court system, however, can be considerable.

Factor #9: Regulation
Score: 4- (High level of regulation)

Establishing a business in Suriname is generally easy, although the bureaucracy is both substantial and corrupt. According to the U.S. Department of Commerce, "Suriname's legacy of government corruption, combined with its proximity to narcotics producer countries, porous borders, remote airstrips, unprotected coastline, navigable rivers, and vast unoccupied interior areas, promote its use as a narcotics transshipment point."[351] This situation has worsened over the past several years.

Factor #10: Black Market
Score: 5-Stable (Very high level of black market activity)

Suriname has an extensive black market, primarily in pirated video and audio cassettes, computer software, and consumer goods.

Summary

Suriname				Overall Score	4.00
Trade	5	Monetary Policy	5	Property Rights	3
Taxation	5	Foreign Investment	3	Regulation	4
Government Intervention	3	Banking	4	Black Market	5
		Wage and Prices	3		

---

349 U.S. Department of Commerce, *Country Commercial Guide,* 1996.

350 *Ibid.*

351 National Trade Data Bank and Economic Bulletin Board—products of STAT–USA, U.S. Department of Commerce.

SWAZILAND

The South African country of Swaziland gained its independence from the United Kingdom in 1968, establishing a monarchy with all executive, legislative, and some judicial powers resting with the king. This system of government remains in effect today. Although Swaziland traditionally has been a largely agrarian society, manufacturing now produces 41 percent of GDP and is becoming the dominant sector of the economy. Swaziland has one of Africa's more free-market economies and recently has reduced its barriers to foreign investment.

Swaziland

Mbabane

125 Miles

Index of Economic Freedom Score	2.80
Mostly Free	

1 | | | | 2 | | | | 3 | | | | 4 | | | | 5

Factor #1: Trade Policy

Score: 4-Stable (High level of protectionism)

Swaziland has an average tariff rate of 19.2 percent.[352] There is no evidence that the government maintains any significant non-tariff barriers.

Factor #2: Taxation

Score - Income taxation: 2-Stable (Low tax rates)
Score - Corporate taxation: 4-Stable (High tax rates)
Final Taxation Score: 3-Stable (Moderate tax rates)

Swaziland's top income tax rate is 39 percent; there are no taxes on the average level of income. The top corporate tax rate is 37.5 percent. These are the only significant taxes.

Factor #3: Government Intervention in the Economy

Score: 2-Stable (Low level of government intervention)

The government of Swaziland consumes 23.5 percent of GDP. It also owns the larger public utilities, such as some transportation and telecommunications enterprises. The rest of the economy, however, is privately owned, and the government is developing plans to privatize most of the remaining state-owned industries.

Factor #4: Monetary Policy

Score: 2-Stable (Low level of inflation)

Swaziland's average annual rate of inflation from 1985 to 1994 was 12.8 percent. In 1995, the inflation rate was 12.3 percent.

---

352 This is a 1996 World Bank estimate based on 1994 data; from *African Development Indicators, 1996* (Washington, D.C.: The World Bank, 1996).

Factor #5: Capital Flows and Foreign Investment
Score: 2+ (Low barriers to foreign investment)

Foreign investment in Swaziland is generally encouraged, and the nationalization of foreign-owned property is prohibited by law. Foreign firms receive the same legal treatment as domestic firms. In fact, according to the U.S. Department of Commerce, "Far from discriminating against foreign participation in the country's development, Swaziland's government has been accused of favoring expatriate business over local entrepreneurs. The Swazi government has for over a decade advanced a policy welcoming foreign investment."[353] The Swazi economy is completely open to foreign investment, with few formal barriers, and the government is trying to develop a consistent and cohesive foreign investment code.

Factor #6: Banking
Score: 3-Stable (Moderate level of restrictions on banking)

Banks in Swaziland are relatively free of government control by African standards. Nevertheless, the government still controls the lending policies of some banks, and there is strict government control of credit.

Factor #7: Wage and Price Controls
Score: 3-Stable (Moderate level of wage and price controls)

Cotton, corn, milk, petroleum, energy, and tobacco products all remain subject to price controls. Swaziland has a minimum wage.

Factor #8: Property Rights
Score: 2-Stable (High level of protection of private property)

Property in Swaziland is legally protected against government expropriation. Enforcement of property rights in the court system, however, can be weak. According to the U.S. Department of Commerce, "Swaziland has a dual legal system comprised of Roman–Dutch law and customary law. This parallel system can be confusing and has at times presented problems for foreign-owned business."[354] Nevertheless, by global standards, Swaziland exhibits a high level of protection of private property.

Factor #9: Regulation
Score: 3-Stable (Moderate level of regulation)

Swaziland has streamlined its regulatory system. The government encourages private companies to establish their own safety and health standards. Some government regulations (especially those dealing with safety conditions), however, are applied erratically, and this can create uncertainty and confusion.

Factor #10: Black Market
Score: 4-Stable (High level of black market activity)

Swaziland has an active black market, primarily in the supply of labor, transportation services, the construction industry, and pirated computer software. The illegal soft-

---

353   U.S. Department of Commerce, *Country Commercial Guide,* 1996.

354   *Ibid.*

ware trade is mainly the result of poor intellectual property protection. According to the U.S. Department of Commerce, "Protection for patents, trademarks and copyrights is currently inadequate under Swazi law."[355]

Summary

Swaziland				Overall Score	2.80
Trade	4	Monetary Policy	2	Property Rights	2
Taxation	3	Foreign Investment	2	Regulation	3
Government Intervention	2	Banking	3	Black Market	4
		Wage and Prices	3		

355 *Ibid.*

SWEDEN

Sweden's economy has changed dramatically over the past several years. Once considered a workable socialist economy, Sweden experienced a severe recession in the 1980s that exploded the myth that a cradle-to-grave welfare state could be maintained without destroying the economy. By the end of the 1980s, it was becoming increasingly clear that high levels of government spending on social welfare, worker retraining, and unemployment compensation—to say nothing of tax rates as high as 98 percent—were leading Sweden down the road to economic ruin. Because of the government's economic policies, for example, GDP shrank by 4 percent from 1991 to 1993, and unemployment rose to around 8 percent in 1994. In the end, Sweden was forced to abandon most of its socialist policies and follow a more market-oriented economic path; it now stands as a shining example of how socialism, no matter how watered down, does not work. Sweden joined the European Union in 1995 and recently has managed to reduce both the rate of inflation and some of its banking regulations.

Factor #1: Trade Policy

Score: 2-Stable (Low level of protectionism)

Sweden's tariff rates average about 3 percent for manufactured goods and 5 percent for finished goods. The average rate is therefore under 4 percent.[356] Sweden maintains significant import licensing procedures, however, for such items as agricultural goods, ferroalloys, and semi-finished iron and steel.

Factor #2: Taxation

Score - Income taxation: 5-Stable (Very high tax rates)
Score - Corporate taxation: 3-Stable (Moderate tax rates)
Final Taxation Score: 4.5-Stable (Very high tax rates)

The Swedish tax burden is one of the heaviest among industrialized economies:[357] a 55 percent top income tax rate,[358] a 31 percent average income rate, a 28 percent top corporate rate, and a 30 percent capital gains tax—in addition to a 6 percent to 25 percent value-added tax.

---

356 U.S. Department of State, *Country Reports on Economic Policy and Trade Practices 1996*, p. 283.

357 State Department Report, 1996, p. 276.

358 *Worldwide Executive Tax Guide and Directory,* 1996 Edition (New York, N.Y.: Ernst & Young, 1996).

Factor #3: Government Intervention in the Economy
Score: 5-Stable (Very high level of government intervention)

The level of government spending in Sweden has fallen from around 75 percent of GDP to about 50 percent of GDP.[359] The government also is engaged in privatizing some companies, including one credit institution, Nordbanken. Of all the companies with more than 50 employees, 90 percent are privately owned.

Factor #4: Monetary Policy
Score: 1-Stable (Very low level of inflation)

Sweden's average annual rate of inflation from 1985 to 1994 was 5.8 percent. In 1996, the inflation rate is expected to be about 1 percent.

Factor #5: Capital Flows and Foreign Investment
Score: 2-Stable (Low barriers to foreign investment)

Sweden presents few barriers to foreign investment. There continue to be some restrictions, however, on foreign ownership of air transportation companies, the maritime industry, and items considered necessary during time of war, such as arms manufacturing.

Factor #6: Banking
Score: 2+ (Low level of restrictions on banking)

With one exception, all commercial banks in Sweden are domestically owned and operated; two are owned directly by the government. Although foreign banks have been permitted to establish subsidiaries and branches since 1986, the application process remains a barrier. The government is trying to liberalize the banking system, however, so that opening new banks will be easier[360] and banks will be able to operate more freely.

Factor #7: Wage and Price Controls
Score: 2-Stable (Low level of wage and price controls)

Most wages and prices in Sweden are set by the market. There is no national minimum wage law, although the government influences wage rates by establishing a minimum wage for employees of state-owned industries. Prices are affected by some government-owned businesses, which are subsidized.

Factor #8: Property Rights
Score: 2-Stable (High level of protection of private property)

Although Sweden has an extensive history of nationalization and expropriation of private property, there is little chance of government expropriation today. A massive, recently initiated privatization program is returning property to the private sector, and Sweden's court system is both efficient and sound.

---

359 Based on central government expenditure; from State Department Report, 1996, p. 283.

360 In addition to the sources noted in the "Banking Factor" section in Chapter 4, "Banking and Finance in Sweden," KPMG Bohlins, Stockholm, Sweden, 1993, was used.

Factor #9: Regulation
Score: 3-Stable (Moderate level of regulation)

Obtaining a business license in Sweden is relatively easy. Businesses must register with the Patent and Registration Office and the appropriate tax offices. Sweden also maintains a comprehensive and burdensome safety, environmental, and consumer regulatory structure, however. For example, the Environmental Protection Act of 1969 requires all businesses to obtain permission from the government before they release any pollutants into the environment. In cases in which the expansion of a business may result in more pollution, a company must undergo a lengthy and sometimes extremely burdensome investigation. Businesses also must comply with many other regulatory strictures, among them a government-imposed five-week vacation.

Factor #10: Black Market
Score: 1-Stable (Very low level of black market activity)

Sweden once had a rather large black market in the construction industry, but economic reforms are making it easier to exchange most goods and services legally. Sweden's protection of intellectual property is among the most efficient in the world.

Summary

Sweden					Overall Score	2.45
Trade	2	Monetary Policy	1		Property Rights	2
Taxation	4.5	Foreign Investment	2		Regulation	3
Government Intervention	5	Banking	2		Black Market	1
		Wage and Prices	2			

SWITZERLAND (INCLUDING LIECHTENSTEIN)[361]

S witzerland's various cantons united to with-draw from the Holy Roman Empire in 1291; by 1499, the Empire was forced to recognize its independence. From 1798 until 1803, Switzerland was occupied by the French under Napoleon. In 1874, it drafted a new constitution that remains largely in effect today. Having succeeded in remaining neutral throughout most of the 20th century's major international conflicts, Switzerland has become a favorite site for conventions, peace accords, and international agreements. Today, Geneva is the seat of the World Trade Organization.

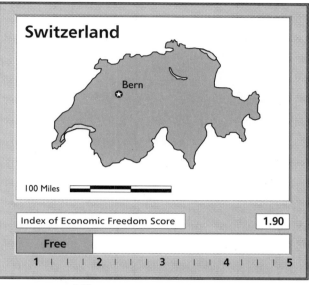

Switzerland

Bern

100 Miles

| Index of Economic Freedom Score | 1.90 |

Free

1 | | | 2 | | | 3 | | | 4 | | | 5

Factor #1: Trade Policy
Score: 2-Stable (Low level of protectionism)

As of January 1996, Switzerland's average tariff rate was about 2.2 percent, 6 percent less than it was a year ago.[362] Although Switzerland maintains trade restrictions in the form of licensing and subsidies for such items as agricultural products and telecommunications, it has no non-tariff barriers on manufactured goods and no antidumping law.

Factor #2: Taxation

Score - Income taxation: 1-Stable (Very low tax rates)
Score - Corporate taxation: 4-Stable (High tax rates)
Final Taxation Score: 3-Stable (Moderate tax rates)

Switzerland's top income tax rate is 11.5 percent, and the average taxpayer is in the 2.64 percent bracket. The top marginal corporate tax rate is 36.8 percent.[363] Switzerland also maintains a capital gains tax at the regular business income rate.[364]

Factor #3: Government Intervention in the Economy
Score: 3- (Moderate level of government intervention)

The Swiss government consumes about 14 percent of GDP and, although it has begun to privatize the public corporation, remains heavily involved in certain parts of the economy. The government owns and operates most voice transmission and telecom-

---

361 Liechtenstein's economy is linked very closely to Switzerland's.

362 Economist Intelligence Unit, *ILT Country Reports: Switzerland*, May 1996.

363 Swiss corporate tax rates vary by canton, from 10 percent to 27 percent. This does not include an additional 9.8 percent federal tax. Thus, this figure is based on the highest canton tax and the federal tax taken together.

364 In Switzerland, capital gains are taxed as income at the regular income tax rate.

munications companies, for example, and its telecommunications corporation (the Postal and Telephone Authority, or PTT) does not allow private competition in markets it controls. Switzerland is one of the few countries with a constitution that limits the government's ability to impose economically costly policies; instead, the government must act by "emergency decrees" that are subject to public referendum. This severely limits its power to pass laws that restrict economic freedom.

Factor #4: Monetary Policy
Score: 1-Stable (Very low level of inflation)

Switzerland's average annual rate of inflation from 1985 to 1994 was 3.7 percent. In 1995, the inflation rate was about 1.8 percent; for most of 1996, it was around 1.6 percent

Factor #5: Capital Flows and Foreign Investment
Score: 2-Stable (Low barriers to foreign investment)

Switzerland is very open to foreign investment, although it restricts investment in hydroelectric and nuclear power plants, oil pipelines, the operation of television and radio broadcasting, and transportation. The government also restricts foreign ownership of real estate and limits the number of foreigners that may sit on corporate boards.

Factor #6: Banking
Score: 1-Stable (Very low level of restrictions on banking)

The Swiss banking system is one of the freest and most competitive in the world. Banks are free to offer a wide range of services with virtually no government interference.

Factor #7: Wage and Price Controls
Score: 2-Stable (Low level of wage and price controls)

Wages and prices in Switzerland are set mainly by the market. The agricultural sector is heavily regulated and subsidized, however, and this influences the prices of agricultural goods. There is no minimum wage.

Factor #8: Property Rights
Score: 1-Stable (Very high level of protection of private property)

From the standpoint of private property rights, Switzerland may well be one of the world's safest countries.

Factor #9: Regulation
Score: 3-Stable (Moderate level of regulation)

Establishing a business in Switzerland is easy. Although such industries as agriculture, television and broadcasting, and utilities are heavily regulated, regulations are applied evenly in most cases.

Factor #10: Black Market
Score: 1-Stable (Very low level of black market activity)

The black market in Switzerland is negligible. There is virtually no black market in pirated intellectual property.

Summary

Switzerland				**Overall Score**	**1.90**
Trade	2	Monetary Policy	1	Property Rights	1
Taxation	3	Foreign Investment	2	Regulation	3
Government Intervention	3	Banking	1	Black Market	1
		Wage and Prices	2		

SYRIA

Syria gained its independence from France in 1946 and has played a leading role in Arab politics and the Arab–Israeli struggle. Syria was plagued by political instability and a series of military coups until General Hafez al-Assad seized power in 1970; since then, it has developed a state-dominated socialist economy and has depended heavily on foreign aid, first from the Soviet Union and more recently from the oil-rich Persian Gulf states. In 1992, the Syrian government sought to spur private and foreign investment by loosening restrictive regulations, but its swollen public sector remains an obstacle to genuine free-market reform. The United States maintains trade sanctions against Syria because of the regime's long-standing support of terrorism.

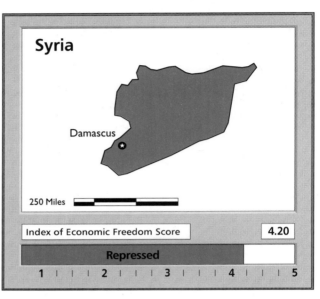

| Index of Economic Freedom Score | 4.20 |

Repressed

1   2   3   4   5

Factor #1: Trade Policy
Score: 5-Stable (Very high level of protectionism)

The average tariff rate in Syria is 21 percent. The customs services are both onerous and confusing, and all imports require a license. Many imports are banned.

Factor #2: Taxation

Score - Income taxation: 5-Stable (Very high tax rates)
Score - Corporate taxation: 5-Stable (Very high tax rates)
Final Taxation Score: 5-Stable (Very high tax rates)

Syria has a top income tax rate of 64 percent[365] and a top marginal corporate tax rate of over 50 percent.[366]

Factor #3: Government Intervention in the Economy
Score: 3-Stable (Moderate level of government intervention)

The Syrian government consumes about 25 percent of GDP, and the public sector accounts for about 36 percent of GDP overall.

---

365   The tax level on the average income is not available, and tax evasion is rampant.

366   Because Syria's tax system is complicated and unclear, this figure includes a host of taxes and fees, and is only a rough estimate.

Factor #4: Monetary Policy
Score: 5-Stable (Very high level of inflation)

Syria's average rate of inflation from 1985 to 1993 was 22.1 percent. In 1994, the inflation rate was about 10 percent.

Factor #5: Capital Flows and Foreign Investment
Score: 4-Stable (High barriers to foreign investment)

Syria requires government approval for all investments. Approval is denied in cases in which government monopolies are threatened.

Factor #6: Banking
Score: 5-Stable (Very high level of restrictions on banking)

The banking system in Syria is completely controlled by the government, which also owns all the major banks.

Factor #7: Wage and Price Controls
Score: 4-Stable (High level of wage and price controls)

Wages and prices in Syria are set mainly by the government.

Factor #8: Property Rights
Score: 4-Stable (Low level of protection of private property)

Private property is not safe in Syria. The legal and judicial system recognizes the free exchange of property and some contractual agreements, but private property also is subject to expropriation.

Factor #9: Regulation
Score: 2-Stable (Low level of regulation)

Establishing a business in Syria is easy if the business does not compete directly with the state-owned sector. The private sector is growing rapidly, and regulations often are ignored or not enforced.

Factor #10: Black Market
Score: 5-Stable (Very high level of black market activity)

The black market in Syria is quite large, although the smuggling of many consumer goods has prompted the government to expand its list of permitted legal imports. According to the Economist Intelligence Unit, "The strong public role in the economy and official over-valuation of the Syrian pound has led to a thriving parallel economy. Smuggling has ensured that industry has been able to obtain vital production inputs as well as a constant flow of consumer goods."[367]

---

367   Economist Intelligence Unit, *EIU Country Profile Reports,* 1996.

Summary

Syria				Overall Score	4.20
Trade	5	Monetary Policy	5	Property Rights	4
Taxation	5	Foreign Investment	4	Regulation	2
Government Intervention	3	Banking	5	Black Market	5
		Wage and Prices	4		

TANZANIA

Since gaining its independence from Great Britain in 1961, the East African nation of Tanzania has developed a socialist economy, nationalizing industry, collectivizing agriculture, and becoming one of the world's poorest nations. Despite tens of billions of dollars in foreign aid from the West, Tanzania remained mired in the economic doldrums until the late 1980s, at which time the government of President Ali Hassan Mwinyi began to introduce limited market reforms. Since then, some progress has been made in liberalizing the economy. Although Tanzania continues to rely heavily on foreign aid, relations with international donors have deteriorated in the past year because of the country's high levels of inflation and corruption. In 1996, Tanzania elected a new government amid fears of social and political instability and ethnic and religious tensions. It also has reduced barriers to trade.

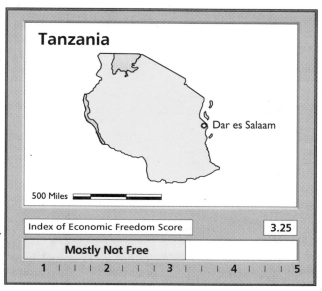

Tanzania

Dar es Salaam

500 Miles

| Index of Economic Freedom Score | 3.25 |

Mostly Not Free

1   2   3   4   5

Factor #1: Trade Policy

Score: 3+ (Moderate high level of protectionism)

Tanzania has an average tariff rate of 8.6 percent.[368] A major non-tariff barrier also is presented by an inefficient customs system. "Despite the existence of regulations and laws," reports the U.S. Department of Commerce, "the customs department is the greatest hindrance to importers throughout Tanzania. Clearance delays and extra-legal levies are commonplace when dealing with the Tanzanian Customs Department. These hindrances can cause undetermined delays when importing goods into the country and should be considered when deciding how best to bring products into the country."[369]

Factor #2: Taxation

Score - Income taxation: 3-Stable (Moderate tax rates)
Score - Corporate taxation: 3-Stable (Moderate tax rates)
Final Taxation Score: 3.5-Stable (High tax rates)

Tanzania's highest income tax rate is 30 percent.[370] The corporate tax rate is 40 percent for foreign firms and 35 percent for domestic firms.[371] Tanzania also has a progressive capital gains tax of up to 45 percent and a sales tax of up to 30 percent.

---

368   Based on total taxes on international trade as a percentage of total imports; from International Monetary Fund, *Government Financial Statistics 1995*.

369   U.S. Department of Commerce, *Country Commercial Guide*, 1996.

370   Tanzania's income tax score is based solely on the maximum rate.

Factor #3: Government Intervention in the Economy
Score: 3-Stable (Moderate level of government intervention)

The Tanzanian government consumes 8 percent of GDP. Although some industries have been privatized, inefficient state-owned enterprises continue to play a major role in the industrial sector, and government monopolies in agriculture still exist. Privatization has been impeded by intensifying nationalist rhetoric.

Factor #4: Monetary Policy
Score: 4-Stable (High level of inflation)

Tanzania's average annual rate of inflation from 1985 through 1994 was 23.4 percent. It is estimated that the current inflation rate is 35 percent.

Factor #5: Capital Flows and Foreign Investment
Score: 3-Stable (Moderate barriers to foreign investment)

Tanzania's new investment code will create a more favorable environment for foreign investment. A single-stop foreign investment approval office has been established; majority government participation in mining projects no longer is required. In addition, the government offers investment incentives, and there is a free trade zone on the island of Zanzibar. Foreign investment is constrained by bureaucratic impediments, however; these include the necessity to acquire business licenses, company registrations, and other documentation from a variety of often corrupt ministries. Foreign ownership of land is prohibited.

Factor #6: Banking
Score: 3-Stable (Moderate level of restrictions on banking)

At least five foreign banks have opened their doors in Tanzania over the past two years, and a Tanzanian-owned bank opened in 1995. These are the first private banks to take advantage of a 1991 law that allows private banking (the banking sector had been nationalized in 1967). Interest rates now are market-determined. Despite reforms, however, financial services still are provided largely by inefficient and corrupt state banks.

Factor #7: Wage and Price Controls
Score: 2-Stable (Low level of wage and price controls)

Most price controls have been removed in Tanzania, and the pricing of agriculture products has been liberalized. Wage controls are imposed indirectly by the government's extensive control of economic enterprise. Tanzania has a minimum wage.

Factor #8: Property Rights
Score: 3-Stable (Moderate level of protection of private property)

There has been no nationalization of private enterprises in Tanzania since 1973. There is, however, a great deal of resentment against individuals, particularly Asians, who have acquired privatized properties. Moreover, the questionable independence of the judiciary leaves property rights insecure.

---

371   This tax rate applies to the Tanzanian mainland and excludes Zanzibar.

Factor #9: Regulation
Score: 4-Stable (High level of regulation)

Excessive regulation is throttling the private sector in Tanzania, and corruption is rampant throughout the bureaucracy. Titles, deeds, business licenses, work permits, and other documentation must be secured through several different departments, although gaining approval to hire expatriate employees is not as problematic as in other African countries.

Factor #10: Black Market
Score: 4-Stable (High level of black market activity)

Tanzania's black market is huge. High textile tariffs have produced a vibrant market in smuggled textiles, and the free trade zone on Zanzibar has led to the smuggling of goods to the mainland. Tanzania's protection of intellectual property rights remains lax.

Summary

Tanzania					Overall Score	3.25
Trade	3	Monetary Policy	4	Property Rights	3
Taxation	3.5	Foreign Investment	3	Regulation	4
Government Intervention	3	Banking	3	Black Market	4
		Wage and Prices	2		

THAILAND

Thailand could be the next Asian tiger. From 1987 to 1991, its GDP grew at an annual rate of about 10 percent. Since then, the economy has grown by about 8 percent a year. The government has worked to continue economic liberalization. Political opponents, however, are trying to limit the expansion of increased foreign investment and ultimately could endanger continued reform. A coalition government is being formed after the November 1996 elections. Thailand's rapid growth has not been without difficulty. Roads, bridges, and rail systems, for example, have failed to keep up with industrial expansion, and there are pockets of poverty in most cities.

Factor #1: Trade Policy

Score: 3-Stable (Moderate level of protectionism)

Thailand has an average tariff rate of 9.3 percent. It also maintains non-tariff barriers in many areas. One in particular ("check prices") prevents imports by assessing tariffs at artificially high rates. The tariff on an imported product is assessed not according to its current price, but according to the price the last time the product entered the country. If the invoice price is lower, the Thai government can impose a tariff rate assessed at the higher previous price.

Factor #2: Taxation

Score - Income taxation: 2-Stable (Low tax rates)
Score - Corporate taxation: 3-Stable (Moderate tax rates)
Final Taxation Score: 3-Stable (Moderate tax rates)

Thailand's top marginal income tax rate is 37 percent, with the average income level taxed at a rate of 5 percent. The top corporate tax rate is 30 percent. Thailand also has a 30 percent capital gains tax and a 7 percent value-added tax.

Factor #3: Government Intervention in the Economy

Score: 1-Stable (Very low level of government intervention)

The government of Thailand consumes 10.1 percent of GDP, up from 9.7 percent a year ago. Privatization is moving forward; the government, for example, recently sold off shares in its major oil refinery.

Factor #4: Monetary Policy

Score: 1-Stable (Very low level of inflation)

Thailand's average annual rate of inflation from 1985 to 1994 was 5.1 percent. In 1995, the inflation rate was about 5.8 percent.

Factor #5: Capital Flows and Foreign Investment
Score: 3-Stable (Moderate barriers to foreign investment)

There are several restrictions on foreign investment in Thailand. The government, for example, restricts foreign entry into such service industries as banking and insurance. In addition, foreign banks are not accorded the same treatment as domestic banks and are subject to regulations prohibiting their expansion.

Factor #6: Banking
Score: 3-Stable (Moderate level of restrictions on banking)

Foreign banks are not permitted to own majority shares of any Thai banks; they also may not open branches in Thailand. Domestic banks are prohibited from participating in some financial activities (for example, real estate ventures).

Factor #7: Wage and Price Controls
Score: 3-Stable (Moderate level of wage and price controls)

The government of Thailand imposes price controls on such items as agricultural products, matches, milk, sugar, toiletries, utilities, and vegetable oil. It also has a minimum wage.

Factor #8: Property Rights
Score: 1-Stable (Very high level of protection of private property)

Expropriation is not likely in Thailand; the court system adequately protects property rights.

Factor #9: Regulation
Score: 3-Stable (Moderate level of regulation)

Thailand has a large but efficient bureaucracy. Because Thai bureaucrats tend to view business as exploitable, however, they often apply taxes, fines, and charges arbitrarily. These and other actions impose a moderate burden on business.

Factor #10: Black Market
Score: 2-Stable (Low level of black market activity)

Thailand's black market is confined mainly to drugs and prostitution. According to the U.S. Department of State, however, "copyright piracy of audio and video tapes and computer software remains widespread."[372]

---

372 State Department Report, 1996, p. 108.

Summary

Thailand						Overall Score	2.30
Trade	3	Monetary Policy	1		Property Rights	1
Taxation	3	Foreign Investment	3		Regulation	3
Government Intervention	1	Banking	3		Black Market	2
		Wage and Prices	3			

TRINIDAD AND TOBAGO

Trinidad was visited by Christopher Columbus in 1498 during his third voyage to the region. Spain established a permanent settlement in 1592, and the island remained under Spanish control until 1802. In 1888, Trinidad and Tobago were merged to create a single island nation that in 1958 became a member of the Federation of the West Indies, established by the United Kingdom. Trinidad and Tobago declared its independence in 1962 and adopted a new constitution in 1976. Since then, it has developed a generally free and prosperous economy. The government recently reduced taxes on corporate profits.

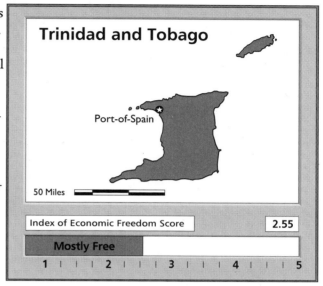

| Index of Economic Freedom Score | 2.55 |

Mostly Free

1 2 3 4 5

Factor #1: Trade Policy

Score: 5-Stable (Very high level of protectionism)

Trinidad and Tobago has passed a trade liberalization law that will reduce tariff rates drastically by 1998. The current average tariff rate is about 20 percent; but as a member of the Caribbean Common Market (CARICOM), the government is working to bring tariffs in line with the market's common external tariff, which now ranges between 5 percent and 20 percent for most goods. Trinidad and Tobago's principal non-tariff barriers include strict licensing requirements for such products as chicken parts, live chickens, sugar, oil seed, and tobacco paper.

Factor #2: Taxation

Score - Income taxation: 5-Stable (Very high tax rates)
Score - Corporate taxation: 3+ (Moderate tax rates)
Final Taxation Score: 4.5+ (Very high tax rates)

Trinidad and Tobago's top income tax rate is 38 percent, and the average taxpayer is in the 33 percent bracket. The top marginal corporate tax rate is 35 percent. Trinidad and Tobago also has a 35 percent capital gains tax and a 15 percent value-added tax.

Factor #3: Government Intervention in the Economy

Score: 2-Stable (Low level of government intervention)

The government of Trinidad and Tobago consumes about 15.7 percent of GDP and is heavily involved in various state-owned companies and industries. The government owns and operates the telecommunications industry, for example, and manages the sugar industry. It also is working to privatize many state-owned companies, however.

Factor #4: Monetary Policy
Score: 2- (Low level of inflation)

Trinidad and Tobago's average rate of inflation from 1985 to 1994 was 6.5 percent, up from 5.9 percent from 1985 to 1993 (primarily because of high inflation in 1993–1994). In 1995, the inflation rate was 5.3 percent.

Factor #5: Capital Flows and Foreign Investment
Score: 1-Stable (Very low barriers to foreign investment)

There are few restrictions on foreign investment in Trinidad and Tobago. Incentives are granted in the form of tax breaks and holidays.

Factor #6: Banking
Score: 2-Stable (Low level of restrictions on banking)

The banking system in Trinidad and Tobago is open and competitive. Banks can be wholly owned by foreigners.

Factor #7: Wage and Price Controls
Score: 2-Stable (Low level of wage and price controls)

Wages and prices in Trinidad and Tobago are set mainly by the market, although the government sets prices on some goods and services, such as sugar, schoolbooks, and pharmaceuticals. There is no national minimum wage.

Factor #8: Property Rights
Score: 1-Stable (Very high level of protection of private property)

Private property is safe in Trinidad and Tobago. The legal and judicial system is efficient.

Factor #9: Regulation
Score: 3-Stable (Moderate level of regulation)

Establishing a business in Trinidad and Tobago is a simple process, and regulations are applied evenly in most cases. Both regulations and bureaucratic red tape, however, are burdensome. Environmental regulations, for example, in addition to being rigid are enforced by 28 different agencies. The government has announced a plan to create a new agency that would consolidate all environmental regulations.

Factor #10: Black Market
Score: 3-Stable (Moderate level of black market activity)

Although Trinidad and Tobago has made significant strides in cracking down on black market activity, intellectual property laws are not enforced. This has created a black market in pirated videos, computer software, recorded music, and other products. According to the U.S. Department of State, "Although the [Copyright Act of 1995] provides protection of literary, musical and artistic works, computer software, sound recordings, audio-visual works and broadcasts, it is not enforced. Video rental outlets in Trinidad and Tobago are replete with pirated videos and operate openly."[373]

---

373   State Department Report, 1996, p. 432.

Summary

Trinidad and Tobago		Overall Score	2.55
Trade	5	Monetary Policy	2	Property Rights	1
Taxation	4.5	Foreign Investment	1	Regulation	3
Government Intervention	2	Banking	2	Black Market	3
		Wage and Prices	2		

TUNISIA

Tunisia gained its independence from France in 1956. In 1964, the government nationalized all foreign-owned land, causing prolonged tension with France. In the early 1990s, after more than 30 years of unproductive socialist economic policies, Tunisia began to reform its economy. Among the results: liberalized trade, a large privatization program, and cuts in government subsidies. Tunisia recently has cut government spending and reformed its banking sector; however, its privatization program has not succeeded in reducing the level of government intervention in the economy; thus, its score in this section is worse than it was last year.

Tunisia — Tunis

500 Miles

| Index of Economic Freedom Score | 2.75 |

Mostly Free

1   2   3   4   5

Factor #1: Trade Policy

Score: 5-Stable (Very high level of protectionism)

Tunisia has an average tariff rate of 25 percent. There are few non-tariff barriers.

Factor #2: Taxation

Score - Income taxation: 3-Stable (Moderate tax rates)
Score - Corporate taxation: 3-Stable (Moderate tax rates)
Final Taxation Score: 3.5-Stable (High tax rates)

Tunisia's top income tax rate is 35.5 percent, and the average income level is taxed at a rate of 15 percent. The top corporate tax rate is 35 percent. Tunisia also has a 35 percent capital gains tax, a 6 percent to 29 percent value-added tax, and a property tax.

Factor #3: Government Intervention in the Economy

Score: 3- (Moderate level of government intervention)

The Tunisian government consumes 16.2 percent of GDP. The government also has an aggressive privatization program in place and has identified some 20 to 30 companies to sell off this year, although several large state-owned companies continue to receive subsidies.

Factor #4: Monetary Policy

Score: 2-Stable (Low level of inflation)

Tunisia's average annual rate of inflation from 1985 to 1994 was 6.3 percent. In 1995, the inflation rate was 6.5 percent.

Factor #5: Capital Flows and Foreign Investment
Score: 2-Stable (Low barriers to foreign investment)

Tunisia is open to foreign investment, treats domestic firms the same as foreign firms, and offers attractive tax holidays to investors. It also prohibits, however, the ownership of land by non-Tunisians.

Factor #6: Banking
Score: 2-Stable (Low level of restrictions on banking)

Banks in Tunisia are becoming more independent from the government. Recent laws have eased some Central Bank regulations on foreign and domestic banks.

Factor #7: Wage and Price Controls
Score: 2-Stable (Low level of wage and price controls)

Tunisia has a minimum wage and maintains some price controls.

Factor #8: Property Rights
Score: 3-Stable (Moderate level of protection of private property)

Tunisia has an efficient and effective legal system. Property rights are relatively secure, although foreigners are not allowed to own land. Terrorism from Tunisia's radical Islamic fundamentalist movement, however, is a potential threat to private property.

Factor #9: Regulation
Score: 2-Stable (Low level of regulation)

Tunisia has a very efficient and well-functioning bureaucracy. Regulations are applied fairly in most cases, although sanitary, health, and product quality regulations can be somewhat burdensome.

Factor #10: Black Market
Score: 3-Stable (Moderate level of black market activity)

As the Tunisian market becomes more accessible to foreign goods, the black market, although still moderately large, is shrinking. There is moderate black market activity in pirated trademarks and prerecorded music and video tapes.

Summary

Tunisia				Overall Score	2.75
Trade	5	Monetary Policy	2	Property Rights	3
Taxation	3.5	Foreign Investment	2	Regulation	2
Government Intervention	3	Banking	2	Black Market	3
		Wage and Prices	2		

TURKEY

Turkey became an independent state in 1923 after the collapse of the Ottoman Empire. After decades of one-party rule, a multi-party system was adopted in 1950. Turkey receives large amounts of U.S. foreign aid, which has done little to promote economic growth. Instead, it often has been used to postpone badly needed economic reforms. During the 1980s, after broad free-market reforms were instituted under Prime Minister Turgut Özal, Turkey enjoyed an economic boom. Since then, the economy has been hard-hit both by the United Nations economic sanctions imposed on Iraq in 1990 and by an intensifying war against Kurdish separatists in eastern Turkey. Former Prime Minister Tansu Çiller's government halfheartedly implemented a privatization program, but future prospects for economic reform have been clouded

by the June 1996 formation of a coalition government headed by Prime Minister Necmettin Erbakan, leader of the pro-Islamist Refah Party. Turkey remains burdened with a large national debt, skyrocketing inflation, huge unemployment rates, and a growing regulatory burden, although some barriers to trade have been reduced recently.

Factor #1: Trade Policy
Score: 1+ (Very low level of protectionism)

Turkey has an average tariff rate of 3.6 percent, having reduced its tariffs from a trade-weighted average of 5 percent to meet the common external tariff of the European Union (EU). Although most import licenses have been eliminated, Turkey requires that importers obtain a certificate before selling their products in the country. This certificate is relatively easy to get, but the procedure is an administrative and financial burden for the importer. Beyond this, there are no significant restrictions on imports.

Factor #2: Taxation
Score - Income taxation: 5-Stable (Very high tax rates)
Score - Corporate taxation: 4-Stable (High tax rates)
Final Taxation Score: 5-Stable (Very high tax rates)

Turkey's top marginal income tax rate is 55 percent, and the average income level is taxed at a rate of 25 percent. The top corporate tax rate is 27.5 percent, down from 45 percent in 1995.[374] Turkey also has a value-added tax, which can reach as high as 23 percent, and a social contributions tax.

---

374   This rate includes a 10 percent surtax on the corporate income tax rate of 25 percent.

Factor #3: Government Intervention in the Economy
Score: 2-Stable (Low level of government intervention)

Turkey's government consumes around 7.6 percent of GDP and still owns significant portions of the economy. Although Turkey has a privatization program, the government owns many companies in such areas as ports, railways, iron and steel, airports, mineral mining, airlines, petroleum, and electronics.

Factor #4: Monetary Policy
Score: 5-Stable (Very high level of inflation)

Turkey's average annual rate of inflation from 1985 to 1994 was 65.8 percent. In 1995, the inflation rate was 93.5 percent.

Factor #5: Capital Flows and Foreign Investment
Score: 2-Stable (Low barriers to foreign investment)

Turkey is relatively open to foreign investment, but some barriers remain. Although there are no limits on how much of a Turkish business foreign investors may own, for example, local labor groups may pressure the government not to permit full foreign ownership of some newly privatized state-owned enterprises.

Factor #6: Banking
Score: 2-Stable (Low level of restrictions on banking)

Banks are open to foreign ownership in Turkey, and over 20 foreign banks have been established. Turkey has a very competitive domestic banking market, although several banks are state-owned. According to the U.S. Department of Commerce, the Turkish banking system is "still dominated by a few large state and commercial banks—some 75 percent of all assets are held by six or seven banks—and suffer[s] from a lack of transparent accounting practices and credit-rating agencies...."[375] By global standards, however, the level of restrictions on banking in Turkey is relatively low.

Factor #7: Wage and Price Controls
Score: 3-Stable (Moderate level of wage and price controls)

There are few official price controls in Turkey. Prices are controlled indirectly by large state-owned corporations, however, whose wholesale prices are controlled by the government (although the government plans to allow most of these corporations to set their own prices). Turkey has a minimum wage law.

Factor #8: Property Rights
Score: 2-Stable (High level of protection of private property)

Expropriation is unlikely in Turkey. The legal system, although imperfect, protects most private property. "There are effective means for enforcing property and contractual rights in Turkey," says the U.S. Department of Commerce. "There is no government interference in the court system. Turkey has a written and consistently applied commercial and bankruptcy law."[376] Court rulings, however, can take several months.

---

375   U.S. Department of Commerce, *Country Commercial Guide*, 1996.

Factor #9: Regulation
Score: 3- (Moderate level of regulation)

Turkey has reduced the size of its bureaucracy, imposed a performance evaluation test for civil servants, and centralized government economic decision-making under the prime minister. Its regulations are aimed at providing more freedom for businesses. Turkey now has few environmental laws, but more may be added in the future. There are, however, recent signs of bribery within the bureaucracy. "Despite significant progress in changing the system," reports Political Risk Services, "bribes are still necessary in order to bypass many bureaucratic obstacles at the middle and lower levels."[377]

Factor #10: Black Market
Score: 3+ (Moderate level of black market activity)

Turkey used to have a rather large black market, especially in such foreign goods as pirated recordings and printed material like books and magazines. As an obligation of joining the EU, however, it had to enact and enforce a variety of intellectual property rights laws. As a result, black market activity in pirated intellectual property has fallen dramatically, although there still is significant black market activity in pirated computer software. Some estimates place the piracy rate in computer software at 97 percent.[378]

Summary

Turkey				Overall Score	2.80
Trade	1	Monetary Policy	5	Property Rights	2
Taxation	5	Foreign Investment	2	Regulation	3
Government Intervention	2	Banking	2	Black Market	3
		Wage and Prices	3		

---

376   *Ibid.*

377   Political Risk Services, "Turkey," 1995, p. A7.

378   National Trade Data Bank and Economic Bulletin Board—products of STAT–USA, U.S. Department of Commerce.

UGANDA

Since gaining its independence from Great Britain in 1962, the central African country of Uganda has endured years of civil strife and economic deterioration. The decline of the Ugandan economy—once one of the more promising in Africa—was accelerated by government control and mismanagement. The government of president Yoweri Museveni, however, has been undertaking fairly dramatic economic liberalization over the past several years, and its policies have paid off with impressive economic growth. GDP rose by 7 percent in 1994 and almost 10 percent in 1995, and the economy continues to grow by about 6 percent a year. Uganda also is making some progress toward political liberalization. Presidential and parliamentary elections were held in May 1996 for the first time in 16 years.

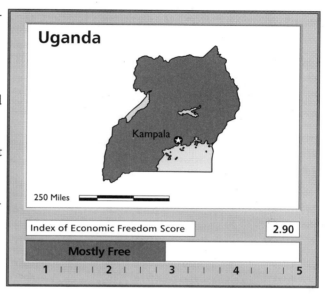

Uganda

Kampala

250 Miles

| Index of Economic Freedom Score | 2.90 |

Mostly Free

1 | | | 2 | | | 3 | | | 4 | | | 5

Factor #1: Trade Policy
Score: 4-Stable (High level of protectionism)

In 1993, Uganda lowered its highest import duty from 80 percent to 30 percent and reduced its lowest import duty from 50 percent to 10 percent.[379] The Ministry of Commerce reserves the right to restrict the import of goods that compete with local industries. Beer, cigarettes, and a few other imports are banned.

Factor #2: Taxation
Score - Income taxation: 4- (High tax rates)
Score - Corporate taxation: 3-Stable (Moderate tax rates)
Final Taxation Score: 4- (High tax rates)

The top income tax rate in Uganda is 30 percent, and the rate for the average income is 20 percent. The corporate tax rate is 30 percent. Uganda also has a 15 percent business turnover tax and a sales tax.

Factor #3: Government Intervention in the Economy
Score: 3-Stable (Moderate level of government intervention)

Uganda's government consumes 8.2 percent of GDP, down from 12 percent a year ago. The government recently privatized 14 state enterprises and liquidated 11 state

---

379 Uganda's average tariff rate was unavailable. The duty schedule cited here (taken from U.S. Department of Commerce, *Country Commercial Guide*, 1996) supports an assumption that Uganda's average tariff rate falls between 15 percent and 19 percent.

enterprises, including Uganda Air. Several other state-owned companies also are slated for privatization, although the government still owns the postal service, some major banking institutions, hotel chains, and similar companies.

Factor #4: Monetary Policy
Score: 5-Stable (Very high level of inflation)

The Museveni government has made significant strides in controlling Uganda's long-standing inflation problem. From 1985 to 1994, Uganda's average annual rate of inflation was 75.2 percent. In 1995, the inflation rate was about 9 percent.

Factor #5: Capital Flows and Foreign Investment
Score: 2-Stable (Low barriers to foreign investment)

The government of Uganda has moved to reduce foreign investment barriers. Foreign investors now may fully own Ugandan companies, and foreign-owned investments are treated in a nondiscriminatory manner. There also are investment incentives, such as some tax holidays. Foreigners, however, may not own agricultural land.

Factor #6: Banking
Score: 3-Stable (Moderate level of restrictions on banking)

Uganda's small financial sector is dominated by the government-owned Uganda Commercial and Cooperative Bank. Uganda is attempting, however, to establish liberal banking legislation. A number of foreign banks operate in Uganda, which also has many non-bank financial institutions, including 21 insurance companies.

Factor #7: Wage and Price Controls
Score: 1-Stable (Very low level of wage and price controls)

Price controls in Uganda were dismantled in January 1994. The abolition of coffee, cotton, and other government monopolies allowed the market to set wages and prices in these important sectors. There now are over 100 private coffee trading companies. Uganda does not have a minimum wage.

Factor #8: Property Rights
Score: 2-Stable (High level of protection of property rights)

The government is proceeding, albeit slowly, to privatize state assets. It also is returning property confiscated by previous regimes. The Departed Asians Property Custodian Board has returned over 4,000 properties in the past few years. Confiscation by the current government is highly unlikely. Tribal land tenure systems challenge private property rights, however, and the outright ownership of land is not permitted. Widespread corruption also works against the protection of property.

Factor #9: Regulation
Score: 3-Stable (Moderate level of regulation)

Although Uganda has made significant progress in making its bureaucracy more efficient, it remains plagued by corruption and graft. According to the U.S. Department of Commerce, "The main political issues which affect the business climate in Uganda are insecurity in sections of the north of the country, widespread corruption, and land tenure issues."[380] Regulations sometimes are applied arbitrarily, and bribes occasionally are necessary. The government has launched a new campaign to stamp out corruption, however, and has managed to make some progress. Thus, by global standards, Uganda's regulatory burden is moderate.

Factor #10: Black Market

Score: 2-Stable (Low level of black market activity)

The smuggling of cigarettes and oil is widespread in Uganda, and some electronic goods are smuggled to escape high tariffs. Black market activity has decreased as Uganda's economy has become more liberalized.

Summary

Uganda				Overall Score	2.90
Trade	4	Monetary Policy	5	Property Rights	2
Taxation	4	Foreign Investment	2	Regulation	3
Government Intervention	3	Banking	3	Black Market	2
		Wage and Prices	1		

---

380 U.S. Department of Commerce, *Country Commercial Guide*, 1996.

UKRAINE

Formerly part of the Soviet Union, Ukraine became an independent republic in 1991 but has been very slow to shake off its communist past. The government of Leonid Kravchuk was composed of old communist *apparatchiks* who resisted reform. As a result, Ukraine has made less progress than Russia in reforming its economy, although some progress has been achieved since the election of President Leonid Kuchma in 1994. For example, Kuchma moved to reduce subsidies to state-owned industries, privatize some state-owned enterprises, and reduce barriers to trade. But more needs to be done, and a corrupt and entrenched bureaucracy continues to stifle reform. Although some barriers to trade have been lowered recently, government spending has been increased.

Ukraine

❖ Kiev

250 Miles

Index of Economic Freedom Score	3.75
Mostly Not Free	

1 | | | 2 | | | 3 | | | 4 | | | 5

Factor #1: Trade Policy

Score: 4+ (High level of protectionism)

Tariffs in Ukraine often are applied arbitrarily, creating confusion for the importer. It is not uncommon for the same import to enter the country at different duty rates. Ukraine also has domestic production standards and certification requirements for all products, although it has made some progress in streamlining its customs procedures and reducing corruption within the customs services.

Factor #2: Taxation

Score - Income taxation: 5-Stable (Very high tax rates)
Score - Corporate taxation: 3+ (Moderate tax rates)
Final Taxation Score: 4.5+ (Very high tax rates)

Ukraine's top income tax rate is 40 percent, and the average income level is in the 30 percent bracket. The top corporate tax rate is 30 percent. Ukraine also has a 30 percent capital gains tax and a 20 percent value-added tax.

Factor #3: Government Intervention in the Economy

Score: 3+ (Moderate level of government intervention)

The government of Ukraine consumes about 11 percent of GDP. This understates, however, the level of government intervention in the economy. For example, the public sector still generates about 80 percent of GDP overall.[381]

---

381 "On the Pillars of Economic Reforms in Ukraine," The World Bank, Kyiv Office, Ukraine, March 1996.

Factor #4: Monetary Policy
Score: 5-Stable (Very high level of inflation)

In 1994, Ukraine's annual rate of inflation was over 500 percent. In 1995, it was 180 percent.[382]

Factor #5: Capital Flows and Foreign Investment
Score: 3-Stable (Moderate barriers to foreign investment)

Ukraine provides up to 10 years in tax holidays for large investments in such priority areas as advanced technologies for agricultural production and high-tech consumer goods. There are no regulatory restrictions on repatriation of capital or profits, and few restrictions on foreign ownership of businesses. Both the unpredictability of the country's laws and the slow progress of reform, however, deter foreign investors, and overt bureaucratic corruption remains a problem. Foreign investors often must pay bribes or kickbacks to facilitate necessary paperwork, permits, and licenses.

Factor #6: Banking
Score: 4-Stable (High level of restrictions on banking)

Ukraine's banking environment remains in regulatory chaos, subject to heavy government intervention and the strict control of credit. Although their number has grown, private banks remain in direct competition with government-controlled and government-subsidized institutions.

Factor #7: Wage and Price Controls
Score: 3-Stable (Moderate level of wage and price controls)

Wages for jobs in Ukraine's industrial sectors are controlled by the government. Some prices also are still controlled by the government, especially in housing, transportation services, and public utilities.

Factor #8: Property Rights
Score: 3+ (Moderate level of protection of private property)

Although its new constitution legally protects private property, Ukraine has not yet fully established a legal system that sufficiently enforces the laws that protect it. But recent government reforms in the judicial system are improving some courts. Some inefficiencies remain, however. Despite an ambitious government program to privatize large sectors of the economy, property remains subject to government expropriation.

Factor #9: Regulation
Score: 4-Stable (High level of regulation)

Regulations in Ukraine are applied haphazardly, posing a significant impediment to business activity. Another problem is widespread bureaucratic corruption, which sometimes results in steep fines for alleged violations of these regulations.[383]

---

382   Based on Consumer Price Index.

383   U.S. Department of Commerce, *Country Commercial Guide*, 1996.

Factor #10: Black Market
Score: 4-Stable (High level of black market activity)

Because Ukraine's economy is controlled by the government, much business activity is performed in the black market. A recent World Bank report estimates that as much as one-third to one-half of Ukraine's economic activity is performed in the black market.[384]

Summary

Ukraine					Overall Score	3.75
Trade	4	Monetary Policy	5		Property Rights	3
Taxation	4.5	Foreign Investment	3		Regulation	4
Government Intervention	3	Banking	4		Black Market	4
		Wage and Prices	3			

---

384 "On the Pillars of Economic Reforms in Ukraine."

UNITED ARAB EMIRATES

The United Arab Emirates (UAE) is a federation of seven emirates: Abu Dhabi, Ajman, Dubai, Fujairah, Ras al-Khaimah, Sharjah, and Umm al-Qaiwain. The individual emirates maintain considerable power over their own legal and economic affairs. Oil revenues are the government's single largest source of income, allowing it to keep import tariffs and taxation to a minimum, and most oil production remains in the hands of the government.

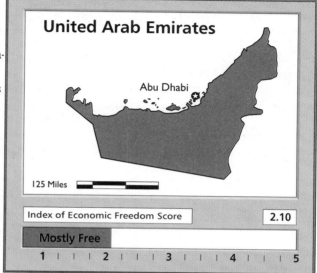

Index of Economic Freedom Score: 2.10

Mostly Free

1 2 3 4 5

Factor #1: Trade Policy

Score: 2-Stable (Low level of protectionism)

The UAE has an average tariff rate of 4 percent. A major non-tariff barrier is the government's requirement that (with the single exception of companies located in free trade zones in Dubai) all import-export companies must be wholly owned by UAE citizens.

Factor #2: Taxation

Score - Income taxation: 1-Stable (Very low tax rates)
Score - Corporate taxation: 1-Stable (Very low tax rates)
Final Taxation Score: 1-Stable (Very low tax rates)

The UAE has no income tax, no corporate tax, and no other significant taxes.

Factor #3: Government Intervention in the Economy

Score: 3-Stable (Moderate level of government intervention)

The UAE government consumes about 18.2 percent of GDP. Most of the country's GDP is derived from oil, nearly all of which is owned by the government. The government also heavily subsidizes such services as education, health care, and utilities. According to the U.S. Department of State, "The emirate and federal governments own full or partial shares of business, financial, and industrial enterprises."[385]

Factor #4: Monetary Policy

Score: 1-Stable (Very low level of inflation)

The UAE's average rate of inflation from 1990 to 1994 was 5.6 percent. In 1995, the inflation rate was about 5 percent, where it remains today.

---

385   State Department Report, 1996, p. 509.

Factor #5: Capital Flows and Foreign Investment
Score: 4-Stable (High barriers to foreign investment)

The UAE is open to some types of foreign investment, but there are significant restrictions. "By law," reports the U.S. Department of State, "foreign companies wishing to do business in the UAE must have a UAE national sponsor, agent, or distributor.... Foreigners cannot own land or buy stocks.... Agency and distributorship laws require that a business engaged in importing and distributing a foreign-made product must be 100 percent UAE national-owned. Other businesses must be at least 51 percent owned by nationals. A 1994 law extended these requirements to service businesses for the first time."[386] Exemptions are given to companies operating in the Jebel Ali Free Zone in Dubai. Some sectors, including oil and gas operations, petrochemicals, electricity, and water desalination, are closed to foreign investment.

Factor #6: Banking
Score: 3-Stable (Moderate level of restrictions on banking)

The UAE banking system is large and competitive. The government's largely liberal economic policies have led to a proliferation of private banks. The government, however, also is trying to slow the creation of new banks. According to the U.S. Department of State, "Within the past three years, the Central Bank has increased the degree of its regulatory activities...."[387] In addition, even though there is no corporate income tax, there is a 30 percent tax on bank earnings.

Factor #7: Wage and Price Controls
Score: 3-Stable (Moderate level of wage and price controls)

Wages and prices in the UAE are set mainly by the market, although the government continues to offer subsidies to many businesses, thus affecting the price of utilities, health care, education, and food. The government also owns many services outright. "In Abu Dhabi," reports the U.S. Department of State, "90 percent of residential and commercial construction is carried out by a government agency that builds and manages commercial and residential rental property on behalf of nominal national landlords."[388] Such government intervention affects free market pricing.

Factor #8: Property Rights
Score: 1-Stable (Very high level of protection of private property)

Private property is protected in the UAE. The legal and judicial system is effective and modern.

Factor #9: Regulation
Score: 2-Stable (Low level of regulation)

Establishing a business in the UAE is easy if the business does not compete directly with state-owned concerns. Regulations are applied evenly in most cases.

---

386 *Ibid.,* pp. 507–512.

387 *Ibid.*

388 *Ibid.*

Factor #10: Black Market

Score: 1-Stable (Very low level of black market activity)

The black market in the UAE is negligible. The government has passed three laws protecting intellectual property, and the economy is virtually free of pirated material.

Summary

United Arab Emirates					Overall Score	2.10
Trade	2	Monetary Policy	1	Property Rights	1
Taxation	1	Foreign Investment	4	Regulation	2
Government Intervention	3	Banking	3	Black Market	1
		Wage and Prices	3		

UNITED KINGDOM

The United Kingdom (UK) is a constitutional monarchy that has gone from periods of experimentation with socialism to spurts of free-market capitalism. Facing near economic collapse in the 1970s, the UK turned to free-market reform under the leadership of Prime Minister Margaret Thatcher. The result was extensive market liberalization that made the British economy one of the strongest in the European Union. The UK's uncertain political future, however, could lead to a new wave of socialist economic policies, jeopardizing this record of economic success.

Index of Economic Freedom Score — 1.95

Free

1   2   3   4   5

Factor #1: Trade Policy

Score: 2-Stable (Low level of protectionism)

The UK has an average tariff rate of 3.6 percent. Although some progress has been made in opening the British market to imports, some non-tariff barriers still remain in telecommunications and the energy industry.

Factor #2: Taxation

Score - Income taxation: 5-Stable (Very high tax rates)
Score - Corporate taxation: 3-Stable (Moderate tax rates)
Final Taxation Score: 4.5-Stable (Very high tax rates)

The UK's top income tax rate is 40 percent, and the average income level is taxed at a rate of 24 percent (the result of a tax cut enacted in April 1996). The top corporate tax rate is 33 percent. The UK also has a 33 percent capital gains tax and a 17.5 percent value-added tax.

Factor #3: Government Intervention in the Economy

Score: 2-Stable (Low level of government intervention)

The British government consumes about 22 percent of GDP. Unlike some of its European neighbors, the UK is making progress in privatization, a sign that the government is becoming less involved in the market. For example, the government currently is engaged in privatizing British Rail and British Energy. In addition, both industries are open to some foreign investment. British Coal, a mining company, and the London busing system also have been privatized.

Factor #4: Monetary Policy

Score: 1-Stable (Very low level of inflation)

The UK's average annual rate of inflation from 1985 to 1994 was 5.2 percent. In 1995, the inflation rate was 2.9 percent.

Factor #5: Capital Flows and Foreign Investment
Score: 2-Stable (Low barriers to foreign investment)

Many non-European companies use Britain as a base for setting up businesses in Europe. The UK also is the largest recipient of U.S. and Japanese foreign investment in Europe. Despite a generally hospitable environment, however, the UK still restricts foreign investment in the aerospace industry and public utilities.

Factor #6: Banking
Score: 2-Stable (Low level of restrictions on banking)

Britain's banking system is fairly open to competition. Most credit is supplied by privately owned banks, and banks are permitted to sell securities, insurance policies, and real estate, as well as to invest in industrial firms. The 1987 Banking Act, however, gives the Bank of England the right to prevent the foreign ownership of more than 15 percent of any British bank.

Factor #7: Wage and Price Controls
Score: 2-Stable (Low level of wage and price controls)

Prices in the UK are set largely by the market, although prices charged by public utilities are fixed by the government. In addition, the government also controls the prices of some products and services, including matches, milk, and taxi fares. The only area subject to minimum wage laws is agriculture.

Factor #8: Property Rights
Score: 1-Stable (Very high level of protection of private property)

The current government of Prime Minister John Major has continued the privatization policies of Margaret Thatcher. Most of Britain's economy is private; and the court system, in addition to being efficient, and provides maximum protection of private property.

Factor #9: Regulation
Score: 2-Stable (Low level of regulation)

It is easy to open a business in the UK. Although its regulatory system can be somewhat burdensome, Britain also has done more than most other industrialized countries to reduce the level of regulation. The UK's regulatory regime, for example, permits companies to self-regulate their industries. Businesses subscribe voluntarily to a code of conduct that, if violated, causes them to be penalized by consumers who see their products as shoddy. There are few environmental laws in Britain. The UK has increased its use of unemployment and other social welfare regulation, however, in attempting to deal with the unemployment and worker displacement caused by privatization of state-owned companies.

Factor #10: Black Market
Score: 1-Stable (Very low level of black market activity)

The UK's black market, like those in the rest of the developed world, is restricted to drugs, guns, and other illegal activities.

Summary

United Kingdom					Overall Score	1.95
Trade	2	Monetary Policy	1		Property Rights	1
Taxation	4.5	Foreign Investment	2		Regulation	2
Government Intervention	2	Banking	2		Black Market	1
		Wage and Prices	2			

UNITED STATES

The United States remains one of the world's most industrialized nations and produces almost one-quarter of the world's GNP. It is the biggest exporter and importer of goods, has the largest economy, and enjoys the highest standard of living. It has one of the world's freest economies—but not *the* freest. The United States has been reducing its level of economic freedom since the 1940s. As a result, economic growth and living standards have leveled off as economic activity has been hindered by increased government intrusion. Despite current moves within Congress to deregulate the economy and cut government spending and taxation, the government of the United States has yet to cut taxes or reform its tax system.

Factor #1: Trade Policy
Score: 2-Stable (Low level of protectionism)

The average U.S. tariff rate is 3.3 percent. The United States maintains trade restrictions on dairy products, glass, machine tools, steel, sugar, textiles, and other items. It also is an aggressive user of unilateral trade retaliation. Although the United States was a major signatory of the General Agreement on Tariffs and Trade and supported creation of the new World Trade Organization, the Clinton Administration has done little to open the U.S. market to imports.

Factor #2: Taxation
Score - Income taxation: 4-Stable (High tax rates)
Score - Corporate taxation: 3-Stable (Moderate tax rates)
Final Taxation Score: 4-Stable (High tax rates)

The top income tax rate in the United States is 39.6 percent, and the average taxpayer is in the 15 percent bracket. The top marginal corporate tax rate is 35 percent. The United States also has state and local taxes, sales taxes, and property taxes, in addition to one of the highest inheritance taxes in the industrialized world. Some of these taxes may reach as high as 100 percent. Some members of Congress are considering reducing taxes and adopting either a flat income tax or some form of national sales tax.

Factor #3: Government Intervention in the Economy
Score: 2-Stable (Low level of government intervention)

The United States government consumes about 18.8 percent of GDP. Congress, led by a Republican majority, has mapped out a budget plan that would significantly reduce government consumption while boosting economic activity.

Factor #4: Monetary Policy
Score: 1-Stable (Very low level of inflation)

From 1985 to 1994, the United States maintained a stable inflation rate of 3.3 percent. In 1995, the rate of inflation was 2.8 percent, where it has remained for most of 1996.

Factor #5: Capital Flows and Foreign Investment
Score: 2-Stable (Low barriers to foreign investment)

The United States welcomes foreign investment, which accounts for some 11.5 percent of U.S. manufacturing employment and 5.2 percent of overall employment; but it also continues to restrict foreign investment in commercial and civil aviation, telecommunications, public utilities, and industries considered vital to national security.

Factor #6: Banking
Score: 2-Stable (Low level of restrictions on banking)

The U.S. banking system is minimally regulated by federal, state, and local governments. There are some limits on foreign banks, such as restrictions on the extent to which foreign interests may own U.S. banks. There has been some progress recently in achieving further deregulation of banking. Congress, for example, passed legislation that would permit banks to open branches across state lines—something foreign banks already were allowed to do. Other reforms would allow banks to engage in both commercial and savings services.

Factor #7: Wage and Price Controls
Score: 2-Stable (Low level of wage and price controls)

Wages and prices in the United States are set by the market, although the government continues to set prices on some goods and services, such as agricultural goods (particularly peanuts), by purchasing excess production, closing borders to imports, and manipulating prices. The government also controls prices of some dairy products by providing subsidies to dairy farmers. In addition, the United States maintains a federally imposed minimum wage standard.

Factor #8: Property Rights
Score: 1-Stable (Very high level of protection of private property)

Private property is a fundamental principle in the United States. The American legal and judicial system is efficient and provides adequate protection of private property. The chances of government expropriation without just compensation are very low. There are situations, however, in which governments at various levels have been known to expropriate property without due process—for example, in cases involving suspected drug dealers or those who proposition prostitutes.

Factor #9: Regulation
Score: 2-Stable (Low level of regulation)

Establishing a business in the United States is easy and affordable. Regulations are applied evenly and consistently in most cases, although they also can make it more difficult for businesses to keep their doors open. Government regulation now costs American consumers $580 billion each year. Moreover, many regulations—for example, the Americans With Disabilities Act, various civil rights regulations, health and product safety standards, and food and drug labeling requirements—although well-intentioned, are also onerous. If current trends continue, the U.S. economy eventually may qualify as heavily regulated; by global standards, however, the level of regulation remains low.

Factor #10: Black Market

Score: 1-Stable (Very low level of black market activity)

The black market in the United States is confined to goods and services— narcotics, prostitution, guns, and stolen goods—that are considered harmful to public safety.

Summary

United States				Overall Score	1.90
Trade	2	Monetary Policy	1	Property Rights	1
Taxation	4	Foreign Investment	2	Regulation	2
Government Intervention	2	Banking	2	Black Market	1
		Wage and Prices	2		

URUGUAY

Uruguay became independent from Brazil in 1828. Today, it has a relatively free and open market. It also used to be a major international banking center until statist economic policies introduced in the 1960s brought economic stagnation. Uruguay is wealthy by Latin American standards and has a relatively high level of literacy. In addition, the current government has been working to liberalize the economy and bring back respectable levels of economic growth. Recent reforms in the banking sector promote greater competition among both foreign and domestic banks, for example, and the government has reduced barriers to trade. Many companies in Uruguay, however, still are owned by the state.

| Index of Economic Freedom Score | 2.70 |

Mostly Free

1   2   3   4   5

Factor #1: Trade Policy

Score: 2+ (Low level of protectionism)

Uruguay has an average tariff rate of around 8 percent, down from 11 percent in 1992. Few other restrictions on imports remain in effect. Import licenses are required, but they are easy to obtain and do not restrict imports.

Factor #2: Taxation

Score - Income taxation: 1-Stable (Very low tax rates)
Score - Corporate taxation: 3-Stable (Moderate tax rates)
Final Taxation Score: 3-Stable (Moderate tax rates)

There is no income tax in Uruguay. The top corporate tax rate is 30 percent. Uruguay also has a value-added tax of 23 percent, up from 22 percent in 1995.

Factor #3: Government Intervention in the Economy

Score: 3- (Moderate level of government intervention)

Uruguay's government consumes 13.4 percent of GDP, down from 14 percent a year ago, and the government has made significant progress in privatizing state-owned industries. For example, many of the country's port facilities and electricity generation plants were privatized in 1993, and the natural gas company was privatized in 1994. The government continues to play a significant role in the economy, however, and still owns many banks and financial companies as well as the telephone company (ANTEL).

Factor #4: Monetary Policy

Score: 5-Stable (Very high level of inflation)

Uruguay's average annual rate of inflation from 1985 to 1994 was 73.9 percent. In 1995, the inflation rate was around 35 percent.

Factor #5: Capital Flows and Foreign Investment
Score: 2-Stable (Low barriers to foreign investment)

Uruguay remains relatively open to foreign investment. Among the exceptions are the so-called strategic industries, which include telecommunications and transportation, in addition to banks and the press. There are some tax incentives for foreign investment.

Factor #6: Banking
Score: 2-Stable (Low level of restrictions on banking)

Foreign banks are assuming a larger role in Uruguay's banking industry. Domestic banks are permitted to sell securities, but they are prohibited from involvement in insurance, real estate, and investment transactions.

Factor #7: Wage and Price Controls
Score: 2-Stable (Low level of wage and price controls)

Uruguay maintains a minimum wage. Most prices are determined by the market, although some price controls remain in effect on such items as bread, milk, alcohol, and fuels. In addition, the list of products subject to price controls changes frequently.

Factor #8: Property Rights
Score: 2-Stable (Low level of protection of private property)

Uruguay's court and legal system is becoming more efficient. Private property no longer is in danger of expropriation, although bureaucratic corruption often results in weak enforcement of private property laws.

Factor #9: Regulation
Score: 3-Stable (Moderate level of regulation)

Establishing a business in Uruguay is a lengthy process. The bureaucracy is cumbersome and inefficient, and the government has yet to dismantle some of its most burdensome regulations, such as strict environmental requirements.

Factor #10: Black Market
Score: 3-Stable (Moderate level of black market activity)

Like most Latin American countries, Uruguay has its share of black market activity. Transportation and labor, for example, are frequently found on the black market. There also is considerable black market activity in pirated computer software, video and tape recordings, and compact discs. By global standards, however, these activities remain moderate.

Summary

Uruguay					Overall Score	2.70
Trade	2	Monetary Policy	5	Property Rights	2
Taxation	3	Foreign Investment	2	Regulation	3
Government Intervention	3	Banking	2	Black Market	3
		Wage and Prices	2		

VENEZUELA

Venezuela today is a multi-party electoral democracy. Along with Italy, Venezuela was a co-founder of the Organization of Petroleum Exporting Countries, and its economy has relied heavily on oil exports. During the period from 1989 to 1992, Venezuela's government made some progress toward free-market reforms, but this began to change when President Rafael Caldera took office in February 1994. Caldera turned away from free-market policies and partially restored the state's control over the economy. In 1996, the Venezuelan government signed a new agreement with the International Monetary Fund, which has been pressuring the government to reinstitute some degree of fiscal responsibility.

Venezuela

Caracas

500 Miles

Index of Economic Freedom Score	3.60
Mostly Not Free	

1   2   3   4   5

Factor #1: Trade Policy

Score: 4-Stable (High level of protectionism)

Venezuela has an average tariff rate of about 10 percent.[388] Non-tariff barriers include direct bans on imports of poultry and pork.

Factor #2: Taxation

Score - Income taxation: 4-Stable (High tax rates)
Score - Corporate taxation: 3-Stable (Moderate tax rates)
Final Taxation Score: 4-Stable (High tax rates)

Venezuela's top marginal income tax rate is 34 percent, and the average income is taxed at a rate of 16 percent. The top corporate tax rate is 34 percent. Venezuela also has a 12.5 percent to 32.5 percent value-added tax and a 34 percent capital gains tax.

Factor #3: Government Intervention in the Economy

Score: 3- (Moderate level of government intervention)

The Venezuelan government consumes around 7 percent of GDP, down from 11.7 percent in 1993, and remains heavily involved in the economy. "The government continues to exercise considerable control over the economy, including price and exchange controls," reports the Economist Intelligence Unit. "And although it has repeatedly stressed its commitment to selling state assets through the country's privatization program, the administration continues to enact policies that ensure the failure of state sales."[389]

---

388   Based on total taxes on international trade as a percentage of total imports; from International Monetary Fund, *Government Financial Statistics 1995*.

389   Economist Intelligence Unit, *ILT Reports*, April 1996, p. 2.

Factor #4: Monetary Policy
Score: 5-Stable (Very high level of inflation)

Venezuela's average annual rate of inflation from 1985 to 1994 was 36.6 percent. In 1995, the inflation rate was 41 percent. In 1996, it has risen to over 100 percent.

Factor #5: Capital Flows and Foreign Investment
Score: 3-Stable (Moderate barriers to foreign investment)

Most industries in Venezuela are open to foreign investment, although some significant restrictions remain in effect. Foreign ownership of a few service industries, including television, radio, the Spanish-language press, and some professional services, is limited to no more than 19.9 percent.

Factor #6: Banking
Score: 3-Stable (Moderate level of restrictions on banking)

Although most restrictions on foreign bank branches have been removed, some 50 percent of all banks are owned by the government. Foreign banks from countries that provide reciprocal treatment now may open 100 percent foreign-owned subsidiaries or purchase 100 percent of existing banks.

Factor #7: Wage and Price Controls
Score: 3-Stable (Moderate level of wage and price controls)

Venezuela maintains a minimum wage, and the government has wide authority to impose price controls, which remain in effect on some basic foodstuffs, medicines, fuel, and public transportation.

Factor #8: Property Rights
Score: 3-Stable (Moderate level of protection of private property)

Private property is a staple of Venezuela's economy, but the government is prone to expropriation, and property is not fully protected by the court system.

Factor #9: Regulation
Score: 3-Stable (Moderate level of regulation)

Opening a business in Venezuela is not difficult, although the recent economic downturn has led to increased corruption. Thus, some regulations are not applied consistently.

Factor #10: Black Market
Score: 5-Stable (Very high level of black market activity)

Wherever prices remain state-controlled (as in the transportation services), the black market is large. The black market also provides about 40 percent of labor services in Caracas. Although Venezuela has established intellectual property laws, enforcement remains lax, and piracy in copyrighted material remains a problem.

Summary

Venezuela		Overall Score	3.60

Trade	4	Monetary Policy	5	Property Rights	3
Taxation	4	Foreign Investment	3	Regulation	3
Government Intervention	3	Banking	3	Black Market	5
		Wage and Prices	3		

VIETNAM

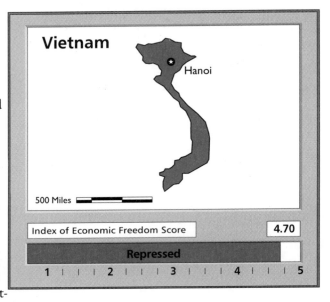

Vietnam

★ Hanoi

500 Miles

| Index of Economic Freedom Score | 4.70 |

Repressed

1   2   3   4   5

Divided into warring factions for most of its early history, Vietnam was occupied by France in the 19th century. After World War II, revolutionaries in northern Vietnam called on the French to withdraw. In 1954, France agreed to withdraw from the northern part of Vietnam and moved south below the 17th parallel. The communists in the north then established the Democratic Republic of Vietnam, while non-communist Vietnamese in the south established the Republic of South Vietnam. After the defeat of South Vietnam in 1975, the Hanoi government established its communist system in all of Vietnam. In 1995, Vietnam joined the Association of South East Asian Nations (ASEAN). Also in 1995, the Clinton Administration decided to extend diplomatic relations to Hanoi. As a result, U.S. companies will be free to invest in Vietnam. Even though the regime has begun to liberalize some areas of its centrally planned economy, Vietnam remains a communist dictatorship, and the state still owns most of the means of production.

Factor #1: Trade Policy
Score: 5-Stable (Very high level of protectionism)

Vietnam's corrupt bureaucracy creates very high barriers to imports. Many imports are confiscated by corrupt border officials. According to the Economist Intelligence Unit, "The country's most serious trade problem is smuggling, with illicit imports (not only consumer items but also some essential industrial inputs such as newsprint, steel, fertilizer, pesticides, and chemicals) amounting to the equivalent of one-fourth to one-third of the official import bill."[390] In some cases, the government attempts to block consumer good imports in favor of raw materials. "From numerous accounts," reports the U.S. Department of Commerce, "Vietnam has been careful to sharply limit imported consumer goods to less than 20 percent of its total import bill, so the composition of imports tends to be skewed toward capital and intermediate goods and inputs for exports."[391]

---

390   Economist Intelligence Unit, "Vietnam," *ILT Reports*, April 1996.

391   U.S. Department of Commerce, *Country Commercial Guide*, 1996.

Factor #2: Taxation

Score - Income taxation: 5-Stable (Very high tax rates)
Score - Corporate taxation: 5-Stable (Very high tax rates)
Final Taxation Score: 5-Stable (Very high tax rates)

Vietnam's top income tax rate is 60 percent, with the average income level taxed at a rate of 40 percent. The tax on foreign corporate profits is as high as 45 percent.[392] Because the economy is centrally planned and most businesses are owned by the government, however, tax rates are actually much higher than these levels suggest.

Factor #3: Government Intervention in the Economy

Score: 5-Stable (Very high level of government intervention)

The government's progress toward privatization has been anemic. The government still owns most of the means of production, still maintains central planning, and has yet to subject the economy to the basic principles of supply and demand.

Factor #4: Monetary Policy

Score: 5-Stable (Very high level of inflation)

From 1990 to 1994, Vietnam's average annual rate of inflation was 33.2 percent. For 1995, the inflation rate was about 8.8 percent.

Factor #5: Capital Flows and Foreign Investment

Score: 4-Stable (High barriers to foreign investment)

Among the world's remaining communist states, Vietnam has gone farther to open its economy to foreign investment than either Cuba or North Korea. Yet much of the economy remains inaccessible to foreigners, investments still need prior government approval, and repatriation of profits remains subject to some restrictions. Even though 100 percent ownership is allowed in principle, few investments have been approved. The government heavily favors 50–50 joint ventures with foreign firms. According to a Political Risk Services analysis, "Despite assurances that foreign investors will be able to repatriate their profits, the level of informal restriction and bureaucratic obstruction is high."[393] The government frequently raids the offices of foreign companies, often without warning, to determine whether they are complying with Vietnamese laws.

Factor #6: Banking

Score: 4-Stable (High level of restrictions on banking)

Banking services in Vietnam are reserved almost exclusively for the government, although attempts have been made to modernize the financial system. The few private banks that do exist are heavily influenced by the government and operate at a disadvantage because of the unfair competition from large state-owned banks.

---

392   This is the top rate for companies without foreign-owned capital. Companies with foreign-owned capital are taxed at a top rate of 25 percent.

393   Political Risk Services, "Vietnam," New York, 1995.

Factor #7: Wage and Price Controls
Score: 4-Stable (High level of wage and price controls)

At least 50 percent of the goods produced by Vietnamese companies are subject to some type of central planning. Vietnam has lifted price controls on some products, including steel and printing paper, but controls on the prices of electricity, water, telecommunications, and transportation services remain in effect. Many wages still are set by the government.

Factor #8: Property Rights
Score: 5-Stable (Very low level of protection of private property)

The Vietnamese government is tolerating more private ownership of property, but property still enjoys almost no legal protection. Moreover, Vietnam still does not fully permit foreign companies to seek arbitration in foreign courts; all disputes must be settled within Vietnam. The court system is subject to extensive government influence, especially when disputes arise among parties with close ties to the government.

Factor #9: Regulation
Score: 5-Stable (Very high level of regulation)

Among the many obstacles to private enterprise in Vietnam, according to the U.S. Department of Commerce, are "a poor physical, legal, and financial infrastructure; a lack of capital; and the bureaucratic mentality of a command economy, coupled with corruption."[394] Although the Vietnamese government is reducing some regulations, it remains a major impediment to entrepreneurship and the creation of new private businesses. The government establishes work weeks, forces companies to provide paid vacations and contribute to employee health and social security plans, and uses environmental regulations (the number of which is increasing) to penalize businesses.

Factor #10: Black Market
Score: 5+ (Very high level of black market activity)

Vietnam has a large black market in such basic goods and services as foodstuffs and labor. Due to the miserable condition of Vietnam's banks, there also is a growing black market in private financing. According to the U.S. Department of Commerce, "People with excess cash can lend money to others—often private businessmen—who have no recourse to bank financing or who prefer to keep their transactions secret to avoid paying taxes. This 'informal' lending takes place at interest rates much higher than bank rates."[395] Such "loan sharking" raises business costs and encourages criminal activity. Finally, although Vietnam has passed laws protecting intellectual property, enforcement remains lax. As a result, there is significant piracy in computer software and other items.

---

394   "Many U.S. Firms Show Interest in Vietnam," *Business America*, National Trade Data Bank and Economic Bulletin Board—products of STAT–USA, U.S. Department of Commerce.

395   National Trade Data Bank and Economic Bulletin Board—products of STAT–USA, U.S. Department of Commerce.

Summary

Vietnam				Overall Score	4.70
Trade	5	Monetary Policy	5	Property Rights	5
Taxation	5	Foreign Investment	4	Regulation	5
Government Intervention	5	Banking	4	Black Market	5
		Wage and Prices	4		

WESTERN SAMOA

The Central South Pacific Island of Western Samoa gained its independence from a New Zealand–administered United Nations trusteeship in 1962. Its primarily agricultural economy mainly produces coconuts, cocoa, bananas, and taro. As a result, most consumer goods and raw materials must be imported, creating a chronic trade deficit.

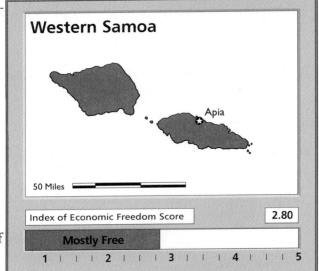

Factor #1: Trade Policy
Score: 3-Stable (Moderate level of protectionism)

Western Samoa has a 7.5 percent tariff rate for most so-called essential items and a varying tariff rate of between 5 percent and 75 percent on many consumer goods; the average rate is about 9 percent. The principal non-tariff barrier is a stringent inspection process that can delay entry of some imports.

Factor #2: Taxation
Score - Income taxation: 3-Stable (Moderate tax rates)
Score - Corporate taxation: 4-Stable (High tax rates)
Final Taxation Score: 4-Stable (High tax rates)

Western Samoa's top income tax rate is 45 percent, and the average taxpayer is in the 10 percent bracket. The top marginal corporate tax rate is 39 percent.[396] Western Samoa also has a 10 percent goods and services tax and a 10 percent to 15 percent tax on interest, royalties, and dividends.

Factor #3: Government Intervention in the Economy
Score: 2-Stable (Low level of government intervention)

The government of Western Samoa consumes 17.9 percent of GDP.

Factor #4: Monetary Policy
Score: 2 Stable (Low level of inflation)

Western Samoa's average annual rate of inflation from 1985 to 1994 was 10.6 percent. In 1995, the inflation rate was 1 percent.

---

396 This is the rate for resident companies; foreign companies pay a top rate of 48 percent.

Factor #5: Capital Flows and Foreign Investment
Score: 3-Stable (Moderate barriers to foreign investment)

Foreigners may lease land in Western Samoa but are not permitted to own it. Permission must be granted for most investments, although registering foreign investments is becoming easier. In this respect, export industries are favored by the government.

Factor #6: Banking
Score: 3-Stable (Moderate level of restrictions on banking)

The banking system in Western Samoa is small. The government continues to be a joint venture partner in at least one commercial bank, the Bank of Western Samoa.

Factor #7: Wage and Price Controls
Score: 3-Stable (Moderate level of wage and price controls)

Wages and prices in Western Samoa are set mainly by the market, although the government mandates a minimum wage. The government controls some prices, mainly in the utilities sector; it also influences prices through its direct ownership of companies (for example, in the agricultural sector).

Factor #8: Property Rights
Score: 3-Stable (Moderate level of protection of private property)

The government owns large tracts of public land, which are closed to business development as a result. Most private land already has been developed.

Factor #9: Regulation
Score: 3-Stable (Moderate level of regulation)

Establishing a business in Western Samoa is relatively easy, and regulations are applied evenly in most cases, although some regulations make it hard for businesses to operate. The government, for example, requires all businesses to contribute 5 percent of gross earnings for each Western Samoan employee to a retirement fund, the Western Samoan National Provident Fund; it also requires that employees contribute 5 percent of their earnings to this fund. Businesses are not free to hire foreigners if there is a Western Samoan who can perform the same job.

Factor #10: Black Market
Score: 2-Stable (Low level of black market activity)

The black market in Western Samoa is negligible.

Summary

Western Samoa		Overall Score	2.80

Trade	3	Monetary Policy	2	Property Rights	3
Taxation	4	Foreign Investment	3	Regulation	3
Government Intervention	2	Banking	3	Black Market	2
		Wage and Prices	3		

YEMEN

Yemen is one of the oldest regions of human habitation. After centuries of domination by various empires, including the Romans and the Ottomans, the southern part of the country became a British protectorate in 1839. The northern part of the country was controlled by Turkey until after World War I and became fully independent in 1934. Inspired by its neighbor's success, Southern Yemen fought to gain its own independence from Great Britain in 1967. A Marxist government took over southern Yemen soon afterward, sending the economy into a nosedive. In 1990, after two decades of political and civil chaos, North and South Yemen united to form a single country. Limited progress toward economic liberalization was cut short by the outbreak of civil war in 1994; since 1994, there has been little economic growth.

Index of Economic Freedom Score	3.90
Mostly Not Free	

Factor #1: Trade Policy
Score: 5-Stable (Very high level of protectionism)

Tariffs in Yemen range from 5 percent to 50 percent; the average tariff is about 20 percent. Special duties apply to some so-called luxury items, such as automobiles, which are assessed a 67 percent duty. Customs duties for tobacco imports are assessed at a rate of 145 percent. Yemen also maintains non-tariff barriers in several areas; for example, import licenses are required for most items, although the government has simplified the licensing procedure.

Factor #2: Taxation
Score - Income taxation: 2-Stable (Low tax rates)
Score - Corporate taxation: 3+ (Moderate tax rates)
Final Taxation Score: 3+ (Moderate tax rates)

Yemen's top income tax rate is 28 percent, with the average income level taxed at a rate of 9 percent. The top corporate tax rate is 32 percent. Yemen also has a 32 percent capital gains tax and other taxes.

Factor #3: Government Intervention in the Economy
Score: 4- (High level of government intervention)

The government of Yemen consumes 27.9 percent of GDP.[397] It also generates a large portion of GDP overall.

---

397 World Bank data, 1991.

Factor #4: Monetary Policy
Score: 5-Stable (Very high level of inflation)

Yemen's average annual rate of inflation from 1990 to 1994 was 109 percent. In 1995, the inflation rate was around 65 percent.

Factor #5: Capital Flows and Foreign Investment
Score: 2-Stable (Low barriers to foreign investment)

Yemen has streamlined its investment laws and procedures in an attempt to attract more foreign investment, and some problems have been alleviated. For example, it has an agency that functions as a central clearinghouse for foreign investors. Some barriers, however, still exist. Foreigners are not permitted to invest in public utilities and in some industries such as telecommunications; and investments in other sectors (for example, hotels and restaurants) are limited.

Factor #6: Banking
Score: 4-Stable (High level of restrictions on banking)

Even though the government plans to let more foreign banks operate in Yemen, not much progress has been made so far. Domestic banks remain heavily regulated.

Factor #7: Wage and Price Controls
Score: 3-Stable (Moderate level of wage and price controls)

Yemen's government controls some prices (mainly the result of the socialist legacy in the northern part of the country). Yemen has no minimum wage, however.

Factor #8: Property Rights
Score: 4-Stable (Low level of protection of private property)

Property has not been expropriated by the government of Yemen since 1990. The threat of expropriation, however, still exists because of uncertain economic conditions. Terrorism is a major threat to private property, as is auto theft. According to the U.S. Department of Commerce, "Protection of property, both physical and intellectual, is weak."[398]

Factor #9: Regulation
Score: 4- (High level of regulation)

Businesses must obtain an environmental impact study before they can engage in new investments or expand their enterprises in Yemen. Although almost no investments have been turned down, the process does cause delays. Bureaucratic inefficiency and rising corruption also remain problems. According to the U.S. Department of Commerce, "Corruption's impact filters through all aspects of doing business in Yemen, distorting judicial and administrative procedures, monetary policy, security, and progress toward democratization, a free market economy and human rights."[399]

---

398   U.S. Department of Commerce, *Country Commercial Guide*, 1996.

399   *Ibid.*

Factor #10: Black Market

Score: 5-Stable (Very high level of black market activity)

Because of high trade barriers, smuggling almost equals official trade in Yemen. Smuggling of some scarce items, such as foodstuffs, is particularly widespread. Protection of intellectual property is weak, and piracy of these products is substantial.

Summary

Yemen			Overall Score	3.90
Trade	5	Monetary Policy 5	Property Rights	4
Taxation	3	Foreign Investment 2	Regulation	4
Government Intervention	4	Banking 4	Black Market	5
		Wage and Prices 3		

ZAIRE

The Central African country of Zaire gained its independence from Belgium in 1960 and quickly fell into turmoil as various regionally based and superpower-backed factions fought for control. A largely futile United Nations peacekeeping operation took place at this time in what then was called the Congo. In 1965, Mobutu Sese Seko seized control of the central government and began decades of repression, forcing Zaire's citizens to live under a strictly government-controlled economy. Under heavy domestic and international pressure to democratize Zaire, Mobutu has long claimed that he is ready to embrace capitalism and reform his country. Zaire remains repressed, however, and in political chaos. With political dissent widespread, Mobutu (who controls the security forces) has been trying to win international support by making the case that he is personally important to maintaining stability in Zaire. Ethnic strife and violence became rampant in late 1996.

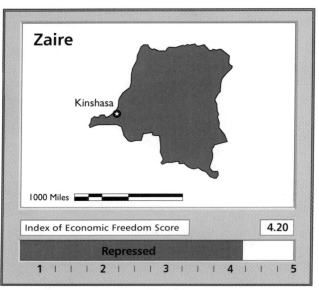

Factor #1: Trade Policy
Score: 4-Stable (High level of protectionism)

Although Zaire's tariffs are established at moderate levels, the largest barrier to trade remains government corruption, particularly in the customs service. As ethnic strife and violence have increased, there has been a corresponding increase in customs corruption.

Factor #2: Taxation

Score - Income taxation: 4-Stable (High tax rates)
Score - Corporate taxation: 5-Stable (Very high tax rates)
Final Taxation Score: 5-Stable (Very high tax rates)

Zaire's top income tax rate is 45 percent.[400] The top marginal corporate tax rate is 50 percent. Zaire also has a 25 percent turnover tax.

Factor #3: Government Intervention in the Economy
Score: 3-Stable (Moderate level of government intervention)

The government of Zaire consumes about 21.7 percent of GDP. Zaire has a large public sector.

---

400   The tax on the average income is unavailable; therefore, Zaire is graded only on its top income tax rate.

Factor #4: Monetary Policy
Score: 5-Stable (Very high level of inflation)

Zaire's average annual rate of inflation from 1985 to 1993 was over 2,000 percent. In 1994, the inflation rate was 5,000 percent.

Factor #5: Capital Flows and Foreign Investment
Score: 4-Stable (High barriers to foreign investment)

Although Zaire's economy has been opening slowly to foreign investment, which remains concentrated in the mining areas, the government still exhibits a general distaste for foreign investment and has made little progress in creating an environment favorable to foreign investors. Movement both within and out of the country is cumbersome and sometimes dangerous. According to the U.S. Department of State, "Corrupt Zairian security personnel may seek bribes to perform their duties, or single out foreigners and stop them on the street for proof of immigration status."[401]

Factor #6: Banking
Score: 4-Stable (High level of restrictions on banking)

The banking system in Zaire is almost completely government-controlled, and all currency must be exchanged at official government banks. "With the continued devaluation of the New Zaire Currency," reports the U.S. Department of State, "U.S. Dollar cash has become a popular means for unofficial transactions greater than 100 dollars. Participating in unofficial money exchanges, however, is illegal. Foreigners have been picked up for infraction and had their money confiscated. Large Denominations of U.S. Currency may not be accepted."[402]

Factor #7: Wage and Price Controls
Score: 4-Stable (High level of wage and price controls)

Wages and prices in Zaire are affected by the massive state-owned sector of the economy.

Factor #8: Property Rights
Score: 4-Stable (Low level of protection of private property)

Private property in Zaire is not secure, both because of corruption and the possibility of government expropriation and because of the country's ongoing civil strife. According to the U.S. Department of State, "The deterioration of Zaire's economy has led to an increase in crime. Vehicle thefts, including armed carjackings, occur, as do burglaries and other crimes."[403]

---

401 U.S. Department of State Travel Advisory, 1996.

402 *Ibid.*

403 *Ibid.*

Factor #9: Regulation
Score: 4-Stable (High level of regulation)

President Mobutu wants to expand the private sector to cut back on subsidies to money-losing government companies. The principal beneficiaries are Mobutu's political friends and long-time operatives in the government.

Factor #10: Black Market
Score: 5-Stable (Very high level of black market activity)

The black market in Zaire is larger than the formal market.

Summary

Zaire				Overall Score	4.20
Trade	4	Monetary Policy	5	Property Rights	4
Taxation	5	Foreign Investment	4	Regulation	4
Government Intervention	3	Banking	4	Black Market	5
		Wage and Prices	4		

ZAMBIA

Zambia gained its independence from Great Britain in 1964. It remained a one-party socialist state until 1989, when political opposition was legalized. In 1991, running on a platform of democracy and free enterprise, Frederick Chiluba won an overwhelming election victory over long-time President Kenneth Kaunda. After years of disastrous economic policies, President Chiluba is trying to lead Zambia to economic recovery. His economic liberalization agenda has suffered significant setbacks, however. Privatization has been sluggish, the government has been tainted by corruption, and economic growth has been minimal over the last few years. Recently, Zambia has reduced its barriers to trade.

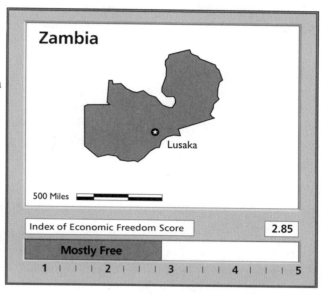

Factor #1: Trade Policy
Score: 2+ (Low level of protectionism)

By African standards, Zambia's average tariff rate is low: 5.5 percent. Import restrictions have been eased. Resentment against increasing South African imports is generating protectionist sentiment, however, and corruption in the Customs Bureau continues.

Factor #2: Taxation

Score - Income taxation: 3-Stable (Moderate tax rates)
Score - Corporate taxation: 3-Stable (Moderate tax rates)
Final Taxation Score: 3.5-Stable (High tax rates)

Zambia's top marginal income tax rate is 35 percent, and the average taxpayer is in the 15 percent bracket. In 1993, Zambia cut its corporate tax rate to 35 percent.[404] Zambia also has a 23 percent sales tax and property transfer taxes.

Factor #3: Government Intervention in the Economy
Score: 2-Stable (Low level of government intervention)

The Zambian government consumes 10 percent of GDP. During the Kaunda regime, state-owned enterprises accounted for more than 50 percent of GDP, and the state sector still dominates the economy. The government, however, is considering selling off the state's massive copper concern.

---

404 Banking profits in excess of ZK1,000 million are taxed at 45 percent. This one exception to an otherwise flat tax rate was judged not significant enough to earn Zambia a grade of 4, which is reserved for countries with a tax system in which the top marginal rate is between 36 percent and 45 percent.

Factor #4: Monetary Policy
Score: 5-Stable (Very high level of inflation)

Zambia's average annual rate of inflation from 1985 to 1994 was 92 percent. The inflation rate currently is running at approximately 30 percent.

Factor #5: Capital Flows and Foreign Investment
Score: 2-Stable (Low barriers to foreign investment)

The Zambian government has improved its foreign investment laws, and there are some investment incentives. There is no legal discrimination between foreign and domestic investors, and few investment opportunities are off-limits, though it is uncertain whether all future privatizations will be open to foreign participation. Zambia is attracting commercial farmers from South Africa and Zimbabwe. Foreign investment must be screened by an investment board, which operates quickly and efficiently. Various licensing requirements and difficulties in acquiring land deter some foreign investment.

Factor #6: Banking
Score: 2-Stable (Low level of restrictions on banking)

Private international and domestic banks operate in Zambia, and interest rates for loans and deposits are set by the market. Merchant banking recently has been legalized. Zambia still has two state-owned banks, however, and the government recently took over the management of a failed major commercial bank.

Factor #7: Wage and Price Controls
Score: 2-Stable (Low level of wage and price controls)

Price controls have been removed in Zambia, and most subsidies have been eliminated. State subsidization of government-owned enterprises, however, distorts the pricing system. There is a minimum wage.

Factor #8: Property Rights
Score: 3-Stable (Moderate level of protection of private property)

Kaunda's socialist regime left a legacy of nationalized property. Businesses were expropriated as recently as 1989. Legislation enacted in 1993, however, provides for full compensation for newly nationalized property in convertible currency. According to the U.S. Department of Commerce, "The courts in Zambia are reasonably independent, but contractual rights and more especially property rights are weak in Zambia."[405]

Factor #9: Regulation
Score: 4-Stable (High level of regulation)

Acquiring business licenses in Zambia involves complex procedures and delays. An investment board screens domestic investment. Corruption is an increasing problem, and labor laws, including the requirement that employers provide housing to employees, are both burdensome and expensive. Residence permits are difficult to acquire.

---

405   U.S. Department of Commerce, *Country Commercial Guide*, 1996.

Factor #10: Black Market
Score: 3-Stable (Moderate level of black market activity)

There is widespread evasion of taxation in Zambia, and the country's labor laws are expensive. This forces employers to seek out laborers informally through the black market. An illegal gemstone trade thrives because of a government monopoly, and the lack of intellectual property protection for such items as computer software has resulted in increased piracy in these areas.

Summary

Zambia				Overall Score	2.85
Trade	2	Monetary Policy	5	Property Rights	3
Taxation	3.5	Foreign Investment	2	Regulation	4
Government Intervention	2	Banking	2	Black Market	3
		Wage and Prices	2		

ZIMBABWE

Since gaining its independence from Great Britain in 1980, Zimbabwe has been a one-party state ruled by President Robert Mugabe. Zimbabwe has one of Africa's more industrialized economies, and the government exercises considerable control over economic activity. Mugabe has begun to liberalize the economy somewhat. He has eased restrictions on foreign investment, for example, and has eliminated most price controls. The future of reform is uncertain, however, because powerful elements within the government are opposed to free-market reform. Zimbabwe has made no progress with privatization.

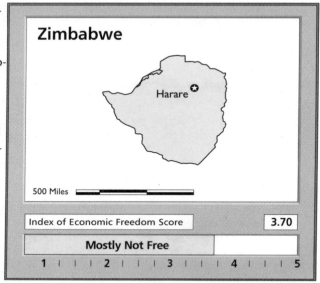

Zimbabwe	
Index of Economic Freedom Score	3.70
Mostly Not Free	

Factor #1: Trade Policy

Score: 5-Stable (Very high level of protectionism)

The average tariff rate in Zimbabwe is 30 percent.[406] Customs procedures are complex, and concern over cheaper South African imports could lead to more protectionist measures. Some textile and clothing imports are banned. There has been some progress in reducing non-tariff barriers to trade.

Factor #2: Taxation

Score - Income taxation: 3+ (Moderate tax rates)
Score - Corporate taxation: 4- (High tax rates)
Final Taxation Score: 4-Stable (High tax rates)

Zimbabwe's top income tax rate is 40 percent, down from 45 percent in 1995, and the average income level is taxed at a rate of 0 percent. The top corporate income tax rate is 37.5 percent, down from 40 percent in 1995. Branches of foreign companies are subject to an additional tax of 8.4 percent. Zimbabwe also has a 30 percent capital gains tax and a 10 percent to 20 percent sales tax.

Factor #3: Government Intervention in the Economy

Score: 3-Stable (Moderate level of government intervention)

The government of Zimbabwe consumes 19 percent of GDP. It also owns 40 enterprises, many of them requiring subsidies. Government-owned enterprises include postal, telecommunications, and broadcasting services, railroads, and the national air service, all of which are closed to private investment. The government has refused to adopt a program of privatization despite donor encouragement.

---

406   As reported by the Zimbabwe Embassy in Washington, D.C., on July 20, 1995.

Factor #4: Monetary Policy
Score: 4-Stable (High level of inflation)

Zimbabwe's average annual rate of inflation from 1985 to 1994 was 19.7 percent. In 1994, the inflation rate was approximately 23 percent.

Factor #5: Capital Flows and Foreign Investment
Score: 4-Stable (High barriers to foreign investment)

Foreign investment regulations have been liberalized substantially by a 1992 investment code. Investor incentives, including duty-free imports in some cases, recently have been introduced, and the Zimbabwe Stock Exchange has been opened to foreign investment. Prior government approval is still required, however, for all foreign direct investment. In 1994, the government banned several sectors from foreign participation, including much of the agriculture, forestry, and transportation sectors. Foreign control of insurance companies is discouraged.

Factor #6: Banking
Score: 3-Stable (Moderate level of restrictions on banking)

Only a few commercial banks in Zimbabwe are foreign-owned. Foreign commercial and merchant banks are allowed majority shareholder status, though this is discouraged. Recent attempts by foreign banks to obtain operating licenses have failed. The government owns some financial institutions. Some of Zimbabwe's banks, however, are becoming more independent. According to the U.S. Department of Commerce, "[Zimbabwe's Central Bank] is becoming increasingly independent of government in its exercising of monetary controls and advising government on fighting inflation, including on occasion criticizing, for example, the GOZ's [Government of Zimbabwe's] lack of fiscal discipline."[407]

Factor #7: Wage and Price Controls
Score: 3-Stable (Moderate level of wage and price controls)

The government of Zimbabwe has succeeded in removing all but a few price controls, although some subsidies on food goods remain in effect. The government sets a minimum wage by employment sector, and government marketing boards continue to control exports of traditional crops.

Factor #8: Property Rights
Score: 3-Stable (Moderate level of protection of private property)

No nationalization of private property has occurred in Zimbabwe since independence. In 1992, however, the legislature passed a sweeping land reform bill that enables the government to force the sale of nearly half of the remaining white-owned farmland and use it to establish state-owned communal farms. This legislation denies landowners due process, and its implementation has been subject to corruption.

---

407   U.S. Department of Commerce, *Country Commercial Guide*, 1996.

Factor #9: Regulation
Score: 4-Stable (High level of regulation)

Wages and employment in Zimbabwe are heavily regulated. Government permission is required not only to terminate an employee, for example, but also to commence virtually any commercial activity. The private sector is under increasing pressure to hire and train more Zimbabweans, and the use of foreign nationals is severely restricted. The bureaucracy lacks transparency and is highly arbitrary.

Factor #10: Black Market
Score: 4-Stable (High level of black market activity)

About 20 percent of Zimbabwe's GDP is in the black market, mainly because of government monopolies in such areas as transportation services.

Summary

Zimbabwe				Overall Score	3.70
Trade	5	Monetary Policy	4	Property Rights	3
Taxation	4	Foreign Investment	4	Regulation	4
Government Intervention	3	Banking	3	Black Market	4
		Wage and Prices	3		

Bibliography

African Development Indicators 1996, World Bank, Washington, D.C., 1996.

Argentina: A Profile, Fundacion Invertir Argentina, 1996.

Argentina, Preview Economic Report, Office of the Financial Representative of Argentina, Year 5, Number 16, 1995.

Argentina: Trade and Investment News, Economic and Commercial Section, Argentine Embassy, January–April 1996.

The Bahamas, Price Control: A Brief Synopsis, Ministry of Planning and Public Service of the Bahamas, 1995.

Bahrain, Annual Report 1994, Bahrain Monetary Agency, The State of Bahrain, 1994.

Benin, Policy Framework Paper for 1995–1996, Beninese authorities, International Monetary Fund, and World Bank, 1996.

Bulgaria Annual Report, Bulgarian National Bank, 1995.

A Business Guide to the Kingdom of Saudi Arabia, Royal Embassy of Saudi Arabia, Washington, D.C., 1993.

A Compendium for Foreign Investors in Argentina, Subsecretaria De Inversiones, Republica Argentina, Buenos Aires, 1995.

Corporate Taxes: A Worldwide Summary, Price Waterhouse, New York, New York, 1995.

Côte d'Ivoire Update, Embassy of the Republic of Côte d'Ivoire, Washington, D.C., Volume 1, Number 2, May 1996.

Country Commercial Guide, Embassy of Bolivia, Fiscal Year 1996.

Country Reports and *Country Profiles*, various country-specific reports, Economist
     Intelligence Unit, Washington, D.C., 1995–1996.

Country Reports on Human Rights Practices for 1995, report submitted to the Committee on
     Foreign Relations, U.S. Senate, and the Committee on International Relations,
     U.S. House of Representatives, by the U.S. Department of State, February 1996.

Current Foreign Investment: Climate in Bulgaria, Sofia, Bulgaria, February 1996.

Cyprus: A Centre for International Business, Central Bank of Cyprus, Nicosia, 1994.

Cyprus: The Way for Businessmen and Investors, Coopers and Lybrand, Nicosia, 1994.

Dinar Digest, Bahrain Monetary Agency, September 1995.

Direction of Trade Statistics Quarterly, International Monetary Fund, Washington, D.C.,
     March 1995.

Direction of Trade Statistics Yearbook: 1996, International Monetary Fund, Washington,
     D.C., 1996.

Doing Business in Switzerland, Ernst & Young, Zurich, Switzerland, 1995.

Economic Bulletin, Banca D'Italia, Rome, Italy, Number 22, February 1996.

Emerging Stock Markets Factbook: 1996, International Finance Corporation, Washington,
     D.C., 1996.

Ernst & Young's Global 1000 Emerging Markets Survey, Global 1000 Investment in Emerging
     Markets: Opportunity versus Risk, Ernst & Young Ltd., 1994.

EY/GEMS Global Expatriate Management System, Ernst & Young LLP, 1996.

Five-Year Political & Economic Forecasts, Political Risk Services, IBC USA Publications Inc.,
     1994–1995.

Foreign Aid Reduction Act of 1995, U.S. Senate, 104th Congress, June 23, 1995.

Foreign Trade Barriers, Office of the United States Trade Representative, Washington,
     D.C., 1996.

The Foundation for Investment and Development of Exports, Industrial Development Group,
     Tegucigalpa, Honduras, 1995.

Geographical Distribution of Financial Flows to Aid Recipients 1990–1994, Organization for
     Economic Cooperation and Development, Paris, 1996.

Geographical Distribution of Financial Flows to Developing Countries: 1989–1993, Organization
     for Economic Cooperation and Development, Paris, 1995.

Germany: Sectors of the Economy, Press and Information Office of the Federal Government
     of Germany, April 1995.

Ghana Human Rights Practices, 1995, U.S. Department of State, Washington, D.C., March
     1996.

Global Economic Prospects and the Developing Countries, World Bank, Washington, D.C.,
     1995.

Government Finance Statistics Yearbook: 1995, International Monetary Fund, Washington,
     D.C., 1995.

Guideline to Investors in Benin, Ministry of Planning and Economic Restructuring, Republic of Benin, April 1995.

Highlights of Bolivia Today, Moreno Munoz, Price Waterhouse, 1995 Edition.

Human Development Report: 1996, United Nations Development Programme, New York, 1996.

The Index of Economic Freedom, Bryan T. Johnson and Thomas P. Sheehy, The Heritage Foundation, Washington, D.C., 1996.

Individual Taxes: A Worldwide Summary, Price Waterhouse, New York, 1995.

International Financial Statistics, International Monetary Fund, Washington, D.C., 1996.

Invest in Iceland Series, Invest in Iceland Bureau, Ministry of Commerce and the Trade Council of Iceland, Reykjavik, Iceland, 1996.

Investing in Change, Training for Free-Market Economies and Democracies in the New Independent States of the Former Soviet Union, Edward B. Fiske, Academy for Educational Development, Washington, D.C., 1995.

Investing in Jordan, 1995, Investment Promotions Department, The Hashemite Kingdom of Jordan, 1996.

Investment in..., various country guides, KPMG Peat Marwick, Washington, D.C., 1995.

Investment Opportunities in Italy, Institute for Industrial Promotion, Rome, 1995.

Investment Trade and Licensing Reports, various country-specific reports, Economic Intelligence Unit, Washington, D.C., 1995–1996.

Italy: International Tax and Business Guide, Deloitte Touche Tohmatsu International, New York, 1995 Edition.

Latvia: Country Profile, Embassy of Latvia, prepared by the Latvian Government for presentation at the 1996 EBRD Annual Meeting.

The Military Balance 1995–1996, published for the International Institute for Strategic Studies by Brassey's Ltd., London, 1995.

Monetary Policy Statement of New Zealand, Reserve Bank of New Zealand, June 1996.

National Trade Data Bank and Economic Bulletin Board, U.S. Department of Commerce, STAT–USA, Washington, D.C., 1995-1996.

News from Ethiopia, Embassy of Ethiopia, Washington, D.C., Volume 5, Issue 2, March 1996.

News from Poland, Embassy of the Republic of Poland, Washington, D.C., Volume 2, June 1996.

New Zealand: Economic and Financial Overview, New Zealand Debt Management Office, Wellington, New Zealand, February 1996.

The Philippines: Political and Economic Assessment, Economist Intelligence Unit, EIU Philippines, Inc., August 1995.

Quarterly Statistical Bulletin, Bahrain Monetary Agency, Directorate of Economic Research, Volume 21, Number 3, September 1995.

Rebuilding Eastern Germany, The Second Half of the Way, Federal Ministry of Economics, Bonn, Germany, September 1995, Nr. 382.

Relevance of Asian Development Experiences to African Problems, Naya, Seiji, and McCleery, International Center for Economic Growth, San Francisco, 1994.

Scorecard on the Israeli Economy: A Review of 1995, Institute for Advanced Strategic and Political Studies, Washington, D.C., March 1996.

Sri Lanka Investors' Guide, Board of Investment of Sri Lanka, Colombo 01, Sri Lanka, 1995.

Statistical Handbook 1995: States of the Former USSR, World Bank, Washington, D.C., 1995.

Swiss Business, HandelsZeitung Group, St. Gallen, Switzerland, Number 1, February/March 1996.

Trade and Development Report: 1993, United Nations Conference on Trade and Development, 1993.

Trends in Developing Economies, World Bank, Washington, D.C., 1995.

Uruguay: Economic Profile, Embassy of Uruguay, Washington, D.C., 1994.

U.S. and Asia Statistical Handbook 1995, ed. Richard D. Fisher, Jr., and John T. Dori, The Heritage Foundation, Washington, D.C., 1995.

The World Competitiveness Report 1994, World Economic Forum, Geneva, Switzerland, September 1994.

World Debt Tables 1994–1995, Volumes 1 & 2, World Bank, Washington, D.C., 1994.

The World Development Report 1996, World Bank, Washington, D.C., 1996.

World Economic Outlook: May 1996, International Monetary Fund, Washington, D.C., 1996.

The World Factbook 1995, Central Intelligence Agency, Washington, D.C., 1995.

The World Factbook 1996, Central Intelligence Agency, Washington, D.C., 1996.

World Tables 1995, Johns Hopkins University Press, Baltimore, Maryland, April 1995.

World Tables, World Bank, Washington, D.C., 1996.

Worldwide Corporate Tax Guide and Directory, Ernst & Young, New York, 1996 Edition.